European Community Competition Law in Practice

European Community Competition Law in Practice

Inns of Court School of Law
Institute of Law, City University, London

OXFORD
UNIVERSITY PRESS

OXFORD
UNIVERSITY PRESS
Great Clarendon Street, Oxford OX2 6DP

Oxford University Press is a department of the University of Oxford.
It furthers the University's objective of excellence in research, scholarship,
and education by publishing worldwide in

Oxford New York

Auckland Bangkok Buenos Aires Cape Town Chennai
Dar es Salaam Delhi Hong Kong Istanbul Karachi Kolkata
Kuala Lumpur Madrid Melbourne Mexico City Mumbai Nairobi
São Paulo Shanghai Singapore Taipei Tokyo Toronto

and an associated company in Berlin

Oxford is a registered trade mark of Oxford University Press
in the UK and certain other countries

Published in the United States
by Oxford University Press Inc., New York

A Blackstone Press Book

British Library Cataloguing in Publication Data
Data available

Library of Congress Cataloging in Publication Data
Data available

ISBN 0-19-926604-2

1 3 5 7 9 10 8 6 4 2

Typeset by L K Murdoch, Tonbridge, Kent
Printed in Great Britain
on acid-free paper by
Ashford Colour Press, Gosport, Hampshire

FOREWORD

These Manuals are designed primarily to support training on the Bar Vocational Course, though they are also intended to provide a useful resource for legal practitioners and for anyone undertaking training in legal skills.

The Bar Vocational Course was designed by staff at the Inns of Court School of Law, where it was introduced in 1989. This course is intended to equip students with the practical skills and the procedural and evidential knowledge that they will need to start their legal professional careers. These Manuals are written by staff at the Inns of Court School of Law who have helped to develop the course, and by a range of legal practitioners and others involved in legal skills training. The authors of the Manuals are very well aware of the practical and professional approach that is central to the Bar Vocational Course.

The range and coverage of the Manuals have grown steadily. Whilst the option Manuals have been updated and revised every two years, this year the entire series has undergone a more thorough revision to ensure that the Manuals reflect the changing needs of Bar students and developments in legal skills training.

This updating and revision is a constant process and we very much value the comments of practitioners, staff and students. Legal vocational training is advancing rapidly, and it is important that all those concerned work together to achieve and maintain high standards. Please address any comments to the Bar Vocational Course Director at the Inns of Court School of Law.

With the validation of other providers for the Bar Vocational Courses it is very much our intention that these Manuals will be of equal value to all students wherever they take the course, and we would very much value comments from tutors and students at other validated institutions.

The enthusiasm of the publishers and their efficiency in arranging the production and publication of these Manuals is much appreciated.

The Hon Mr Justice Elias
Chairman of the Advisory Board of the Institute of Law
City University, London
December 2003

OUTLINE CONTENTS

DETAILED CONTENTS

TABLE OF CASES AND COMMISSION DECISIONS

TABLE OF UK LEGISLATION

UK statutes

UK secondary legislation

TABLE OF EUROPEAN COMMUNITY TREATIES

International legislation

TABLE OF EUROPEAN COMMUNITY SECONDARY LEGISLATION

1 Introduction

1.1 What the Manual is intended to do

The EC has, among its aims, the raising of living standards and a harmonious development of economic activities (Article 2, EC Treaty). It seeks to achieve these aims largely through the mechanism of a common market. To this end, certain specific tasks (or 'activities') are imposed on the Community in Article 3, EC Treaty; primarily (for our purposes) a 'system ensuring that competition in the internal market is not distorted'. In Part Three of the Treaty, under 'Title VI. Common rules on competition, taxation and approximation of laws', you find 'Chapter I. Rules on Competition'. This is divided into two sections:

Section 1. Rules applying to undertakings

Section 2. Aids granted by States

We are mainly concerned here with those Articles which deal with undertakings, that is, Articles 81–86 (ex 85–90) and, in the space available, we shall concentrate almost exclusively on the 'substantive' competition laws: Articles 81 (ex 85) and 82 (ex 86). The European Court of First Instance has described these Articles as 'independent and complementary provisions designed, in general, to regulate distinct situations by different rules'.

These Articles are interpreted and applied primarily by the European Commission. Article 83 (ex 87), EC Treaty, requires the EC Council to pass legislation to give effect to the principles set out in Articles 81 (ex 85) and 82 (ex 86): it refers explicitly to the need to 'define the respective functions of the Commission and of the Court of Justice in applying' the legislation. This is taken further in Article 85 (ex 89), EC Treaty, which states that, as soon as the Commission takes up its duties, it shall ensure the application of the principles laid down in Articles 81 (ex 85) and 82 (ex 86). The Commission is to investigate cases of suspected infringement. If proved, the Commission is to propose appropriate measures to bring the infringement to an end.

In addition to the relevant Articles in the Treaty, the competition rules of the European Community are found in regulations issued under the authority of the Treaty by the Council or Commission and in case law, that is, decisions of the Commission made in individual cases and the judgments of the Court of Justice and Court of First Instance. The Commission also issues notices from time to time indicating its policy on certain topics (eg, the Notice on Agreements of Minor Importance).

The major piece of secondary legislation pursuant to Article 83 (ex 87) is Council Regulation 1/2003 (in force from 1 May 2004). This sets out in detail the powers and duties of the Commission in the field of competition. It will be examined in detail later (see **Chapter 6**). Regulation 1/2003 replaced Regulation 17/62, to which much of the case law refers.

The recital to Regulation 1 makes the point that all decisions taken by the Commission under the Regulation are subject to review by the Court of Justice of the European Communities (ECJ), in accordance with the Court's jurisdiction as laid down by the Treaty. This allows the Court to review the procedural or substantive merits of a decision. Now, the *initial* judicial review will be undertaken by the Court of First Instance (a more recent creation, which first sat in 1989).

For ease of reference, Articles 81 (ex 85) and 82 (ex 86) and Council Regulation 1/2003 are printed in full at **2.1**, **5.1** and **Appendix 1**, respectively. Other measures are not printed in full but are set out in the text as appropriate (eg, Articles from the 'block exemption' on vertical agreements, Regulation 2790/99 (see **Appendix 2**).

It was said above that we are going to concentrate on Articles 81 (ex 85) and 82 (ex 86): the 'competition' rules. However, it is also important to be aware of related topics which sometimes interact with or are relevant to the operation of those Articles. So **Chapter 9** looks briefly at the rules governing free movement of goods throughout the Community, and includes a short explanation of intellectual property rights.

1.2 Brief history of the European Union and its institutions

1.2.1 The creation and membership of the European Union

The European Community grew out of the movement towards international cooperation after World War II. The Council of Europe grew from the same impetus.

The foundations were laid by Robert Schuman, the French Foreign Minister at the time, in his declaration made on 9 May 1950. He set out a plan he and Jean Monnet had devised to combine the European coal and steel industries in a European Community for Coal and Steel. The European Coal and Steel Community (ECSC) was established a year later by the signing of the Treaty of Paris on 18 April 1951 and came into force in 1952.

The European Economic Community and the European Atomic Energy Community (Euratom) were formed by the same original six states (France, Germany, Italy, Belgium, The Netherlands, Luxembourg) signing the Treaties of Rome (EEC Treaty and Euratom Treaty) on 25 March 1957.

The United Kingdom, Ireland and Denmark joined on 1 January 1973 and Greece entered in 1981. Spain and Portugal followed in 1986, and most recently Finland, Sweden and Austria, so that total membership is now 15 States, with a combined population of some 370 million people. Moves are now going ahead for the further enlargement of the EU to a possible 26 Member States. Negotiations are reported to be in place with Hungary, Poland, Romania, Slovakia, Latvia, Estonia, Lithuania, Bulgaria, the Czech Republic, Slovenia and Cyprus. Any enlargement is unlikely before the year 2000.

There is not just one European Community (although from 1 July 1993, the EEC has been known as the European Community). Three separate Communities have existed since the entry into force of the Treaties of Rome, each based on its own foundation treaty. No formal merger of the three Communities has ever taken place although the three now share a single Council and a single Commission. Regardless of their differences, the three Communities are regarded as one unit. They share the same basic objectives expressed by the same Member States and share the same legal structure and institutions. All three Communities are by common usage referred to as the European Community. Under the ECSC Treaty the Community has the task of administering the coal and steel industries. The European Atomic Energy Community concerns the utilisation of atomic energy within the Community and research connected with it.

On 1 January 1993, the (then) 12 Member States of the European Community evolved into the 'European Union' (EU) as the result of the Treaty on European Union signed at Maastricht on 7 February 1992. The original EC Treaty of Rome continues in force, though, as amended over the years since 1957, so we need not put aside the idea of the European Community and its laws just yet. (We should also note that the other two 'European' treaties — those establishing the ECSC and Euratom — continue to exist as well.) The Treaty on European Union made some changes to the EC Treaty but the institutions created in 1957 carry on into the European Union and often continue to derive their functions from the EC Treaty. In particular, Article 2 of the TEU states that the EU will 'maintain in full', 'respect' and 'build on' the *acquis communautaire* (or the acts of the EC as interpreted and applied since the beginning). The TEU does go further than the Treaty of Rome in one salient respect, though — in Article 6 the EU states that it will 'respect fundamental rights, as guaranteed by the European Convention for the Protection of Human Rights and Fundamental Freedoms [1950] ... and as they result from the constitutional traditions common to the Member States, as general principles of Community law'.

Without wishing to confuse the reader too much, we should also remember that on 1 January 1994, the Agreement on a European Economic Area (EEA) came into effect. This brought together, as a single territory, the Member States of the European Community with those countries belonging to the European Free Trade Association (except Switzerland) in many important economic areas, for example free movement of goods and rules governing business competition. Extra institutions have been created for the EEA, together with new rules, but any examination of them in this Manual would make it unduly long and complicated; it should also be remembered that three members of the EFTA subsequently joined the EU (see above), leaving Iceland, Lichtenstein and Norway outside the EU but within the EEA.

1.2.2 What are the tasks of the European Community?

The underlying goals for creating the European Community are set out in the preamble of the EC Treaty, as amended. They are mainly economic but also include social goals, and even political ideals such as laying 'the foundations of an ever closer union among the peoples of Europe' and 'pooling their resources to preserve and strengthen peace and liberty'. These ideals are continued and expanded in the preamble to the Treaty on European Union.

The European Community was formed to create a single European market uniting the national markets of the Member States and in which goods and services could be offered and sold under common conditions, usually in a free, competitive market. Freedom of movement for capital and labour were also to be secured.

In order to evolve the common economic market, the national economic policies of the Member States were to be gradually harmonized insofar as they fell within the EC's jurisdiction.

The Community's tasks are outlined in the EC Treaty:

Article 2 (as amended):
The Community shall have as its task, by establishing a common market and an economic and monetary union and by implementing common policies or activities referred to in Articles 3 and 4, to promote throughout the Community a harmonious, balanced and sustained development of economic activities, a high level of employment and of social protection, equality between men and women, sustainable and non-inflationary growth, a high degree of competitiveness and convergence of economic performance, a

high level of protection and improvement of the quality of the environment, the raising of the standard of living and quality of life, and economic and social cohesion and solidarity among Member States.

To facilitate the establishment of the market, the Community is to engage in the following activities:

Article 3 (as amended):

For the purposes set out in Article 2, the activities of the Community shall include, as provided in this Treaty and in accordance with the timetable set out therein:

(a) the prohibition, as between Member States, of customs duties and of quantitative restrictions on the import and export of goods, and of all other measures having equivalent effect;

(b) a common commercial policy;

(c) an internal market characterised by the abolition, as between Member States of obstacles to the free movement of goods, persons, services and capital;

(d) measures concerning the entry and movement of persons as provided for in Title IV;

(e) a common policy in the sphere of agriculture and fisheries;

(f) a common policy in the sphere of transport;

(g) a system ensuring that competition in the internal market is not distorted;

(h) the approximation of the laws of Member States to the extent required for the functioning of the common market;

(i) the promotion of coordination between employment policies of the Member States with a view to enhancing their effectiveness by developing a coordinated strategy for employment;

(j) a policy in the social sphere comprising a European Social Fund;

(k) the strengthening of economic and social cohesion;

(l) a policy in the sphere of the environment;

(m) the strengthening of the competitiveness of Community industry;

(n) the promotion of research and technological development;

(o) encouragement for the establishment and development of trans-European networks;

(p) a contribution to the attainment of a high level of health protection;

(q) a contribution to education and training of quality and to the flowering of the cultures of the Member States;

(r) a policy in the sphere of development cooperation;

(s) the association of the overseas countries and territories in order to increase trade and to promote jointly economic and social development;

(t) a contribution to the strengthening of consumer protection;

(u) measures in the spheres of energy, civil protection and tourism.

In all other activities referred to in this Article, the Community shall aim to eliminate inequalities, and to promote equality, between men and women.

These activities are developed in more detail in later provisions of the EC Treaty.

The EC Treaty extends to social matters including inter alia:

(a) cooperation between Member States on employment, labour law and working conditions, vocational training and social security;

(b) prevention of occupational accidents and diseases and improvements in occupational hygiene;

(c) the right of association and collective bargaining between workers and employers (Article 140 (ex 118)); and

(d) equal pay for men and women (Article 141 (ex 119)).

The Community has by the EC Treaty assumed competence in all of these areas. However, the founding treaties have not given the Community power to deal with all aspects of national sovereignty so that matters like defence, diplomacy, education and culture remain outside the Community's jurisdiction. Even so, the Community has partial competence in some of these areas (eg diplomacy and education).

The Single European Act 1986 (SEA) amended the EC Treaty. It provided additional objectives and thus enlarged the scope of Community competence. The SEA was signed by all 12 Member States. Incorporation into UK law was brought about by the European Communities (Amendment) Act 1986.

The SEA provided for a formal framework for political cooperation between Member States which had not been covered by the EC Treaty (see below). It set out new goals for economic and monetary cooperation, health and safety of workers, regional policy, research and technological development and environmental protection. It made procedural changes which accelerated progress towards a single internal market by 1992 and moved Member States nearer to European integration. The scope of the Treaty as amended by the SEA was very broad and was expanded much further by both the TEU and the Treaty of Amsterdam, as can be seen in the amended Article 3 above. The Community has been given competence to deal with important areas of economic and social activity which had hitherto been within the sole competence of Member States.

A Community law point may arise in cases involving any of these areas.

1.2.3 The institutions of the European Community

The three Communities share common institutions which carry out their tasks. The major ones are: the European Parliament, the Commission of the European Community, the Council (formerly called the Council of Ministers), the European Court of Justice (ECJ) and the Court of First Instance (CFI). In addition to the Economic and Social Committee, which has a purely consultative role, the more recent, and perhaps more minor, community institutions are:

- The Court of Auditors.
- The European Investment Bank.
- The Committee of the Regions.
- The European Ombudsman.
- The European Monetary Institute.
- The Office for the Harmonization of the International Market (perhaps strictly an 'agency' rather than an institution).

An enormous amount of material about the institutions is accessible on the Internet, at http://www.europa.eu.int/institutions/index_en.htm. See also **Appendices 6** and **7**.

1.2.3.1 The function and powers of the European Commission

The Commission, sometimes called the 'guardian of the Treaties', consists of 20 members (Commissioners) who are appointed by the governments of their own Member States and agreed to by all the Member States. The Amsterdam Treaty 1997 declares that there will be only one Commissioner from each Member State in the future; those countries which at present have two Commissioners (Germany, UK, France, Italy and Spain) will give up their second Commissioner. They do not represent their own countries as they are supposed to be above national loyalties and their independence should be beyond doubt. In performance of their duties they must 'neither seek nor take instructions from any government or any body'. A breach of this principle by a Commissioner would mean his or her compulsory retirement which the ECJ would request the Commissioner to take. See generally Article 213 (ex 157), EC Treaty, as inserted by the Treaty on European Union.

The functions of the Commission are threefold:

(a) It is to initiate proposals on any matter provided for under the Treaty (Articles 208 (ex 152) and 308 (ex 235), EC Treaty).

(b) It acts as the Community watchdog. Article 10 (ex 5) of the EC Treaty states:

> *Member States shall take all appropriate measures, whether general or particular, to ensure fulfilment of the obligations arising out of this Treaty or resulting from action taken by the institutions of the Community. They shall facilitate the achievement of the Community's tasks.*
>
> *They shall abstain from any measure which could jeopardise the attainment of the objectives of this Treaty.*

The Commission investigates (and takes to the ECJ) any Member State which infringes the EC Treaty, under Article 226 (ex 169). It also has the task of administering and enforcing EC competition policy. It can impose fines and penalties on individuals and companies who are in breach of this policy.

(c) The Commission also acts as the manager and executor of Community policies. If the Council makes a policy decision, it falls to the Commission to carry it out. This usually means adopting further, detailed, legislation to implement the policy.

Subject to any review by the European Court, the European Commission is the investigator, judge and jury in competition 'trials'. A complaint was made in *Musique Diffusion Française v Commission (100–103/80)* [1983] ECR 1825 (the 'Pioneer' case) that this multiplicity of roles was a breach of due process of law, contrary to Article 6 of the European Convention on Human Rights. The complaint was rejected by the Court of Justice, which indicated that the Commission was not a tribunal within the meaning of Article 6 of the Convention. The same point was raised subsequently before the European Commission on Human Rights in *Société Stenuit v France* [1992] EHRR 509. The Commission felt that the nature of its investigations was such that Article 6(1) of the European Convention should apply to them. The Commission on Human Rights said that, regardless of the procedural safeguards that competition proceedings now have, the European Community Commission is both plaintiff/prosecutor and judge, there is no presumption of innocence and the burden of proof on the EC Commission is only to a civil standard. It was felt that none of these elements complied with Article 6(1) of the Convention. There have been suggestions that there should be an independent 'Competition Authority', distinct from the Commission. For example, in October 1994 the head of the German Cartel Office recommended that the competition decisions which are currently made by the Commission should instead be made by an independent authority so that political interference might be reduced (see Financial Times, 3 October 1994; and Alan Riley, 'The European Cartel Office: A Guardian Without Weapons' [1997] ECLR 3). However, such an entity has not yet been created. Indeed, the former head of DG IV, Dr Claus-Dieter Ehlermann, has expressed the opinion that the Commission, rather than the Council of Ministers, possesses the fundamental power in the matter of competition policy.

The Commission investigates either on its own initiative or following a complaint made to it, using its own officials to elicit information; it then decides whether the law has been infringed. If it finds that there has been an infringement, the conduct is prohibited and the Commission either requires termination of the conduct and/or imposes a fine or (under Article 81 (ex 85) only) grants an exemption.

1.2.3.2 The functions and powers of the Council of the European Union

The Council ensures the coordination of the general economic policy of the Member States and has the final power to make decisions in the decision-making process of the Community. Its final say is subject usually to consultation with the Parliament. Any legislation it adopts must first, however, be proposed by the Commission. The Council decides some matters by qualified majority voting, while others require unanimity (it depends under which enabling Article of the Treaty the proposed legislation is introduced). Under the Amsterdam Treaty, the weighting of Member States in the Council will be adjusted so that a majority decision of the Council will represent a similar proportion of the population of the EU.

Each Member State has one member on the Council but the identity of the actual delegate fluctuates and will depend on the topic being decided. The actual member will be the Head of Government for important issues or the appropriate government minister on specialist issues.

As the Council is not a permanent body and meets for only a few days each month, the day-to-day work is done by the Committee of Permanent Representatives, COREPER, and a system of Management Committees.

1.2.3.3 The European Parliament

The European Parliament was originally called the Assembly in the EC Treaty (formally changing its name in the SEA 1987). It has over 600 members, including 87 from the UK. The Amsterdam Treaty of 1997 sets a ceiling of 700 members of the European Parliament (or MEPs). This figure is intended to remain the ceiling for some time, even after the probable expansion of the EU from the present 15 Member States up to 20. The Parliament represents the political and other views of all the peoples of the Member States.

The Parliament's powers were expanded considerably by the Treaty on European Union. For example, Article 251 (ex 189b), EC Treaty (inserted by the EU Treaty) not only involves the Parliament fully in the procedure for the adoption of an act, but allows Parliament to veto such adoption (ie it can prevent proposed legislation from becoming law). Article 252 (ex 189c) (an alternative procedure for the adoption of acts) contains no such veto. Under Article 192 (ex 138b) (again inserted by the EU Treaty), the Parliament may initiate the legislative process by requesting the Commission to submit proposals on topics that Parliament considers require legislation.

1.3 National use

The extent to which national courts make use of Articles 81 (ex 85) and 82 (ex 86) varies from State to State. This was examined by the Commission through a questionnaire sent to the Member States in 1985. Although the response was very patchy (due to an absence of systematic gathering of information) the Commission concluded that:

> ... in principle, there are no fundamental obstacles to the application of Community competition law by national courts... . Until now it is clear that the Community competition rules have generally been pleaded as a basis for obtaining an injunction or other interim relief or as a defence to an action for breach of contract. There does not appear, to the Commission's knowledge, to be any case in which damages have been awarded by a national court for a breach of either Article 85 [now 81] or Article 86 [now 82] of the EC Treaty. (16th Report on Competition Policy, 1987.)

In 1993, the Commission issued Guidelines for national courts when applying Articles 81 (ex 85) and 82 (ex 86) in 'domestic' litigation. The use of Articles 81 and 82 in English courts is examined in **Chapter 7**.

It is also now possible in some Member States for their competition authorities to use Articles 81 (ex 85) and 82 (ex 86) (or suitably amended variants) against undertakings whose activities do not attract the attention of the European Commission. Since March 2000, the Competition Act 1998 has been fully in force in the United Kingdom. Under this Act, the Office of Fair Trading is able to apply statutory rules, virtually identical to Articles 81 and 82, to anti-competitive conduct which may affect trade within the United Kingdom. The previous regulatory framework (provided by a number of different Acts) has been largely replaced. See now also the Enterprise Act 2002.

The European Commission is keen to delegate work to bodies in the Member States, where appropriate. Guidelines for cooperation between the Commission and national competition authorities were issued in 1997 and it is possible for the Commission to find that a complaint made to it lacks Community interest but should be referred to the appropriate national authority (in the UK, this is usually the OFT). Currently, OFT officials assist those of the European Commission when they investigate cases in the UK and, in such circumstances, the OFT can exercise the investigative powers vested in the European Commission by EC Regulation 1/2003. The Competition Act 1998 allows High Court judges to issue search warrants, backing up the investigative actions of the Commission. The 1998 Act also makes it a criminal offence for anyone intentionally to obstruct a Commission (or OFT) official executing such a warrant (punishable by imprisonment). See **6.3**.

The influence of the EC competition rules can be found in rather unexpected areas in the United Kingdom. For example, the London Stock Exchange was found (by the Minister for Corporate Affairs) to be in breach of Article 86 (now 82) by virtue of its rules on the dissemination of news about companies. Under the Financial Services Act, the Minister is empowered to direct the Stock Exchange to take specific action if he considers that its conduct conflicts with the Community obligations of the United Kingdom.

1.4 What is an 'undertaking'?

'Undertakings' is a term that will be referred to many times in this book. There is no definition of it in the EC Treaty, nor in the secondary legislation, although Regulation 17/62 gives some clues as to the probable scope when it deals (in Article 11) with requests to undertakings for information. Article 11 imposes a duty (to supply information) upon:

(a) the owners of undertakings (or their representatives);

(b) the authorised representatives of legal persons, companies or firms;

(c) the authorised representatives of associations which have no legal personality.

In practice, any form of entity which engages in economic activity will be considered by the Commission and the European Court to be an undertaking. Its legal status and the way in which its activities are financed are irrelevant. See, for example, *CNSD v Commission* (C-35/96) [1998] ECR I-3851. In his Opinion in *J.C.J. Wouters and others v Algemene Raad van de Nederlandse Orde van Advocaten* (C-309/99) [2002] ECR I-1577, Advocate-General Leger observed that lawyers in the Netherlands may act either as independent agents or as employees and two distinct bodies of legal rules apply. Those who function as independent agents demand and receive remuneration from their clients for services performed; they also bear any financial risks in that they will bear any shortfall between income and expenditure. They are undertakings. By contrast, lawyers who carry out their activities as employees, performing their services for, and under the direction of, another who pays them remuneration are employed workers and not covered by competition law.

Other examples have included:

(a) individuals (eg *AOIP/Beyrard* [1976] 1 CMLR D14 — an inventor who gave exclusive rights in his invention to a commercial organisation; franchisees like Mrs Schillgalis in Pronuptia; even opera singers — *RAI/Unitel* [1978] 3 CMLR 306);

(b) corporations — even of non-EC origin (*Europembellage Corp and Continental Can Co v Commission* (6/72) [1973] ECR 215; *Ahlström Oy v Commission* (89/85 et al.) [1993] 4 CMLR 407 — the woodpulp cartel);

(c) partnerships (*Re William Prym-Werke* [1973] CMLR D250);

(d) non-profit-making organisations which operate to collect artists' royalties commercially (eg, *GVL* [1983] ECR 483 — a German society which collects copyright royalties); and

(e) organisations which are part of the 'State', where they carry on economic or commercial activities (an example in the UK might be the Post Office).

Where an organisation puchases goods, not for the purpose of offering those goods as part of an economic activity but to use them in a different context, it may not be engaged in an economic activity. In *Federación Nacional de Empressas de Instrumentación Cientifica, Médica, Técnica y Dental (FENIN) v Commission* (T-319/99) [2003] 5 CMLR 34, the 26 bodies or organisations which run the Spanish national health system ('SNS') were held not to constitute an undertaking for the purposes of Article 82. The 26 (which included three Spanish government ministries) were held not to be acting as undertakings when they provide their services (including the goods they purchase) free of charge to their members on the basis of universal cover. It followed that they were not acting as undertakings when they purchased the medical goods and equipment. Although as an entity they might 'wield very considerable economic power, even giving rise to a monopsony', it is not acting as an undertaking because the activity for which they bought the goods is not an economic activity, and they are therefore not subject to Article 81 or 82.

1.5 What is the 'market'?

1.5.1 Basic principles

Definition of the relevant market is of fundamental importance to analysis under both Article 81 and Article 82. It is crucial for Article 81(1) analysis when considering the possible effect of a suspected anti-competitive agreement. It is vital as a preliminary step to determination of whether a firm occupies a dominant position, under Article 82. It is necessary when seeing if an agreement is one of 'minor importance' (see **2.3.2**). In 1997, the Commission issued a Notice on the definition of the relevant market (OJ 1997 C372). The Notice is quite explicit on how to define the relevant market. First, it consists of two components — the relevant product market and the relevant geographical market.

- The relevant product market 'comprises all those products and/or services which are regarded as interchangeable or *substitutable* by the consumer, by reason of the products' characteristics, their prices and their intended use'.

- The relevant geographical market 'comprises the area in which the undertakings concerned are involved in the supply and demand of products or services, in which the conditions of competition are sufficiently homogenous and which can be distinguished from neighbouring areas because the conditions of competition are appreciably different in those areas'.

One should look at the nature and characteristics of the products concerned. For example, are they perishable? Are they large bulk, low value, such as breeze blocks? What about consumer tastes — are they the same across the various territories under consideration? Price differences between products can be relevant — the Commission uses the SSNIP test. This asks what would be the effect of a [S]mall but [S]ignificant, [N]on-transitory [I]ncrease in [P]rice on consumer purchase? Typically, if a 5% price rise in product A will result in a fall in demand for that product but an increased demand for product B, these two products may occupy the same market as one appears to be a substitute for the other. This notion of substitutability is crucial in determining the limits of a product market.

1.5.2 An example of market definition

Chapter 4 considers the definition of the relevant market in the particular context of Article 82 (see **4.2.2** and **4.2.3**). However, an example now may be helpful before we move on to look at Article 81. There is an excellent breakdown of factors to consider in the Commission's decision on a proposed merger between Nestlé and Perrier (*Nestlé-Perrier* [1992] OJ L356/1).

1.5.2.1 Relevant product market

Nestlé submitted to the Commission that there was no separate market for bottled source water, and that the relevant market to assess the proposed concentration should be that of all non-alcoholic refreshment beverages, including both bottled source water and soft drinks. Nestle proposed this market definition on the basis that all beverages have as [their] basic function to quench the consumer's thirst.

The Commission rejected this proposed definition, as it considered that a limited substitutability looking only at functionality was not sufficient to establish substitutability in competition terms. If the only criterion to establish substitutability was to be quenching thirst, 'many products of very different nature which fulfil that function would have to be considered as belonging to the same market (tea, milk, beer, certain fruits, etc.)'. The Commission identified several factors which indicated the existence of a distinct market for bottled source waters. In this market, according to the Commission, operators were able to act to a significant degree independently of the actions of companies selling soft drinks, in particular in the area of pricing.

(a) Demand considerations

The Commission looked at four factors here.

(i) Motivation of final consumers to purchase bottled water originating from a natural source.

(ii) Differences in composition of the products, their taste and their intended use.

(iii) Low responsiveness to price changes:

> Three main factors indicate that it cannot be reasonably expected that an appreciable non-transitory increase in the price of source waters compared with that of soft drinks would lead to a significant shift of demand from source waters to soft drinks for reasons of price only.

1. Substantial price difference in absolute terms between bottled water and soft drinks [often 2 or 3 times higher for soft drinks in France than for bottled waters]
2. The market of bottled source water in France is characterized by strong marketing and promotional activities, with high advertising budgets for the three main suppliers.

   As a consequence of the resulting image of natural, pure and healthy product associated with source water ... consumers do not recognize soft drinks as a substitute of bottled source water for daily use at home. The general image directly associated by consumers with branded source water as a consequence of the common axes of the publicity of each brand, and their additional attachment to each particular brand reduce the importance of price as purchasing criteria (small elasticity of demand).
3. Price evolution 'Manufacturers' prices of source water and soft drinks have had a very different evolution during the last five years'.

(iv) Views of retailers:

The vast majority of retailers consulted by the Commission regard bottled source waters as a distinct market, where demand is basically led by brand awareness and health concerns.

(b) Supply considerations

Three basic factors were important to the Commission's analysis here.

(i) Conditions of production and marketing

'Production and marketing are subject to different constraints in the soft drink market and in the market of bottled source water in particular in France' [this distinction should be borne in mind when looking at the Commission's analysis of the geographical market]. Those constraints were:

1. Regulatory requirements [production of spring and mineral water was subject to authorisation and had to be bottled at source. That had an effect on the possible location of bottling plants.]
2. Manufacturers of soft drinks may and often do grant trade mark licences to independent bottlers who produce the soft drink in their own premises and sell the product under the original brand.
3. Different actors in each market:

   In France, no major soft drink producer (Cadbury Schweppes, Coca-Cola, Pernod Ricard) has been able to develop a presence in the market of bottled water, in spite of the past growth of demand and increasing manufacturers' prices for bottled source water.

(ii) Manufacturers' pricing

Pricing in the soft drink and the bottled source water market seems to follow a different logic.

(iii) Supply side substitutability

'The conjunction of the production and marketing constraints described under [(b)(i) above] make it impossible for soft drink or beer producers to switch their installed capacity from production of soft drinks to production of source water, be it spring or mineral water. Even if soft drink producers currently had excess capacity, the legal requirement to bottle spring and mineral water at the source makes it impossible for them to use any possible spare capacity already installed to bottle source water.'

(c) Conclusion

The Commission concluded that the relevant product market was that of bottled source water. However, that left open a further refinement of the possible product market — should there be a distinction between still source waters and sparkling and flavoured waters? In the Commission's opinion, its assessment would not be materially different whether or not sparkling and flavoured source waters were excluded from the relevant product market.

Several demand factors indicate that sparkling and flavoured waters could be excluded from the relevant product market. There are a number of differences between still source waters and sparkling and flavoured waters, in terms of physical characteristics, taste, intended use, volumes consumed and price levels. In certain exceptional cases, the companies concerned position sparkling and flavoured waters closer to soft drinks in terms of packaging, marketing and price. The sparkling water Perrier (3.8% of the market) and certain flavoured waters (less than 1%) constitute examples of such exceptions.

However, it is not possible to exclude competitive interactions between sparkling flavoured and still source waters. Most companies marketing still source waters also market sparkling source waters, and to a lesser extent, flavoured source waters. A bottler of still source water can easily switch production to a sparkling or flavoured source water, at least from a technical point of view.

For these reasons, it might be difficult to justify a radical exclusion of sparkling and flavoured source water from the relevant product market. However, still sparkling and flavoured waters certainly constitute different categories of products, or segments, within the overall market of bottled source water. In the present case the assessment of the proposed merger would in any event not materially differ even if sparkling and flavoured waters were excluded.

1.5.2.2 Relevant geographical market

The Commission concluded that the relevant geographic market within which the power of the new [merged] entity has to be assessed was France. Nestlé had argued that the relevant geographic market should be extended from France (its home market) to include Belgium and some German Laender. It argued that if excessive prices were to be applied in the French market, parallel imports into France would develop. In other words, the products it sent to Belgium and Germany would find their way back to the home market in France. Several factors indicated that the parties were (and would in the future) be able to determine their competitive behaviour in France without suffering significant competitive constraints from outside the country:

(a) the different competitive environment prevailing in each Member State,

(b) the practical impossibility of the development of parallel imports, and

(c) the absence of Community competitors capable of overcoming the strong barriers to entry into the French market.

Let us consider those factors in turn.

(a) The competitive environment in the Member States

The Commission considered that the competitive environment in the bottled source water market was 'very heterogeneous throughout the Community' for the following reasons.

- Demand presented different characteristics in each Member State [there were some countries such as the UK, Ireland, Netherlands, Denmark and Portugal, where the demand for bottled source water was extremely low or non-existent and the market was 'in a stage of take-off'. In other Member States, the demand was basically for sparkling waters only. In Germany these accounted for 75% of the market and in Italy for over 60%.]

- trade flows were negligible in terms of consumption. [The Commission found that water was 'a low-value/high-volume product which in general cannot bear transport costs over long distances. The high impact of transport costs tends to regionalize the bulk of the market.' Nestlé had estimated the impact of transport costs at 10% for 300 km for the most expensive still waters. Where glass containers were used, transport costs were over twice as much]; and
- supply is highly fragmented in most Member States. [This is self-explanatory but was due to several factors, including the organisation of distributors on a regional basis, rather than nationwide. Also, the use of glass bottles was much greater in Germany and Italy, than in France. That had an effect on transport costs and the fact that these glass bottles were usually returnable also inhibited exports.]

(b) French exports and the threat of parallel imports

As we have seen already, the Commission regarded bottled source water as a relatively inexpensive and bulky product where transport costs had a high impact. The Commission thought it unlikely, even if margins were high, that a parallel importer could move throughout the various Member States the large volumes required to earn significant revenue and profits. Further, exports of French mineral water were carried out through subsidiaries of the main suppliers. This arrangement allowed a certain degree of price control over the water exported. For example, prices for Vittel in Belgium and Germany (prices delivered to customers) were significantly higher than the ex-works prices in France. The result of this comparison was that the price at which any hypothetical parallel importer could buy Vittel in Belgium or Germany was much higher than list prices charged by Vittel in France (40 and 18% respectively). Having paid these higher prices, the hypothetical re-exporter would then also incur further costs associated with:

- transport of the product back to France,
- unpackaging pallets, relabelling bottles and repackaging them again,
- its own margin.

Also, as we saw above, in Germany, the packaging of source water was different from that in France. The usual packaging in the German source water market was glass bottles of 75 cl size. These were not used in France. 89% of all sales of bottled water in Germany were in returnable glass bottles, and the bulk of French exports to Germany were packaged in glass bottles. Vittel's exports to Germany consisted basically of glass bottles of 1 litre and 1.25 litres. Transport costs for glass bottles were substantially higher than for plastic (Nestlé had estimated that they doubled). Finally, French retailers confirmed that distribution of still source water in France in glass bottles would face several problems (consumers are used to purchasing still source water in plastic bottles and the distributors would incur higher costs in handling glass instead of plastic).

For all of these reasons, the Commission considered that 'the conditions prevailing in the source water market show that the parties' exports and the threat of parallel imports do not and will not constrain the parties' competitive behaviour in the relevant geographic market'.

(c) Barriers to entry isolating the French market

The Commission identified several barriers to entry which indicated that France was a separate geographical market, where French suppliers were able to impose appreciable non-transitory price increases without suffering any external competitive constraint.

These factors were:

(i) the absence of imports [typically due to cost considerations];

(ii) the logistics of distribution [French producers moved sufficiently large volumes of water around to make it cost-effective to use trains to move their product, typically in complete wagons. Non-French producers would suffer in comparison, having either to transport by trucks or incur the costs involved in setting up their own rail distribution system and additionally move the volume of water sufficient to make this method of transport efficient.];

(iii) access to distribution [the French bottled water market was seen as 'mature'. This meant that it was difficult for any new water brand to penetrate. National brands were well-established in consumer consciousness and there was limited space to stock bottled water in retail outlets. Entry of a new brand would be 'high-risk'.];

(iv) advertising costs [the French market was 'brand-dominated'. In 1991, the aggregate advertising budget of the big three French producers exceeded FF680 million. Establishing a new brand would require heavy investment, take a long time and, because there were already three major producers, would be high- risk.];

(v) additional entry barriers [the French market was highly concentrated, with the big three holding a combined market share of 82% by value. The absence of imports implied that the barriers identified were effective, as did the fact that of fifteen attempted entries into the market in the preceding five years, only four were still present. Of that quartet, two were owned wholly or partly by members of the big three and the other two were 'insignificant in terms of sales'.]

1.6 The competition Articles

It should be noted that the Treaty of Amsterdam created a consolidated version of the EC Treaty. The consolidated version can be found, for example, in Foster, *Blackstone's EC Legislation*. The Treaty of Amsterdam came into effect on 1 May 1999 and the Articles containing the competition rules were re-numbered. The two main Articles are (now) Articles 81 and 82. In decisions or regulations of the Commission or Council, or judgments of the European Court, which precede 1 May 1999, you will find these Articles referred to as Articles 85 and 86 respectively. For ease of reference, the current Article numbers are added in square brackets.

1.7 Preliminary work

Before reading anything else, turn to **2.1** and **4.1** and read the text of Articles 81 (ex 85) and 82 (ex 86) of the Treaty.

2

Article 81(1): anti-competitive agreements

2.1 Introduction

The purpose of Article 81 (ex 85) is to ensure that competition is not restricted, prevented or distorted within the common market as the result of two or more undertakings agreeing to do (or not do) something which runs counter to the normal, competitive, working of the market.

Article 81 (ex 85) is divided into three paragraphs. Paragraph (1) sets out the prohibitory rule itself:

> 1. *The following shall be prohibited as incompatible with the common market: all agreements between undertakings, decisions by associations of undertakings and concerted practices which may affect trade between Member States and which have as their object or effect the prevention, restriction or distortion of competition within the common market, and in particular those which:*
> (a) *directly or indirectly fix purchase or selling prices or any other trading conditions;*
> (b) *limit or control production, markets, technical development, or investment;*
> (c) *share markets or sources of supply;*
> (d) *apply dissimilar conditions to equivalent transactions with other trading parties, thereby placing them at a competitive disadvantage;*
> (e) *make the conclusion of contracts subject to acceptance by the other parties of supplementary obligations which, by their nature or according to commercial usage, have no connection with the subject of such contracts.*

Paragraph (2) simply states the legal effect of such prohibition:

> 2. *Any agreements or decisions prohibited pursuant to this Article shall be automatically void.*

Lastly, paragraph (3) creates an exemption for certain agreements etc which would otherwise be prohibited and void. In order to be exempted, these agreements must comply with certain requirements:

> 3. *The provisions of paragraph 1 may, however, be declared inapplicable in the case of:*
> *— any agreement or category of agreements between undertakings;*
> *— any decision or category of decisions by associations of undertakings;*
> *— any concerted practice or category of concerted practices;*
> *which contributes to improving the production or distribution of goods or to promoting technical or economic progress, while allowing consumers a fair share of the resulting benefit, and which does not:*
> (a) *impose on the undertakings concerned restrictions which are not indispensable to the attainment of these objectives;*
> (b) *afford such undertakings the possibility of eliminating competition in respect of a substantial part of the products in question.*

We shall look in detail at Article 81(3) (ex 85(3)) in **Chapter 3**. The rest of this chapter will focus on Article 81(1) (ex 85(1)) — the prohibitory rule.

Article 81(1) (ex 85(1)) can be split into several elements, each one of which needs to be satisfied before the prohibition will take effect.

First, there must be a meeting of minds between two or more undertakings to do (or refrain from doing) some act. This may take the form of a written agreement or may be something much less formal. This will be considered in **2.2**.

Secondly, the 'agreement' must have an actual or potential effect on trade between Member States of the European Union. This will be considered in **2.3**.

Thirdly, the parties to the 'agreement' must intend that their agreement shall prevent, restrict or distort competition. Alternatively, it is enough if the 'agreement' does in fact prevent, restrict or distort competition within the common market. This will be considered in **2.4**.

What sort of things might be caught by Article 81(1) (ex 85(1))? Maybe the most obvious example would be the activities of a *cartel* — that is, a group of companies that should be competing with each other under normal competitive conditions but who decide to substitute cooperation for competition. The cartel may decide to split up territories between its members, so that each member has an exclusive area where it faces no effective competition (its 'home' market). Or the cartel may decide upon a common pricing structure for the product, with a view to lessening (or removing entirely) competition in terms of the price charged for the product. The effect of these decisions is to decrease the level of both active and passive competition.

The Commission and the European Court have seldom spoken in practical terms about the way their ideal, competitive, market should work. But the message seems clear that there should be competition between companies operating in the same market: that competition should be reflected in different prices being charged, different services being offered (lots of knowledgeable staff available to advise customers prior to purchase, or self-service and no staff, for example).

2.2 Agreements, decisions of associations and concerted practices

2.2.1 Introduction

Article 81(1) (ex 85(1)) distinguishes between three forms of collusion:

- agreements between undertakings
- decisions by associations of undertakings, and
- concerted practices

all of which are described as being 'incompatible with the common market' when they prevent, restrict or distort competition. In practice, the Commission and the Court do not maintain hard and fast divisions between the three. There may be differences as to ease of proof between the three: a piece of paper bearing the word 'Agreement' on its head in gothic script may do the job more swiftly than the detective work that may be needed to demonstrate a concerted practice but there is no magic in the labels themselves.

2.2.2 Agreements between undertakings

A legally-binding contract will be covered. So a patent licence will suffice, as will an exclusive dealership, a tied public house, a fast food franchise agreement. A less formal agreement will also be covered: a morally-binding (or gentlemen's) agreement will fall within Article 81(1) (ex 85(1)). According to the Court of First Instance in *Hercules v Commission* (T-7/89) [1991] ECR II-1711:

> ... it is sufficient if the undertakings ... have expressed their joint intention to conduct themselves on the market in a specific way.

The agreement may be between specific parties for a stated period of time. Alternatively, it may have a changing membership with different parties active over different periods. Although this presents problems of proof, this may still be an 'agreement'. Where the Commission investigates such a 'rolling' agreement, it will need to adduce sufficient evidence to show that any particular company was a party to the agreement; the Commission will also need to adduce evidence of the duration of that company's participation — this will be relevant to the severity of punishment handed down. As the Court of First Instance observed in *Dunlop Slazenger International Ltd v Commission* (T-43/92) [1994] ECR II-441:

> With regard to the alleged duration of an infringement, the ... principle of legal certainty requires that, if there is no evidence directly establishing the duration of an infringement, the Commission should adduce at least evidence of facts sufficiently proximate in time for it to be reasonable to accept that infringement continued uninterruptedly between two specific dates.

As to exactly what the parties have agreed to (in the legally-binding contracts referred to above) there should be no problem, but companies do need to be on their guard. In *Sandoz Prodotti Farmaceutici SpA v Commission* (C-277/87) [1990] ECR I-45, the Court of Justice held that tacit acquiescence may lead to the incorporation of terms into the contract. In Sandoz, a supplier sent out invoices to his customers, containing the expression 'export prohibited'. When a customer raised no protest about this and continued to order supplies, the expression could become a part of an agreement between the supplier and customer within the scope of Article 81 (ex 85) (re-affirmed by the Court of First Instance in *Dunlop Slazenger International Ltd v Commission* (T-43/92) [1994] ECR II-441). For an example of an agreement being inferred from behaviour, see *Tipp-Ex v Commission* (C-279/87) [1990] ECR I-261. The concept of an 'agreement' was explored once more by the CFI in *Bayer AG v Commission* (T-41/96) [2001] All ER (EC) 1, where it was said that:

> ... it centres around the existence of a concurrence of wills between at least two parties, the form in which it is manifested being unimportant so long as it constitutes the faithful expression of the parties' intention. [para 69]

Although unilateral acts are not covered by Article 81(1) (ex 85(1)), it is important to consider whether an act which is apparently unilateral may have some underlying, collusive, motive. For example, if a producer decides to terminate its relationship with an exclusive distributor, that looks like a unilateral act. But we must ask why the termination has occurred. If it is the result of pressure being brought to bear on the producer by its other exclusive distributors, maybe because the terminated dealer is undercutting the others on price, then we may have an agreement within the scope of Article 81(1) (ex 85(1)). See further on this: *Holleran v Daniel Thwaites* [1989] 2 CMLR 917; *Richard Cound Ltd v BMW (G.B.) Ltd*, 10 May 1995, unreported; and *Dunlop Slazenger*.

To fall within Article 81(1) (ex 85(1)), an agreement must be made *between* undertakings, not *within* a single undertaking. So one needs to know when more than one undertaking is involved. This can become problematic when a parent company and its subsidiaries are parties to an agreement. The Commission and the Court have said that parent companies and their subsidiaries form a single economic unit: *Hydrotherm v Andreoli* (170/83) [1984] ECR 2999. Any agreements between them (sometimes known as a 'bathtub conspiracy'!) cannot fall foul of Article 81 (ex 85). Thus in *Centrafarm v Sterling* (15/74) [1974] ECR 1147 the ECJ said:

> [There is no violation of Article 81 (ex 85) by] agreements or concerted practices between undertakings belonging to the same concern and having the status of parent company and subsidiary, if the undertakings form an economic unit within which the subsidiary has no real freedom to determine its course of action on the market, and if the agreements or practices are concerned merely with the internal allocation of tasks as between the undertakings. (Emphasis added.)

(Conversely, this idea of economic unity has been used to fine a parent company for the misdeeds of its subsidiary: see, eg, *Eurim Pharm GmbH v Johnson & Johnson* [1981] 2 CMLR 287; see also *Commercial Solvents Corp v Commission* (6–7/73) [1974] ECR 223.)

What constitutes an agreement for present purposes? It is clear that legally binding contracts are included but it seems that the meaning is broader than this. 'Gentlemen's agreements' are included — in *Boeringer v Commission* (7/72) [1972] ECR 1281 a quinine cartel divided up the world market and fixed prices, but its contract expressly excluded the common market. The members of the cartel then wrote down a gentlemen's agreement, which extended the application of the contract to the common market. This was held to be an agreement for the purposes of Article 81 (ex 85) even after its operation was suspended by the members, as the prices set under its terms continued to be used. If two or more entities pursue a joint plan then it may not matter that it cannot be classified as an 'agreement' — it may be labelled as a 'concerted practice' (see **2.2.4**) and still be within the net of Article 81 (ex 85).

The polypropylene cartel which was investigated by the Commission in the early 1980s (see OJ 1986 L230) was alleged to be a 'rolling' agreement which lasted some six years. It was asserted that it had a variety of members at any point in time, who sometimes undercut their (covertly) agreed prices and where meetings occurred at different levels of importance ('bosses' meetings and 'experts' meetings). The Commission found that the basic, detailed plan constructing the cartel was an agreement for the purposes of Article 81(1) (ex 85(1)). We should note that, in the present judicial climate, the Commission would be put to strict proof as to who belonged to the cartel and for what period(s) — see the Court of First Instance in its judgments on the polypropylene cartel decision; eg, *BASF AG v Commission* (T-4/89) [1992] 4 CMLR 357. That the Commission has accepted and discharged that burden of proof may be seen in *Re Cartonboard Cartel* 1994 OJ L243/1 where the participants in a series of regular 'secret and institutionalised meetings' were divided into four groups by the Commission, according to the period of their participation.

2.2.3 Decisions by associations of undertakings

Typically, such associations are trade associations but the expression could include other organisations such as cooperatives. Formal decisions which are approved by the members of a trade association would fall within the scope of Article 81(1) (ex 85(1)) (although they could as easily be classified as a collection of agreements between the members: see eg, *Groupement des Fabricants de Papiers Peints v Commission* (73/74) [1976] ECR 1491). Non-binding recommendations made by a trade association to its members may be regarded as 'decisions': see eg, *FEDETAB v Commission* (209/78)[1980] ECR 3125; *Vereeniging van Cementhandelaren v Commission* (8/72) [1972] ECR 977.

If two trade associations reach an agreement, the terms of which will affect their respective members, this may be regarded as both a decision of the associations and an agreement between the individual members, rendering both members and associations liable to fines if the agreement infringes Article 81(1) (ex 85(1)): see eg *FRUBO v Commission* (71/74) [1975] ECR 563. A trade association may be liable for its involvement in a cartel, if undertaken separately from the involvement of individual association members. Two examples can be found in the Commission decisions involving (i) a Finnish board mills association, Finnboard, for its participation in a producers' cartel (*Cartonboard* OJ 1994 L243/1); and (ii) the European Cement Association, Cembureau, for its participation in a cartel comprising Cembureau, eight national associations and 33 producers (Cement OJ 1994 L343/1).

2.2.4 Concerted practices

2.2.4.1 Coordination

The expression concerted practice is intended to bring within Article 81(1) (ex 85(1)) those forms of cooperation which are more amorphous than a formal oral or written agreement. In a case involving a cartel of dyestuff producers (*ICI v Commission* (48/69) [1972] ECR 619), the Court of Justice observed that:

> By its very nature ... a concerted practice does not have all the elements of a contract but may *inter alia* arise out of coordination which becomes apparent from the behaviour of the participants.

The Court of Justice went on to define a concerted practice as:

> a form of coordination between enterprises that has not yet reached the point where there is a contract in the true sense of the word but which, in practice, *consciously substitutes a practical cooperation for the risks of competition*. (Emphasis added.)

This may cause difficulties for the Commission, which bears the burden of proof on the issue, but it will also create problems for companies which find themselves suspected of involvement in a concerted practice. Although there is no burden of proof on the company(ies) in the strict sense, it may make good sense tactically for them to offer explanations for their behaviour which are consistent with the absence of a concerted practice (see eg, *CRAM and Rheinzink v Commission* (29 and 35/83) [1984] ECR 1679).

The evidence adduced to establish the existence of a concerted practice may be direct: a company may decide to cooperate with the Commission (cf the Commission's Notice on the non-imposition or reduction of fines for 'whistle-blowers' in cartel cases, OJ 1996 C207/4), or detailed records of meetings may be found by the Commission on searching through a company's files (see **Chapter 6** for details of the Commission's investigative powers). More often, the evidence is indirect: there may be evidence that meetings occurred and who attended them but perhaps not what was discussed or what the participants disclosed to each other. One then looks at circumstantial evidence to see what may be inferred from the activities of the suspect companies. If there is evidence of:

(a) meetings between companies that should be competing with each other (in the same product market and same territories), and

(b) identical or very similar actions by these different companies, often on the same date (perhaps announcing identical price rises for the product within days of each other),

then a concerted practice may be inferred. However, the Court of Justice has stated that simply producing evidence of parallel conduct will not suffice as proof of a concerted practice unless that is the only plausible explanation for the conduct (*Re Woodpulp Cartel, Re: Ahlstroem Osakeyhtiö and others v Commission* (C-89/85) [1993] ECR I-1307). In that case, the Court's experts found that the structure of the market in woodpulp was a more credible explanation for the companies' pricing policies than any attempt at concertation. In a similar vein, Advocate General Mayras observed in the *ICI* case that:

> [I]t is necessary at the least to show: first, that the conscious parallel behaviour is not exclusively or even mainly due to economic conditions or to the structure of the market; secondly, that, where there is no express meeting of minds, sufficiently clear, unequivocal presumptions lead to the conviction that the parallel conduct was the result of concertation, of a coordinated policy.

It should be easier for the Commission to discharge its burden of proof where the market is not oligopolistic in nature (see also *Van Gerven and Verona* [1994] CMLR 31, at p 601).

In the cases concerning a polypropylene cartel, the Court of First Instance in *Rhône-Poulenc SA v Commission* (T-1/89) [1991] ECR II-867, set out what companies must avoid doing in order to avert suspicion. What is forbidden is:

(a) to have contact, whether direct or not, with one's competitors;
(b) if such contact is intended to (or does); either
(c) influence the conduct of a competitor (whether actual or potential); or
(d) disclose to such competitors the intended or possible future conduct of one's own company.

According to the Court of First Instance, each company must work out its policies for itself. That does not mean that they cannot adapt their policies intelligently to respond to the existing and anticipated conduct of their rivals. See also *Suiker Unie v Commission* (40/73 etc) [1975] ECR 1663; *Tate & Lyle plc and others v Commission* (T-202/98 etc) [2001] All ER (EC) 839.

The best indicator of a concerted practice seems to be if the Commission can adduce evidence of contact between the alleged participants. Again, though, even this can be inferred from the circumstances. An example is found in the *Dyestuffs* case (*ICI v Commission* (48/69)), where the correspondence of behaviour showed a high degree of coordination between the various producers. The Court of Justice observed that the dye producers had raised their prices by similar amounts on three separate occasions. The first point to be noted was that the rates of individual price increases were identical in all the relevant countries. Further, with very few exceptions, the price increases applied to the same dyestuffs. The price rises were put into effect on almost — or even exactly — the same day by producers in the different countries concerned. The orders sent out by several producers contained very similar wording, even with some sentences exactly the same, and were sent out on the same day, sometimes simultaneously. The Court was also furnished with evidence of attendance by producers at meetings in Basel and London but that hardly seemed necessary in light of the remarkable series of coincidences that would need to exist for these events to be explicable on any basis other than concertation.

A company suspected of belonging to a cartel might ask — what conduct could be inconsistent with membership? In the *PVC II cartel* (C-238/99) [2002] ECR I-8375, the ECJ noted evidence of fierce competition on the relevant market, with aggressive conduct on prices and that the intended 'compensation mechanism' between producers had functioned poorly. Despite these shortcomings, the ECJ had no doubt that there was ample evidence of the alleged cartel.

2.2.4.2 Parallel conduct

The Commission's biggest problem occurs when it tries to infer a concerted practice from circumstantial evidence in an oligopolistic market (or industry). It is forced to rely upon parallel conduct (or coincidences) which, in the absence of evidence of contact between the suspected undertakings, may simply be the natural result of having so few players on the market. Where there are 12 or fewer 'in play', economic theory suggests that similar behaviour (perhaps increasing price at the same time, or by the same amount or percentage) by undertakings may just be the way an oligopolistic market operates. The dividing line between mere parallel behaviour and a concerted practice is a hard one to spot but it must be done. In *Re Polypropylene Cartel,* OJ 1986 L230, the Commission stated that while it is not very important to maintain a strict distinction between 'agreements' and 'concerted practices', what matters is distinguishing a concerted practice from the simple parallel behaviour of companies who are not colluding.

2.3 Effect on inter-State trade

2.3.1 Why you need to consider this

This phrase introduces the intra-Community element into Article 81 (ex 85), an idea similar to that which can be seen in some of the cases on free movement of workers (eg, *Morson & Jahnjan v Netherlands* (35 and 36/82) [1982] ECR 3723). The idea is that there should be a single common market with goods circulating freely within it. If one's behaviour cannot affect trade between Member States, then it is outside the scope of the EC Treaty.

The phrase may be taken, then, as indicating the boundary between the jurisdiction of the EC rules on competition and the competition laws of the Member States. This was certainly the position adopted by the Court of Justice in *Hugin/Liptons v Commission* (22/78) [1979] ECR 1869. However, it is quite limited because the Court usually gives a generous interpretation of those matters which may affect trade between Member States — for example, it will acknowledge the jurisdiction of the Community rules even where behaviour has only an indirect or even potential effect on trade between Member States: see, eg, Advocate-General Trabucchi in *Groupement des Fabricants de Papiers Peints v Commission* (73/74) [1976] ECR 1491, who suggested that, in time, the idea of 'an effect on trade between Member States' would simply mean that the effect of the behaviour must be '... such as to be significant at Community level', regardless of frontiers or geographic areas.

It has been suggested (by Dr Ehlermann of DG IV) that the inclusion of a requirement of an 'effect on inter-State trade' in Article 81 (ex 85) was an early forerunner of the *subsidiarity* principle (introduced by the Maastricht Treaty to indicate that matters of purely local/national importance should fall outside the scope of the European Community).

Agreements have been found to have an effect on trade between Member States even though they are restricted expressly to cover a single country. Examples are:

(a) *Vereeniging van Cementhandelaren v Commission* (8/72) [1972] ECR 977 — price fixing between Dutch cement producers, limited to sales in The Netherlands but which, the Court said, made the Dutch market more difficult for foreign cement producers to operate in or penetrate.

(b) *Papiers Peints* (supra) — loyalty discounts to customers who bought in bulk from Groupement members, but only within Belgium. The Court acknowledged that, in theory, the alleged behaviour could have an effect on trade between Member States, but quashed the decision of the Commission because it was not sufficiently reasoned (and thus fell foul of Article 253 (ex 190), EC Treaty).

This is likely to remain the situation, notwithstanding the view of the Commission that 'agreements whose actual or potential effect [is] limited to the territory of only one Member State' will not come under Community law but will be a matter for national law. The Commission recognises that agreements made between undertakings established in only one Member State may be within Article 81(1) (ex 85(1)) where they concern intra-community imports or exports from that State. Similarly, as the Commission has also noted:

> so-called 'national' agreements, in which only the undertakings of one Member State participate and which were created with the sole aim of regulating the production or the marketing of products in that Member State, are covered by Article 85(1) [now 81(1)] when they cover the whole or the greater part of the national territory, because they grant an artificial protection to national industry and therefore impede the economic interpenetration envisaged in the [EC] Treaty.

(Commission Notice relating to the revision of the notice of 3 September 1986 on agreements of minor importance which are not caught by the provisions of Article 85(1) of the EC Treaty, 1996.)

A typical example of a clause which had a direct effect on inter-State trade is found in *Consten and Grundig v Commission* (56 & 58/64) [1966] ECR 299. Specific terms of contracts prohibited exports of Grundig machines from Germany into France other than by the authorised French dealer, Consten. Grundig transferred its French trademark, 'Gint', to Consten. When an unauthorised exporter shipped (cheaper) German Grundig machines into France and undercut Consten's prices, Consten started litigation in France alleging, *inter alia*, breach of its trademark rights. The matter was then brought to the attention of the Commission and subsequently to the European Court on appeal. The insulation of the French market from imports clearly affected trade between Member States.

2.3.2 Agreements of minor importance

As we saw in **2.3.1**, the effect of the behaviour under analysis must be 'significant at Community level' (per Advocate General Trabucchi). It is important to note that not all effects on inter-State trade will fulfil this criterion of Article 81 (ex 85). The Commission has issued several Notices defining what constitutes economically significant activity ('Notice on agreements of minor importance'). The earlier versions concentrated on defining small and medium-sized firms and removing them from the operation of Article 81 (ex 85). The objective there was to encourage these smaller firms to thrive and expand, thereby providing effective competition for the larger firms. More recently, the 1997 version of the Notice changed emphasis to remove the prohibitory threat from firms, regardless of their size, if their share of the relevant market was small. Even a large firm could find that its agreement(s) in a particular market did not have an 'appreciable effect'on competition. This change continued in the 2001 revision (see OJ 2001/C 368/07). Like the 1997 version, the 2001 Notice distinguishes between horizontal agreements (between competing firms) and vertical agreements (where the parties operate on different levels of the relevant market). The 2001 Notice increased the thresholds for an agreement to have an appreciable effect on competition:

(a) where the agreement is made between (actual or potential) competitors in a market, the aggregate market share held by the parties must not exceed 10% (para 7(a) of the Notice);

(b) where the agreement is made between non-competitors in a market, the market share of each party must not exceed 15% (para 7(b) of the Notice);

(c) where it is unclear whether the agreement is between competitors or not, the 10% threshold applies (para 8 of the Notice);

(d) where a market has several parallel networks of agreements whose cumulative effect is to foreclose that market, all of the preceding thresholds are lowered to 5%. A cumulative foreclosure effect is thought to be unlikely where less than 30% of the relevant market is covered by parallel networks of agreements having similar effects. In addition, any supplier or distributor with a market share of 5% or less would not usually be considered to make a significant contribution to the cumulative foreclosure effect and thus not be caught by Article 81(1).

These thresholds may be exceeded by up to 2% in two successive calendar years without adverse consequences (para 9, 2001 Notice). It is important to note that the Commission prefers market shares to be measured in terms of sales value data. If that is not appropriate, purchase value data may be used. If neither is available, other measures may be used including volume data.

Agreements which contain specified hardcore restrictions on competition will not be covered by this Notice, regardless of the market shares involved (para 11, 2001 Notice). Again, a distinction is made between 'competitor' agreements and 'non-competitor' agreements. A 'competitor' agreement must not contain any restriction which is intended to fix prices for third parties, to limit output or sales, or to allocate markets or customers. The hardcore restrictions for 'non-competitor' agreements are similar but much more specific.

The 2001 Notice focuses on the determination of whether an agreement produces an appreciable restriction on competition. However, it also points out that agreements between small and medium-sized firms are seldom capable of having an appreciable effect on inter-State trade. Such firms are those with fewer than 250 employees and either an annual turnover of Euro 40 million or less (or an annual balance-sheet total of Euro 27 million or less).

2.3.3 A reasoned test?

The determination of an effect on inter-State trade may now be subject to a 'rule of reason' test, (see **2.4.3**). We can draw this conclusion from the decision of the ECJ in the *Delimitis* case (C-234/89) [1991] ECR I-935. The court considered an 'access' clause in the beer supply agreement between the litigants, which purported to allow the customer to purchase beer from other suppliers, including those in other Member States. If it was a genuine clause, and foreign suppliers could have access to the customer, then the effect on inter-State trade of an exclusive purchase agreement could be minimised so that Article 81(1) (ex 85(1)) need not apply. See further **2.4.4.6** on *Delimitis*.

Against this introduction of a 'rule of reason' must be balanced the interesting opinion of both the CFI and ECJ that a contractual clause which has *never* been implemented may nevertheless have an effect on trade between Member States because its existence may create a 'visual and psychological' effect which contributes to a partitioning of the market. See eg, the CFI in *Parker Pen Ltd v Commission* (T-77/92) [1994] ECR II-0549. It is still an accepted principle that it is not necessary that the conduct in question should in fact have substantially affected trade between Member States, it is sufficient for the Commission to establish that the conduct was capable of having an appreciable effect on inter-State trade; see *Tate & Lyle and others v Commission* (T-202/98 etc) [2001] All ER (EC) 839.

When considering whether there is an 'effect on trade between Member States,' remember that 'trade' has been broadly construed to cover trade in services as well as goods.

2.4 The object or effect of prevention, restriction or distortion of competition within the Common Market

2.4.1 Object

The European Court treats 'object' as separate from 'effect'. If you are concerned with the object of an agreement, you need not analyse the market to see the effects of the agreement — purpose (or intention) alone is enough: see, eg, *Re Polypropylene Cartel* (1986), where the Commission was satisfied that the producers' cartel had an anti-competitive object; it was unnecessary to demonstrate that competition had been affected. See also *Tate & Lyle and others v Commission* (T-202/98 etc) [2001] All ER (EC) 839; *Volkswagen AG v Commission* (T-62/98) [2000] ECR I-2707. You should remember, though, that even if a company is found 'guilty' of having an unlawful objective, the degree of any consequential effect may be examined in order to determine the amount of any financial penalty to be imposed on the company.

The ability to prohibit conduct which is *intended* to have anti-competitive effects is vested in the Commission, by virtue of Article 85 (ex 89). Subject to problems of proof, the Commission may act to prevent business plans from coming into effect, or at least stop them at an early stage. This requirement, that parties have the object of preventing, restricting or distorting competition, has been interpreted quite liberally — see, for example, *Consten and Grundig v Commission* (56 & 58/64) [1966] ECR 299: '... it is not necessary to take into consideration the actual effects of an agreement where its purpose is to prevent, restrict or distort competition'. The agreements between Consten and Grundig were *designed* to isolate the French market and artificially maintain separate national markets within the Community for products of a widely distributed brand. This meant that there was a distortion of competition within the common market.

These matters were considered by the Court of Justice in the *Sandoz* case (C-277/87) [1990] ECR I-45) where Sandoz raised three objections to the allegation that its conduct had the object or effect of preventing, restricting or distorting competition. Sandoz said:

(a) the conduct (inclusion of the words 'not to be exported' on an invoice) was void under national (Italian) law;

(b) there had been no allegation that its conduct had an adverse effect on trade between Member States;

(c) it had done nothing to enforce observance of the clause by its customers.

All three points were rejected by the Court: it was unnecessary that the agreement be valid in national law — Article 81 (ex 85) was concerned only with the parties' intention; if it appeared that an agreement had the objective of preventing (etc) competition within the common market, it was unnecessary to have regard to the specific effects of the agreement; the absence of enforcement was not sufficient to excuse the clause from the prohibition in Article 81(1) (ex 85(1)). One can see that the Court of Justice is still determined to take a tough line on 'offenders' by its adherence to a teleological interpretation of the phrase 'object or effect' in Article 81(1) (ex 85(1)). That the Court of First Instance adopts the same attitude can be seen in, eg, *Solvay v Commission* (T-12/89) [1992] ECR II-907.

2.4.2 Effect

The effect must be established by means of a market analysis (and see **2.4.3**). In *Volk v Vervaecke* (5/69) [1969] ECR 295 the Court demanded that there must be an 'appreciable' or not insignificant effect on the market. This means that agreements between undertakings who hold only a small share of the market may fall outside of the scope of Article 81 (ex 85). That idea was first given some formal detail in 1970, when the Commission issued its first *Notice on Agreements of Minor Importance*. Originally set up to facilitate cooperation between small and medium-sized undertakings, the Notice has been amended so that now even quite large companies can get the benefit of it, so long as their combined share of the relevant market is small.

The Court considered the concept of behaviour which has the effect of restricting competition within the common market in *Ahlström Oy v Commission* (C-89, 104, 114, 116–7/85, C-125-129/85) [1993] 4 CMLR 407 (the woodpulp cartel). The defendant undertakings were companies based outside the EC who sold woodpulp to paper manufacturers based in the EC and who had been found guilty (by the Commission) of fixing the prices of these sales by means of agreements and other concerted practices. On appeal, the defendants alleged that they were outside the jurisdiction of the EC competition rules. The Court held that if woodpulp producers established in non-EC countries sold directly to purchasers established in the Community and engaged in price competition in order to win orders from those purchasers, that would constitute competition within the common market. Where, as here, those woodpulp producers jointly fixed the prices at which they would sell to EC customers and then sold at such prices: '... they are taking part in concertation which has the object and effect of restricting competition *within* the common market'. This is a very simplistic analysis but is perhaps best explained by the fact that the Court was only concerned with the jurisdiction of the Commission to investigate and fine the non-EC enterprises, rather than the merits of the Commission's decision.

Whilst one should not demean the significance of this element in Article 81(1) (ex 85(1)), the usual finding of the Commission is that competition has been restricted in some way without too rigorous an analysis. This may be because an agreement which infringes Article 81(1) is automatically void (Article 81(2)) unless it is granted an exemption under Article 81(3). Until 2004, only the Commission had the power to grant an exemption and it could impose conditions on an undertaking in order to qualify for an exemption. Thus, by finding that an undertaking has infringed Article 81(1), the Commission concentrated a lot of power in its hands.

This simplistic approach to economic analysis for the purposes of Article 81(1) came under attack on two grounds. First, it is not good enough to perform a full economic analysis under Article 81(3): one can see why the Commission wants to do things that way but there should be a proper analysis initially to determine whether conduct is anti-competitive, whether by purpose or effect. This approach has been advocated by the Court of First Instance: see, for example, its judgment in *Delimitis v Henninger Braü AG* (and see **2.4.4.6**). This shift was further reinforced by the reliance on reports by economic experts in the Court of Justice when it heard the *Ahlström Oy* case. The second challenge to the Commission's preferred way of working is the application of a 'rule of reason' — this is examined below.

2.4.3 Rule of reason

Examples of behaviour which has been found to have the effect of preventing, restricting or distorting competition and which may be prohibited by Article 81(1) (ex 85(1)) include:

(a) non-competition clauses;
(b) restrictions on use of know-how, patents;
(c) non-challenge clauses;
(d) restrictions on conditions of resale;
(e) price-fixing (other than within a specific contract);
(f) export bans;
(g) tying the sale of one product to that of another;
(h) exclusive purchase clauses;
(i) exclusive sale clauses.

The Court of Justice indicated in *Pronuptia de Paris v Schillgalis* (161/84) [1986] ECR 353 that it was prepared to consider the necessity of such clauses or, in other words, how reasonable it is that commercial agreements contain such clauses. Prior to this case, such matters had been considered but only under Article 85(3) (now 81(3)) when the Commission was deciding whether to grant an exemption to an otherwise void agreement. In *Pronuptia* the Court considered whether such clauses were economically justified in order to determine whether the agreement was prohibited by Article 85(1) (now 81(1)) at all.

The *Pronuptia* case involved a dispute concerning a distribution franchise. Mrs Schillgalis owned a shop where she had a franchise from Pronuptia to sell goods supplied by them (eg, wedding dresses) and related services. The Court held that franchising was a business method which promoted competition and that, without certain types of protection, the franchisor would not grant a franchise that obliged him to supply know-how and training and generally to support a franchisee. Certain clauses which were prima facie restrictive of competition were fundamental to the franchisor's willingness to grant a franchise, eg clauses which prohibited the franchisee from competing with the franchise network or disclosing confidential information to people outside the network. In the opinion of the Court, when performing the analysis under Article 85(1) (now 81(1)) to see if these clauses had the effect of preventing, restricting or distorting competition, one had to balance any identifiable anti-competitive effects against any effects which were pro-competitive. In *Pronuptia*, such pro-competitive effects could be seen because franchising helps small businesses to start up, thus increasing consumer choice. In the past, the presence of pro-competitive effects had always been considered, but for the purpose of an exemption under Article 85(3) (now 81(3)) (see further **3.2** below). If the Commission was now to weigh such considerations under Article 81(1) (ex 85(1)), one might ask what was left to consider on the issue of exemption? Indeed, the European Commission has posed this very question itself, while at the same time acknowledging that it had 'adopted this approach to a limited extent' and that:

> the current division between paragraph 1 and paragraph 3 in implementing Article 81 is artificial and runs counter to the integral nature of Article 81, which requires economic analysis of the

overall impact of restrictive practices. (See *White Paper on Modernisation of the Rules implementing Articles 81 and 82 of the EC Treaty*, April 1999.)

There should be no doubt that the ECJ intended, in *Pronuptia*, to alter significantly the way in which we should analyse agreements under Article 81(1) (ex 85(1)). This intention was reinforced by its subsequent judgment in *Delimitis v Henninger Braü AG* (see **2.4.4.6**). But the Commission remained cautious:

> if more systematic use were made under Article 81(1) of an analysis of the pro- and anti-competitive aspects of a restrictive agreement, Article 81(3) would be cast aside, whereas any such change could be made only through revision of the Treaty. (*White Paper*, 1999.)

In 1997, the Commission issued a Notice on the 'definition of the relevant market for the purposes of Community competition law' (OJ 1997 C 372). The Notice sets out how the Commission will ascertain the relevant market, in terms of product(s) and geography. This was nothing new when analysing behaviour under Article 82 (ex 86) (see **5.2**) but the Notice was quite explicit in its relevance to Article 81 (ex 85), too:

> Market definition is a tool to identify and define the boundaries of competition between firms. It allows to establish [sic] the framework within which competition policy is applied by the Commission. The main purpose of market definition is to identify in a systematic way the competitive constraints that the undertakings involved face.
>
> The objective of defining a market in both its product and geographic dimensions is to identify those actual competitors of the undertakings involved that are capable of constraining their behaviour and of preventing them from behaving independently of an effective competitive pressure. [So far, this is quite standard for Article 82 (ex 86) analysis but the Notice continues] It is from this perspective, that the market definition makes it possible, *inter alia*, to calculate market shares that would convey meaningful information regarding market power for the purposes of assessing dominance *or for the purposes of applying Article 85* [now 81]. (emphasis added)

The Notice stated that the market needs to be defined in an Article 81(1) (ex 85(1)) analysis, to see if there is an appreciable effect on competition, as well as under Article 81(3) (ex 85(3)) to see if the criterion in (3)(b) is satisfied. If the Commission has an understanding of the relevant market, when considering if there is evidence of an infringement of Article 81(1) (ex 85(1)), it will be in a sound position to assess both the pro-competitive and anti-competitive effects of the suspect behaviour. This can only be good for the application of a rule of reason to Article 81(1) (ex 85(1)). See further **4.2**.

The most recent consideration of the rule of reason is to be found in the CFI judgment in *Métropole Télévision and others v Commission* (T-112/99) [2002] All ER (EC) 1. The applicants argued that the Commission had failed to use a rule of reason approach in its analysis of the facts under Article 85(1) (now 81(1)). The CFI did not mince its words:

> ... the existence of such a rule has not, as such, been confirmed by the Community courts. Quite to the contrary, in various judgments the [ECJ and CFI] have been at pains to indicate that the existence of a rule of reason in Community competition law is doubtful. [A]n interpretation of Article 85(1) ... in the form suggested by the applicants, is difficult to reconcile with the rules prescribed by that provision ... It is only in the precise framework of [Article 85(3)] that the pro- and anti-competitive effects of a restriction may be weighed ... Article 85(3) would lose much of its effectiveness if such an examination had to be carried out already under Article 85(1) ...

This seems to be an explicit renunciation of the judgments in earlier cases, notably *Pronuptia de Paris*. The CFI considered this:

> It is true that, in a number of judgments, the [ECJ and CFI] have favoured a more flexible interpretation of the prohibition laid down in Article 85(1) ... Those judgments cannot, however, be interpreted as establishing the existence of a rule of reason in Community competition law. They are, rather, part of a broader trend in the case-law according to which it is not necessary to hold,

wholly abstractly and without drawing any distinction, that any agreement restricting the freedom of action of one or more of the parties is necessarily caught by the prohibition ... in Article 85(1) ...

In assessing the applicability of Article 85(1) to an agreement, account should be taken of the actual conditions in which it functions, in particular the economic context in which the undertakings operate, the products or services covered by the agreement and the actual structure of the market concerned ... That interpretation [observes] the substantive scheme of Article 85 ... and [preserves] the effectiveness of Article 85(3) ... It must, however, be emphasised that such an approach does not mean that it is necessary to weigh the pro- and anti-competitive effects of an agreement when determining whether the prohibition ... in Article 85(1) ... applies.

So, it appears for the time being at least, the rule of reason is dead but the assessment of the restrictive nature of clauses is to be done by placing them in 'their economic and legal context'. With respect, it may not always be easy to see where the distinction falls.

2.4.4 Some examples

It is useful to look at several types of behaviour mentioned in Article 81(1) (ex 85(1)), to see how and why such behaviour might fall foul of Article 81(1). The examples chosen are: price fixing, limiting production, controlling markets, sharing markets, ties and exclusive purchasing.

2.4.4.1 Price fixing

Price fixing is a real 'no-no', particularly when the parties operate in cartel form, ie in a *horizontal* arrangement. The reason for this emphasis on such horizontal cooperation is that it can remove price competition from an entire level of the market place (eg all manufacturers of this product) and is thus seen as against the interest of consumers. See, for example, the judgment of the ECJ in *ICI v Commission*, at paras 12 and 17.

Horizontal price fixing is traditionally not allowed — it is never acknowledged as 'necessary' or as setting a 'reasonable price'. A good illustration of horizontal price fixing is the case of *Vereeniging van Cementhandelaren v Commission* (8/72) [1972] ECR 977, which involved the Dutch Cement Dealers' Association (CDA).

CDA alleged that its system of 'target prices' was rarely adhered to in practice, and did not constitute a restraint on members (see para 16 of judgment). The ECJ said (para 21) that price fixing, even of a target, has an effect on competition as it enables all participants to 'predict with a reasonable degree of certainty' what their competitors' pricing policy is going to be.

A similar attitude can be seen in the more recent Commission Decision *Re Scottish Salmon Board* 1992 OJ L246/37:

there was a price-fixing agreement on farmed salmon, between the Scottish Salmon Growers' Association and the Norwegian Fish Farmers' Sales Organisation. This agreement infringed Article 85 [now 81] but there was no fine even though neither party had notified the Commission of the agreement, perhaps as this was the first infringement of Article 85 [now 81] in the economic sector of fish farming. The Commission observed that any concern about low Norwegian prices for salmon could be attacked through the anti-dumping procedure in the EC Treaty, not via an illegal arrangement.

The ban on horizontal price fixing includes indirectly fixing prices, for example, through exchange of information about prices (eg, discussions on proposed increases; press conferences; exchange of new price lists), or through concertation on discounts (ie, how much or even deciding not to give them).

Coming more up to date, in 1998 the Commission imposed large fines on price-fixing cartels involving, for example, stainless-steel producers (see OJ 1988 L/100, total fines ecu 27 million) and sugar producers (OJ 1998 L/284, total fines ecu 50 million).

A quote from the XXVIIIth Report of the European Commission on Competition Policy, published in 1999, is also illuminating:

> Of all restrictions of competition, restrictive practices in the form of secret agreements are undoubtedly the most destructive. Very often, these concerted practices involve a substantial number of economic operators in a given area of activity and, as such, they have a very marked impact on the relevant markets. Furthermore, these agreements almost invariably concern prices and thus severely undermine competition. The Commission is committed to an extremely tough stance against cartels ... The positive impact of the launch of the euro ... must not be countered by restrictive agreements designed to side-step market confrontation by artificially fixing prices or other trading conditions, which in the longer term could push up inflation and undermine the foundations of economic and monetary union.

The same prohibitory attitude does not exist for *vertical* agreements. This difference of approach between horizontal and vertical agreements is quite general, and does not apply just in the area of price fixing. The distinction can also be seen in the block exemptions which exclude the application of Article 81(1) (ex 85(1)): they are usually couched in the form of vertical arrangements, with agreements between competitors often specifically excluded. See, eg, Recital 3 and Article 1(a) and 2(4) of Regulation 2790/99. See also the Green Paper produced by the Commission on Vertical Restraints in Competition Policy 1996.

2.4.4.2 Limiting production

This might involve, for example, establishing quotas for existing companies. It is likely to be linked to price increases with a corresponding fall in production. The idea is to preserve everyone's market share. The victim is the consumer: he has to pay more money to buy the product, there are fewer satisfactory goods available and he is driven to consume inferior substitutes. It should be noted that if there are acceptable substitutes, such a system breaks down: see *Rhône-Poulenc SA v Commission* (T-1/89) [1991] ECR II-867.

Limiting technical development is a related prohibition for reasons which are partly economic, partly social. The ban is economic in the sense of preventing wasted resources — money could be better spent in other ways; it is social in the sense of Article 2 EC — seeking to guarantee an increase in living standards.

2.4.4.3 Controlling markets

This might be done through the use of guarantees, eg, if they are valid only in the country of manufacture, not the country of purchase or use. This would act as a disincentive to buy 'foreign' goods. Typical instances can be seen in the consumer journals for SLR cameras or computer games and equipment, which often warn consumers against the otherwise tempting offers in the 'grey' unofficial import market.

In another economic sector, see the proceedings involving *Honda*, Commission Press Release, August 1992. The Commission looked at, *inter alia*, Honda's spare parts distribution system in Europe. This had allowed Honda importers in single Member States to set up exclusive distribution networks designed to protect their distributors against parallel imports. In the light of the Commission's interest, Honda agreed to introduce a single standard form distribution and servicing agreement for the whole Community. This gave distributors an exclusive right to provide in their territory the guarantee services offered by Honda to purchasers of its motorbikes. In exchange, distributors had to service all users who had a guarantee certificate from Honda, which must accompany the motorbike until it reached the end user.

Also, consider the response to a question asked in the European Parliament, by then Competition Commissioner Van Miert (OJ 1992 C66/40). He stated that the

Commission was concerned about major manufacturers who operate over a Community-wide market, offering guarantees which claim to be 'European'. They are actually valid in all Member States but their content and scope vary considerably from one Member State to another. This was seen by the Commission as very unsatisfactory and the Commission had still to investigate the explanations given.

2.4.4.4 Sharing markets

This might involve quotas as the means of restricting competition. It prevents price competition, eg, through export bans or absolute territorial exclusion, a ban on either an active or passive 'foreign' sales policy. Isolation lessens competition (either inter- or intra-brand) because everyone has their own exclusive territory.

The Commission has often been strongly against such territorial protection but may justify it in certain circumstances, eg, a new product or market or process. If the risks involved are such that no one would venture into the market without 'protection', it may be in the long-term interests of consumers to permit such protection for at least a short period. It is more likely to be allowed in vertical, rather than horizontal, arrangements. See, eg, *Nungesser v Commission* (258/78) [1982] ECR 2015; *Pronuptia*.

Absolute territorial protection is probably the one major example of a *vertical prohibition*. In this context, we could usefully consider the proceedings involving *Fyffes/Chiquita Europe*, Commission Press Release, IP(92) 461. C was the largest importer of bananas into the EC, selling principally under the Chiquita trade mark in continental Europe. Prior to 1986, its UK sales were made through Fyffes Group Ltd (FGL), a wholly-owned subsidiary. C also sold bananas under the Fyffes trade mark through Europe, as a secondary brand after introducing its Chiquita brand.

In 1986, C sold off FGL. In an agreement on trade marks, FGL granted C exclusive rights to use the Fyffes trade mark outside the UK and Ireland for three years and a non-use clause, stopping FGL using the Fyffes trade mark for any fresh fruit outside the UK and Ireland until 2006 (or such earlier date as C might decide). After 1989, C stopped using the Fyffes trade mark but would not allow FGL to use it in continental Europe. Following FGL's complaint, the Commission felt the non-use clause restricted competition because of loss of competitive advantage in selling under a strong trade mark. The clause could not be regarded as legitimate protection of C's continental goodwill following sale of the UK company. After agreement on the worldwide use of the trade mark between the parties, the Commission agreed to close its file.

On a similar note, see *Viho/Parker Pen* 1992 OJ L233/27. V, a Dutch company, tried to buy Parker pens in Germany and Italy for resale in The Netherlands. P's distributors in both countries refused to sell to V, alleging that a clause in their contracts with P, making them distributors for their national market, forbad them to sell outside their territory. V complained to the Commission. On investigation, P submitted that the express export ban was inserted into the distribution agreements on a marketing director's personal initiative, acting without P's authority. P immediately revoked the restrictions. The infringement had lasted over two years. P was fined ECU 700,000 (reduced to ECU 400,000 on appeal to CFI), the German distributor Herlitz was fined ECU 40,000. The Commission observed that export bans are always restrictions of competition. The director's lack of authority was irrelevant — the company was still liable, either because it had allowed him to act in that fashion or because it had failed to supervise him properly.

The Commission continues to be vigilant to promote the goals of market integration and 'opening up' markets. In 1998, the Commission concluded its investigation into the behaviour of Volkswagen AG. It had received numerous complaints about difficulties encountered by German or Austrian consumers who wished to buy Volkswagen or Audi cars in Italy. Its investigation showed that Volkswagen had pursued a policy of market-partitioning for about ten years. Volkswagen's Italian dealers were effectively forbidden from selling the cars to foreign buyers, in particular those from Germany and Austria. The Commission imposed a fine of ecu 102 million and noted, in its XXVIIIth Report on Competition Policy, that this was the largest fine ever imposed on a single company (see also OJ 1998 L/124; later reduced on appeal).

2.4.4.5 Ties

This is the name given to an arrangement where you can buy the thing you want but only if you buy something else which you do not want (either at all or at that price). The more natural home for the prohibition of ties is Article 82 (ex 86), where market power would allow an undertaking to compel the acceptance of unwanted terms or products. However, it is also an example given in Article 81 (ex 85). Maybe the example is intended to regulate contractual relations with third parties?

Examples of ties can be found in *Vaessen/Moris* [1979] 1 CMLR 511. There was a patented machine to make saucissons de Boulogne; the machines were sold with a requirement to buy all sausage casings from the manufacturer too. See also *Hilti* (although this involved Article 82 (ex 86)), a Commission decision recently confirmed by the Court.

These ties can be justified — for example, if the price for the machine is paid via use of the machine; this can be policed through the number of casings sold (you would need to check thoroughly by stamping your mark on the casings).

Another recent example of tying might be the freezer exclusivity arrangements concluded by Langnese and Schöller, regarding retail ice cream sales in Germany. See, eg, 1993 ECLR at R-41 and below at **2.4.4.6**. These have also been the subject of litigation in Ireland, involving the Mars Corporation.

2.4.4.6 Exclusive purchasing

The Commission has issued block exemptions dealing with exclusive distribution and exclusive purchasing (Regulations 1983/83 and 1984/83 and see now Regulation 2790/99). The exclusive purchasing regulation was considered in *Delimitis v Henninger Braü AG* in 1991. In this case, the ECJ looked at beer supply agreements in Germany. It considered the advantages offered to both supplier and reseller by such an agreement, eg the supplier gets guaranteed outlets, a motivated reseller and the ability to plan production and distribution more effectively; the reseller gets access to the beer resale market under favourable conditions (favourable loans, technical installations), guaranteed supply, and help in securing product quality.

The ECJ concluded that such agreements *may not* have the *object* of restricting competition, but it is still necessary to examine their *effect*. The ECJ said that one must look at the totality of such beer supply agreements to get the full picture; in the present case it was 'necessary to analyse the effects of a beer supply agreement, taken together with other contracts of the same type, on the opportunities of national competitors or those from other Member States, to gain access to the market for beer consumption or to increase their market share and, accordingly, the effects on the range of products offered to consumers'.

First, you must define the market in terms of product and territory. Here, the market was the distribution of beer through premises for the sale and consumption of drinks (*not* retail outlets) in Germany. Secondly, see if the existence of several beer supply agreements impedes *access* to that market. You need to examine the effect of all of them, not just the one you are presently concerned with. Relevant factors are the proportion of tied outlets compared to 'free' houses, duration of agreements, quantities of beer involved and how that compares to quantities sold by free houses.

Even if there is 'a considerable effect' on chances to gain access, that is insufficient in itself to allow a finding that the market is inaccessible. It is simply one factor among several, economic and legal. For example, you should also consider opportunities for access — a competitor might take over an existing national brewery with its tied sales outlets, or build new pubs. You need to examine any laws relating to such actions and (an economic factor) find the minimum number of outlets needed to operate a distribution system economically. Then see how the market itself works, competitively, to see how easy access is. Find the number and size of producers on the market, the degree of saturation of the market and customers' brand loyalty. A saturated market with high brand loyalty to a few large producers is more difficult to break into 'than a market in full expansion in which a large number of small producers are operating without any strong brand names'.

Lastly, if this examination of the totality of such contracts shows that they do not have the cumulative effect of denying access to new national or foreign competitors, the individual agreements cannot restrict competition within Article 81(1) (ex 85(1)) and so are not prohibited.

If access is found to be hard to attain, it is still necessary to assess the extent to which the 'suspect' brewery's contracts contribute to the cumulative effect of all such agreements. Breweries whose beer supply agreements make an *insignificant* contribution to the cumulative effect are not prohibited by Article 81(1) (ex 85(1)).

Whether the contribution is significant or not is determined by:

(a) the brewery's market share (and that of any group it belongs to);

(b) the number of outlets tied to it (or its group) compared to the total number of such outlets in the relevant market;

(c) the duration of the agreement compared to the average for that market, eg, a brewery with a relatively small market share but which ties up sales outlets for many years may make as significant a contribution to sealing-off the market as a brewery with a relatively strong market position which regularly releases outlets at shorter intervals.

Applying those principles to the case, the ECJ considered the economic and legal effect of an *access clause* in the beer supply agreement (this was the referring court's fourth question, shown as A(4) in the Report). Such a clause allows the reseller to buy beer from other Member States. In theory, this should reduce the scope of the prohibition on competition in a beer supply agreement. If, in practice, the effect of the access clause is hypothetical or economically insignificant, one can ignore the clause. This may be the situation where the clause only authorises the reseller directly to buy beers from other Member States, rather than allowing him to buy beers imported by other companies into his Member State. Similarly, if the agreement has a clause requiring minimum quantities to be purchased by the reseller from the brewery (especially if backed by financial penalties for failure), those minimum amounts may be high in comparison to sales normally achieved by the pub in question; any 'freeing-up' of access here would be illusory.

If the access clause allows a national/foreign supplier '*a real possibility*' of supplying the pub in question, the agreement is not in principle capable of affecting trade between Member States. It therefore falls outside the prohibition in Article 81(1) (ex 85(1)).

The *Delimitis* case has many other facets to it, but is of great importance here because it shows the ECJ going to considerable lengths to conduct more than a knee-jerk analysis under Article 81(1) (ex 85(1)). A great deal of economic and legal analysis was required by the ECJ, and the Commission was expected to follow this lead in future investigations. The Commission responded by putting out a Notice on 'beer supply agreements of minor importance', putting into practice some of the ECJ's thoughts on economic significance. See OJ 1992, C121/2, amending Regulations 1983/83 and 1984/83.

Subsequently, the Commission had to consider exclusive purchase in the context of 'impulse' ice cream sales in Germany in *Langnese-Iglo, Schöller-Lebensmittel* OJ 1993 L183/1. It said that, in *normal* market conditions, exclusivity agreements are beneficial to competition because they strengthen the position of the undertaking which concluded the agreement. But, if access to the market by other suppliers is impeded *as a result of the market structure* and other significant barriers to entry, then exclusivity is unacceptable. That appears to have been the case here. Two companies had a duopoly over wholesale ice cream sales in Germany and access to that market was difficult because of the 'freezer exclusivity' arrangements they had with retailers. Generally, there is room for one ice cream freezer in a shop selling other goods (newspapers, etc). If that freezer is supplied to the shopkeeper by the wholesaler on condition that it is used to stock only a specific manufacturer's goods, then no other manufacturer can get access to that retail outlet. In its final Decisions in these two cases, the Commission distinguished between 'outlet exclusivity' and 'freezer exclusivity'. The former was anti-competitive because it foreclosed that outlet for other suppliers, while the latter was permissible as a *quid pro quo* for making the ice creams available.

For a cogent criticism of the Commission's Decisions in the 'ice cream' cases, based on its failure to follow or distinguish *Delimitis*, see *Korah* [1994] 3 ECLR 171. However, it should also be noted that the decision of the Commission has been upheld, in very large part, by the CFI (*Langnese-Iglo v Commission* (T–7/93) [1995] ECR II-1533). An appeal to the ECJ was subsequently dismissed (Case (C-279/95P) [1998] ECR I-5609).

3

Article 81(3): escape from prohibition

3.1 Introduction

Having seen that an agreement will be void if it falls within Article 81(1), we must now consider the possibility of its resurrection! Article 81(3) allows an agreement to be exempted from the consequences of an infringement. In order to qualify for an exemption, the agreement must satisfy four criteria. These are set out in Article 81(3).

3.2 A system in flux

In 1962, Council Regulation 17/62 established that only the Commission could grant an exemption under Article 81(3). This imposed a centralised system and, in particular, meant that national competition authorities and courts could not grant exemptions, even where they considered the criteria were clearly met. Furthermore, exemption could only be granted once the Commission had been notified of the agreement in question. To notify the Commission, an undertaking had to complete a lengthy and complex document, known as Form A/B, and submit multiple copies of it to the Commission. The notified agreement would then take its place in the queue of such agreements awaiting consideration by the officials of DG IV, the competition directorate of the Commission.

This centralised system had some advantages for the Commission. For example, its officials quickly discovered how many potentially anti-competitive agreements were in circulation. Tens of thousands were notified to the Commission in the first few years of the system. However, there were disadvantages, too. The number of notified agreements meant that undertakings had to wait for very long periods until they eventually found out whether their agreement had been exempted or not. In the meantime, it might be unenforceable in the national courts. Such delays could be costly and did not achieve legal certainty. If a notified agreement did become the subject of litigation in a national court, those proceedings were likely to be suspended until the Commission made its decision, causing further delays. The Commission invented several informal methods for closing its files — informal settlements and comfort letters in particular — or for discouraging notification, through the use of block exemptions. However, it has long been of the view that there were just too many notifications being made. Between 2000 and 2002, the annual total of notifications hovered around the 100 mark, which is quite low but with the forthcoming enlargement of the EU, that number was likely to increase again. In its 1999 White Paper on Modernisation, the Commission harked back to a warning given to it in 1961 by the Economic and Social Committee:

> Although some might see the authorisation system [ie notification and exemption] as a means of obtaining better knowledge of the existence of agreements that were harmful to competition,

such a system risked diverting the Commission from its true mission by overloading it with administrative work that would prevent it from carrying out a serious, in-depth examination of agreements between undertakings and of their real effects.

In the 1999 White Paper, the Commission observed that this warning had proved to be correct. The Commission now wanted to be pro-active, not reactive as circumstances forced it to be. The Commission sought revision of the system so that it could address itself more efficiently to the implementation of Article 81. In particular, it wanted the freedom to take on more 'own-initiated' procedures. In 2002, such cases formed less than one third of all new cases (the rest being notifications and complaints, at 31% and 40% respectively). To secure the necessary freedom, the Commission proposed the abolition of the notification system. Following a process of consultation, the proposed replacement was published in September 2000 and the final, legally effective, measure was passed by the Council of Ministers in December 2002. The new measure, Regulation 1/2003, came into effect on 1 May 2004. It contains no provisions for notification. Instead, undertakings must determine for themselves whether their agreements are anti-competitive or not. If an undertaking concludes that an agreement is, or may be, anti-competitive, it can rely on a presumption of legality until such time as a national authority or court declares the agreement anti-competitive. If that happens, the undertaking can ask the authority or court to also consider if the agreement is exempt from the operation of Article 81(1) and (2). In summary, responsibility for the initial assessment of an agreement as anti-competitive has been passed over to individual undertakings and their advisers. Responsibility for determining whether an anti-competitive agreement is exempted has passed from the Commission to the national authorities including the courts. Whether these changes will achieve the desired effects for the Commission remains to be seen. For one view, see J. F. Appledorn, 'Are the proposed Changes Compatible with Article 81(3) EC?' [2001] ECLR 400; for a detailed critique of the White Paper, see R. Wesseling, *The Modernisation of EC Antitrust Law*.

3.3 Qualifying for exemption

Although the system for obtaining an exemption has changed, the criteria remain the same. Also, the burden of proof will stay on the undertaking seeking the exemption, to show that it is merited. Article 81(3) sets up four criteria to meet. An agreement will qualify for exemption if it:

(a) helps to improve the production or distribution of goods (for example, it makes a larger amount of the product available than would otherwise have been the case) or it promotes technical or economic progress (typically through the raising of living standards);

(b) gives consumers a fair share of the resulting benefit;

(c) only restricts competition to the extent and in ways which are totally necessary to achieve the pro-competitive ends; and

(d) does not allow the parties to the agreement to eradicate competition to any great degree.

A noted US writer on anti-trust law, Barry Hawk, advises caution when seeking guidance from the reported decisions of the Commission upon the application and interpretation of Article 81(3). Hawk says that, to a large extent, they are 'fact-specific' and provide few, if any, general principles which we might use. According to Hawk, 'this makes hazardous the extrapolation of general rules beyond the four express statutory conditions in Article 85(3) [now Article 81(3)] itself'. This is a matter of potential concern for companies — under the decentralised system for exemptions, they are intended to self-assess whether their agreements satisfy the criteria; the Commission considers that there are now enough reported decisions and judgments of the European Court to guide companies accurately.

Let us see what we can make of each of the four criteria.

(a) *The agreement must contribute to either an improvement in production or distribution of goods or the promotion of technical or economic progress.* This criterion harks back to Article 2 EC (see **Chapter 1**) and is the single most important one of the four. It is intended to identify those pro-competitive aspects of the agreement which may balance or outweigh the anti-competitive aspects which were identified during the analysis under Article 81(1). The most important question to ask is: 'Does this agreement, as presently constituted, give benefits which would not be available in the absence of such agreement?' The Commission has phrased this in a slightly different way on occasion: do the restrictions on competition 'bring about an improvement over the situation which would have existed in their absence?' (See *GERO-fabrik* 1977 OJ L16/8, Commission Decision). Examples of such benefits are:

- that a longer production run may result in a reduced cost per unit;
- entry into new product or geographical markets may be facilitated;
- distribution may improve through the continuity of supplies; or
- a wider range of products may become available.

If and only if this first criterion is met, we can consider the second one.

(b) *Consumers must receive a fair share of the resulting benefits.* This may be apparent through a better standard of living, or perhaps a wider choice of products becoming available. 'Consumer' has a broad meaning in this criterion. It covers not only the ultimate user of the goods or services but also everyone else down the manufacturing-distribution chain who makes use of the goods or services which are affected by the agreement. Valentine Korah notes the example of *ACEC/Berliet* [1968] CMLR D35, where the 'consumers' of a bus were held to be the bus companies and tour operators, not the likely passengers. The 'benefit' may be shared with consumers in various ways. It could happen through a price reduction, employing qualified staff, providing a service facility, or offering a guarantee of quality. This second condition is one of the less demanding ones to satisfy. Once it has been met, we can turn to the third criterion.

(c) *The restrictions on competition which the agreement makes must be indispensable to attaining the identifiable benefits.* This criterion illustrates a recurring theme in EU law, namely, that one may derogate from a fundamental principle but only in very limited circumstances. The derogation must serve a legitimate goal and the derogation can only go so far as is absolutely necessary to achieve that goal. The key word in this criterion is 'indispensable'. The question to consider here is: 'Are there less restrictive alternatives available which would achieve the same benefits?' For example, could we secure the same benefits over a shorter timespan, or by applying the restrictions over a smaller territory? There is an obvious link with the first criterion and these two criteria are the most important of the quartet. If this criterion can be satisfied, we can turn finally to the fourth (and probably least important) criterion.

(d) *The parties to the agreement must not have been given the chance to eradicate competition regarding a substantial part of the products in question.* It is sufficient to say that, if an agreement satisfies the other three criteria, it is most unlikely to fail through not meeting this criterion.

3.4 Self-assessment

The emphasis now is on firms performing their own assessment of whether what they are doing is anti-competitive, rather than engaging the Commission. Until the recent revision of the system, a firm could complete Form A/B and submit it to the Commission, asking for either an exemption or negative clearance under Article 81. (Negative clearance was sought where the firm thought that it was not infringing Article 81 but wanted the Commission to confirm that). Obviously, firms took legal advice and that advice grew more sophisticated as lawyers became more educated in the philosophy and interpretations of the Commission (and of the European Court). Further, the use of regulations to provide for 'block exemptions' (see **3.5**) meant that lawyers took on greater responsibility for ensuring that a client firm's business methods were compliant with Article 81. This practical shift in responsibility has now been recognised by the re-modelled system for exemptions.

No longer are firms only able to get an exemption from the Commission, their business arrangements are in effect deemed to be valid until such time as a court or competition regulator says otherwise. The new system marks a shift from the original centralised scheme to 'a directly applicable exception system' (Regulation 1/2003, recitals (3) and (4)), 'in which the competition authorities and courts of the Member States have the power to apply not only Article 81(1) and Article 82 ... but also Article 81(3) ...'

Sometimes, self-assessment may still be difficult but Regulation 1/2003 offers some help:

> In exceptional cases ... it may also be expedient for the Commission to adopt a decision of a declaratory nature finding that the prohibition in Article 81 or Article 82 ... does not apply, with a view to clarifying the law and ensuring its consistent application throughout the Community, in particular with regard to new types of agreements or practices that have not been settled in the existing case-law and administrative practice. [Recital 14]

Further:

> Legal certainty for undertakings operating under the Community competition rules contributes to the promotion of innovation and investment. Where cases give rise to genuine uncertainty because they present novel or unresolved questions for the application of these rules, individual undertakings may wish to seek informal guidance from the Commission.

But note that this is informal; the process is untrammeled by legal procedures and form-filling.

In order to help with self-assessment (which in practice will be done by lawyers and compliance staff), firms can refer to forty-odd years of Commission decisions and European Court judgments. The Commission is also doing much more to inform and educate the self-assessors. A good example is the Guidelines on Vertical Restraints, issued by the Commission in 2000 and comprising 229 paragraphs covering some 44 pages (see OJ 2000 C291/1–44). The purpose of them, according to the Introduction, is to 'help companies make their own assessment of vertical agreements under the EC competition rules'. One particularly useful section of the Guidelines is 'VI Enforcement policy in individual cases'. This explores the effects, either negative or positive, that vertical restraints can have either directly (on their own) or indirectly (in combination with other obligations). The section sets out general rules for evaluating vertical restraints. It lists factors to be considered under either Article 81(1) or (3) and provides a 'methodology of analysis'.

In summary, the Guidelines explain that assessment usually consists of four sequential steps (Guideline 120):

1. The undertakings involved need to define the relevant market in order to determine the relevant market share. They could, of course, refer to the Commission's 1997 Notice on market definition.
2. If the market share is 30% or less (usually measured by the value of sales, in preference to the volume of sales), the agreement fails within the block exemption *unless* it contains hardcore restrictions on competition or otherwise fails to meet the conditions set out in the block exemption (in which case, it will become necessary to assess the agreement on an ad hoc basis).
3. If the market share exceeds 30%, it will be necessary for the undertakings to assess whether or not the agreement falls within the scope of Article 81(1).

   In determining whether a vertical agreement causes an appreciable restriction of competition within Article 81(1), the Guidelines identify seven factors as the most important to consider (Guideline 121):
   - the supplier's market position,
   - competitors' market positions,
   - the buyer's market position,
   - barriers to entry,
   - the maturity of the market,
   - the level of trade, and
   - the nature of the product.

   There may also be other relevant factors in a specific case.
4. If the agreement does fall within the scope of Article 81(1), the undertakings will need to assess if it satisfies the criteria for exemption under Article 81(3).

3.5 Alternatives to individual exemption

3.5.1 The development of alternatives to exemption

Following the introduction of Regulation 17/62, the Commission was quickly overwhelmed with notifications seeking exemption for existing agreements. By 1967, over 35,000 agreements had accumulated in the system and, with the annual number of formal decisions usually in single figures, the backlog was unlikely to diminish. The Commission developed two main measures to help itself. One was the block exemption regulation (see **3.5.2**), the other was the comfort letter (see **3.5.3**).

3.5.2 Block exemptions and Regulation 2790/99

Block exemptions are intended to prevent notifications. They do this by allowing firms to determine for themselves whether their agreement is contrary to Article 81(1) and, if so, could be exempted by application of Article 81(3). If it is clear that the agreement could be exempted, then for practical purposes, it will be treated as if it had been examined individually by the Commission and obtained an exemption.

All four criteria in Article 81(3) are applied by the Commission in its block exemptions, as can be seen for example in Regulation 2790/99 on vertical agreements (for the full text, see **Appendix 2**):

- recitals 6–8 and 9 deal with the first criterion (for example, stating that vertical agreements can improve economic efficiency);
- recital 8 deals with the second criterion (in certain circumstances, vertical agreements 'allow consumers a fair share of the resulting benefits');
- recital 10 deals with the third criterion (insofar as it gives examples of restrictions on competition which are *not* indispensable to attainment of the pro-competitive benefits);
- recital 12 deals with the fourth criterion (for example, the regulation sets a ceiling on the supplier's market share of 30%; this should normally ensure that participating undertakings are unable to eliminate competition in the relevant market).

Block exemptions have developed over the years since their introduction in 1967. The Commission conducted a review of its treatment of vertical restraints in 1996, where its Green Paper suggested that current block exemptions were too form-based, too legalistic and constrained firms' freedom of action unduly. In 1998, the Commission concluded that a 'profound change of policy'was required. The result was that the Regulation on vertical agreements is quite different to earlier forms of block exemption. For example, Regulation 2790/99 can apply to agreements between two or more undertakings, whilst earlier exemptions were limited to bipartite agreements. It also introduced a limitation in the form of a maximum market share: if the supplier (or buyer in the case of an exclusive supply agreement) has more than 30% of the relevant market, the block exemption will not apply and individual analysis will be required (see Article 3). A familiar element of Regulation 2790/99 is its identification of so-called 'hard core' restrictions on competition — if any of these are present, the whole agreement fails outside the 'safe haven' of the block exemption (see Article 4; examples are price-fixing and market sharing). However, the block exemption moves away from an all-or-nothing approach — if there are obligations in the agreement which are less anti-competitive in their effects, these may be severable and leave the rest of the agreement safe and valid (see Article 5).

The clear intention behind this block exemption is to take an economic approach to the analysis, based on the anticipated effects of the agreement on the relevant market. Because markets can change over time, and because economic thinking sometimes changes too, block exemptions are usually of finite duration. Regulation 2790/99 is no exception — it came into force on 1 January 2000, applied from 1 June 2000 and is scheduled to expire on 31 May 2010.

3.5.3 Comfort letters

The other main measure introduced by the Commission was the comfort letter. These documents do not grant either a negative clearance (that is, the agreement is not anti-competitive) or an exemption. Instead, they represent an administrative convenience. The Commission can avoid the need to take a formal decision and yet close its file on the case under consideration.

A comfort letter may be used in different circumstances. For example:

(a) On the facts currently known to the Commission, the agreement does not seem to infringe Article 81(1) (or Article 82, if relevant). This looks like a negative clearance decision but, without the formal decision of the Commission, it has little legal effect.

(b) The agreement falls within a block exemption. This should be rarely used because, if its analysis is correct, there was probably no need to involve the Commission.

(c) The agreement merits exemption under Article 81(3). This has been the most troublesome form of comfort letter in the past since it condemns the agreement but does not exempt it. As only the Commission could grant exemptions, that left the agreement apparently unenforceable until such time as the Commission might be persuaded to re-open its file and reach a formal decision. For an example, see *Rovin* [1984] 1 CMLR 128. Now, of course, national competition authorities and courts can grant exemptions, this form of comfort letter is unlikely to be so problematic.

One might expect that, with the removal of the centralised system of notification and exemption, the Commission's use of comfort letters would decline. Numerically, this will probably prove to be true but it should be remembered that the Commission is not abandoning its work! It will still conduct investigations, either on its own initiative or following complaints or whistle-blowing. Those investigations may still result in a comfort letter being sent to the firms under investigation.

The effect of a comfort letter is rather vague. As against the Commission, it can be used on an estoppel basis. That is, the Commission cannot perform a volte-face and condemn an agreement that it has previously approved in a comfort letter unless the circumstances have changed since the letter was issued. A change in circumstances may occur when the market changes, for example, the entry of new competitors, or when the Commission discovers previously unknown facts. If the Commission can demonstrate a change in circumstances, any action by the recipient of a comfort letter to stop the new investigation (on the grounds of its legitimate expectations) is likely to fail: see for example, *Langnese-Iglo GmbH v Commission* (C-279/95P) [1998] ECR I-5609.

3.5.4 Informal settlements and commitments

In addition to the introduction of block exemptions and comfort letters, the Commission has also settled investigations on an informal basis, with the suspect company either giving undertakings to the Commission about its future conduct or perhaps agreeing to modify its behaviour or delete specific terms from its agreement. One example is the case of *IBM* [1984] 3 CMLR 619. Here, the Commission suspended its investigation of IBM (under Article 82) indefinitely in return for certain promises about future conduct from the company. The Commission made it clear that IBM would be monitored carefully in the future to ensure its compliance. Another example is the Italian Coca Cola case: *San Pellegrino SpA v Coca Cola Export Corporation Filiale Italiana* [1989] 4 CMLR 137. Following a complaint that Filiale Italiana was excluding its competitors from the market by offering discounts to distributors who agreed to sell no-one else's cola, the Commission conducted a preliminary investigation. When it informed Filiale Italiana that it agreed with the complaint, the firm amended its distribution agreements to remove the offending clauses. The Commission then simply closed its file on the case.

The competence of the Commission to adopt such measures to close a file does not derive from the EC Treaty or secondary legislation. Under Regulation 1/2003, the Commission is now empowered to accept 'commitments' from a firm. The Commission should have made its preliminary assessment of the situation and intimated to the firm that it intends to make an adverse finding. If the firm then offers 'commitments' which are designed to resolve the Commission's concerns, the Commission is empowered to take a decision making those commitments legally binding on the firm and close its file on that basis. Should the Commission later decide that its decision is ill-founded, either due to a change of circumstances or because the original decision to close the file was based on flawed information, it may re-open the file. See Regulation1/2003, Article 9.

4

Article 82: abuse of a dominant position

4.1 The elements of Article 82

Any abuse by one or more undertakings of a dominant position within the common market or in a substantial part of it shall be prohibited as incompatible with the common market in so far as it may affect trade between Member States. Such abuse may, in particular, consist in:

(a) directly or indirectly imposing unfair purchase or selling prices or other unfair trading conditions;

(b) limiting production, markets or technical development to the prejudice of consumers;

(c) applying dissimilar conditions to equivalent transactions with other trading parties, thereby placing them at a competitive disadvantage;

(d) making the conclusion of contracts subject to acceptance by the other parties of supplementary obligations which, by their nature or according to commercial usage, have no connection with the subject of such contracts.

Generally speaking, the competition rules are not concerned with the acquisition of monopoly power by an individual enterprise but rather with the way in which such power is used — or abused (see **4.6**). Only those businesses which are dominant within the common market or a substantial part of it are at risk of infringing Article 82 (ex 86), EC Treaty — the Community is not concerned with big fishes in insignificant pools. Article 82 (ex 86) may be broken up into several significant elements:

(a) relevant product market; (plus)
(b) relevant geographical market; (leads to)
(c) a dominant position;
(d) for one or more undertakings;
(e) in a substantial part of the Common Market;
(f) abusive behaviour;
(g) effect on trade between Member States.

We shall examine each of these in this chapter.

4.2 Dominant position

4.2.1 Market power

It has been said that, in order to determine whether a firm occupies a dominant position, you must ask four questions:

(a) Which firm is accused?

(b) Which products sold by it are involved in the complaint?

(c) Who buys them?

(d) What else could be used by those customers with minimal adaptation to their business? (that is, what substitutes are there?)

(Korah, *An Introductory Guide to EC Competition Law & Practice*, p 80)

You may have realized, on reading that list, that what is being done is the construction of a market definition. Answering the questions should identify a relevant product market and a relevant geographical market. These are fundamental matters that we first considered in **Chapter 1**. They are relevant here because the typical way in which a dominant position is proved is by producing evidence of the suspect firm's market power. The market definition is the context in which the evidence of market power makes sense.

4.2.2 The ability to act independently

Once you have defined the market, you can then try to assess the undertaking's market power. Barry Hawk says that 'Neither the definition nor the determination of dominant position under Article [82] bears much resemblance to the economic analysis of market power'.

We must remember that we are looking at the ways in which people who are basically lawyers have interpreted and applied Article 82 (ex 86). Bearing that in mind, what are the symbols of such power in a market that enable us to say the undertaking has a dominant position? According to decided cases, they are:

(a) the power to prevent effective competition; and/or

(b) the power to behave independently of competitors, suppliers and customers, to an appreciable extent.

We can see this test in the following extract from the Court's judgment in *Hoffmann-La Roche v Commission* (85/76) [1979] ECR 461 (the 'Vitamins' case):

> [D]ominant position relates to a position of economic strength enjoyed by an undertaking which enables it to prevent effective competition being maintained on the relevant market by affording it the power to behave to an appreciable extent independently of its competitors, its customers and ultimately of the consumers.

In *Michelin v Commission* (322/81) [1983] ECR 3461 the Court stated:

> [I]t is not a precondition for finding that a dominant position exists in the case of a given product that there should be a complete absence of competition from other partially interchangeable products so long as such competition does not affect the undertaking's ability to influence appreciably the conditions in which that competition may be exerted or at any rate to conduct itself to a large extent without having to take account of that competition and without suffering any adverse effects as a result of its attitude.

It should be noted that although most of the reported cases on 'dominant position' refer to an independence of action over one's competitors, this 'horizontal' form of dominance is not the only way to achieve a dominant position. One may be 'vertically' dominant — that is, a company may dominate its supplier (or its customers). An example of supplier-dominance may be seen in the *Volvo v Veng* case (see **4.2.4** and **7.6**), while customer-dominance could be illustrated by the purchasing power of the National Health

Service in the United Kingdom (or BT or the Ministry of Defence) regarding appropriate products.

Although the ECJ said in *Hoffmann-La Roche v Commission* that the possession of a very large share of the market was a highly important element in establishing a dominant position, it is clear that absolute domination of the market is not needed. This is best illustrated by *United Brands v Commission*, where the 'dominant' enterprise was engaged in losing a price war with its main competitor (Chiquita against Dole bananas). What you have to do is analyse the market share of the suspect undertaking.

4.2.2.1 Relevant product market

The issue here is essentially what product(s) are we interested in? To assist in defining the product market, we could try to answer Professor Korah's four questions (at **4.2.1**):

(a) Identify your suspect undertaking. It may be a corporate group or a parent and subsidiary.

(b) Identify which of its products are the subject of the investigation.

(c) Who buys them? This is important for three reasons. First, because, having identified the customers, you can start to see what alternative products would satisfy them. Then, having decided who are the customers, you can see where they are. It is useful to know what territory should be considered. Why do you need to know this?

  (i) To define the geographical market for the product. This will be the next step in defining the market — an undertaking's share of sales will vary according to both what is sold and over what territory. A good example is *Michelin*. A company's market share of saloon car tyres will probably differ from its market share for all types of motor vehicle tyres. Again, market share will vary according to whether we look at (say) just The Netherlands or the whole common market.

  (ii) Jurisdiction. If you have a dominant position in an insubstantial part of the common market, a *de minimis* argument will apply. No matter how abusive your behaviour, if you are a big fish in a little pond the European Commission is not likely to be interested. See, eg, *Cutsforth v Mansfield Inns Ltd* [1986] 1 WLR 558, *Hugin/Liptons v Commission* (22/78) [1979] ECR 1869 and, by analogy, the Commission's Notices on Agreements of Minor Importance.

(d) What acceptable substitutes there are (on both the supply side and demand side)? We need to know because we are concerned with the undertaking's ability to act independently of others.

Substitution

The way(s) in which the Commission and ECJ define 'market' has (have) been criticised by economists. They complain that the notion of a single, compartmentalised market is usually unattainable because there will often be substitutes. Further, as Barry Hawk has observed, 'market definition more often than not reflects a legal conclusion, not an economic fact'.

As a general rule, the broader the definition of the relevant product market (and the same applies for the geographical market), the less likely you are to find a dominant position. Why? Because of *substitutes*, basically.

For the product market, let us return to the example of *Michelin v Commission* (322/81) [1983] ECR 3461. If we define the relevant product as 'tyres', the company faces competition from all other sources of tyre; every other tyre is a potential substitute and so the company's market share is likely to be low. We may wish to define the product more narrowly: not simply 'tyres', but 'new tyres'. At least we now remove second-hand tyres from our analysis. We could go further and define the product ever more narrowly: new tyres; new tyres for vehicles other than saloon cars; new tyres for commercial goods vehicles; new tyres for heavy goods vehicles; new replacement tyres for HGVs. As we continue down this road, the number of potential substitutes drops and thus our company's market share rises. If we then look at the geographical market we could find that over different areas tastes may change; transport costs may inhibit long-range shipment of goods so that market share drops: so, the larger the territory, the smaller the market share is likely to be. It may be concluded that if the product is defined very narrowly and the chosen geographical market is small, substitution becomes less likely and market share will rise.

Reference was made above to substitutes being either supply-side (who else could step into your shoes?) or demand-side (what else could customers use to replace your product?) An example of a case where the Commission looked at *supply-side* substitutes is *Europemballage Corp and Continental Can Co* (6/72) [1973] ECR 215. The product was found to be light metal containers for meat and fish, and lids for jars. The Commission cast around for other manufacturers who could step into the shoes of Continental Can but seemed unable to conclude that companies who make light metal containers for fruit and vegetables (for example) might be able to supply Continental Can's customers. However, the Commission was criticised for its confused thinking by the ECJ on appeal (see paras 33–36 of ECJ judgment). This may explain why the Commission does not undertake this supply-side analysis very often.

A case where the Commission looked at *demand-side* substitutes is *United Brands v Commission* (27/76) [1978] ECR 207. The Commission found the product market was limited to fresh bananas (as opposed to fresh fruit generally, or non-citrus fruits). The Commission's decision was upheld by the ECJ, rather surprisingly given the apparent fluctuations in the price of bananas during the year coinciding with the availability of other fruits (see, eg, paras 15 and 16 of the judgment). Apparently, the banana has particular qualities of softness and seedlessness and is good for the young, the old and the sick (described by Barry Hawk as a Clint Eastwood classification). The ECJ described the banana as a 'privileged fruit' (see paras 23-25 of the judgment). The Commission's Notice on the definition of the relevant market (OJ 1997 C 372) states that demand substitution:

> constitutes the most immediate and effective disciplinary force on the suppliers of a given product, in particular in relation to their pricing decisions.

The Commission appears to favour a test known as the SSNIP test. In this test, one looks at the consequences of a firm imposing a small but significant non-transitory increase in the price of its product. If a permanent price rise, of the order of 5–10%, would be unprofitable because customers would switch to other, substitute, products, then those products should be included in the definition of the relevant product market. However, this is only one possible measure for defining the product market, amongst many. Product characteristics and intended use are, by themselves, seen as inadequate guides to demand substitution. The Commission has identified several sources of evidence:

- actual substitution in the recent past;
- quantitative economic and statistical tests;
- the views of customers and competitors, expressed directly and through market research studies;
- barriers and other costs involved in switching demand to substitute products;

- the existence of different categories of customers (the presence of whom might indicate specific niche markets).

A consideration of product definition and substitutability outside the European Community came in the Full Federal Court of Australia (see *Singapore Airlines Ltd v Taprobane Tours WA Pty Ltd* (1992) ATPR 41-159). T was a wholesale travel agent. One of its products was package tours to the Maldives from Australia, with the flights provided by Singapore Airlines (SA). After three years, SA reduced the number of flights between Australia and the Maldives, limited them to departures from one State in Australia and raised the prices it charged to T but not to other wholesalers. T sued, alleging an abuse of market power (analogous to Article 82 (ex 86), EC Treaty). The Full Federal Court held that the relevant product market was 'airline services to destinations outside mainland Australia' and package tours to such places, *not* return air flights to the Maldives. SA was dominant in such flights but there were many other holiday destinations and many other package tours to them, ie plenty of substitutes, so the court held that SA had insufficient market power for the case to succeed.

Time is also important when considering the possibility of substitution. When the Commission looks at supply-side substitutes, it usually does so in the short term (who could step in and meet demand *now*?), while a longer-term view might result in more substitutes being able to come forward (eg other companies could re-tool their plant, retrain staff, end existing contracts). A good illustration of the Commission's use of this short time-span is found in the 'Vitamins' case, see below. The Commission has stated, in its Notice on the definition of the relevant market (OJ 1997 C 372), that:

> When supply side substitutability would imply the need to adjust significantly existing tangible and intangible assets, additional investments, strategic decisions or time delays, it will not be considered at the stage of market definition.

4.2.2.2 Relevant geographical market

As mentioned earlier, we need to consider this for three reasons:

(a) it helps to define the market (and, indirectly, dominance);

(b) it determines whether a substantial part of the common market is involved;

(c) it helps to see if there is any effect on trade between Member States.

Defining the geographical market

The geographical market may be delimited by, for example, consumer tastes and transport costs — those matters which establish a separate market. In fact, we also need to see where goods sold in the market come from. If 'local' prices are high, this may encourage some suppliers, who are geographically remote, to transport their product from there to here. This may suggest that the geographical market is to include here and there too.

Barry Hawk has stated that in most decisions of the Commission, there is little or no analysis of the relevant geographical market. He says that this may be because it was obvious in the particular case — he gives the example of *Commercial Solvents* (the company was found to possess a worldwide monopoly and thus a dominant position in the common market).

Often an abstract formulation is offered by either Court or Commission but this is of little practical assistance in forecasting the way a decision will go (or advising one's clients).

The ECJ has insisted that different territories must present homogenous conditions for trade to form a comparable basis for analysis of market power. The ECJ and Commission seem very keen to use single Member States as the geographical market — where they go beyond this, similarity of trading conditions is important.

Three examples

(a) A simple example is *Alsatel Société Alsacienne et Lorraine de Télécommunications et d'Eléctronique v Novasam SA* (247/86) [1988] ECR 5987. A was found by the Regional Court, Strasbourg, to have a major share of the regional market in the relevant product (telephone installations) but the ECJ held, on a preliminary reference, that 'the relevant context within which the conditions of competition are sufficiently uniform to enable the economic strength of the undertaking in question to be assessed is the market in telephone installations for *the whole of France*'. Since A was dominant only in the Alsace-Lorraine area and had no dominant position in the relevant product market for the whole of France, the ECJ found that Article 86 (now 82) did not apply.

(b) *United Brands* (see paras 36-53 of the judgment). The Commission was right to consider Germany, Denmark, Ireland, The Netherlands and Belgium/Luxembourg as the geographical market because all six had free competition in bananas (whilst not necessarily being the same in trading conditions, eg transport costs), while in the other three Member States (ie, France, Italy, the United Kingdom) there was State interference in the market (see, eg, paras 36, 38, 44, 46, 51-53 of the judgment).

(c) *Michelin*. The Commission took The Netherlands as the relevant geographical market for heavy truck tyres. Michelin NV (which was the undertaking under investigation) complained to the ECJ that this was too narrow (see para 23 of the judgment). Michelin NV relied on the fact that the Commission had considered factors pertaining to the whole Michelin group when looking at market power, eg its technological lead over rivals and group financial strength. Michelin said that this suggested 'a much wider market' or even the world market. Its main competitors are worldwide. The Commission's response was that tyre makers have chosen to sell tyres through national subsidiaries in the national markets; thus, Michelin NV faces competition on The Netherlands market. The ECJ upheld the Commission's decision — tyre dealers who are established in The Netherlands in practice obtain their supplies only from suppliers operating in The Netherlands. So, Michelin NV's competition is 'mainly' on The Netherlands market and it is at that level that the objective conditions of competition are the same for traders.

Conclusion

It may be concluded that both the Commission and the European Court are often prepared to limit the relevant geographical market to the territory of a single Member State. They may be unlikely to consider a larger territory even where there is (apparently) clear evidence of competition from outside the Member State or cross-elasticity of supply.

Remember, we must also determine the geographical market in order to establish whether the area under consideration is at least a '*substantial part of the common market*' (the fourth element of Article 82 (ex 86)). This is related to the jurisdictional point referred to earlier (ie, whether there is any effect on inter-State trade). See **4.5**.

4.2.3 Diagnosing market power

4.2.3.1 Market share

We have seen the criteria set out by the Court for a dominant position, but how are we to determine whether those criteria have been satisfied in any particular case? It seems that the existence of a dominant position may derive from several factors which, taken separately, are not necessarily determinative; but among these factors a highly important one is the existence of very large market shares. See *Hoffmann-La Roche v Commission*.

An economist might assert that market power can be directly measured by examining (for example):

(a) whether the company's customers can buy the product from someone else;
(b) whether the company is charging an excessively high price compared to its marginal cost;
(c) whether the company is making monopoly profits;
(d) whether the company is engaging in price discrimination.

In practice, all of these four measurements are difficult to determine with certainty. The most simple symptom to spot (and therefore the one most relied on) is *market share*. This gives a 'rough and ready' diagnosis and may affirm the presence of a dominant position where a more sophisticated analysis would reject it; but often such sophisticated analysis is very difficult to do. Barry Hawk describes the use of market share as a benchmark as 'a necessary evil'.

So, how has this worked in practice? We can use *Hoffmann-La Roche* to illustrate the situation. In this case the Commission relied on Hoffmann-La Roche's market share in seven vitamins to demonstrate its dominance, especially when compared to the market shares of its competitors (see p 504 of the judgment).

The ECJ reiterated its 'test' of whether an undertaking can prevent effective competition and act, to an appreciable extent, independently. It then went on (para 41):

> ... the view may legitimately be taken that very large shares are *in themselves*, and save in exceptional circumstances, evidence of the existence of a dominant position.

We can see the same analysis in the later case of *AKZO Chemie BV v Commission* (C-62/86) [1991] ECR I-3359, where market share of over 50% appears to show a dominant position in the absence of exceptional circumstances and the onus of proof shifts to the suspect undertaking to disprove its dominance.

The same approach has been used by the Court of First Instance. See *Irish Sugar plc v Commission* (T-228/97) [1999] ECR II-2969 (although this case was quite straightforward, with the dominant undertakings holding over 90% of sales recorded in the relevant market). In *Hilti AG v Commission* (T-30/89) [1991] ECR II-1439 market shares between 70 and 80% were, in themselves, clear indications of a dominant position. Hilti disputed these figures before the CFI, saying they were unreliable. Hilti's credibility was rather stretched by the fact that it had supplied the figures in response to a request from the Commission (pursuant to Article 11, Regulation 17).

The Court of First Instance also observed that the several patents which Hilti possessed went towards strengthening its position on the market. This leads on to a consideration of the secondary symptoms which may support the initial diagnosis of a dominant position.

4.2.3.2 Ancillary factors

On their own, these are unlikely to support a finding of dominance but, when put together with ambiguous evidence of market power, may be enough to tip the balance in favour of a finding of dominance.

In *Hoffmann-La Roche*, the significant factors for the Commission were (see para 42 of judgment):

(a) the size of Hoffmann's market share;

(b) the size of the disparity between its market share and that of its rivals;

*(c) the fact that it produces a much wider range of vitamins than its competitors;

*(d) the fact that Hoffmann is the largest manufacturer of vitamins in the world with a turnover exceeding that of all the other producers;

(e) its technological advantages over the others, originally given by patent but now achieved by its 'leading role' in the field;

(f) its very extensive and highly specialised sales network;

(g) the absence of potential competition.

In addition to market share, heads (b), (e), (f) and (g) were all relevant factors according to the ECJ. Head (b) enables an undertaking's competitive strength to be assessed; (e) and (f) represent technical and commercial advantages; (g) is the result of having obstacles which prevent entry to the market by potential competitors.

*Conversely, head (c) was rejected by the ECJ as immaterial — there are separate markets for each vitamin. Head (d) was also rejected by the ECJ — other companies who make vitamins play on the world market with other products and enjoy the freedom to set off one market against another.

The ECJ then applied each of these factors to the seven different product markets under consideration.

Looking at the *Michelin* case, we can see the Court attaching significance to the relative economic strengths of Michelin and its Dutch competitors. Michelin is part of a group of undertakings operating throughout Europe and the world. This gives it an advantage in investment and research. It also has an unusually large product range — for certain types of tyre, Michelin is the only supplier in The Netherlands. Michelin has a larger network of sales representatives than its competitors, offering an excellent service. (The French Government intervened, alleging that Michelin was being penalised for providing a good product and service — the argument was rejected by the ECJ.)

A similar analysis can be clearly seen in the *United Brands* case. The Commission found United Brands' market share to be 45%. United Brands pointed out that in 1975 this dropped to 41%. The ECJ observed that a trader can only be in a dominant position with a product if it has 'succeeded in winning a large part' of the market. The Court said the evidence showed that United Brands' market share was always more than 40% and nearly 45%. 'This percentage does NOT permit the conclusion that the company automatically controls the market.' So the Court had to look at other factors — for example, it must take into consideration the strength and number of United Brands' competitors. United Brands' market share was several times greater than its nearest competitor, with the rest far behind. This situation can indicate its preponderant strength in the market.

Barriers to entry and the speed with which potential rivals can enter the market can be significant ancillary factors. However, the timescale which is used when considering the possibility of other companies entering the market may have a bearing on the conclusion. The Commission and the ECJ have both used a very small time-frame when determining if there are potential competitors. In *Hoffmann-La Roche*, the test was, if Hoffmann-La Roche pushed prices up (or decreased production), would those companies with smaller market shares 'be able to meet *rapidly* the demand from those who would like to break away from the undertaking which has the largest market share?'. This short timespan for potential competitors to become actual competition can be criticised.

Again, in *Commercial Solvents*, the ECJ said that if there was a raw material on the market which could be substituted without difficulty for nitropropane or aminobutanol when making ethambutol, this could mean that Commercial Solvents did not have a dominant position, but no such raw material then existed.

In *Michelin*, you might be forgiven for thinking that as the relevant product was a specific type of tyre, it would be quite easy for other tyre manufacturers to switch production over to that type and so provide a substitute for Michelin's product. The ECJ took a different view (at para 41):

> ... there is no elasticity of supply between tyres for heavy vehicles and car tyres owing to significant differences in production techniques and in the plant and tools needed for their manufacture. The fact that time and considerable investment are required in order to modify production plant for the manufacture of light-vehicle tyres instead of heavy-vehicle tyres or vice versa means that there is no discernible relationship between the two categories of tyre, enabling production to be adapted to demand on the market.

4.2.4 Legal monopolies and a dominant position

It might seem that to hold a legal monopoly in a product — eg through a patent, copyright or registered design — might lead to the relevant company having a dominant position with regard to that product. Of course, whether this was the situation in fact should depend on the availability of substitute products to satisfy customer demand. The Court of Justice has not said that mere possession of a legal monopoly over a product is enough to create a dominant position in the market for that product: eg, *Deutsche Grammophon v Metro-SB Grossmarkte* (78/70) [1971] ECR 487.

In *Volvo AB v Erik Veng (UK) Ltd* (238/87) [1988] ECR 6211 the ECJ was specifically asked by the High Court, on a preliminary reference, whether the possession of exclusive rights to manufacture and import certain car body panels gave Volvo a dominant position. (Volvo had the exclusive rights because they held the UK registered designs for those parts.) The ECJ was also asked a second question — whether a refusal to license others to import the panels constituted an abuse under Article 86 (now 82). The ECJ answered the second question, saying that there was no proof of abuse, and therefore it found it unnecessary to answer the first question.

The topic was raised again in 1988 in an Italian case involving Renault car parts (*Consorzio Italiano della Componentistica di Ricambio per Autoveicoli and SpA Maxicar v Regie Nationale des Usines Renault* (53/87) [1988] ECR 6039). One question posed by the Italian court was whether the obtaining of protective rights in respect of ornamental models for car bodywork components and the exercise of the resultant exclusive rights constituted an abuse of a dominant position within Article 86 (now 82)? With respect to the drafter of the preliminary reference, this seems to roll up two questions into one, and the ECJ gave a straightforward answer: 'the mere fact of obtaining protective rights in respect of ornamental designs for car bodywork components does not constitute an abuse of a dominant position within the meaning of Article 86 [now 82] of the Treaty.' It does appear, though, from the subsequent text of the judgment that the ECJ still thought that the mere possession of an exclusive right did not constitute a dominant position. (See, in particular, para 18 of the judgment.)

This straightforward view may be in the process of changing, though. In the case of *Radio Telefis Eireann et al v Commission* (T-69-70/89, 76/89) [1991] ECR II-485, the Commission initially found that various broadcasting organisations had a factual monopoly over television listings. This meant that any third parties who were interested in publishing a weekly guide to such listings were in a position of economic dependence on those organisations. (Such dependence is often owed to those who are in a dominant position.) The Commission found that this factual monopoly was strengthened into a legal monopoly by the use of copyright. The Commission found that the organisations did not permit third-party competition and inferred that they each held a dominant position.

The decision was challenged in the Court of First Instance. The Court decided that the relevant product was 'weekly television guides with comprehensive listings for the week'. Because of their copyright, the organisations had a monopoly over publication of such listings and a dominant position on the market for the listings. They also had a dominant position in the secondary market for magazines in which such listings are published. This has subsequently been upheld by the ECJ (1995).

We can see that the nub of the judgment may be the decision to extend the copyright monopoly over listings into a different market — that of printed weekly television guides. We can apply this argument to the *Volvo* situation and see that Volvo are likely to have a dominant position in the market for new spare parts for Volvo vehicles. This could be regarded as a secondary market (the primary one being the market for new, factory-fresh Volvos) and we would then have the answer to the question that the ECJ dodged answering in *Volvo* itself. However, the ECJ stated explicitly in the *RTE* appeal (1995) that the mere ownership of an intellectual property right does not confer a dominant position.

Before leaving this topic, we should note also the assertion by Claus-Dieter Ehlermann, in 1993 14 ECLR 61, that it is the 'well-established case-law of the [ECJ] that an undertaking which holds *an exclusive right* in a substantial part of the Common Market can be considered to be in a dominant position within Article 86 [now 82]'. He cites *CBEM/CLT* (311/84) [1985] ECR 3261 as authority for this (the 'Telemarketing' case). However, these exclusive rights appear to be basically those permitting public utilities to have a form of monopoly (eg, BT, British Gas, etc). The position there may be much clearer than it is in the 'pure' private sector. In *Micro Leader Business v Commission* (T-198/98) [2000] All ER (EC) 361, the Court of First Instance examined the position of MC and MF, two companies within the Microsoft group which sold computer software, particularly French-language, both in Canada and in France. The price of the software was significantly cheaper in Canada. MLB imported the products from Canada into France for re-sale, exploiting the price difference. MC held the copyright in the software and prohibited the marketing of Canadian products outside Canada. MLB complained to the Commission, alleging that the Microsoft companies had a dominant position and were abusing it through their prohibition. MLB presented a factual argument in support of their assertion that MC held a dominant position and did not rely upon the mere fact that MC held the copyright. The Commission (and subsequently the Court of First Instance) proceeded on the basis that MLB had to produce evidence of a dominant position, through the usual market analysis.

4.2.5 Can more than one firm be dominant?

This element of Article 82 (ex 86) does not require a great deal of elaboration. The Article clearly envisages a situation where two or more undertakings abuse a dominant position. This seems to be aimed at corporate groups which act as a single unit, eg parent and subsidiary, as in *Commercial Solvents Corp v Commission* (6-7/73) [1974] ECR 223.

An alternative meaning is that one can take a number of separate undertakings, add together their market shares, and see if they have a dominant position between them. The ECJ seems to have accepted this in situations where several companies have agreed to act in concert but, as this behaviour will usually fall within Article 81(1) (ex 85(1)), the additional infringement of Article 82 (ex 86) adds little. The ECJ seems to avoid suggesting that independent companies, against whom there is no evidence of collusion, should be examined to see if they have joint dominance even though no individual has a dominant position. The ECJ concept of dominance relies on a *unilateral* exercise of power: see the decision of the Court in *Zuchner v Bayerische Vereinsbank* [1981] ECR 2021 and the opinion of (then) Advocate-General Slynn who said:

> [O]ne of the hallmarks of a dominant position covered by Article 86 [now 82] is its unilateral nature. As a result ... it is right to point out that only [Article 81 (ex 85)] applies if the facts establish the existence of a concerted practice.

The concept of 'one or more undertakings' has been the subject of attention from the Court of First Instance. In the 'Italian Flat Glass' case (*Società Italiana Vetro SpA et al v Commission* (T-68, 77 and 78/89) [1992] ECR II-1403 three companies each made flat glass in Italy. They allegedly operated a cartel. The Commission alleged that this cartel (clearly a breach of Article 85 (now 81)) also contravened Article 86 (now 82) as, taken together, the three companies held a dominant position on the Italian market for flat glass. The Court rejected the suggestion that the same factors which showed a breach of Article 85 (now 81) could also be used to demonstrate a breach of Article 86 (now 82). However, the Court accepted the argument that circumstances could arise where several undertakings together abuse a dominant position, although that was only likely to be the case where they were united by 'economic links' of some form. The concept of a joint dominant position has been held to be applicable to two or more undertakings operating in a vertical relationship. This arose in *Irish Sugar plc v Commission* (T-228/97) [1999] ECR II-2969 and is interesting because, unlike *Società Italiana Vetro*, there was no cartel nor, unlike *Commercial Solvents*, was there a corporate group involved.

4.2.6 Disproving dominance

As noted above, in the *Akzo Chemie* case, the ECJ held that mere possession of a market share in excess of 50% would, in the absence of exceptional circumstances, shift the onus of proof onto the company to disprove dominance. How might a company discharge that onus?

In *Hoffmann-La Roche*, the company argued that it faced 'lively competition'. The ECJ said that this does not preclude a dominant position. A dominant position means that such competition goes on without the dominant undertaking having to modify its behaviour or suffering any detrimental effects from not modifying its behaviour. But if a competitor's price reductions compelled an undertaking to cut its own prices, this behaviour would be incompatible with the independence which marks out a dominant position. (See paras 69-71 of the judgment.)

Again, turning to *Michelin*, the company argued that over recent years it had made a loss. The ECJ observed that 'temporary unprofitability or even losses are not inconsistent with the existence of a dominant position'. (See para 59 of the judgment.)

Similar arguments had been tried and found wanting in *United Brands*. The company complained that it had suffered 'fierce competition'. The ECJ said that it is unnecessary to have eliminated all competition in order to be in a dominant position: United Brands always held out successfully against the attacks of its competitors. Also, United Brands pointed out that it had made losses for five years while its competitors made profits; if a dominant position gave a company the power to fix prices, then making a loss did not show a dominant position. The ECJ rejected this — over the five years customers continued to buy more bananas from United Brands even though it was the dearest vendor:

this was a more significant factor. It is a particular feature of a dominant position and was determinative in this particular case.

4.2.7 Conclusions

The single most important factor in proving dominance seems to be market share. How does this apply to the cases that have come before the courts? The decisions are as follows:

(a) For market share of 75% or higher: if maintained over a relatively long period, no further evidence is needed. See *Hoffmann-La Roche* (vitamins B2, B6, H (75%)); *Hilti* (nail guns (70–80%)); *Tetra Pak II* (cartons (90%)).

(b) For market share between 40–55%: is strong evidence of a dominant position but will require confirmation through evidence of the competitors' market shares and the firm's own structure. See *Hoffmann-La Roche* (vitamins A (47%) and C (about 65%)); *United Brands* (bananas (40–45%)); *Akzo* (hydrogen peroxide (50%)).

(c) For market share of under 25%: a dominant position is very unlikely to be found to exist.

4.3 Within the Common Market or a substantial part of it

Of course, the relevant territory has been considered already in our analysis under Article 82, as part of the market definition which enabled us to determine whether the suspect firm occupied a dominant position or not. The phrase 'within the Common Market or a substantial part of it' is used in Article 82 to shift our attention to jurisdictional matters. If the dominant position is not held over the whole of the Community or an economically significant part of it, there is no 'Community interest' in how the dominant company behaves. That is not to say that national authorities will be similarly uninterested in the behaviour; it just means that the Commission, as Community watchdog, will not need to get involved.

Examples of geographical areas which have fulfilled this requirement are:

(a) The entire common market: *Hoffmann-La Roche v Commission* ('Vitamins').

(b) The United Kingdom: *Hugin/Liptons v Commission.*

(c) The Netherlands: *Michelin v Commission; BP v Commission* (77/77) [1978] ECR 1511 (oil traders).

(d) South-western Germany: *Suiker Unie v Commission* (40/73 et al.) [1975] ECR 1663 (the sugar cartel).

(e) Italian ports: *Merci Convenzionali Porto di Genova v Siderurgica Gabrielli SPA* (C-179/90) [1991] ECR I-5889.

It remains open to question whether the smallest Member States (in terms of numbers of consumers) — Denmark, Ireland and Luxembourg — are substantial parts of the common market. In *BAT and Reynolds v Commission* (142 and 156/84) [1978] ECR 4487 the Commission found Rothmans International was dominant in Belgium *and* Luxembourg with 47.8% of that market. This territory was a substantial part of the EEC. It is likely that political expediency, if nothing else, will dictate that the smaller states are all found to be substantial parts of the common market.

We can see an example of such expediency, perhaps, in the *Radio Telefis Eireann* case (see **4.2.4**). RTE alleged that the geographical area under consideration (Eire and Northern Ireland) did not constitute a substantial part of the common market. This allegation was based on the number of households in the territory (ie 1 million; or less than 1% of the Community total). This type of test had been used before by the ECJ — see, for example, the *Suiker Unie* case — but the Court of First Instance held that the island of Ireland was 'undeniably a substantial part of the common market'.

4.4 Abusive behaviour

4.4.1 Introduction

In the French language version of the EC Treaty this is rendered as 'abusive exploitation', which may make its scope clearer. Unlike Article 81 (ex 85), which caught behaviour that was *intended* to restrict competition or had that effect, Article 82 (ex 86) is concerned with *conduct*. Article 82 gives several examples of behaviour that will constitute an abuse. You should note that there is no possibility of getting an exemption from prohibition if the abuse in question in fact has some beneficial effects for consumers (unlike Article 81(3) (ex 85(3)).

The Court of Justice considered the meaning of 'abuse' in *Europembellage Corp and Continental Can Co v Commission*: it said that Article 86 (now 82) aimed at stopping not just behaviour which was directly detrimental to consumers (eg selling at unfair prices or deliberately cutting back on production in order to obtain a higher price for the product), but also behaviour which could harm consumers indirectly, usually by terminating effective competition in the market (ie wiping out the existing competition or making it more difficult for others to enter the market and compete).

In *Hoffmann-La Roche v Commission* the Court returned to the notion of 'abuse' and this time noted that an abuse was abnormal behaviour (that which would not occur in conditions of normal competition) which had the effect of either causing existing competition to wither or remain (stagnant) at present levels.

'Abuse' requires a company to engage in an activity; merely possessing a dominant position is not an abuse in itself. This was made clear by the ECJ in *Michelin*:

> A finding that an undertaking has a dominant position is not in itself a recrimination but simply means that, irrespective of the reasons for which it has such a dominant position, the undertaking concerned has a *special responsibility* not to allow its conduct to impair genuine undistorted competition on the common market.

This notion of a *special responsibility* has been echoed more recently by Competition Commissioner Mario Monti, in an answer to a question asked by two Danish MEPs in the European Parliament (2001). The Commissioner stated that the Commission discriminates in its application of Article 82 between non-dominant firms and those which are dominant. Conduct which could be tolerated when done by a non-dominant firm may well be condemned as an abuse under Article 82 if performed by a dominant firm. See OJ 2001 C318E/90.

None of this really helps us to determine what specific types of behaviour might be found to be an abuse. Article 82 itself offers some assistance in heads (a)–(d) (see **4.1**). These are not intended to be exhaustive; see *Continental Can* at para 26: 'The list merely gives examples, not an exhaustive enumeration … .'

Article 82, heads (a) and (b) are indicative of attempts to regulate performance directly: unfair prices (price increases) or restrictions on output have a direct effect on the customer/consumer (although price cuts may benefit consumers; but not perhaps in the long term?). By looking at Article 82 heads (c) and (d), one sees that the provision aims not only at 'practices which may cause damage to consumers directly, but also at those which are detrimental to them [ie consumers] through their impact on an effective competition structure' (*Continental Can*, para 26).

Examples (c) and (d) show that unfair or discriminatory conduct is covered by Article 82 (eg price discrimination and tie-ins). We should remember that *Continental Can* was a merger case (in a time before the Merger Regulation). This may explain the bold statement in the judgment that simply strengthening a dominant position may be an abuse within Article 82, *regardless of the means and procedure by which it is achieved*, if it has the effect of substantially fettering the competition.

Is it useful to try to *classify* the types of abuse that fall within Article 82? Arguably, this is what the Article itself does with the four examples. However, the Commission and Court often fail to refer to heads (a)–(d) specifically; or else they refer to more than one of them; or, if they do use just one, they fail to state how it is that the example is demonstrated by the facts in the particular case. We may need to create a classification for ourselves.

4.4.2 Three classes of abuse?

It has been suggested (by John Temple Lang) that there are three basic classes of abuse:

- exploitative abuses, eg, excessive prices;
- anti-competitive abuses, eg, tie-ins, mergers and discriminatory pricing;
- reprisal abuses, eg, refusals to deal, predatory pricing.

It should be noted that these provide a basic framework but are not necessarily mutually exclusive: eg, tie-ins are anti-competitive but also allow exploitation; predatory pricing is anti-competitive but may be used as a reprisal weapon. The United Kingdom Government's Green Paper on 'Abuse of Market Power' (November 1992) uses 'anti-competitive' and 'exploitative' abuses as a system to underpin several practical examples of abusive behaviour (see p 19 of the Green Paper).

Examples of abuse were found in the following cases:

(a) *Commercial Solvents Corp v Commission*: refusal to supply a competitor.

(b) *United Brands v Commission*: discriminatory pricing — different prices applied to sales of bananas brought by ship from the Caribbean. Also refusal to deal — termination of dealer in Denmark after it became an exclusive for another brand of bananas.

(c) *Micro Leader Business v Commission*: the Court of First Instance held that marketing a copyright product (computer software) in Canada did not exhaust the copyright in the EU and the copyright could generally be used to prevent parallel imports; however, if it could be shown that the copyright holder applied lower prices for the product on the Canadian market than on the European market and that its Community prices were excessive, the enforcement of copyright protection to stop parallel imports could be considered as abusive conduct.

(d) *AKZO* (C-62/86) [1991] ECR I-3359: threats to enter the victim's market, coupled with a predatory pricing policy.

An alternative to classification is to look at *particular types of conduct* and see what is indicated by precedent. We can examine three types:

- discounts (**4.4.3**);
- refusals to deal (**4.4.4**);
- unfair pricing (**4.4.5**).

4.4.3 Discounts

This activity had been tried by Hoffmann-La Roche and was considered by the Court of Justice in what is sometimes called the 'Vitamins' case. The company had a variety of exclusive or preferential supply contracts with several bulk vitamin 'users'. The customers were required either to buy *only* from Hoffmann-La Roche, or to buy most of their requirements from the company. In return, they got a *fidelity rebate,* ie a discount based on past purchases. The customers had to get past a threshold percentage of their previous requirements. The principle behind the rebate was said to be — the more you buy the cheaper it gets. The rebate also applied to more than one vitamin, so if a customer bought more of any Hoffmann-La Roche vitamin, this increased their discount on purchases of any other Hoffmann-La Roche vitamin.

These fidelity rebates were rejected by the ECJ as abusive, even if they were entered into willingly by the customer. They were not based on an economic transaction which justified this burden but were designed to *deprive or restrict* the customer's *choice* in sources of supply. This rebate system also hindered other vitamin producers from getting *access* to the market. The rebates were wrong because they were based on loyalty (ie, Hoffmann tied up an outlet against its competitors) rather than simple *quantity of purchase*. One *can* discount on quantity usually because of economies of scale — these can be passed on to the customer. Here, customers qualified on a percentage of their *need,* whether great or small.

Incidentally, Hoffmann-La Roche also had so-called 'English' clauses in their rebate agreements. These allowed the customer to buy the product elsewhere if they had a better offer from another supplier but they were obliged to tell Hoffmann about the better offer. The ECJ held that 'English' clauses were unacceptable — although superficially they *prevented foreclosure* by allowing the customer to shop elsewhere, the fact of an obligation to inform Hoffmann-La Roche of its competitors' moves helped it to identify competitors and deal with them.

Discounts were also considered in *Michelin*: the ECJ observed that discounts *per se* are not abusive (para 71 of its judgment) but loyalty rebates are. The problem is that discounts, especially for quantity, can be offered on a one-off basis but loyalty rebates operate on a rolling basis and require continuity of purchase. This results in competitors being denied access to one's customers. Discounts must be justified by some economic service. Here, discount periods were measured over a one-year qualifying period. Customers came under heavy pressure to buy Michelin tyres over the whole period. Also, Michelin kept changing the qualifying rules and not telling customers, so uncertainty prevailed and customers were less likely to switch to another supplier. This stopped free selection by customers and was not competitively-justified behaviour.

Rather surprisingly, in June 2001 Michelin was again fined by the Commission. This time, it had operated in France 'a complex system of quantitative rebates, bonuses and commercial agreements, which constitute a loyalty-inducing and unfair system *vis-à-vis* its dealers from 1990 to 1998. The Commission regarded the fact that this was a second infringement, for the same anti-competitive behaviour, as an aggravating circumstance. See Commission Press Release IP/01/873.

4.4.4 Refusal to deal

A useful article has been written by Romano Subiotto, 'The right to deal with whom one pleases under EC competition law: a small contribution to a necessary debate' 1992 ECLR 234.

Refusals to deal occur in various ways, eg as a response to shortages; as a threat of punishment for misconduct; as a result of forward vertical integration. Refusals can be competitively justified: for example, in *United Brands*, the company argued that its ban on resale was to protect both its brand name and consumers by guaranteeing the quality of the product. The ECJ said it was permissible if it did not raise obstacles, the effect of which went beyond the (legitimate) objective to be achieved.

Examples of legitimate refusal might be:

(a) in a selective distribution system where a distributor fails to meet (proper) requirements;

(b) genuine shortages, if properly dealt with (cf. the 'Dutch Oil' case, *ABG/BP* [1977] 2 CMLR D1);

(c) when a customer transfers its central activity to promoting a rival brand. The supplier could review its relationship with the customer and legitimately terminate that relationship, giving adequate notice (taken from the Subiotto article, citing the Commission decision in *Brass Band Instruments/Boosey & Hawkes* OJ 1987 286/36, Commission Decision). But this must be compared with United Brands: *United Brands* terminated supplies to a long-standing customer (Olesen) after Olesen gave priority to a competing brand of bananas. This was held to be a 'penalty' used to discourage others from following Olesen's example of independent action. It was designed to have a serious adverse effect on competition. (See paras 169–178, 182–196 of the judgment.)

If a company engages in forward vertical integration, the desire of the Commission to protect its *competitors* seems overwhelming. See, for example, *Commercial Solvents*, where the refusal to supply is condemned even though one can see it as the simple replacement of one company by another. The case is often seen thus by its critics, but we should note that potential competition was eliminated — the situation changed from one actual supplier plus one potential supplier to just one actual supplier. A very strict test was applied in *Commercial Solvents* — intention seemed to be irrelevant — the Court noted that the company's objective had been to reserve the raw materials it produced for its own in-house fabrication of the finished product.

This approach finds an echo in a more recent decision, that of the French *Conseil de la Concurrence* (or Competition Board): *Re Supply of Metallic Calcium* [1992] BOCCRF 185. Here, a dominant supplier of standard industrial calcium supplied the product to a smaller company producing high-grade calcium granules. The dominant company was slow in making deliveries and failed to provide necessary technical information about the product. So the customer went to other, more expensive, sources and had to raise its own prices. According to the *Conseil*, the requests for supply were normal and it found that the delays were due to the supplier's wish to develop its own in-house production of the high-grade product.

The urgency of the customer's need for supplies seems to be irrelevant, as may be seen from para 26 of the judgment in *Commercial Solvents*.

The Subiotto article (above) refers to the American 'doctrine of *essential facilities*'. This idea, that an undertaking which possesses such a facility is under some obligation to its competitors in a 'downstream' market, seems to be assuming significance in Europe. A good example is *B & I/Sealink Harbours and Stena Sealink* [1992] 5 CMLR 255.

Sealink is both a British ferry operator and the port authority at Holyhead, Wales. Both Sealink and B & I use berths at Holyhead. The B & I berth is at the harbour mouth and, when Sealink's ferries pass, the water level rises so that B & I have to interrupt loading or unloading of their ferry. Only one such incident occurred per B & I ferry until October 1991 when Sealink announced new sailing times which would involve two ships passing each docked B & I ferry. B & I sought interim measures, prohibiting the new sailings, which the Commission granted.

The Commission said that a dominant undertaking which owns or controls an essential facility and which uses that facility will be guilty of an abuse within Article 82 (ex 86) if it either:

(a) refuses to grant access to competitors; or

(b) grants access on terms less favourable than those which it gives to its own services.

An essential facility is one to which competitors must have access in order to provide a service to customers. One might easily draw parallels between such a (typically physical) situation and that where access to information protected by an intellectual property right in one market is necessary to enable a separate market to be developed (cf *Volvo v Veng and Radio Telefis Eireann v Commission* (C-241-242/91) [1995] ECR I-743. The ECJ said that a refusal to grant a licence for an intellectual property right would only constitute abusive behaviour in 'exceptional circumstances'.

4.4.5 Unfair pricing

A basic problem in proving unfair or predatory pricing lies in the assessment of the cost structure of the suspect. Various theories exist on how costs are to be assessed but there is no real consensus. The task is easiest where a bald threat exists but a 'guilty' verdict in such a situation seeks to punish behaviour (intent) with little consideration of the effect. A good example of this is the *ECS/AKZO* litigation, where there was a 'smoking gun' letter and the issue of intent seems to have been accorded great significance.

The fact that behaviour, rather than effect, is caught by the notion of predatory pricing can be shown by the words of the ECJ in *Sirena v Eda* (40/70) [1971] ECR 69:

> ... as regards the abuse of a dominant position, although the price level of the product may not of itself necessarily suffice to disclose such an abuse, it may, however, if unjustified by any objective criteria, and if it is particularly high, be a determining factor.

So, price increases may be caught, as well as price reductions!

In *United Brands* (1976), the ECJ said that 'charging a price which is excessive because it has no reasonable relation to the economic value of the product supplied is ... an abuse' (see p 252 of the judgment). When calculating the economic value of a product, we must take into consideration the production costs.

The formula set out by the ECJ for establishing whether predatory pricing has occurred looks like this:

First, find	£ x (ie price actually charged for a unit of product)
then deduct	£ y (ie costs actually incurred on making it)
Result?	£ z

We should then determine whether £ z is excessive or not. Assuming that someone (usually the Commission) can answer 'Yes' to the question 'Is £ z excessive?', we should next see if £ x is unfair, either in itself or in comparison with competing products. If this can be answered affirmatively, we have a case of unfair or predatory pricing.

The formula is useless to apply in practice for two reasons. First, no one can agree on the method of costs analysis which should be used. Secondly, the notion that '£ z is excessive' implies a comparison with something else but it is not clear what we should use for the comparison. The ECJ has appreciated the difficulties involved in an analysis of production costs but has suggested (correctly) that some tests exist for determining excessive prices and that the Commission should use them when alleging excessive pricing. A problem remains, in that there is a plurality of such tests.

Let us take the *AKZO* case as an illustration. The Court said that prices which are lower than the average variable cost (AVC) and which are used as a tool to lever out a rival must be regarded as an abuse; a dominant undertaking has no interest in such action except to eliminate rivals in order to then raise prices. The reason it has no interest other than this is that every one of its sales represents a loss, ie all the fixed costs plus at least part of the variable costs for each unit sold.

Where an undertaking charges prices above AVC but below average total cost (ie, the sum of its fixed costs plus variable costs — ATC), these prices must be an abuse where they form part of an elimination plan. The dominant undertaking is able to remove undertakings who are as effective as the dominant undertaking but who cannot resist the competition due to their inferior financial capacity.

The ECJ defines variable costs as only those which vary according to the level of output. The Court says that labour costs fail to do this and so they are fixed costs. On the facts, AKZO's prices were below AVC only once. Other pricing abuses fell in the range between AVC and ATC. These were still abusive as they could not be explained away as reactions to offers made by AKZO's competitors and they continued over a long period. No abuse was proved by the Commission regarding the alleged selectivity of offers to AKZO's customers. The variation in availability of offers properly reflected the differences in the types of customer. For a cogent argument showing the limitations of the AKZO formula for predatory pricing, see Soames and Ryan [1994] 3 ECLR 157. National courts seem quite willing to detect predatory pricing. See, eg, the French 'Competition Council' in *Béton de France* [1995] 2 ECLR R-45, and the Italian Antitrust Authority in *Tekal/Italcementi* [1995] 5 ECLR R-130.

4.5 Effect on trade between Member States

The same element occurs in Article 81 (ex 85), and there is little else to say beyond that which was said earlier (see **2.3**) except for two points. First, occasionally the European Court has interpreted this requirement quite strictly. In *Hugin/Liptons v Commission*, a Swedish parent company with a UK subsidiary terminated supplies of spare parts for its cash tills to the 'victim', Liptons. Liptons was a small company which operated in the Greater London area, providing a cash till repair service. The ECJ said that Liptons would normally have bought the spares from Hugin's subsidiary in the UK; the volume of trade was so small as to be insignificant and not attractive enough for other companies to want to import spares and satisfy Liptons' demand; finally there was no evidence that Liptons was likely to expand its business into another Member State. Thus there was no effect on trade between Member States and therefore no breach of Article 82 (ex 86).

Secondly, under Article 82 (ex 86) the Court and the Commission are more likely to consider the harm done to one's competitors as affecting inter-State trade, even where this does no immediate harm to the ultimate consumer. The most typical example is the actual or threatened elimination of a rival (eg *AKZO* (Commission Decision); *Commercial*

Solvents Corp v Commission) or someone in a rival 'camp' (eg, *United Brands v Commission* — trade buyer deciding to promote a rival brand). This is a rather broader test than that used for Article 81 (ex 85), so conduct which distorts the structure of the market may be regarded as affecting the inter-State trade.

4.6 The relationship between Article 82 and exemption under Article 81(3)

Exemption is only possible for breaches of Article 81 (ex 85). In the first *Tetra Pak* case (*Tetra Pak Rausing v Commission* (T-51/89) [1990] ECR II-309) the Court of First Instance considered the relationship between Article 82 (ex 86) and exemption under Article 81 (ex 85), when the same behaviour is under examination.

The Court concluded that if behaviour is illegal under Article 82 (ex 86), then that is conclusive of the matter. The fact of exemption under Article 81(3) (ex 85(3)) (in this case via the patent licensing block exemption, Regulation 2349/84) is irrelevant. If conduct was exempt under Article 81(3) (ex 85(3)), the usual consequences would follow but undertakings in a dominant position still had a separate obligation to comply with Article 82 (ex 86). Tetra Pak's complaint about being left in a position of legal uncertainty was dismissed. Tetra Pak was subsequently fined a record sum by the European Commission for these activities — see **Chapter 7**.

For further reading on Article 82 (ex 86), see chapter 4 in Korah; chapter 12 in Hawk; or chapter 14 in Steiner — all works cited in **Appendix 9**. See also the European Economic Area Agreement, Article 54, which replicates Article 82 (ex 86) *mutatis mutandis* (text in [1993] 14 ECLR supplement).

5 Compliance

5.1 Who cares about compliance?

5.1.1 The company that may be guilty of an infringement

A company may well be concerned about possible infringement of Article 81(1) (ex 85(1)), through its contracts with suppliers or distributors perhaps, or if it is in a dominant position it may be concerned to ensure that its actions are not perceived as an abuse of a dominant position and contrary to Article 82 (ex 86). Many large companies now have compliance departments in order to cope with the large volume of regulatory material by which businesses have to abide. A company may infringe one of the EC competition rules without intending to but that would be no defence to a Commission decision imposing a fine (though it might lead to a reduction). Companies have the opportunity to apply to the Commission for negative clearance and thus get a clean bill of health for the agreement or conduct that they were concerned about; they can do this in respect of either Article 81(1) (ex 85(1)) or 82 (ex 86) or both (using Form A/B). In practice, they are unlikely to get a formal decision from the Commission but they may get a comfort letter indicating that, on what the Commission currently knows about their situation, there seems to be no infringement. That letter will not stop the Commission from investigating the company if the circumstances change or new information is sent to the Commission (and it is not binding on national courts) but usually the comfort letter works as its name suggests.

Alternatively, a company may have a good idea that its agreement infringes Article 81(1) (ex 85(1)) but it may also think that there are sound, pro-competitive reasons for it to act in this way. It should first check whether a block exemption may apply: generally, these protect contracts between undertakings in a vertical relationship (ie between companies operating at different economic levels). If that is of no help, the company should look at the current criteria for agreements of minor importance: they may be too weak on the relevant market to attract the Commission's attention. That does not mean, though, that they will necessarily escape the attention of national competition authorities. If none of this helps, the company should consider making a notification to the Commission (on Form A/B) and applying for an individual exemption under Article 81(3) (ex 85(3)). Again, a comfort letter is the most likely outcome of benefit to the company. If the company suspects it may be infringing Article 82 (ex 86), its advisers should remind it that no exemption is possible.

5.1.2 The competitors of a company that may be guilty of an infringement

Companies in competition with a 'suspect' firm are unlikely to have any contractual dealings with that firm, although it is not impossible. It is more likely that these competitors feel they are being excluded from a profitable market by the actions of the suspect firm, or that they are being hit by an unfair pricing policy operated by that firm. There are many ways in which competitors can be damaged by breaches of Article 81(1) (ex 85(1)) or 82 (ex 86) by a suspect firm. Indeed, an English judge recently declared that Article 81(1) (ex 85(1)) was intended solely to regulate the relationships between competitors operating in the same market (see *Scottish & Newcastle plc v Bond*, 25 March 1997, unreported). Such companies may wish to alert the Commission to the existence of an infringement: they should do so by means of a complaint. This should comply with the headings in Form C. The Commission is not obliged to investigate complaints, though, and a complainant company may find its complaint being referred down to the appropriate national competition authorities for further action. This is likely to be the case where the anti-competitive effects of an agreement or conduct are felt within the territory of a single Member State of the EU.

5.1.3 The suppliers of a company that may be guilty of an infringement

Whether a supplier feels aggrieved will, no doubt, depend entirely upon whether the supply contract suits it or not. It may be that the supplier is in a weak bargaining position, compared to the other party to the contract, and has been obliged to accept certain anti-competitive clauses or to sell at an uncompetitive price, or to accept other restrictions (perhaps upon who or where else it can supply the contract goods). Sometimes a change in the market (or a related market) may make the present contract less advantageous than it seemed at first: so complaints can be used as tactical weapons in an essentially commercial struggle. It is likely that a supplier will complain about its contract with another party only where it wishes either to amend the contract and make it less onerous (or restrictive) or to escape from the contract altogether (since infringing Article 81(1) (ex 85(1)) or 82 (ex 86) will render the relevant provisions void). A complaint may bring about the termination of the relationship, whether desired or not: once a company is being investigated by the Commission, its own interests often take priority over the particular wishes of the complainant. It will often be the case that a supplier is better advised to use the *threat* of a complaint as a lever in re-negotiating the terms of the contract, rather than actually going to the Commission. If it did so, the complaint would follow the headings in Form C.

5.1.4 The customers of a company that may be guilty of an infringement

The end user may well be a private citizen, in which case a complaint to the Commission is unlikely. It may be that if enough people are affected by the allegedly infringing behaviour (maybe excessively high prices charged by a dominant supplier), some sort of collective complaint may be possible. An unusual complaint can be seen in the OJ 1992 C2/32. Scottish MEPs were asking questions in the European Parliament, in the course of which it emerged that the Commission had received a formal complaint in 1990 from a 'pressure group'. This group was the Scottish Steel Campaign Trust and its complaint was about the alleged anti-competitive behaviour of British Steel in closing down the hot strip mill at Ravenscraig. Sir Leon Brittan, for the Commission, replied that the Commission had investigated the complaint and taken a decision. Also, it is not impossible to envisage complaints coming from trade unions, concerned about a company's decisions and their effect on the workforce.

Where customers have entered into a contract, which they now allege is anti-competitive, they may also be guilty of the infringement if Article 81(1) (ex 85(1)) is involved. It is much better for them if their partner is in a dominant position and they can try to lay any blame at the door of the dominant firm. If a customer wishes to complain to the Commission about a supposed infringement, it will do so in a document adopting the headings in Form C.

5.2 Determining compliance

Until Regulation 1/2003 came into effect, there were three ways to initiate a Commission investigation. First, the Commission could begin one on its own initiative. Secondly, a complaint could be made. Thirdly, a firm which was a party to an agreement (or which believed itself to be in a dominant position) could seek a decision from the Commission (it would be hoping for either a negative clearance, that there was no infringement, or for an exemption). There was no particular procedure which the Commission had to follow for own-initiative investigations; also, complaints could be made quite informally, although the Commission has given guidance to help would-be complainants (see **5.3**). However, for firms seeking negative clearance or an exemption, there was a specific format to follow which required detailed and voluminous information to be provided to the Commission. The firm had to 'notify' the Commission. It had to do so using a template known as Form A/B; that was set out in Regulation 3385/94.

With the advent of Regulation 1/2003, the centralised system of notification was removed. Now, the Commission is only empowered to investigate and possibly find an infringement following a complaint or if acting on its own initiative (see Regulation 1/2003, Articles 7 and 1 0). So, a firm which believes that it may have somehow infringed either Article 81(1) or Article 82 is no longer able to seek a formal opinion from the Commission.

5.3 Using Form C

A special form (Form C) exists for complainants to use. Its use is not mandatory but complainants should always ensure that their reasons for alleging a breach of Article 81 (ex 85) and/or 82 (ex 86) are clearly set out in writing for the Commission. In 1997, the Commission registered 177 complaints and 101 cases were opened on the Commission's own initiative (source: XXVIIth Report on Competition Policy).

Form C is merely a guide to help an undertaking to satisfy the requirements of the Commission. There are six heads to use in the complaint document, as follows:

1. Identify the parties

It is probably a good idea to give a brief indication of the relationship (if any) between them, with a description of the nature of their business.

2. Give details of the alleged infringements

The complainant should set out exactly what has gone on, perhaps with reference to specific contract clauses or the content of letters, faxes or telephone calls.

3. Demonstrate a legitimate interest

This may be quite easy to do, especially if the complainant can be seen as a victim of the other company's anti-competitive acts. Any damage which has been or may be suffered by the complainant as a result of the anti-competitive acts should be particularised.

4. Produce documents and refer to the evidence relied on
Usually a job for solicitors, working closely with the lay client, but clear instructions must come from counsel or whoever is in charge of organising the complaint document as to what is wanted (ie specific documents, types of invoices, relevant periods of time).

5. Termination
The complainant should set out any steps taken to alert the suspect company to its breach of the competition rules. This is of a similar nature to a letter before action in English civil proceedings.

6. Declaration
That the previous information is correct, signed by a properly mandated officer of the complainant undertaking.

5.4 National competition authorities and the Commission

Although this chapter has been largely concerned with the Commission, it should not be forgotten that national authorities also supervise the behaviour of undertakings. By 1998, eight Member States had incorporated Articles 81 (ex 85) and 82 (ex 86) into their national laws — Belgium, France, Germany, Greece, Italy, The Netherlands, Portugal and Spain. National competition authorities in those countries applied those Articles directly to undertakings. The UK now has provisions in its national law which are based upon the Articles, in the Competition Act 1998.

In the Competition Act 1998, ss 2, 9 and 18 reproduce, almost word for word, Articles 81 (ex 85)(1), (2) and (3) and 82 (ex 86). This national system is intended to work in 'a consistent manner' with the EU regime (see the Explanatory and Financial Memorandum which was attached to the Competition Bill during its passage through Parliament). For example, s 60 of the Competition Act 1998 requires the UK courts, when interpreting the national rules, to:

> *act ... with a view to securing that there is no inconsistency between ... the principles applied ... by the court ... and the principles laid down by the Treaty and the European Court. The court must, in addition, have regard to any relevant decision or statement of the Commission.* (Competition Act 1998, s 60(2))

In a similar fashion, an agreement will be exempt (a 'parallel exemption') from prohibition under the Competition Act 1998, s 2, if the agreement is already exempted from Article 81(2) (ex 85(2)) by reason of Article 81(3) (ex 85(3)). The Community exemption may arise either by means of a regulation (ie a block exemption), an individual decision or through application of an opposition procedure.

There are still differences between the UK competition regime and that established by the EC Treaty. Both of the UK prohibitory rules apply only where the anti-competitive behaviour *may affect trade within the United Kingdom*. Under s 2, agreements and concerted practices are prohibited only if they have (or are intended to have) an effect on competition *within the United Kingdom*. Under s 18, undertakings must possess a dominant position *within the United Kingdom*.

The UK authorities are:

(a) the Office of Fair Trading, which is responsible for the enforcement of the Competition Act 1998, ss 2 and 18; and

(b) the Competition Commission, which hears appeals from decisions of the OFT. It also took on the work of the current Monopolies and Mergers Commission.

The idea behind the Act is that competition matters of significance at EU level will continue to be examined by the European Commission while 'domestic' matters are dealt with by the UK authorities.

This position is possibly different to the one the Commission would like to see in place. The Commission issued a Notice in 1997, setting out details of the relationship between itself and the various national competition authorities; see OJ 1997 C313/3. This Notice is similar in nature to the one issued in 1993 dealing with cooperation between the Commission and national courts. The 1997 Notice was intended 'to reduce the number of complaints addressed to the Commission if they can be dealt with effectively by the national authorities' (Commission White Paper, 1999). The fact remains that the Competition Act 1998 focuses on internal matters, within the United Kingdom. The emphasis in s 2 is upon agreements which may affect trade within the UK. That concept may be interpreted liberally by the UK courts so that an agreement which may affect trade between Member States, one of which is the UK, will fall under both Article 81 (ex 85) and the Competition Act 1998, s 2. It may be that the Act's emphasis on trade within the UK is intended to mark out a 'horizontal' boundary between its competence to oversee agreements and the competencies of other Member States, rather than having any impact upon the 'vertical' jurisdictional divide between the UK and the European Commission. All of that remains to be seen. Perhaps the national courts remain the appropriate route for enforcement of Articles 81 (ex 85) and 82 (ex 86) within the UK? Articles 81(1) and (2) (ex 85(1) and (2)) are directly effective and have been used by litigants in English courts for several years. The Commission has recognised the different roles of the national courts on the one hand, and itself and national competition authorities on the other:

> It is the task of national courts to safeguard the individual rights of private persons in their relations with one another ... [B]oth the Commission and national competition authorities act in the public interest in performing their general task of monitoring and enforcing the competition rules.

Whether one should try to interest the national competition authority in a complaint or instead sue in a national court remains unclear. What is clear is the fact that:

> Complainants remain reluctant to apply to the national courts or competition authorities when they consider they have been harmed by an infringement of Community law ... [T]he mechanisms for cooperation with national authorities have not to date encountered the success expected, owing to the Commission's monopoly for the application of Article 81(3) of the Treaty. (Commission White Paper, 1999)

One major reason for this reluctance to turn to national courts or authorities is identified by the Commission in that passage — its monopoly over the grant of exemptions.

The Commission's 'monopoly of exemption' has been removed, with effect from 1 May 2004. National competition authorities are able to determine if the criteria in Article 81(3) (ex 85(3)) are met. Similarly, undertakings in national courts are able to rely on the direct applicability of Article 81(3) (ex 85(3)), using it as a defence to allegations that an agreement is prohibited and void. This fundamental shift is justified on the basis that the Competition rules have been in operation for a considerable length of time. Over this period, there have been many Commission decisions and judgments of the European Court. Interpretation, scope and application of the Articles are all much clearer now than they were in 1962. National authorities and courts are better informed and so are more able to be trusted to apply the Treaty Articles correctly and uniformly. However, as the Commission's White Paper stated: '... if this reform is really to improve the application of the [EC] competition rules, the seven Member States that have not yet done so will have to empower their competition authorities to apply Community law.'

6

Investigations

6.1 Investigations

This chapter looks at the procedures used by the European Commission when it investigates cases of suspected infringement of the EC competition rules. The main body of procedural rules is found in Council Regulation 1/2003; throughout this chapter the Regulation will be referred to as 'Regulation 1'.

6.2 Starting an investigation

The Commission may act either on its own initiative or on application by a Member State (see Article 85 (ex 89), EC Treaty). In practice, these have not produced many investigations. Regulation 1 adds a third category to those who may initiate an investigation: applications may be made by 'natural or legal persons who claim a legitimate interest (Article 7), Regulation 1; they may use Form C to complain, see **Chapter 5**). This addition has enabled many companies, firms, associations and individuals to alert the Commission to alleged infringements (comparison might be made to the practice in the anti-trust system of the USA, where the prospect of considerable awards of damages has encouraged many alleged victims of anti-competitive behaviour to take the malefactor to court themselves, thus relieving the pressure on central enforcement agencies). This category of applicants are typically referred to as 'complainants'. Complainants, by definition, have a particular interest in the outcome of any investigation but there are limits on what they may do.

6.2.1 Rights of complainants

A complainant is entitled to be kept informed of the acceptance (or otherwise) of the complaint, to be told of the Commission's preliminary findings, to apply to be heard by the Commission (in writing or orally) in the course of any investigation, and to challenge the final decision of the Commission at the Court of First Instance (see Article 230 (ex 173), EC Treaty and *Metro SB-Grossmarkte v Commission* (26/76) [1977] ECR 1875). However, the complainant does not have the same degree of access to the Commission's file on the investigation as does the undertaking being investigated (see eg *ICI v Commission* (T-36/91) [1995] ECR II-1847). Even more importantly, a complainant cannot force the Commission to investigate a complaint. While it is inconceivable that the

Commission would refuse to investigate, following an application to do so from a Member State, a complaint by a natural or legal person does not carry the same weight with the Commission. The Commission is entitled to prioritise complaints and the Court of First Instance has decided (in *Automec srl v Commission* (T-24/90) [1992] ECR II-2223) that the Commission is not bound to conduct an investigation, nor to take a formal decision on the existence of any alleged infringement (with one exception — where the complaint raises an issue that the Commission alone can deal with). So, there is no right for a complainant to obtain a formal decision on the existence, or otherwise, of an infringement *even if the Commission has become persuaded that such an infringement has occurred* (*Bureau European des Medias de l'Industrie Musicale v Commission* (T-114/92) [1995] ECR II-147). It should be noted that, other than in very exceptional cases, where an agreement is of minor importance the Commission will not institute proceedings against it, neither on its own initiative nor following an application. Going further, the Commission has said it will not institute proceedings against an agreement, even where the parties to it exceed the relevant *de minimis* thresholds for market share, if they are small or medium-sized undertakings (see Commission Notice relating to the revision of the Notice on agreements of minor importance, 1996).

The Commission is entitled to reject a complaint either before embarking upon an investigation, or after the preliminary stages of an investigation. It can do so if it finds that the case shows 'insufficient Community interest' to warrant any (or further) investigation (see eg *Bureau European des Medias*). The idea of referring many complaints to national competition authorities accords with the concept of *subsidiarity*. It also eases the work-load of the Commission and it has been suggested (by Dr Claus-Dieter Ehlermann) that if the Court had not decided *Automec* in the way it did, the Commission might have had to seek amendment of Regulation 17 (the predecessor to Regulation 1) to achieve a similar result. This was because the number of complaints being received by the Commission was too great. It seems that the Commission gets about 100 complaints annually, although 'exact figures are hard to come by and tend to be contradictory' (see Bo Vesterdorf, a judge of the Court of First Instance, in 1994 CMLR 31:77, 'Complaints concerning infringements of competition law within the context of European Community law'). It is not possible to determine whether this apparent popularity confirms the real value of the procedure to complainants. What else could they do?

The obvious 'next-best' alternatives for the would-be complainant are:

- to start litigation in the legal system of an appropriate Member State against the alleged infringer; or
- to re-submit the complaint to the appropriate competition authority in a Member State.

A person or firm considering making a complaint to the Commission may also seek advice on bringing a private legal claim against the alleged infringer. The advisers should be clear that the advantages and disadvantages of both courses are considered. Whilst there is no legal bar on running the two procedures simultaneously, the commencement of proceedings on a 'private' level may help to persuade the Commission that the matter is one that is better dealt with at the national level.

6.2.2 The complainant as a private 'enforcer' of the competition rules

An alleged victim of anti-competitive behaviour which contravenes either Article 81(1) (ex 85(1)) or Article 82 (ex 86) may bring a claim in the appropriate national court. Both Articles are directly effective in the courts of the Member States, giving rights to, and imposing obligations on, individuals (see *BRT v SV SABAM* (127/73) [1974] ECR 51). The procedural rules which apply and the remedies which are available vary from one State to another (for England and Wales, see **Chapter 7**). The effectiveness of enforcement will correspondingly shift, according to the ease with which a claim can be brought and whether the national legal system offers meaningful remedies to the complainant (who may, for example, be seeking modifications to behaviour instead of or as well as financial compensation). The US anti-trust legislation can offer 'treble' damages to a successful litigant (ie the proven damage is simply multiplied by three to arrive at the total award), while EU Member States show a great reluctance to award damages at all in anti-competition suits. The availability and scope of interim remedies will be another factor in determining whether a complainant would be well-advised to launch a private claim against an alleged infringer.

There is an additional consideration for complainants, where anti-competitive behaviour crosses national boundaries: in which legal system should they sue? If a product market embraces two or more Member States, and the complainant alleges that it has sustained damage across the market, should separate claims be brought in each Member State, and the damages claim broken down so that the losses are shown for each national territory? If so, there is the danger of different outcomes to the claims, for example, different limitation periods may apply, or there may be different rules on proving the amount of loss or remoteness of damage (note a call for the Member States to develop common procedural rules when making damages claims based upon Community law ([1995] 1 ECLR 49)). Such variations will do little to encourage private enforcement of the competition rules. In these situations, it is desirable that the Commission is willing to take charge of the complaint and investigate it.

6.2.3 Further action by a complainant

If the Commission refuses to investigate, a complainant is not bound to seek an alternative source of succour. The refusal itself may be challenged in the Court of First Instance, using the procedure in Article 230 (ex 173), EC Treaty (see **8.2**). The Court envisages three stages, leading up to a refusal by the Commission:

- First, the Commission examines a complaint to see what action it will take. This may include informal correspondence between the Commission and complainant, to clarify and expand the issues of concern.
- Secondly, the Commission sends a letter to the complainant setting out the reasons (if any) why it considers there are insufficient grounds to proceed with the complaint. The letter will invite further comments from the complainant.
- Finally, the Commission may reject the complaint. This third stage is a decision (see Article 249 (ex 189), EC Treaty) and may be challenged by an action for annulment using Article 230 (ex 173), EC Treaty. See eg *Guérin Automobiles v Commission* (T-186/94) [1995] ECR II-1753.

Frustrated complainants should note that, if the Commission is engaged in the second stage of this procedure, the complaint may enter a state of limbo. If the Commission sends a letter, telling a complainant that its complaint cannot be dealt with individually at present, this will not be subject to an action for annulment under Article 230 (ex 173), EC Treaty. Conversely, the letter will be a sufficient definition of the Commission's position, and will defeat an action for failure to act under Article 232 (ex 175), EC Treaty (see *Guérin Automobiles*).

6.2.4 The importance of complaints

Although the exact number of complaints remains somewhat mysterious (see **6.2.2**), the Commission has observed that the number of complaints 'continues to be high' (XXVIIIth Annual Report on Competition Policy). Also, its 1999 White Paper states that formal complaints make up nearly a third of new cases taken to the Commission, while most of the investigations begun on its own initiative start with information being sent to the Commission informally. The Commission wants to encourage firms, or others with a legitimate interest, to continue to complain to the Commission since information 'supplied in this way is a very valuable means of detecting infringements of the competition rules'.

In order to facilitate the lodging of complaints, the Commission proposed a number of new measures:

- the introduction of a time limit for deciding whether or not to reject a complaint (probably four months);
- simplifying the procedure for rejecting a complaint;
- the incorporation into Regulation 17/62 of a straightforward restatement of the situation regarding interim relief for a complainant (see **6.5**);
- publication of an explanatory notice about complaints, including advice to help the would-be complainant decide whether the complaint would be better brought to the Commission or a national authority.

6.3 Conducting the investigation

An official of DG IV will be appointed as *rapporteur* for the case. The initial task will be to gather information in order to understand the context of the complaint. This will usually include early attempts to define the relevant market in terms of product and territory.

6.3.1 Requests for information

The Commission is empowered to get information from governments and competition authorities of the Member States (Article 18(6), Regulation 1/2003). It should also be noted that the Commission and national competition authorities form a network and 'the exchange and use of information should be allowed between the members of the network, even where the information is confidential' (Recitals 15 and 16, Regulation 1/2003).

The Commission can also send a request for information to undertakings and associations of undertakings (Article 18(1), Regulation 1/2003). The request should set out:

- the purpose of the request;
- its legal basis;
- what information is required;
- a time-limit for compliance; and
- the possibility of a fine if incorrect information is supplied, whether intentionally or negligently (under Article 23, Regulation 1/2003).

The Commission has the choice to proceed instead by *decision* (Article 18(3)). When it proceeds by decision, the Commission may impose periodic penalty payments instead of a fine (under Article 24, Regulation 1/2003); also, the recipient can seek judicial review of the decision in the ECJ.

Whether the Commission is proceeding by simple request or by formal decision. Article 18 imposes an obligation on the owners of the undertaking (or, if it is a legal person, its officers) to supply the specified information.

In the past, the Commission could not proceed to take a decision to 'request' information unless it had already made an unsuccessful simple request (see case law on Article 11, Regulation 17/62). It is unclear whether such a two-stage procedure applies to Article 18.

See also Article 17, Regulation 1/2003 on requests for information where the Commission is investigating a sector of the economy or a common type of agreement.

6.3.2 Necessary inspections

6.3.2.1 Generally

Under Article 20, Regulation 1/2003, the Commission may 'conduct all necessary inspections' when performing its duties under the Regulation. On an Article 20 inspection, the Commission typically will send its staff to the premises of the firm. Once there, the Commission officials can:

- enter any premises, land and means of transport of the undertaking;
- examine the books and other records relating to the business;
- take or obtain in any form copies or extracts from such books or records;
- seal any business premises, books or records for the duration of the inspection;
- ask any representative or employee of the undertaking to explain a fact or a document relating to the subject-matter of the investigation and record their answers.

There are two types of visit:

(a) one where the officials arrive and simply ask to come in: there is no obligation on the undertaking to comply and, if denied access, the officials will leave (Article 20(2), Regulation 1/2003); and

(b) one where the Commission has taken a formal decision to order the investigation. When officials arrive, usually with no prior warning, and demand entry, access cannot be denied (Article 20(4), Regulation 1/2003).

The rights of the undertaking being inspected are rather circumscribed. In either type of visit, the officials may allow the undertaking to consult a legal adviser, but not if this will cause delay and prejudice the effectiveness of their inspection. Although the second type of visit may seem quite draconian (and is known as a 'dawn raid'), it is not necessary for the Commission to try and fail to gain entry under Article 20(2) first: see *National Panasonic v Commission* (136/79) [1980] ECR 2033. The essence of this type of visit is precisely that it takes place without warning. Undertakings are thus allowed only minimal time to dispose of any incriminating evidence before its potential discovery by the Commission officials. As the Commission has observed:

> If the Commission has reason to believe that the competition rules of the [EC] Treaty may have been seriously infringed, it obliges the companies in question to submit to verifications at all of

their premises. These verifications are normally not announced in advance, in order to ensure that evidentiary documents are not hidden or even destroyed. [Commission Press Release IP/93/893, concerning a periodic penalty payment imposed on AKZO Chemicals B.V.]

6.3.2.2 Use of 'dawn raids'

While one can appreciate the need, in certain circumstances, to avoid alerting the suspect undertaking to the fact of an impending visit to company premises, this power should be strictly limited in its use. One might say that this limitation is in-built due to the requirement for a decision to have been taken by the Commission, prior to a dawn raid. However, several of those who have been investigated have complained about the absence of any independent third party which could have a role in the Commission's use of its power to inspect. A comparison might be made with the procedures in England for searching a premises in criminal and civil proceedings and parallels could be drawn with search warrants and search orders; in both situations, application must be made to a court for grant of the warrant or order.

Article 20 itself provides that:

- the Commission must consult with 'the competent authority of the Member State in whose territory the inspection is to be conducted' before taking the formal decision (Article 20(4)); and
- the formal decision is subject to the suspect's right to have it reviewed (post-execution) by the European Court (Article 20(4)).

Neither of these requirements really addresses the problem, though. It should be a simple matter to legislate so that the Commission must seek approval from a judge of the Court of First Instance (or even a national judge) before executing a formal decision to raid a company.

6.3.2.3 The scope of an inspection

When investigating under Article 20, officials of the Commission are entitled to enter all of the suspect's premises and seek out information which is not already known about or fully identified (*Hoechst v Commission* (46/87, 227/88) [1989] ECR 2919). The Commission is under no obligation to identify in advance those files or documents which it wishes to see, although the written authorisation should indicate clearly the subject-matter and purpose of the investigation. It has been said that the Commission cannot use its powers to justify a 'fishing expedition' (see *National Panasonic*), but it still has a broad area to trawl through once it has decided to launch its boats. The investigation (or 'verification' as the Commission sometimes describes it) may have the character of enabling the Commission officials to verify existing information, gleaned from other sources, or to obtain further details on a topic or event.

In its 1999 White Paper on Modernisation, the Commission expressed concerns about its current powers. These were two-fold. First, before conducting a dawn raid, it is necessary to apply to a judge of the relevant Member State for authorisation (see, for example, the Competition Act 1998, s 61, in the United Kingdom). If the Commission's investigation involves two or more Member States, it becomes a difficult task to coordinate these applications and to ensure that the outcomes are the same. This problem could be overcome by removing the task of judicial oversight to the European Court for a single decision. An alternative solution would be to 'harmonise and simplify the procedural law in the Member States' but, as the White Paper recognised, this is a much more complex option which would almost certainly require amendments to procedural law in most Member States.

The second concern was that some doubt had arisen over exactly what the Commission officials can ask about during an investigation. The White Paper proposed the amendment of Regulation 17/62 to make it clear that the authorised officials of the Commission can ask a company's staff or representatives 'any questions that are justified by and related to the purpose of the investigation, and to demand a full and precise answer'. Official minutes of the answers could be drawn up and those minutes placed in the Commission's file, for possible use later in the investigation. See Article 20(2)(e), Regulation 1/2003.

6.3.2.4 Fines and further attempts

Although there is no obligation to allow officials of the Commission to enter an undertaking's premises, where the visit takes place pursuant to Article 20(2), if the undertaking does permit entry and provides information (whether written, oral or otherwise) it must be careful. If the undertaking supplies incomplete information (in the form of its books or other business records), whether deliberately or through negligence, it may be fined pursuant to Article 23(1)(c) (see further **6.8.1.1** and **6.8.2.1** below).

When the visit takes place pursuant to Article 20(4), there is the additional possibility that, if entry is denied by the undertaking, it may face a fine for that denial and penalty payments (increasing on a daily basis) for continued denial (see Article 23(1)(c); Article 24(1)(d)). Also, if an undertaking is delaying or denying entry to properly-authorised Commission officials, Member States are required to afford any assistance necessary to enable the officials to do their job.

In the UK, in the past this meant applying for an injunction, similar to a search order under the Civil Procedure Rules, from the Commercial Court. The Attorney-General also had power to apply without notice to the High Court for an order. Since 1 March 2000, the Competition Act 1998 makes specific provision for applications to a High Court judge. The judge may issue a warrant authorising entry to named premises, for the purposes of searching for books and records, using reasonable force where necessary. Such a warrant may only be issued where the judge is satisfied that a Commission investigation is being, or is likely to be, obstructed. Intentional obstruction of any person exercising powers under such a warrant is to be a criminal offence, punishable in the Crown Court by two years' imprisonment and an unlimited fine. See further the Competition Act 1998, ss 62 and 65.

6.3.3 Withholding information from the commission

Given the fact that fines may be imposed for supplying incorrect or incomplete information to the Commission and the incentive to volunteer information, it may seem odd for an undertaking to even think about withholding information. However, attempts have been made to do this on a variety of grounds:

- confidentiality;
- privilege against self-incrimination;
- legal professional privilege.

An undertaking may decide to supply information to the Commission, even though it feels the information is confidential and should not be disclosed to third parties. Problems may arise either where the Commission seeks to disclose that information to others (disclosure of confidential material) or refuses to do so (infringement of right to a fair hearing, to defend oneself effectively). See further **6.6.5**.

The topics of confidentiality and disclosure are the subject of an article by Julian M. Joshua at [1994] 2 ECLR 68.

6.3.3.1 Confidentiality

In general, the information which the Commission obtains through any of its information-gathering activities 'shall be used only for the purpose for which it was acquired' (Article 28, Regulation 1/2003). However, the Commission is part of a network comprising itself and the competition authorities of the Member States. The Commission is empowered to exchange its information with national competition authorities in a variety of circumstances. The Commission may also disclose information to its Advisory Committee to enable it to do its job. Finally, the Commission may transmit factual information to the national courts; see Article 15(1), Regulation 1/2003).

The information may be confidential in nature. Confidentiality will normally be respected but the information may still be used by the recipients. Where a national competition authority is applying Article 81 or 82, it may use confidential information which has been supplied to it by the Commission (Article 12(1), Regulation 1/2003). In the past, such use was forbidden; information could be transmitted but not used. See for example, the judgment in *Direccion General de Defensa de las Competencia v AEB* (C-67/91) [1992] ECR I-4785. That is no longer the position.

When there is a disclosure of information, all those who deal with it are obliged not to disclose it further, where it is covered by the obligation of professional secrecy (Article 28(2), Regulation 1/2003). 'Professional secrecy' is a concept undefined in either the legislation or case law of the European Court. A firm may wish to withhold information from the Commission on the ground that it may or will fall into the hands of a competitor. That is most obviously a risk where a competitor may seek access to the Commission's file in order to make representations in the course of an investigation. That aspect is considered in detail in **6.6.5**. Suppose the competitor is an arm of the State whose competition authority may receive the information? The concern may be that access to the Commission's file is now not the most obvious route to disclosure; rather, there is a risk that the information may 'leak' between the various arms of the State. This was the concern raised in *SEP v Commission* (C-36/92) [1994] ECR I-1911. The Commission had requested information from a firm, in particular it wanted a copy of the contract for the supply of gas between SEP and Statoil. Statoil was in competition with the Dutch State-owned gas supplier, Gasunie. SEP refused to disclose the contract to the Commission on the ground that:

- it contained commercially sensitive information, and
- the Commission would disclose it to the Dutch competition authority.

The ECJ vindicated the concerns of SEP. The ECJ felt that no 'Chinese wall' could be erected between the State officials in the Dutch competition authority who would look at Statoil matters and those whose task was to consider the commercial policy of Gasunie. The fore-runner of Article 28, Regulation 1/2003 (Article 20, Regulation 17/62) apparently did not provide an effective barrier against possible misuse of confidential information. Interestingly, SEP's claim failed and the ECJ ordered disclosure. Its reasoning was that the Commission was under no duty to pass the contract onto the Dutch, so the possibility of a conflict of interest might never arise. Given the changes to the procedural framework made in Regulation 1/2003, a claim like SEP's might now succeed.

6.3.3.2 Privilege against self-incrimination

No right to remain silent has ever appeared in the procedural regime governing competition investigations, notwithstanding their apparent similarity to criminal inviestigations. For example, the power given to the Commission to 'ask for oral explanations on the spot' in 1962 (Article 14, Regulation 17/62) did not admit of any exceptions. In 1989, the ECJ recognised that the recipient of Commission questions could raise a privilege against self-incrimination. In a case based upon a request for information (then Article 11, Regulation 17/62, see now Article 18, Regulation 1/2003), the ECJ held that questions which effectively require a firm to admit its guilt are likely to be ruled void and the firm is not obliged to respond. See *Orkem SA v Commission* (374/87) [1989] ECR 3283. In 1993, the European Court of Human Rights held that there is a right to remain silent and not to incriminate oneself. See *Funke v France* [1993] 1 CMLR 897. The right arises under Article 6 of the European Convention on Human Rights and Fundamental Freedoms.

In the new procedural framework, Regulation 1/2003 says almost nothing about the right to remain silent. In recital 23, the Council of Ministers recognises that 'undertakings cannot be forced to admit that they have commited an infringement'. The recital goes on to state the limits on this 'right' — undertakings are 'in any event obliged to answer factual questions and to provide documents, even if this information may be used ... against them [or others] to establish ... the existence of an infringement'.

Some Member States now impose criminal liability upon firms and individuals responsible for anti-trust infringements (including the UK — see the Enterprise Act 2002). Recital 16 of Regulation 1/2003 says that information gathered by the Commission may be transmitted to national competition authorities, where it may be used for the application of national competition law in parallel with the application of the EC Articles. This includes confidential information. The recital goes on to observe that natural persons 'may be subject to substantially different types of sanctions across the various [legal] systems [of the Member States]'. In the UK, an individual may face a fine or imprisonment (Enterprise Act 2002, s 190). The recital concludes that 'information can be used only if it has been collected in a way whch respects the same level of protection of the rights of defence of natural persons as provided for under the national rules' of the recipient competition authority. This perhaps raises the questions of the scope of a right to silence under the Enterprise Act 2000 specifically, under English law more generally and, finally, under the European Convention on Human Rights (as incorporated into English law by the Human Rights Act 1998).

One might note that, despite the reference in recital 16 to 'collection in a way that respects the [national] level of protection', no Article in Regulation 1/2003 deals with this matter. Furthermore, what consequences flow from an individual's refusal to answer questions will vary from one Member State to another, as will the protection. For example, in *Norway v Rieber & Son AS* [1995] 2 ECLR R-51, the Norwegian Supreme Court ruled that the judgment in *Funke* was too brief to be relied upon for the purpose of overturning 'long-established procedures under Norwegian competition law concerning the duty to render information to investigating officers'. Of course, Norway is not a Member State of the European Union but it is an adherent to the European Convention on Human Rights. Individual employees may find that they are now asked 'for explanations on facts or documents relating to the subject-matter' of an inspection, with their answers (or silence) being recorded (Article 20(2)(e), Regulation 1/2003). Likewise, their homes may be inspected (Article 21, Regulation 1/2003). It seems incredible that the legal systems of the Member States would not afford such individuals at least the basic protection offered by the European Convention. Cp the judgment of the ECJ in *Otto v Postbank* (C-60/92) [1993] ECR I-5683. Here, the ECJ held that a national court is not required to recognise the privilege against self-incrimination as established (*sic*) in Community law, when determining whether there has been an infringement of Article 81 or 82.

6.3.3.3 Legal professional privilege

Not all documents have to be shown to the Commission. An undertaking which is undergoing an investigation is entitled to withhold documents which are protected by legal professional privilege (see *AM & S Europe Ltd v Commission* (155/79) [1982] ECR 1575). The privilege attaches to written advice from independent (ie not in-house) lawyers who are registered and practising in the EC. Protection extends to all written communications exchanged between lawyer and client after the start of the administrative procedure under Regulation 1 and it will also cover earlier written communications which relate to the subject-matter of that procedure.

The onus of proof rests with the undertaking. If unsatisfied, the Commission can then take a decision requiring the undertaking to produce the relevant document(s). The undertaking may then seek annulment of the decision under Article 230, EC Treaty, before the Court of First Instance.

6.4 After the investigation: the statement of objections

Having concluded its initial look into the allegations, a decision will be taken whether to initiate a procedure against the undertaking(s) involved (this is not a decision within Article 249 (ex 189), EC Treaty and cannot usually be challenged on appeal). A statement of objections will then be issued and served on each undertaking. In many respects, the statement of objections resembles the particulars of claim familiar to English lawyers. The relevant facts will be set out, together with the conclusions that the Commission avers can be drawn from those facts. Copies of documents and other evidence which support the factual picture constructed by the Commission, and its conclusions, must be supplied to the undertaking(s). The factual assertions must be set out in sufficient detail that an effective response can be made; a time limit will usually be set for an undertaking to pass its observations onto the Commission. The statement of objections essentially crystallises the Commission's case against the undertaking(s). Any subsequent decision finding an infringement of Article 81(1) (ex 85(1)) or 82 (ex 86) must be based upon the allegations of fact as set down in the statement of objections. A little further refinement of the Commission's case may be permitted, as the undertaking submits its comments or evidence, but the Commission must be careful to allow the undertaking sufficient time to make a proper response to any further developments. The right of a 'defendant' undertaking to be heard is considered in **6.6.5**.

6.5 Interim measures

It will be cold comfort to a complainant that the Commission's investigation has resulted in the termination of an infringement, or the modification of another undertaking's behaviour, if the complainant has suffered serious or irreparable damage whilst awaiting an outcome to an investigation. Articles 242 and 243 (ex 185 and 186), EC Treaty expressly allow the European Court to grant temporary relief to an affected firm. Such power will be exercised initially by the Court of First Instance but, in order to have jurisdiction, an action must be proceeding at the Court. During the investigative stages prior to a Commission decision, therefore, an affected firm could not turn to the CFI.

It might be thought logical to allow the Commission to grant interim relief, pending a final decision. Examination of the express terms of the EC Treaty shows that no such power was given to the Commission. In 1980 though, the ECJ ruled that the Commission had *implicit* power to grant interim relief during an investigation (see *Camera Care v Commission* (792/79R) [1980] ECR 119). The rationale was that decisions of the Commission become 'ineffectual or illusory' if, by the time of the final decision, the complainant firm had ceased trading because of the effect of the infringement. *Camera Care* is a good example of the teleological approach of the ECJ to the interpretation of the Treaty.

Under this judge-made law, it was for the firm seeking relief to apply for it. The applicant had to satisfy the Commission that the relief it sought was:

- *temporary, conservatory* and *proportionate* (that is, the minimum needed in the present situation);
- *urgently needed* in order to avoid a situation which was either:
  - likely to cause *serious and irreparable damage* to the applicant; or
  - *intolerable* for the *public interest.*

It can be seen that an applicant had to show it was acting *either* out of self-interest or in the public interest.

Regulation 1/2003 has modified this position. A power to grant interim measures is now explicitly included in the Regulation (see Article 8). The scope of the power is somewhat limited, though, in comparison to the previous position. No longer are applications to be made by firms who feel threatened — the Commission is empowered to act only 'on its own initiative'. Also, interim measures will be granted only where necessary 'due to the risk of serious and irreparable damage to *competition*' [emphasis added]. This seems to limit the use of such measures to a public interest requirement. Regulation 1/2003 itself is silent on this aspect but the explanatory memorandum that accompanied the draft of Regulation 1/2003 was more explicit:

> The Commission acts in the public interest and not in the interest of individual operators ... The Commission has an obligation ... only in cases where there is a risk ... to competition. Companies can always have recourse to national courts, the very function of which is to protect the rights of individuals.

Finally, the Commission will only act in urgent cases and where it is satisfied that there is a prima facie case of infringement of Article 81(1) or 82. Case law prior to Regulation 1/2003 stated that the standard of proof should not be too high on the issue of 'serious and irreparable damage'; it is irreparable if it could not be made good by the final decision on the merits (see *La Cinq SA v Commission* (T-44/90) [1992] ECR II-1). It is also likely to be the position still that any interim measure must fall within the scope of the final decision that the Commission could reach, having found an infringement; see *Ford v Commission* (228/82) [1984] 2 ECR 1129; *Brass Band Instruments/Boosey & Hawkes* OJ 1987 L286/36, [1988] 4 CMLR 67).

The other option for a 'victim' firm is to follow the Commission's 'advice' and apply to a national court or competition authority for relief. In an English court, this is most likely to be an application for an interim injunction. Typically, an applicant will need to satisfy the criteria derived from the decision in *American Cyanamid Co v Ethicon Ltd* [1975] AC 396. The Commission may encourage a worried firm to pursue this course — it has observed that national courts can usually adopt interim measures and order the ending of infringements more quickly than the Commission is able to do (*Notice on Cooperation between national courts and the Commission in applying Articles 85 and 86*, OJ 1993 C39/6, para 16).

However, if a firm took this advice, it would find that:

(a) the standard of proof may be higher, compared to that applied by the Commission (a 'serious question to be tried'); also,

(b) the applicant firm would almost certainly have to provide an undertaking in damages, to protect the 'defendant' firm should the interim measures prove unjustified eventually; and

(c) the applicant firm would need to start a civil claim against the defendant firm.

Thus, a firm which feels threatened may find it harder (and costlier) to obtain interim relief nationally but now is unable to seek redress for itself from the Commission.

6.6 Hearings

6.6.1 Introduction

Before taking certain decisions under Regulation 1, the Commission is required to give the undertaking(s) concerned the chance to be heard on matters relevant to the potential decision. These decisions are:

- The decision to order termination of an infringement of Article 85(1) or Article 86 pursuant to Article 7, Regulation 1.
- The decision to order interim measures pursuant to Article 8, Regulation 1.
- The decision to impose a fine pursuant to Article 23, Regulation 1.
- The decision to impose periodic penalty payments pursuant to Article 24(2), Regulation 1.

In 1963, the Commission enacted Regulation 99/63 to regulate such hearings. Subsequently, it published decisions setting out the terms of reference for hearing officers (the latest of these is Decision 01/462, OJ 2001 L162/21; see **Appendix 3**). The Commission issued Regulation 2842/98 in December 1998. This Regulation replaces 99/63, and several similar measures governing hearings in other fields. Regulation 2842/98 contains various procedural improvements, in the light of experience gleaned from using 99/63 over so many years, and is intended to make the whole procedure of hearings much clearer. It came into force on 1 February 1999.

Undertakings against whom objections are raised by the Commission, shall have the chance to express their views in writing, as shall natural or legal persons who show a sufficient interest. A time limit for receipt of views will be imposed. When it takes its decision, the Commission can only rely on those matters which were notified to the undertaking(s) and thus upon which they were able to express their views. The Court of Justice has said that Regulation 17 (and presumably Regulation 1/2003):

> ... applies the general rule that a person whose interests are perceptibly affected by a decision taken by a public authority must be given the opportunity to make his point of view known.

See, eg, *Musique Diffusion Française v Commission* (100-103/80) [1983] ECR 1825.

6.6.2 Hearings for complaints

Specific provision is made for complainants to be informed if the Commission proposes to dismiss their complaint; the complainant must be told the reasoning behind the proposal and allowed to submit any further written comments before any decision is taken to grant negative clearance or an exemption (see Article 27(4), Regulation 1/2003). This communication to the complainant is not a decision (within the meaning given by Article 249 (ex 189), EC Treaty) capable of judicial review under Article 230 (ex 173), EC Treaty: see *Automec v Commission I* (T-64/89) [1990] ECR II-367. On the other hand, it is a definition of the Commission's position, sufficient to defeat an application to the European Court under Article 232 (ex 175), EC Treaty, alleging failure to act: see *Guérin Automobiles v Commission* (T-186/94) [1995] ECR II-1753. Ultimately though, there must a formal decision on the merits, taken by the Commission, which is susceptible of judicial review: see *Automec v Commission II* (T-24 and 28/90) [1992] ECR II-2223.

6.6.3 Oral hearings

As part of its proceedings under Regulation 1, the Commission may send one of several letters to an undertaking or other natural or legal person. These include:

- a statement of objections (as part of infringement proceedings against that undertaking);
- an invitation to a natural or legal person, having shown sufficient interest to be heard as a third party, to submit written comments;
- a letter to a complainant, explaining that in the Commission's view there are insufficient grounds to find an infringement and inviting the submission of any further written comments;
- a letter to a natural or legal person, explaining that in the Commission's view that person has not shown sufficient interest to be heard as a third party.

A recipient of any of the foregoing letters may submit written comments in reply. These written comments may contain an application to be heard at an oral hearing. Regulation 2842/98 distinguishes between three categories of applicant in this context:

(a) parties against whom objections have been laid by the Commission (ie, suspect undertakings). If they request an oral hearing, they shall be given one in order to develop their arguments;

(b) complainants, whether the Commission has taken up the complaint or is disposed to dismiss it. If they request an oral hearing, the Commission may afford them the opportunity of expressing their views, where appropriate;

(c) 'other third parties' who have applied to be heard and have shown a sufficient interest in the subject-matter. Where the Commission has issued objections against an undertaking, it may invite other third parties to develop their arguments at the oral hearing. Generally, the Commission may afford to any other third party the opportunity to express their views orally.

See, respectively, Articles 5, 8 and 9 of Regulation 2842/98.

The oral hearing will take place in private and be conducted by the Hearing Officer. Those summoned to attend may be assisted or represented by lawyers. Those who attend to be heard may be heard separately or in the presence of others so summoned; this is a decision for the Hearing Officer to take but he or she must bear in mind the need to observe the desire of undertakings to protect their business secrets. A useful article on oral hearings, by C.S. Kerse, may be found at [1994] ECLR 40.

6.6.4 The hearing officer's report

The Hearing Officer is administratively a part of DG IV but is intended to be independent of the investigation. This independence is ensured by attaching the hearing officer, for administrative purposes, to the Commissioner responsible for competition. Where the hearing officer is unable to act, the Competition Commissioner will designate another official to carry out his duties. The replacement must not be involved in the case in question. After a hearing, the hearing officer will make an interim report to the Competition Commissioner. The report will look at procedural issues, such as access to the file and disclosure of documents; its main objective is to report on respect for the right to be heard. A copy of the report will go to the Director-General for Competition. The hearing officer may also make observations concerning the future conduct of the case; for example, he may identify that further information is needed, that certain objections should be withdrawn or that new objections be added.

Once a draft decision on the merits has been prepared, to go to the Advisory Committee, the hearing officer will submit a final report dealing with the procedure that has been followed and looking at respect for the right to be heard. The final report goes to the Competition Commissioner and Director-General, as before. It will also go to the competition authorities of the Member States and, eventually, to the Commission when it considers the draft decision and reaches a decision on the merits. The hearing officer's final report will eventually be sent to the addressees of the decision and be published in the Official Journal (see Decision 2001/462, Article 16). This represents a significant shift from the previous position, where the hearing officer's opinion was kept within the Commission, was characterised as an internal working document and was not to be disclosed to an undertaking under investigation unless an allegation of serious misuse of power had been made against the Commission (see eg *BAT and Reynolds v Commission* (142 and 156/84) [1987] ECR 4487).

6.6.5 An effective right to be heard?

6.6.5.1 Access to the Commission's file

Whether making comments in writing or addressing the Hearing Officer orally, an undertaking is entitled to do so effectively. In the case of an undertaking under investigation, the proper exercise of the right to be heard may be hampered if the Commission is in possession of material which has not been disclosed to the undertaking. If the material is incriminatory (maybe comments from third parties), then in one sense we could say that the undertaking benefits from non-disclosure. This would be because the Commission is not permitted to take account of any undisclosed material or arguments when reaching its decision on whether there has been an infringement or not (see Article 2(2), Regulation 2842/98). However, such material may colour the Commission's (or DG IV's) thinking and it may be that, if the undertaking was informed of the incriminatory material, it could provide a satisfactory explanation, consistent with innocence.

What may be worse is if the Commission is in possession of material which could positively assist the defence of the undertaking. Non-disclosure here could result in a serious injustice. As the Court of First Instance observed in *ICI plc v Commission* (T-36/91) [1995] ECR II-1847:

> The purpose of providing access to the file in competition cases is to enable the addressee of a statement of objections [ie the suspect undertaking] to examine evidence in the Commission's file so that on the basis of that evidence it may effectively express its views on the conclusions reached by the Commission in its statement of objections.
>
> That access is one of the procedural safeguards intended to protect the rights of the defence, which is a general principle, the proper observance of which requires that the undertaking concerned be afforded the opportunity ... effectively to make known its views on the truth and relevance of the facts, charges and circumstances relied on by the Commission ... In the defended proceedings for which Regulation 17/62 provides, it cannot be for the Commission alone to decide which documents are of use for the defence. Where difficult and complex economic appraisals are to be made [the case involved parallel conduct alleged to demonstrate a concerted practice], the Commission must give the advisers of the undertaking concerned the opportunity to examine documents which may be relevant so that their probative value for the defence can be assessed.

To an extent, the Commission had already sought to do the bidding of the Court of First Instance. In its decision on the terms of reference for Hearing Officers (Decision 94/810, OJ 1994 L330/67), the Commission introduced a new provision on disclosure. Article 5 of that decision states that if an undertaking, or natural or legal person, has received one of the letters listed in Article 4(3) (see **6.7.3**), and it has reason to believe:

(a) that the Commission has not disclosed all of its documents, and

(b) that those documents are necessary for the proper exercise of the right to be heard,

then it may make a reasoned request for disclosure. A reasoned decision, either for or against disclosure, will be communicated to the undertaking which made the request and to any other undertaking or person concerned by the procedure.

In its XXVth Report on Competition Policy (1995), the Commission recorded that it was examining the impact of ICI and related cases (involving a soda-ash cartel) on its current practice. The result came in January 1997, when the Commission published a Notice on its internal rules of procedure for processing requests for access to the file in competition cases (see OJ 1997 C23/03; **Appendix 3**). This Notice attempted to ensure compatibility between the Commission's current practice on access to the file and the judgments of the European Court in the 'soda-ash' cases (eg the *ICI* case mentioned above). The Notice recognised that, in principle, the addressee of a statement of objections must have access to all documents in the Commission's file. This is subject to three exceptions:

- business secrets of other undertakings;
- internal Commission documents;
- other confidential information.

'Business secrets' are not fully defined yet (see eg *BAT and Reynolds v Commission* (142 and 156/84) [1987] ECR 4487). The Notice suggests that they include 'strategic information on [an undertaking's] essential interests and on the operation or development of [it's] business' which is not known outside the undertaking.

6.6.5.2 Procedure for implementing access to the Commission's file

When supplying information to the Commission, undertakings are asked to indicate which documents (or parts of documents) are claimed to contain business secrets or are otherwise confidential. Any claim for confidentiality should be substantiated and a non-confidential version of such document(s) supplied. Any claim for confidentiality will be determined swiftly on a provisional basis. Subsequently, there will be a 'final assessment' of the accessibility of the document(s). The Commission reserves the right to allow suspect undertakings to have access to documents, overriding the supplier's objection, where the document 'serves as a basis for the decision' (on infringement) or may assist the suspect undertaking. An exception exists in cases of alleged infringement of Article 82 (ex 86): the Commission acknowledges that an undertaking in a dominant position may be able to take retaliatory steps against its customers, suppliers or competitors if it learns they have been in communication with the Commission. Thus, communications with such third parties, even though of value in giving the Commission a better understanding of the relevant market, are unlikely to be disclosed in order to minimise the risk of retaliation by a dominant undertaking.

The Commission will draw up a list of documents in its file, giving each one an access code. This code will show the document to be either:

- accessible;
- partially accessible;
- non-accessible.

Non-accessible documents will be those containing business secrets, other confidential information and the Commission's internal working documents. The list will have a summary, so that the content and subject of such documents may be identified. This should enable undertakings to determine whether to request access to a document, notwithstanding its present classification. A reasoned request for such access should be made to the Hearing Officer. Inevitably, a balancing exercise is involved; where a document is alleged to contain business secrets, the Commission must assess:

- the relevance of the information to the determination of whether an infringement has occurred;
- the probative value of the information;
- whether the information is indispensable;
- the potential harm that disclosure might cause;
- how serious the infringement is.

Every document containing business secrets must be considered individually to assess if the need for access outweighs the possible harm in granting access. It should be noted that the Court of Justice has previously said that access should not be given to documents containing business secrets (see *BAT and Reynolds v Commission* (142 and 156/84) [1987] ECR 4487; *Akzo v Commission* (53/85) [1986] ECR 1965). It seems that the Notice takes a less principled, more pragmatic approach. Other confidential information may be disclosed if the Commission needs to rely on it to establish an infringement or if it may assist the defence (a non-confidential version will be used, where possible).

Access to documents will usually be given on the premises of the Commission, although undertakings can choose to have all outstanding accessible documents sent to them.

The Commission may dispute an undertaking's claim to confidentiality, on the basis that the information supplied is not a business secret; it may then propose to disclose the information to a third party for comments. The supplier should be given the opportunity to make representations in support of its claim to confidence prior to any disclosure and, if still unsuccessful, can then make an interim application to the Court of First Instance under Article 230 (ex 173) to annul the decision to disclose. See *Peugeot v Commission* (T-90/96, 136/96) [1997] ECR II-663; **8.2**.

6.6.5.3 Access to the file for complainants

The Commission is quite explicit in its Notice that the degree of disclosure given to undertakings which are the subject of investigations does not extend to those who are complainants, still less to third parties. The Notice states:

> ... there are no grounds for treating the rights of the complainant as equivalent to those of the firms [which are the addressees of a statement of objections].

When a complainant is informed that the Commission intends to reject the complaint, it may ask to see those documents which the Commission has considered. The Notice explicitly states that a complainant will not be given access to any confidential information or business secrets, either of the suspect undertaking or of third parties. This contrasts with the position previously examined by the Court of Justice in the *BAT* case (142 and 156/84) and *Akzo* (53/85) where the Commission could disclose documents to a complainant, although they contained confidential information, in order to obtain the complainant's opinion on them, if to do so was necessary for the proper conduct of the investigation. See also *Matra Hachette v Commission* (T-17/93) [1994] ECR I-595.

6.6.5.4 Challenging a denial of access

The appropriate action to take is to seek judicial review of the denial, using Article 230 (ex 173), EC Treaty, in the Court of First Instance. An applicant may rely on either the infringement of an essential procedural requirement (eg Article 2(2), Regulation 2842/98) or the infringement of a rule of law relating to the application of the EC Treaty (eg 'hear both sides'; see eg *ICI v Commission* (T-36/91) [1995] ECR II-1847).

Complainants may face obstacles in mounting a challenge based on their right to be heard. Complainants must have an opportunity to defend their legitimate interests which means, in practice, that the Commission must consider all legal and factual material which the complainant draws to its attention. The rights of a complainant are not co-extensive with those of the suspect company and the investigation is not adversarial in nature. A complainant's rights expire when they start to conflict with the right of a suspect to a fair hearing. See *BAT and Reynolds v Commission* (142 and 156/84) [1987] ECR 4487.

When should the challenge be made? The moment of denial would seem appropriate but that is wrong in the opinion of the Court of First Instance. Access to files may underpin the right to be heard but there is no legal effect on a suspect undertaking until such time as the Commission finds there has been an infringement of Article 81(1) (ex 85(1)) or Article 82 (ex 86) and, perhaps, imposes a fine (or when it finds there has not been an infringement, if a complainant has been denied access to the file). The Court of First Instance has said, in an action to challenge the denial of access under Article 230 (ex 173), EC Treaty, that such an action is premature and inadmissible if it precedes a formal decision on the substantive merits of the case. See *Cimenteries CBR SA and others v Commission* (T-10-12/92 and 15/92) [1993] 4 CMLR 259. While a 'wait-and-see' approach may satisfy the pragmatist (and most undertakings may be used to looking at the end rather than worrying about the means too much), it does little for principles and it may be hard to conclude that justice has been served if the full picture has not emerged.

Although the established case-law shows that a decision may be annulled on either of two grounds (infringement of an essential procedural requirement or infringement of a rule of law), a more pragmatic approach has now been suggested. In his Opinion delivered in *Irish Cement* (C-205/00 P) (Opinion 11 February 2003), Advocate General Ruiz-Jaralo Colomer recognised that Article 6 ECHR applied to this type of proceedings ('administrative proceedings of a disciplinary nature') but also said that the concept of being unable to defend oneself is substantive. By this he meant that there may be numerous procedural defects but they are irrelevant if, despite them, the applicant has enjoyed appropriate rights of defence (para 34 of the Opinion). His Opinion leads to the conclusion that a decision can only be annulled if either (i) in the absence of the procedural defects, the outcome could have been more advantageous to the applicant or (ii) because of the defects, it is impossible to say whether the decision would have been different (in other words, the applicant gets the benefit of the doubt). The Advocate General does not recognise a 'due process' ground to annul a decision — as he says, 'defects in the procedure do not have a life of their own.' A 2002 judgment shows the CFI is of the same opinion. In *Tetra Laval* (T-5/02) [2003] ECR II-4381, the CFI held that, to annul on the basis of an infringement of the rights of defence, it is sufficient to establish that non-disclosure might have influenced the course of the procedure and the content of the Commission's decision to the applicant's detriment.

6.7 The decision of the Commission on infringement

6.7.1 The procedure

After allowing the undertakings, and other interested parties, to be heard, the Commission will consult with the Advisory Committee on Restrictive Practices and Monopolies (the UK is usually represented on the Advisory Committee by an official from the Office of Fair Trading). A copy of the draft decision will be before the Committee, together with the most important evidence. The Committee may deliver an opinion to the Commission but this is not published and does not bind the Commission. The decision itself must be taken by the full Commission, it is not within the scope of the delegated powers of the Commissioner for Competition. The procedural rules for taking a decision must be strictly complied with: failure to do so is likely to lead to the measure being annulled by the Court of First Instance (see eg *Commission v BASF and others* (C-137/92P) [1994] ECR I-2555). The decision must be published, although the obligation to respect business secrets often results in much of the substance being removed from the published version of the decision. The undertakings to whom the decision is addressed will receive the full version.

Finally, an undertaking which is aggrieved by the decision may challenge it, either on procedural or substantive grounds, before the Court of First Instance, using Article 230 (ex 173), EC Treaty to seek its annulment. It should be noted that the right of challenge is not limited to the suspect undertaking(s). In particular, a complainant will normally have the standing to challenge the Commission's finding. An illustration of this can be found in *BAT and Reynolds v Commission* (142 and 156/84) [1987] ECR 4487.

BAT complained to the Commission about a joint venture company which was established by two of its rivals in the European cigarette industry, Philip Morris and Rembrandt. The Commission began an investigation but then decided there were no longer any grounds for investigating, after the two suspect companies modified their agreement. The Commission wrote to BAT, telling them it was closing its file. BAT challenged this in the Court of Justice (there was no Court of First Instance then), using Article 230 (ex 173). On the question of its ability to use this procedure, the Court of Justice said that BAT had received the letter from the Commission. All it needed to do was show that the letter was a reviewable act, ie it produced legal effects for BAT. This had been done by asserting that the change in the market structure which the Commission had, in effect, approved meant it was likely that BAT would suffer financial losses in the future.

6.7.2 The content of a decision

Having investigated under Article 7, Regulation 1, where the Commission finds an infringement of Article 81(1) (ex 85(1)) or 82 (ex 86) has been proven, it is empowered to 'require the undertakings ... concerned to bring such infringement to an end'. There may be a variety of ways in which a specific infringement could be brought to an end: while the Commission should give a reasonable indication of the infringement, it should usually leave decisions on how best to comply with that finding to the undertaking (see eg *Automec v Commission* (T-24/90) [1992] ECR II-2223). Occasionally, though, the Commission has been permitted to impose quite specific requirements as part of the obligation to terminate an infringement. A typical example can be found in a series of cases where a supplier (or small number of suppliers) comprised the sole source of a product or service: if the Commission finds that a refusal to supply or maintain supplies (or give access to a service) constitutes an infringement (of Article 81(1) (ex 85(1)) or 82 (ex 86)), it may order a resumption of supplies (or the commencement thereof). Such cases include *Commercial Solvents v Commission* (6 and 7/73) [1974] ECR 223; *Radio Telefis Eireann v Commission* (C-241 and 242/91P) [1995] ECR I-743. This is rather an exceptional situation and the Commission can probably order an undertaking to take such positive steps (rather than stop an act or end a contract) only where that is the sole effective way to terminate the infringement.

It seems that other, minor, forms of positive action that an undertaking can be required to take are:

- filing regular reports with the Commission, to confirm that problems are not recurring; and
- taking steps to inform others with an interest in the termination of the infringement that termination has occurred, and the consequences thereof for them (for example, the opportunity or need to renegotiate a contract).

6.7.3 Alternatives to a decision

The Commission has improved its performance in reaching formal decisions in competition investigations over recent years. In the early 1990s, its formal decisions could be numbered usually in the 'teens. In the last three years for which statistics are available, it has increased to give at least 36 and at most 68 formal decisions (see XXXth Annual Report on Competition Policy, 2000). Over the same period, though, the number of complaints has increased from around 100 annually to sometimes as many as 192. The number of own-initiative investigations undertaken by the Commission has also increased significantly over the last decade. The backlog of work which built up over many years has not significantly reduced and the Commission is actively promoting radical alternatives to the formal decision, such as self-assessment for undertakings and greater enforcement through national competition authorities and private legal suits in national courts. See further, for example, **3.2**.

6.8 Fines

6.8.1 Fines and periodic penalty payments

Regulation 1/2003 provides for the imposition of fines and periodic penalty payments upon undertakings. Under Article 23 (fines) and Article 24 (periodic penalty payments) of Regulation 1, the Commission is empowered to take a decision (see Article 249 (ex 189), EC Treaty) to impose financial penalties on undertakings or associations of undertakings. Fines take the form of a one-off penalty, while periodic penalty payments will be applied on a daily basis and the total will increase until the undertaking complies with the decision of the Commission.

6.8.1.1 The range of fines

Fines imposed under Article 23(1) may be any amount not exceeding 1% of the firm's total turnover in the preceding business year. Fines imposed under Article 23(2) are subject to an overall limit on the fine of not more than 10% of the turnover of the undertaking in the preceding business year ('turnover' here refers to the global turnover of the undertaking, across its entire product range: see eg *Pioneer* (C 100-103/80) [1983] ECR 1825).

Examples of fines imposed by the Commission are:

(a) *Re Konica UK Ltd* [1988] 4 CMLR 848 — ECU 75,000.

(b) *Re Quaker Oats UK Ltd* [1989] 4 CMLR 553 — ECU 300,000.

(c) *Hilti* [1989] 4 CMLR 677 — ECU 6 million for a very serious breach of Article 82 (ex 86), EC Treaty, even taking into account mitigating factors like:

  (i) Hilti's cooperation;

  (ii) its voluntary offer of a remedial undertaking prior to the outcome of the investigation; and

  (iii) its introduction of a compliance programme governing its future conduct.

  The fine was upheld through appeals to the Court of First Instance and then the Court of Justice (see (C-53/2P) [1994] ECR I-667).

(d) *Re Polypropylene Cartel* [1988] 4 CMLR 347 — a cartel among the major producers of polypropylene in the EC infringed Article 81(1) (ex 85(1)). It led to fines totalling nearly ECU 58 million being imposed on some 15 firms, eg Hoechst (ECU 9 million), ICI (ECU 10 million), and Shell (ECU 9 million). The producers appealed. Several had their appeals rejected (eg Hoechst) while others had their fines reduced, usually on the basis that the Commission had insufficient evidence to establish that their membership of the cartel covered the full period alleged.

(e) *Akzo Chemie BV*, OJ 1985 L374/1, [1986] 3 CMLR 273. The original fine of ECU 10 million was reduced by 25% on appeal to the Court of Justice. Two reasons for the reduction were:

  (i) that the Community policy on predatory pricing was largely unknown when Akzo embarked on its conduct; and

  (ii) that the market shares of Akzo and its rival, ECS, had not been significantly affected by the conduct.

(f) *Tetra Pak* (C-333/94) [1997] 4 CMLR 662. A fine of ECU 75 million was imposed by the Commission for abuse of a dominant position. Tetra Pak, a Swiss company owned by Swedes, was found guilty of carrying out a 'deliberate policy aiming to eliminate actual or potential competitors'. The fine was a record amount and the subject of unsuccessful appeals to the Court of First Instance and Court of Justice. The absence of precedent did not result in any reduction in this case (cf. *Akzo*).

(g) *Re Cartonboard Cartel*, OJ 1994 L243/1. A cartel of cartonboard producers was fined in excess of ECU 130 million, with several individual members fined more than ECU 15 million each. On appeal to the Court of First Instance, the total amount was reduced to some ECU 120 million (*Cartonboard* (T–295/94)).

(h) *Vitamins II*, (2001) Commission Press Release IP/01/1625. A cartel of vitamin manufacturers was fined for its conduct on a variety of vitamin markets within the European Union, extending over several years. One of the two ringleaders was Hoffmann-La Roche, which had also featured in *Vitamins I*. The Commission imposed its largest single fine to date on the company, euro 462 million, and noted that it had applied a 50% reduction to reflect the company's cooperation with the investigation. It is nevertheless anticipated that there may be an appeal to the Court of First Instance against the level of the fine.

A table of fines imposed on undertakings by the Commission can be found in Bellamy & Child, *Common Market Law of Competition*, at 12-064; see also Ritter Braun and Rawlinson, *European Competition Law: A Practitioner's Guide*, at p 935.

6.8.1.2 The range of periodic penalty payments

According to Article 24, Regulation 1, periodic penalty payments may be as high as 5% of the average daily turnover in the preceding business year per day.

6.8.1.3 Calculating the amount of a fine or periodic penalty payment

Calculating the total payable under a periodic penalty payment ('ppp') should be simple. One takes the daily rate, as specified in the decision, and multiplies that by the number of days that the undertaking took to comply. In fact, after the undertaking has complied, the Commission must take a second decision, to fix the total amount of the ppp. The Commission is allowed to fix this at a lower sum than the original calculation would produce; if the Commission does not take this second decision, then nothing is due under the ppp.

A fine may be imposed where an undertaking has broken the rules either negligently or intentionally. One may expect a fine to be higher where the undertaking has set out deliberately to act in a way that infringes the rules; that seems to be the situation in practice, too. Conversely, if an undertaking is found to have broken the rules in a novel way, perhaps where it could not have known that its actions would be seen as an infringement, the lack of precedent (or foreseeability) may result in a reduction in the fine, even though novelty may not excuse the act itself (cf. *Akzo Chemie BV v Commission* (C-62/86) [1991] ECR 1-3359; *Tetra Pak International SA v Commission* (C-333/94) [1997] 4 CMLR 662).

Before deciding to impose a fine, the Commission must allow the undertaking a chance to express its views, both written and oral. Officials within DGIV will advise the Commissioner for Competition on the amount of any fine. The Commissioner will then make a recommendation to the College of Commissioners who must make the final, formal, decision. What sum should the Commission take as its starting point? In its XXlst Annual Report on Competition Policy (1991), the Commission stated that:

> The financial benefit which companies infringing the competition rules have derived from their infringements will become an increasingly important consideration. Wherever the Commission can ascertain the level of this ill-gotten gain, even if it cannot do so precisely, the calculation of the fine may have this as its starting-point. When appropriate the amount could then be increased or decreased in the light of the other circumstances of the case, including the need to introduce an element of deterrence or penalty in the sanction imposed on the participating companies.

However, many people outside the Commission still felt that the methodology for quantifying fines should be made more transparent. See, for example, lvo van Bael, *Fining a la carte: the lottery of EU competition law* [1995] 4 ECLR 237; and compare Luc Gyselen, *The Commission's Fining Policy in Competition Cases*, in Slot & McDonnell, ed, 1993. In 1997, the then Competition Commissioner, Karel van Miert, published guidelines for the calculation of fines under Articles 81 (ex 85) and 82 (ex 86). These guidelines attempted to provide the transparency that had been sought. The gravity and duration of an infringement provide the starting points for calculation (see also Regulation 1/2003, Article 23(3)). One begins with *gravity* and considers:

- the nature of the infringement;
- the size of the relevant geographic market; and
- the impact of the infringement upon the market, where this can be determined.

The information thus gathered should enable the Commission to put the infringement into one of three categories:

- *minor* — these would normally involve only vertical restraints, having only limited impact on the market and not covering a wide territory. Likely range of fine 1,000–1 million ECU;
- *serious* — these are more likely to involve horizontal restraints, and will have a greater impact on the market, over a more extensive territory. Less significant abuses of a dominant position would fall to be considered in this category. Likely range of fine 1 million–20 million ECU;
- *very serious* — the worst types of horizontal restraint, such as sharing markets through quotas, other forms of market partitioning, and price cartels, will appear here. The worst abuses of a dominant position will also be regarded as *very serious*. Likely range of fine — in excess of 20 million ECU.

Within these ranges, the nature of the infringement will indicate whether the fine should fall towards the bottom, middle or top of the range. Deterrence will also play a part here, as will the size of the undertaking (that is, bigger firms usually have the resources to know what acts will infringe the competition rules). Completing the calculation will give a base figure.

Having got this basic idea of the fine to be imposed on an undertaking, one then turns to consider the *duration* of the infringement. Again, there are three categories and which one applies to the infringement determines whether the base figure will stay the same or may be increased:

- short duration (less than one year) will result in no change;
- medium duration (one to five years) allows an increase of up to 50% on the base figure;
- long duration (over five years) allows an increase of up to 10% for each year on the base figure.

The possibility of significant increases in the fine where the infringement is of long duration, coupled with the reductions for 'whistle-blowers', is intended to stimulate firms to turn 'informer' and deal with the Commission.

Having calculated the new basic figure, one looks for any aggravating or mitigating factors. Amongst these are:

- ringleader (aggravating factor);
- ancillary role (mitigating factor);
- repeating the infringement (aggravating factor);
- negligent or unintentional infringement (mitigating factor);
- cooperation with the Commission — refusal to do so (aggravating factor) or enthusiasm for doing so (mitigating factor);

- swift termination of the infringement following intervention by the Commission (mitigating factor);
- the need to 'claw back' ill-gotten gains, earned because of the infringement (aggravating factor);
- second or subsequent infringement (aggravating factor recognised in *Michelin* [2001] Commission Press Release IP/01/873; see also *Volkswagen* OJ 2001 L262-0014).

The next step, where relevant, is to apply the Commission's Notice on immunity from fines and reduction of fines in cartel cases (OJ 2002/C 45/03). This is considered in more detail in **6.8.1.4**. The definitive amount of the fine should now be re-determined and may indeed be nil. Assuming it is not nil, though, it needs to be measured against the ceiling for a fine as set out in Regulation 1/2003, Article 23(2), namely that the fine shall not exceed 10% of an undertaking's total turnover in the preceding business year. The fine should now be reduced if it exceeds that figure. Finally, adjustments are made to the amount to comply with what the guidelines call 'certain objective factors'. These will include:

- 'a specific economic context';
- any economic or financial benefit derived (although this seemed also to appear earlier in the calculation);
- the 'specific characteristics' of the firm(s); and the firm's 'real ability to pay in a specific social context'.

Whatever figure you now have on your piece of paper is the amount of the fine! As an attempt to increase transparency, these guidelines do a reasonable job until that final step. It remains to be seen if those people who had previously criticised the Commission for its opaqueness will be mollified by the publication of these guidelines.

Calculation of the fine in seven easy stages:

Stage 1 Decide on the gravity of the infringement in broad terms. Is it (a) minor, (b) serious, or (c) very serious?

Stage 2 Decide, more specifically, where it falls within the appropriate range. Is it towards the top, middle or bottom? (a) Minor range is 1,000 to 1 million ECU; (b) serious range is 1 million to 20 million ECU; (c) very serious range is more than 20 million ECU. You should now have a figure to work with.

Stage 3 Move onto consider duration. Was it of (a) short, (b) medium, or (c) long duration? Depending upon the answer, your figure will either stay the same or increase.

Stage 4 Increase or reduce the figure to take account of aggravating or mitigating factors.

Stage 5 Make any reductions necessary to 'reward' firms who cooperate or are whistle-blowers.

Stage 6 Determine the ceiling for the fine, set at 10% of global turnover for the firm in its last financial year. Make any necessary adjustment to your figure.

Stage 7 Make final adjustments, up or down, but no more than 10% of turnover, to take account of 'certain objective factors'.

An extremely thorough and clear example of the Commission working its way through the application of both the 1997 'calculation' guidelines and the 1996 'informer' notice can be found in its decision on the British sugar producers' cartel — *British Sugar, Tate & Lyle, Napier Brown and James Budgett*, OJ 1999 L76, 22 March 1999.

Notwithstanding the clarity of method in that case, the undertakings challenged the amount of their fines in the Court of First Instance. The Commission had calculated on the basis that the infringement was a 'serious' one — the undertakings argued it should have been 'minor' because of the absence of substantial anti-competitive effects on the market. The Court observed that it was a horizontal price-fixing cartel and would normally have been classified as 'very serious'. The limited impact it had achieved on the sugar market was already reflected in the down-grading to 'serious'. British Sugar complained that an increase in the fine of 40%, following classification of the infringement as 'medium duration', was disproportionate. BS also asserted that any infringement was unintentional and finally that the Commission was wrong to increase its fine to deter others. The Court held that there was nothing disproportionate about the 40% uplift allowing for the duration; that for an infringement to be intentional, a firm did not need to be aware that it was infringing a competition rule, it is sufficient if the firm could not have been unaware that its conduct was aimed at restricting competition; and it is legitimate to determine the level of fine with one eye on the deterrent effect where a particular type of infringement is still relatively frequent and profitable. See *Tate & Lyle plc and others v Commission* (Joined cases T-202/98, T-204/98 and T-207/98) [2001] All ER (EC) 839.

6.8.1.4 Reducing fines for whistleblowers

It was noted in **6.8.1.3** that a fine may be mitigated if an undertaking takes prompt action to terminate an infringement or comply with a requirement from the Commission, once the Commission's view has been drawn to its attention. So, a quick acceptance of one's guilt may save money. In 1994, the Commission decided to be more pro-active in encouraging firms to cooperate with it. Specifically, the Commission recognised the difficulties it had in finding the evidence to condemn cartels. These collaborative entities are serious infringements of Article 81 and likely to have a very detrimental effect on the operation of the relevant market. As the Commission put it in its XXXIInd Annual Report on EU Competition Policy (2002).

> Hardcore cartels are among the most serious violations of competition rule ... Cartels are particularly harmful to European industry and consumers. They diminish social welfare, create allocative inefficiency and transfer wealth from consumers to the participants in the cartel by modifying output and/or prices in comparison with market driven level ... [T]he detection, prosecution and punishment of secret hardcore cartel agreements is one of the central elements of the Commission's competition policy.

However, their typically secretive nature meant that their existence was often unknown and, even where it was suspected, hard evidence was difficult to find. Too often, the Commission would be faced with only circumstantial evidence. The most obvious way to procure compelling evidence would be to persuade a member of the cartel first to inform the Commission of its existence, and then to provide the evidence needed to determine membership, duration and scope. The Commission in effect piloted this approach in its investigation into the *Cartonboard* cartel in 1994 and then in 1996 produced a Notice setting out the conditions in which a whistleblower could expect a fine to be either reduced or eradicated (see OJ 1996 C207/4).

In 2002, the Commission announced that, after five years of operating the 1996 Notice, it had enough experience to modify its policy. In particular, the Commission felt that the process would be more effective if it was made more transparent and the conditions for reduction made more certain. It issued a new Notice (OJ 2002/C 45/03, effective from February 2002), declaring that 'the collaboration of an undertaking in the detection of the existence of a cartel has an intrinsic value. A decisive contribution ... may justify the granting of immunity ... [whilst] cooperation may justify a reduction of a fine'.

For immunity, a firm must be the first to submit evidence which either:

(a) may enable the Commission to take a decision to investigate under Article 14(3) of Regulation 17/62 (the 'dawn raid'; see now Regulation 1/2003, Article 20); or

(b) may enable the Commission to find an infringement of Article 81, in connection with an alleged cartel affecting the European Community. In addition, the firm must cooperate fully, continuing to supply any evidence that fails into its hands; it must terminate its involvement in the cartel no later than the time of its initial submission of evidence; and it must not have taken steps to coerce others to participate in the cartel.

If a firm submits evidence but discovers it is not the first to do so, it has a choice. It may either withdraw that evidence or ask the Commission to consider it for the purpose of a reduction in the level of any fine. The 'reduction' route is the most likely choice to take, not least because the Notice reminds the firm that the Commission is 'not prevented from using its normal powers of investigation to obtain the information' so withdrawal is not a sensible option (see para 17 of the 2002 Notice).

So, if immunity is not possible, a firm may still hope to have any fine reduced. To qualify for a reduction, a firm must submit evidence of the infringement 'which represents significant added value' compared to the evidence already in the possession of the Commission. The firm must also terminate its involvement no later than the time of its submission. The Notice makes clear the purpose behind the incentive — "added value" refers to the extent to which the evidence provided strengthens, by its very nature and/or its level of detail, the Commission's ability to prove the facts in question' (para 22 of the 2002 Notice). So, the Commission will prefer contemporary evidence of the infringement, rather than evidence 'subsequently established'. Again, directly relevant evidence has more value than that which is only of indirect relevance. At the end of the administrative procedure, the Commission will be able to gauge whose evidence has indeed proved to be of 'significant added value'. It will then rank the firms, if there is more than one which qualifies, as follows:

(a) the first firm to qualify will get a reduction of 30–50%

(b) the second such firm, a reduction of 20–30%

(c) subsequent firms, a reduction of up to 20%.

Finally, if a firm supplies evidence, previously unknown to the Commission, which is directly relevant to either the duration or the gravity of the infringement, the Commission will disregard these new parameters when setting the fine for that firm (para 23 of the 2002 Notice).

By way of an illustration, one may look at the *British Sugar* cartel case. In 1998, the Commission investigated the British sugar industry and fined four sugar producers a total of ECU 50.2 million (about £38 million). One of the four, Tate & Lyle plc, faced a fine of ECU 14 million, calculated as ECU 10 million as the starting point for the gravity of the infringement, increased to ECU 14 million to reflect its duration. However, Tate & Lyle had alerted the Commission to the cartel's existence before the Commission was aware of it. Tate & Lyle also supplied two self-incriminatory letters to the Commission;

these were the first hard evidence the Commission had of the cartel's existence. Finally, Tate & Lyle ended its involvement in the cartel before turning whistleblower. The Commission's decision notes that, rather oddly, Tate & Lyle 'did not maintain continuous and complete cooperation with the Commission' throughout the investigation. It had still done enough to qualify for a reduction of 50% under the applicable Notice, thus ending with a fine of only ECU 7 million.

In November 2001, the Commission announced its first 100% reduction of a fine. This came in the *Vitamins II* case (see Commission Press Release IP/01/1625). Aventis SA, formerly Rhône-Poulenc, was praised for its full and voluntary disclosure of a cartel of vitamin manufacturers. Again, in 2002, Aventis was granted full immunity having disclosed a thirteen-year long, world-wide cartel of producers of methionine, an important amino acid. One of its fellow cartel members was not so lucky — Degussa AG was fined Euro 118 million.

6.8.2 When a fine can be imposed

6.8.2.1 'Procedural' fines

When looking into possible infringements, the Commission can request information from an undertaking, pursuant to Article 18; it may set a deadline for compliance. The Commission may conduct an inspection and require an undertaking to produce business records, under Article 19 or 20. Under Article 23(1), Regulation 1, fines can be imposed on an undertaking which:

- supplies incorrect, incomplete or misleading information to the Commission; or
- fails to supply requested information within the deadline; or
- fails to comply with an inspection.

6.8.2.2 'Substantive' fines

Under Article 23(2)(a), Regulation 1, if the Commission finds an undertaking to have infringed Article 81(1) (ex 85(1)) or 82 (ex 86), a fine may be imposed. Also, when the Commission grants an individual exemption to an undertaking, pursuant to Article 81(3) (ex 85(3)), it may attach conditions and obligations to the exemption (see Article 9, Regulation 1). If the undertaking subsequently is found to be in breach of any such obligation, it may be fined (Article 23(2)(c)).

6.8.3 When a periodic penalty payment can be imposed

The situation is governed by Article 24, Regulation 1. Again, it may be divided into 'procedural' and 'substantive' payments. The objective of imposing a daily penalty is to maximise the probability of swift and full compliance with whatever demands are imposed on an undertaking.

6.8.3.1 'Procedural' periodic penalty payments

When seeking information from an undertaking, pursuant to Article 18, Regulation 1, the Commission is to indicate the penalty for non-compliance and set a deadline. This penalty may be a one-off fine (see Article 23(1)(b)) or it may be a periodic penalty payment (see Article 24(1)(c)).

6.8.3.2 'Substantive' periodic penalty payments

If the Commission takes a decision that an undertaking is infringing either Article 81(1) (ex 85(1)) or 82 (ex 86), it may impose a periodic penalty payment in order to compel the undertaking to put an end to the infringement (Article 24(1)(a), Regulation 1). Likewise, if the Commission grants an individual exemption and requires an undertaking to refrain from any specific acts, it may attach a periodic penalty payment to compel such restraint (see Article 24(1)(c)). In practice, it seems that this last power could only be used where the prohibited act is in existence at the time the decision to exempt is taken and is likely to continue thereafter.

6.8.4 Limitation periods

6.8.4.1 Council Regulation 1/2003, Article 25

Regulation 17 was silent on the topic of limitation periods for lump sum fines and periodic penalty payments. According to the Court of Justice, this meant that there was no limitation period (see *Boehringer Mannheim v Commission* (45/69) [1970] ECR 769). Since 1974, and now by Regulation 1/2003, the Commission is required to observe limitation periods when imposing a fine on an undertaking. The period varies, depending upon whether the fine is imposed for a procedural infringement, or is imposed for a substantive infringement of either Article 81(1) (ex 85(1)) or 82 (ex 86).

The periods are:

(a) Three years for infringements of provisions concerning:
  (i) requests for information (Article 18, Regulation 1);
  (ii) carrying out inspections (Article 20, Regulation 1).

(b) Five years for any other infringement, ie:
  (i) being in breach of Article 81(1) (ex 85(1)) or 82 (ex 86); or
  (ii) failing to comply with a requirement imposed as part of the grant of an exemption pursuant to Article 81(3) (ex 85(3)).

Time starts to run from the day the infringement occurs. If the infringement is repeated, or is in the nature of a continuing infringement, then time runs from the date the infringement ceases. This may enable the Commission to establish a long-running infringement going back over many years; this may have serious repercussions for the undertaking(s) involved since duration is an important factor in determining the amount of any fine.

6.8.4.2 Limitation period for enforcement

What is the Commission to do if it takes a decision to impose a fine, but the fine is not then paid? Further, what happens if the Commission takes a decision fixing the total amount due from an undertaking, as the result of a periodic penalty payment order, and that amount is unpaid? Article 26, Regulation 1/2003, establishes a five-year period within which the Commission is empowered to enforce the decision. Time starts to run on the day the decision became final.

6.8.4.3 Interrupting the limitation period

The limitation period 'clock' may be reset in certain circumstances. Typically, this interruption (sic) occurs when the Commission notifies at least one undertaking which has participated in an infringement that it has commenced proceedings for infringement; alternatively, issuing a written request for information would interrupt the limitation period, as would notification of a decision by the Commission to investigate pursuant to Article 20, Regulation 1. Interruption against any one undertaking constitutes interruption against all concerned undertakings (Article 2(2), Regulation 2988/74).

If an undertaking decides to challenge the decision of the Commission, then the limitation period is *suspended* (sic) for the duration of proceedings before the European Court (see Article 25(6), Regulation 1).

Every interruption starts the clock afresh (Article 25(5), Regulation 1). This is subject to a ceiling of double the relevant limitation period (ie six or ten years), plus any period of suspension. If the Commission has not imposed a fine or penalty by the expiry of this time, it is now too late for it to do so.

6.8.4.4 Example

Let us suppose that company A and company B agree to divide up a certain product market between themselves, and in so doing they act contrary to Article 81(1) (ex 85(1)). If the agreement comes to an end on, say, 31 December 1996 (or, subsequently, the Commission cannot prove that it continued beyond that date) then the limitation period commences on that date. If it is to impose a fine for the breach of Article 81(1) (ex 85(1)), the Commission must do so within five years — that is, by 30 December 2001. If the Commission sends a request for information to company A, which is received by A on 31 December 1999, then the clock is reset for both A and B. The Commission need not worry about running out of time now until 30 December 2004. If the Commission subsequently serves a Statement of Objections on company B on 31 December 2002, again the clock returns to zero. However, the Commission does not have until 30 December 2007 to impose a fine for infringement of Article 81(1) (ex 85(1)) because the ceiling of double the limitation period will expire on 30 December 2006 (ie ten years from the date of cessation of the infringement).

6.8.5 Double jeopardy

In some circumstances, a company may face liability for the same anti-competitive behaviour before both the Commission and (one or more) national competition authorities. Ideally, with the spirit of cooperation between the Commission and such authorities, there should not be two sets of investigations and therefore the possibility of two punishments would not arise. However, this cannot be guaranteed and so the principle is observed that, if the Commission and national authorities both proceed to use their separate powers, a company should not be fined twice for the same behaviour. What should occur is a kind of set-off, whereby the 'sentencer' who is later in time takes into account the punishment which has been imposed already. See *Boehringer Mannheim GmbH v Commission* (45/69) [1970] ECR 769.

6.8.6 Challenging a decision to impose a financial penalty

As the Commission's decision (whether to impose a fine or settling the total amount due under a periodic penalty payment order) will be addressed to the undertaking concerned, there should be no problem in the undertaking possessing the standing to mount a legal challenge to the decision. Article 229 (ex 172), EC Treaty and Article 31, Regulation 1, give unlimited jurisdiction to the Court of Justice to review decisions of the Commission to fix a fine or periodic penalty payment. The Court can review matters of fact as well as law; it has the power to cancel, reduce or raise the amount involved. In 1988, the jurisdiction was transferred to the Court of First Instance.

7

Using the competition rules in national courts

7.1 Introduction

There are two preliminary points to note briefly here. First, the supremacy of EC law over national law. Secondly, the possibility of using EC laws (whether Treaty Articles or secondary measures) in the legal systems of the 15 Member States of the European Union. These topics are of general relevance to the application of EC laws in the legal systems of the Member States and are covered in more detail in **Appendix 6**.

7.2 Supremacy of EC law

That EC law prevails over contradictory national law has been established at least since 1964, when the European Court of Justice delivered its judgment in *Costa v ENEL* (6/64) [1964] ECR 585. See also *Walt Wilhelm* (14/68) [1969] ECR 1. The consequence is that if conduct is legal in national law but illegal under EC rules, both the national courts and the European Court must treat it as illegal (both Articles 81(1) (ex 85(1)) and 82 (ex 86), EC Treaty refer to the conduct as 'prohibited'). This helps to ensure that similar conduct is treated in a similar fashion throughout the European Union. However, if conduct is legal under EC rules, it may still appear to be illegal under national rules. The European Court of Justice seems to think that national courts cannot contradict a decision by the Commission to exempt an agreement under Article 81(3) (ex 85(3)) (see *Anne Marty v Esteé Lauder SA* (37/78) [1981] ECR 2481). The then Director General of the United Kingdom Office of Fair Trading, Sir Bryan Carsberg, stated his opinion that there is 'no clear indication' whether UK rules may prohibit an agreement which has been exempted by the Commission. More recently, the Director General of the OFT (then John Bridgeman), observed that a draft Bill introducing a prohibitory system 'along the lines of Article 85 [now 81] of the Treaty of Rome' had been published in the UK. He went on to point out that the Bill was explicitly designed to ensure its provisions are interpreted in a manner that would 'avoid inconsistency and potential conflict with Article 85 [now 81]'. Nevertheless, he concluded by declaring that:

> ... the UK prohibitory provisions ... should enable me to impose more stringent conditions than required for exemption under Article 85(3) [now 81(3)] where I consider it necessary in order to take specific UK circumstances properly into account.

(Speech to the International Bar Association, Berlin, 22 October 1996; and see now the Competition Act 1998.)

Mr Bridgeman's thoughts may be contrasted with those of Advocate-General Tesauro. In the Opinions that he delivered in two cases in the mid-1990s (*BMW v ALD* (C-70/93) [1995] ECR I-3439; *Bundeskartellamt v Volkswagen and VAG Leasing* (C-266/93) [1995] ECR I-3477), the Advocate-General stated clearly that agreements which had been exempted by the Commission could not be prohibited by the national competition authorities, using more restrictive provisions, other than in very exceptional circumstances. The Court of Justice did not resolve the issue in either case.

To state the position clearly for our purposes, if a clause in a contract or some sort of behaviour infringes either Article 81 (ex 85) or 82 (ex 86), EC Treaty and is thus prohibited by them, then any national laws in the UK will not save that clause or behaviour from prohibition, nor will national laws save the undertaking(s) concerned from any penalty that might be imposed for such infringement.

So far, we have considered the relationship between Community law and the laws of a single Member State. However, an agreement that operates across national boundaries may be treated differently according to which set of national rules are applied to it. The problem is addressed in Article 3 of Council Regulation 1/2003. This states that an agreement which may affect trade between Member States, shall not be prohibited by national laws if either:

(a) it does not restrict competition within Article 81(1); or

(b) it meets the conditions for exemption under Article 81(3); or

(c) it is covered by a block exemption.

It is, however, possible where national competition laws are stricter than Article 82, for unilateral behaviour to be prohibited by a Member State even though allowed by Article 82.

7.3 Direct effect of EC law

Both Articles 81 (ex 85) and 82 (ex 86) have been held to be directly effective and therefore capable of use in the national courts of Member States (see *BRT v SV SABAM* (127/73) [1974] ECR 51, paras 14–16, 21 and 22):

> It must ... be examined whether the national courts, before which the prohibitions contained in Articles 85 [now 81] and 86 [now 82] are invoked in a dispute governed by private law, must be considered as 'authorities of the Member States'.
>
> The competence of those courts to apply the provisions of Community law, particularly in the case of such disputes, derives from the direct effect of those provisions.
>
> As the prohibitions of Articles 85(1) [now 81(1)] and 86 [now 82] tend by their very nature to produce direct effects in relations between individuals, these Articles create direct rights in respect of the individuals concerned, which the national courts must safeguard.
>
> [I]f the Commission initiates a procedure in application of Article 3 of Regulation No17 such a court may, if it considers it necessary for reasons of legal certainty, stay the proceedings before it while awaiting the outcome of the Commission's action.
>
> On the other hand, the national court should generally allow proceedings before it to continue when it decides either that the behaviour in dispute is clearly not capable of having any appreciable effect on competition or on trade between Member States, or that there is no doubt of the incompatibility of that behaviour with Article 86 [now 82].

See also *Guérin Automobiles v Commission* (C-282/95 P) [1997] ECR I-1503, para 39.

7.4 Which court?

With the introduction of the Civil Procedure Rules in 1998, a decision which previously faced any claimant — whether to sue in the High Court or County Court — has been removed from them. A claimant will request a court (either High Court or County Court) to issue a claim form. It is now for the Procedural Judge (either a District Judge or a Master) to determine into which management track the case will fall — the small claims track, the fast track or the multi-track. As with every other civil case launched in England from April 1999 onwards, the parties will usually have to fill in an allocation questionnaire (see CPR, r 26.3). While the financial value of any claim is clearly very significant to the question of allocation (any claim for less than £15,000 is likely to be allocated to either the small claims track or the fast track, in the County Court), other significant factors include:

(a) the likely complexity of the facts, law or evidence;

(b) the importance of the claim to persons who are not parties to the proceedings.

Also of possible relevance is CPR, r 26.6(5), which indicates that even if a claim is worth less than £15,000, the fast track (County Court) is unlikely to be appropriate if the trial is expected to last for longer than one day and there is likely to be oral evidence from several experts. Conversely, CPR PD 29, suggests that claims with an estimated value of under £50,000 will generally be transferred to a county court unless, for example, they fall within a specialist list. Reference should also be made to the ***Civil Litigation Manual***.

Where, then, should a claim involving Article 81 (ex 85) or 82 (ex 86) be tried? The initial choice is between fast track (County Court) and multi-track (High Court or County Court). Thereafter, if the case goes for trial in the High Court, a choice must be made (by the court) about whether it should be tried in the Queen's Bench Division (QBD) or the Chancery Division. Most claims which raise issues of EC competition law will be best described as claims in contract or tort. The QBD is usually the most appropriate division of the High Court for such claims if the remedy sought includes damages. However, in the past (pre-CPR) there was no bar on starting claims involving contract or tort in the Chancery Division, and a swift glance at reported English cases involving the EC competition rules shows that at least half of them were dealt with in the Chancery Division. One reason for that is that the judges in the Chancery Division handle most of the commercial litigation and, over many years, have probably built up greater collective expertise in handling points of EC and EU law.

Where a High Court claim will be heard will depend upon the list in which it is placed. Under the CPR, cases are allocated to different lists according to their subject-matter. According to the editors of 'The Civil Procedure Rules', issued by the publishers of the *White Book*, one specialist list covers what the CPR refer to as 'specialist proceedings'. Under CPR, Part 49, 'specialist proceedings' include 'commercial and mercantile actions' and 'Patent Court business'. It is likely that some claims involving the EC competition rules will thus be specialist proceedings and continue to be dealt with by judges who are knowledgeable about EC and EU law. If a claimant decides to issue a claim form in the High Court, seeking money from the defendant, the claim form should state that the claimant expects to recover in excess of £15,000 and/or state that the claim is in one of the specialist High Court lists, specifying which one.

7.5 Offensive use of the rules

7.5.1 Causes of action

As a sword, certainly within the United Kingdom, attempts to rely on the EC competition rules have met with a varied reaction. Several years ago Lord Denning suggested that Articles 85 and 86 (now 81 and 82) represented 'new economic torts' — see, eg, his speech in *Application des Gaz SA v Falks Veritas* [1974] 3 All ER 51 — and could be used as causes of action in order to sue someone. This idea was not enthusiastically received by his judicial brethren.

The way forward seems to be indicated by cases like *Cutsforth v Mansfield Inns Ltd*, *Argyll v Distillers and Guinness* [1986] 1 CMLR 764, and, particularly, *Garden Cottage Foods v Milk Marketing Board* [1984] AC 130. The plaintiffs [now claimants] in these cases have not sought to put forward the EC rules as creating some new cause(s) of action, but instead have sought (or strained) to fit them into existing categories. The most acceptable, in judicial terms, seems to be the tort of breach of statutory duty, with its attendant remedies — namely, damages and interim measures.

In *Cutsforth* the plaintiffs owned coin-operated machines such as juke boxes and game machines which were placed in public houses. As a result of a take-over of Northern Breweries by Mansfield Brewery plc, the brewery told the plaintiffs to take their machines out of some 160 tenanted pubs under brewery control. The tenants were told that they could have such machines in the pubs but that they must come from a nominated supplier. Mansfield Brewery refused to put the plaintiffs on their list of approved suppliers.

The plaintiffs issued a writ, then applied for an *ex parte* injunction. The application was successful and was followed subsequently by an *inter partes* hearing. The High Court judge (Sir Neil Lawson) accepted that, if the plaintiffs could raise a serious question as to whether or not the defendants were guilty of infringing either Article 85 (now 81) or Article 86 (now 82), EC Treaty, they should get their injunction. He said (at p 563) that such conduct would be unlawful; the plaintiffs would be entitled to seek its prohibition in the High Court:

> ... as it is clear on the authorities that breaches of the relevant provisions of the EEC Treaty give rise to a cause of action in the domestic courts by a plaintiff who contends that he is the victim of such breaches.

The judge also considered whether the brewery's modified agreement with its tenants fell within the block exemption for exclusive purchase agreements (Regulation 1984/83), but decided it did not. He concluded that there was a serious question to be tried in relation to Article 85 (now 81) and that damages would not be an adequate remedy for the plaintiffs, whereas they would for the defendant.

Conversely, the plaintiffs lost their argument under Article 86 (now 82). Sir Neil Lawson held that:

(a) there was no evidence that the brewery held a dominant position;

(b) the area in which the brewery operated was not a 'substantial part of the common market' (although there is nothing in the judgment to indicate their area of operations, as distinct from that of the plaintiffs whose territory was 'Humberside and the surrounding district'); and

(c) no effect on inter-state trade had been shown.

The take-over battle for Distillers plc was the subject of (at least) two court cases between Argyll Group plc and Guinness plc — one in England and one in Scotland. In Scotland, when a revised bid by Guinness was not referred to the Monopolies and Mergers Commission, Argyll applied to the Court of Session for an interim interdict, to prevent the merger on the basis that it would contravene Article 86 (now 82), EC Treaty.

The court accepted the proposition (from *Garden Cottage Foods v Milk Marketing Board*, apparently, rather than *BRT v SV SABAM*) that Article 86 (now 82) was directly effective. It said that it was entitled to consider breaches of Article 86 (now 82) on an application for interim relief and noted that, taking *Europembellage and Continental Can Co v Commission* into account, it was possible for a merger to infringe that Article.

All three parties argued about the effect of *Continental Can Co* on the merits of the case (all with contradictory opinions), but the judge concluded that, on the available evidence, there was no prima facie case that a dominant position existed (or would exist); nor that the proposed merger would be an abuse. (The judge considered the relevant market in terms of geography and product.)

In *Garden Cottage Foods* the House of Lords considered the uses of Article 86 (now 82) in English courts. The defendants had cut off supplies of butter which the plaintiffs needed to carry on their business. They sought an interlocutory injunction, restraining the defendants from withdrawing supplies.

The House (Lord Wilberforce dissenting) held that it was clearly arguable that a breach of Article 86 (now 82) would give rise to a cause of action in English law at the behest of an individual who has suffered pecuniary loss by reason of the infringement; and that the remedy of damages would be available to compensate for such loss. Lord Diplock noted that Article 86 (now 82) had been held to be directly effective, citing *BRT v SV SABAM*, and that this was binding on English courts. A breach of the Article:

> ... can thus be categorised in English law as a breach of statutory duty that is imposed ... for the benefit of private individuals to whom loss or damage is caused by a breach of that duty.

According to Lord Diplock, whilst it was barely arguable that a breach of Article 86 (now 82) was not actionable as a breach of statutory duty in English courts, it could not be disputed that, if the cause of action existed, a remedy in damages must be available. In a dissenting speech, Lord Wilberforce thought that an open mind should be kept on whether or not a breach of Article 86 (now 82) simply gave rise to the remedy of an injunction; furthermore, it was still debatable what the nature of the cause of action was — it need not be defined as a tort or a 'breach of statutory duty'. The remaining three Law Lords agreed with Lord Diplock.

By way of completeness, we must also take note of *Bourgoin v Ministry of Agriculture, Fisheries and Food* [1986] QB 716. The case involved decisions of MAFF to keep French turkeys out of the UK. These decisions were subsequently declared to be illegal by the ECJ (under Article 30 (now 28), EC Treaty — free movement of goods). The plaintiffs were French turkey producers and distributors. They claimed damages from MAFF, alleging substantial loss. The causes of action were stated to be:

(a) breach of statutory duty under Article 30 (now 28), EC Treaty;

(b) the commission of an 'innominate tort' by so breaching Article 30 (now 28); and

(c) misfeasance in a public office (ie deliberate abuse of power).

The Court of Appeal held (by a two to one majority) that, although Article 30 (now 28) gave rights to individuals and imposed obligations on Member States, it said nothing about procedures or remedies. National courts had to offer the same remedies as are available for breach of a similar right in national law. A breach of Article 30 (now 28) was akin to an ultra vires act under an English statute. It would give rise to judicial review, a declaration on the invalidity of the measure containing the illegality, and possibly an order of mandamus, but *not* a claim for damages.

The majority in the Court of Appeal held that a prima facie cause of action existed for misfeasance in public office, but there was no cause of action under the 'innominate tort' or breach of statutory duty (cf. Oliver LJ). The distinction between this case and *Garden Cottage Foods* (*supra*) was that the latter dealt with 'private law rights'. The present case involved breach of negative obligations by a Member State and 'public law rights', which were only susceptible to judicial review. Even Lord Justice Oliver (who dissented in the result) pointed to the decisions of the Court of Justice in cases like *Bayerische HNL Vermehrungsbetriebe GmbH & Co KG v Council and Commission of the EC* (83 and 94/76, 4, 15 and 40/77) [1978] ECR 1209 (the skimmed milk powder case), which limit the rights of individuals to claim damages for the legislative acts of the Community under Article 288(2) (ex 215(2)), EC Treaty.

For another examination of the impact of EC Article 28 (ex 30) on our national law (this time by the Court of Justice, although note in the law reports the acceptance of it by the House of Lords), see the judgment in *Allen & Hanburys Ltd v Generics (UK) Ltd* (434/85) [1988] ECR 1245.

Lastly, it should be noted that, however you dress up your claim, it needs to persuade the judge that it can apply to the factual situation that confronts the court (see also **7.6.3**). An apparent failure to do so can be found in one of several cases involving breweries (or companies running chains of pubs) and their tenants: *Scottish & Newcastle plc v Bond*, 25 March 1997, unreported. The tenant of a S & N pub stopped paying rent and got his supplies of beer elsewhere. S & N sued for the rent arrears and mesne profits. The tenant claimed that the beer tie provisions contravened Article 85(1) (now 81(1) and so were void. According to the report, the judge found there was no arguable defence to S & N's claim, observing that Article 85 (now 81) is intended to regulate the position between competitors who operate in the same market but not between a particular supplier and customer. It is unclear how this decision could be reconciled with earlier English cases like *Cutsforth v Mansfield Inns Ltd* [1986] 1 WLR 558 and *Holleran v Daniel Thwaites* [1988] 2 CMLR 917, let alone *Delimitis v Henninger Braü AG* (C-234/89) [1991] ECR I-935, all three of which set Article 85 (now 81) in the context of the relationship of pub or bar tenants with their landlords and suppliers. See also **7.11**.

7.5.2 Equal and effective protection

In *Bourgoin*, Lord Justice Oliver stated that the English courts are under a twofold obligation. First, to protect the rights of any individual infringed by a breach of a directly effective Article of the Treaty, in a manner not inferior to the protection given for similar rights in domestic law (equal protection). Secondly, to do so effectively (effective protection). To withhold a remedy of damages from a claim against the Crown would deny equal and effective protection to the individual. It would not be equal and effective because the infringement should be classified as the tort of breach of statutory duty and attract the same remedies. Although this was a dissenting judgment, it was by far the longest in the case and very well argued. The Court gave leave to appeal to the House of Lords but the case was subsequently settled. The EC points raised in this case have not subsequently been aired in an appellate court in England and remain, at least temporarily, unresolved. (See also *R v Pharmaceutical Society of Great Britain, ex p Association of Pharmaceutical Importers* [1987] 3 CMLR 951 and (266 and 267/87) [1989] ECR 1321, [1990] 2 WLR 445 — a preliminary reference to the ECJ by the Queen's Bench Divisional Court.)

English courts may now be required to accord better than equal protection to claimants who rely on Community law — see the *ex p Factortame cases* (C-213/89 etc). The Court of Justice ruled (on a preliminary reference from the House of Lords) that interim relief could be granted to a litigant in a case concerning Community law if the 'sole obstacle' to such relief was a rule of national law. The relief in that case was the temporary suspension of an Act of Parliament in respect of the applicants.

The judgment of the ECJ in *Francovich and others v Italian Republic* (C-6/90 and C-9/90) [1991] ECR I-5357 may prove to be a landmark in the development of national remedies for breaches of EC laws. In essence, the ECJ held that a Member State may become liable in damages for failure to implement an EC directive. There are clear limits on how far one may infer from this judgment some broader right to damages, in particular between private individuals (as distinct from 'vertically' where an individual sues the State) but the case offers a way forward. It is, of course, binding on English courts and has been clarified by the judgment of the Court of Justice in *Brasserie de Pêcheur SA v Federal Republic of Germany* (C-46 and 48/93) [1996] 2 WLR 506; *R v Secretary of State for Transport, ex p Factortame Ltd (No 4)*. On a preliminary reference, the ECJ said that Member States could be liable in damages where individuals had suffered harm as the result of a breach of Community law which was attributable to the acts or omissions of the national legislature. In *Factortame*, Spanish fishermen alleged that they had suffered financial harm as a result of their exclusion from fishing in British waters, by virtue of provisions of the Merchant Shipping Act 1988. This statute had previously been held to be contrary to Community law (see *Factortame (No 3)* [1992] QB 680) and, eventually, the Spanish fishermen succeeded with a claim in the High Court, recovering damages against the United Kingdom.

7.6 Defensive use of the rules

7.6.1 Introduction

As a shield, one finds the competition rules used in cases like *British Leyland Motor Corporation v Armstrong Patents Co Ltd* [1986] AC 577, *Volvo AB v Erik Veng (UK)* (238/87) [1988] ECR 6211, and *R v Henn and Darby* (34/79) [1979] ECR 3795. Where people are sued in national courts for infringement of intellectual property rights (patents, copyright, trademarks, etc), they may allege that the litigation is an abuse of a dominant position or that the grant of the property right is the fruit of an anti-competitive agreement between undertakings.

One should note in passing that ancillary arguments, made by way of 'Euro-defences', can include reliance on the rules providing for free movement of goods within the Community (see **Chapter 9**). This has occurred both in the field of infringement of intellectual property rights and in criminal prosecution for importation of obscene material where the offending subject-matter had come, quite lawfully, from another Member State. (See, eg, *R v Henn and Darby*, and cases on free movement of goods such as *Hoffman-La Roche v Commission* and *Centrafarm v Sterling*.)

7.6.2 A defence of breach of statutory duty?

Despite the advice of the House of Lords in *Garden Cottage*, it seems unusual to find that one should rely on a defence that the claimant is in breach of a statutory duty. This is not unknown in the form of a counterclaim perhaps (one could imagine, in a claim for trespass to property, finding a counterclaim for damage suffered by the defendant contrary to the occupier's liability legislation) but that would not normally excuse the defendant from liability in the original claim.

What happens in practice is that the defence alleges, first, that the claimant has infringed either Article 81 (ex 85(1)) or 82 (ex 86) (or both) and gives full particulars of the allegation. The defence then goes on to argue that the effect of such infringement is to deprive the claimant of his cause of action. The argument may be that the claimant is suing on a contract or licence which the defendant argues is void and thus unenforceable. Or it may be that the claimant is alleged to be in a dominant position, and his abuse of that position is argued to excuse the defendant from liability (as may be the case in a patent infringement claim where the patentee sues a parallel importer). In these situations, it makes little sense on the facts to defend oneself simply with an allegation that the claimant is guilty of a breach of statutory duty; after all, such duty may not be intended to prevent the type of damage that the defendant relies on (cf *Gorris v Scott* (1874) LR 8 Ex 125). In using Article 81 (ex 85) or 82 (ex 86) defensively, then, you will usually find it makes sense to set out the material facts in a manner which appears consistent with the allegations made in the particulars of claim. This should also help to persuade any judge that there is a sufficient nexus between your EC defence and the cause of claim (see **7.6.3**). Any reference in the Defence to the claimant being in breach of statutory duty will usually appear as a very short 'further or alternative' paragraph, after the substance of the alleged infringement has been dealt with.

7.6.3 The need for a nexus

It almost goes without saying, but there does need to be a connection between the cause of claim of the claimant (and the remedies sought in the claim) and the EC point relied on by the defendant. The point was well made by Megarry V-C in *ICI v Berk Pharmaceuticals* [1981] 2 CMLR 81:

> If the plaintiffs [now claimants] are imposing unfair selling prices in that they charge too much for their product, I cannot see why this breach of the prohibitions of Article 86 [now 82] means that the defendants are thereby set free from any liability to the plaintiffs if they, the defendants, commit the tort of passing off (or, indeed, any other tort) against them.

In a similar vein, there has been a spate of cases involving public house licensees and their landlords (in particular, Inntrepreneur Estates). In these cases, typically the property company sues the pub licensee for rent arrears; the licensee then defends the claim arguing that the 'tie' relating to the purchase of beer contravenes Article 81(1) (ex 85(1)) — thus the tie is void and so is the lease itself. This argument has failed on two bases. First, assuming the tie is void as claimed, there is no suggestion that the obligation to pay rent under the lease is itself void by virtue of Article 81(2) (ex 85(2)); secondly, even if the tie is void, it can be severed from the rest of the lease leaving the rent payable as claimed by the claimant. See eg *Inntrepreneur Estates v Boyes* (1983) 47 EG 140. See also *IBM v Phoenix International* [1984] RPC 251; also, *Chiron Corp v Murex Diagnostics Ltd* [1992] 3 CMLR 813.

7.6.4 Declarations and severance

If a defendant has to rely on Article 81 (ex 85) to argue that a contract clause is void, it would be best to seek a declaration to that effect. Further, if the defendant really wants out of the contract altogether, it may be necessary to seek a declaration that the entire contract is void (in a counterclaim). A claimant who is confronted by a defendant counterclaiming for a declaration that the whole contract is void may attempt to overcome that claim by seeking severance of any offending clause (see *Inntrepreneur Estates* above).

These days it is settled law that just because a specific clause in a contract is anti-competitive, it does not follow that the whole contract is void by virtue of Article 81(2) (ex 85(2)). If the offending clause can be severed from the contract, and leave the rest, then that is what will happen. Issues of severance are for the national courts to decide in accordance with their usual rules on the topic. In England, the rule might be simply described as a 'blue pencil' test: if, after deletion of the offending clause(s), one is left with no meaningful contract or one which is so changed in character that the parties would not have entered into it in the first place, then severance is not possible. See *Société Technique Minière v Maschinenbau Ulm GmbH* (56/65) [1966] ECR 235 and *Société de Vente de Ciments et Bétons v Kerpen & Kerpen* (319/82) [1983] ECR 4173 for the view of the Court of Justice; and *Chemidus Wavin v TERI* [1978] 3 CMLR 514 for the leading Court of Appeal case in England. Per Buckley LJ in *Chemidus Wavin*:

> [I]n applying Article 85 [now 81] to an English contract, one may well have to consider whether, after the excisions required by the Article ... have been made from the contract, the contract could be said to fail for lack of consideration or on any other ground, or whether the contract would be so changed in its character as not to be the sort of contract that the parties intended to enter into at all.

The series of 'pub' cases mentioned in **7.6.3** seemed to indicate that severance was a possibility: beer ties were being excised, leaving enforceable leases, but it may be significant that the lessor in those cases was not usually a brewery so maybe the supply of beer was not paramount to it. Anyway, they might be contrasted with a case involving the supply of cars to a dealer (*Richard Cound Ltd v BMW (GB) Ltd*, 10 May 1995, Court of Appeal, unreported). Here, various clauses were severed from a car distribution agreement whereby the buyer (the car dealer) had agreed to resell the new cars he bought from BMW, and to resell the spare parts he bought from them and to provide a service facility for BMW cars, regardless of their place of purchase. The Court of Appeal thought that, by severing these requirements, what was left would be a simple contract for the sale of new BMW cars and spares. This would be (per Balcombe LJ):

> an agreement so different that ... it is apt to regard the effect of severance as 'altering entirely the scope and intention of the agreement' or as removing the heart and soul of the agreement ...

7.7 To sue or be sued?

7.7.1 Factors to consider

An undertaking which considers that another is infringing either Article 81(1) (ex 85(1)) or Article 82 (ex 86) has a choice. Apart from making a complaint to the Commission, the undertaking may:

- start a claim against the alleged infringer, seeking various remedies;
- carry on as normal and wait until the alleged infringer sues it (the cause of action is not important here).

There are several factors which an undertaking should consider when confronted with this choice. It may be relatively easier to get a declaration that an infringement has occurred; relatively harder to get damages to compensate for any losses. Thus, it is important to minimise one's financial claim: carrying on as normal might achieve that. Also important is timing: it may be that there is insufficient evidence of an infringement available to your client at present. The best evidence of an infringement may be provided by the very act of the infringer launching a legal claim against your client (cf eg *Consten and Grundig v Commission* (56 and 58/64) [1966] ECR 299).

Of course, you should always consider what the client's objectives are. If there is a contract or licence agreement of some sort between your client and the alleged infringer then the first question is: does the client want to escape from the contract? If not, then it might be best not to initiate a claim as any reliance on Article 81(1) (ex 85(1)) or 82 (ex 86) may result in the contract being declared void despite your best endeavours. There is also the problem that, even if your client does want out of the contract, the judge may not agree that there is a cause of action; it may be simpler to act as if the contract is at an end (eg send the other party a letter terminating the contract or find a replacement for the other party and stop dealing with them).

Expense is unlikely to be an issue in deciding whether to sue or be sued. In particular, the cost of the evidence needed to substantiate your allegations of anti-competitive behaviour will not vary according to whether your client is claimant or defendant. This is because it is rather unusual to find a claim where both parties allege breaches of EC competition rules have occurred. Clearly, a claimant bears a heavy financial burden in acquiring the evidence needed to discharge the burden of proof; equally, since the use of an EC competition point in a Defence is likely to raise entirely different issues to those in the Particulars of Claim, the defendant will bear the burden of proof on the competition issues and the accompanying cost of acquiring the evidence.

Example

This example tries to show some of the questions that you should consider, and their possible outcomes. When confronted by a problem which might involve an issue of EC competition law, it is important not to focus too heavily on that, especially when advising the client. Nevertheless, the possible uses of the competition law rules, and the information needed to advise thereon, should be borne in mind when considering advice on strategy.

Your client is Folio Ltd, an undertaking which is acting in possible breach of another's intellectual property rights (eg manufacturing patented goods without a licence). Folio is warned by the patentee of a possible claim for patent infringement if manufacturing continues. The options for Folio are:

- stop manufacturing forthwith (and maybe pay compensation for past infringement);
- start proceedings to overturn the grant of the patent (simple possession of a patent is not going to ground a claim alleging abuse of a dominant position, using Article 82 (ex 86); there may be grounds to challenge the validity of the patent, though);
- ask the patentee to grant Folio a licence to manufacture the goods (which, if granted, is very likely to result in Folio paying royalties);
- just carry on manufacturing.

The first option might be the easiest one to take, but if Folio has been manufacturing in the knowledge that they were infringing a patent it seems an unlikely option for them to take now. Assuming the patent to be valid, Folio has no ground to sue the patentee, which rules out the second option. Folio could try the third option, if it is prepared to pay royalties. If it approaches the patentee for a licence and is refused, or considers the royalties demanded to be too high, then if the patentee is in a dominant position, Folio might start a claim alleging breach of Article 82 (ex 86) (the objective being to compel the patentee to grant a licence; cf *Volvo AB v Erik Veng (UK)* (238/87) [1988] ECR 6211). At first glance, the last option seems a poor one to take. Your client is asking to be sued for infringement and ordered to pay damages. The fourth option makes more sense if the patentee is in a dominant position because, if the patentee then sues your client, you can make the claim in Folio's defence that the patent claim constitutes an abuse of that dominant position. An alternative question would be to ask if the patentee is in fact an assignee of the patent. If so, it might be worth considering if there has been an attempt by the original patentee and its assignee(s) to divide up the single, common market by the use of national intellectual property rights.

7.8 Drafting pleadings in English claims

7.8.1 Remember the rules

As we have seen, a civil claim may involve either Article 81 (ex 85) (1), (3), or Article 82 (ex 86), EC Treaty. A litigant may use the competition rules offensively or defensively, and at an interim stage as well as at trial. The main 'engines' for all of these purposes are really the statements of case, and we can concentrate on:

- the particulars of claim; and
- the defence and Part 20 claim (previously a 'counterclaim').

This section is not intended to replicate the excellent books on precedent and procedure for the practitioner (the *White Book*; Bullen, Leake and Jacobs, *Precedents of Pleadings* (Sweet & Maxwell); *A Practical Approach to Civil Procedure*, Stuart Sime (Blackstone Press); *A Practical Approach to Legal Advice and Drafting*, Susan Blake (Blackstone Press); *Pleadings Without Tears*, William Rose (Blackstone Press)); all are extremely helpful in their different ways. What they tend to omit is any guidance on how to draft issues of EC competition law (often the only help one finds is assistance on drafting a question for preliminary reference to the Court of Justice, under Article 234 (ex 177), EC Treaty). (An attempt to fill this gap has been made: see *European Courts Practice and Precedents* (Sweet & Maxwell, 1996).) So what help can we offer to anyone who has to draft a statement of case involving issues of EC competition law?

Of course, your statement of case here is inherently no different from that which you are already familiar with; only the substantive law is different. The primary obligation is to comply with the Civil Procedure Rules, Part 16, on statements of case. Your statement of case must set out the necessary particulars of any claim, defence or other matter intended to be advanced at trial. Further, the statement of case should contain a concise statement of the facts which are material to the claim or defence advanced. Prior to the CPR, the old rules of civil procedure specified that one should not plead the evidence by which the material facts were to be proved. That never sat very easily with the practices developed by practitioners in the EC/EU field and CPR, PD 16 specifies, for example, that where a claim is based upon a written agreement, a copy should be attached to the particulars of claim; similarly, where a claim is based upon an oral agreement, the particulars of claim should state the actual words used, by who, to whom and when and where they were spoken (see PD 16, para 9). Furthermore, in the past statements of case involving the EC competition rules have contained more points of law than was usual in more 'domestic' claims.

That practice now seems set to become legitimate, since PD 16 permits a claimant to refer in his or her particulars of claim to any point of law on which his claim is based.

As you can see, the rules for statements of case now seem to reflect existing practice for drafters in many respects. It is nevertheless important to consider in detail how these rules will apply to cases using Articles 81 (ex 85) and 82 (ex 86), EC Treaty.

7.8.2 What to include

Typically, when relying on Article 81(1) (ex 85(1)) in one's statement of case, the novice's mistake is to focus the allegations of infringement on the relationship between the claimant and the defendant in the particular case. This happens because the drafter is representing one party to the claim, has received instructions from that party and seeks remedies (of whatever sort) which are intended to benefit that party. In other words, the drafter's focus is on the individual. This can cause a problem in that Article 81(1) (ex 85(1)) looks at matters on a bigger scale. Clearly, the statement of case must show how the client has been harmed and how their damage might be quantified; but of equal importance is the need to demonstrate the infringement of the competition rules. The economic analysis required to do so means that the statement of case may deal with matters somewhat divorced from the obvious subject-matter of the litigation. What is needed is that:

> the factual allegations regarding effect on competition should be pleaded in such terms that it can be seen how the effect complained of flows from the agreement or concerted practice ...

(per Ferris J in *Intergraph Corp v Solid Systems CAD Services Ltd*, 7 December 1983, Chancery Division, unreported).

There may be less conceptual difficulty with Article 82 (ex 86). Here the abusive exploitation which is alleged against one party typically has the other party as its victim. Obvious examples occur when there is:

- a refusal to supply *your client* (cf *Hugin/Liptons; Boosey & Hawkes/Brass Band Instruments*);
- denial of access to essential services for *your client* (for example, *B & I/Stena*);
- predatory pricing directed against *your client* (see *ECS/Akzo*).

Nevertheless, these situations may fall outside the common grasp of how tortious liability is established in England. The harm envisaged by Article 82 (ex 86) may be seen as harm to the 'market' or to the interests of consumers. In the last of the three examples above, the effect of the anti-competitive act (predatory pricing) is directed against the competitors of the dominant undertaking. Where there are several competitors, can they all sue for infringement of Article 82 (ex 86)? Might there be a 'floodgates' problem here? This is perhaps the difficulty in relying upon individual undertakings taking action to 'protect' the 'normal' competitive working of the (collective) market. At the least, we should note that the drafter of a statement of case who relies upon Article 82 (ex 86) will need to show a causal connection between the alleged infringement and the loss or damage borne by the client.

We have seen (in **Chapters 2** and **5**) that the proper analysis of whether there has been an infringement of Article 81(1) (ex 85(1)) or 82 (ex 86), EC Treaty demands a meaningful economic analysis of the relevant market (see eg, *Delimitis v Henninger Braü AG* (C-234/89) [1991] ECR I-935; *Hoffmann La-Roche v Commission* (85/76) [1979] ECR 461). It cannot be denied sensibly that such a definition of the market is an essential part of one's analysis under these Articles, but should it appear in the statement of case? The material facts have to be in the statement of case and that means those facts which are necessary for the formulation of a complete cause of action (see Scott LJ in *Bruce v Odhams Press Ltd* [1936] 3 All ER 287). So, it seems that some attempt must be made in your statement of case to define the relevant market. This does not mean that the full details of an expert's report should be included (although this will be fundamental *evidence* to persuade the trial court of the nature and operation of the relevant market) but it does mean that you should assert what are the relevant products and what territory is involved. Are we concerned with the effects on others as well as, or instead of, just our client? Both Articles 81(1) (ex 85(1)) and 82 (ex 86) require an effect (actual or potential) on inter-State trade: the evidence to show that may come from the effect of the anti-competitive behaviour on other undertakings, not on the client; whilst we should avoid, or at least minimise, the incorporation of evidence into our statement of case, the allegation has to be made.

What about the relief sought? This must be set out in the body of your statement of case, and you must check that the nature of your claim facilitates your chosen remedy(ies). *Garden Cottage* said that the proper cause of action was breach of statutory duty, but suppose that the most appropriate remedy for your client is not one commonly (or ever) awarded to parties in statutory duty cases? It is quite usual to set your statement of case out in a manner which gives the 'best fit' for the material facts and the optimal remedies *and* then to allege, as being further or alternative to the initial allegations, that the 'matters aforesaid' also constitute a breach of statutory duty (really as a sort of insurance policy for your drafting).

In essence, when relying upon Article 81(1) (ex 85(1)) or 82 (ex 86), each and every element of the relevant Article should appear on your checklist and when you have finished a draft you should be able to read through it and tick off each element as your statement of case deals with it. Adopting a 'belt-and-braces' approach, you might even want to assert the direct effect of the relevant competition rule, thus entitling your client to rely on it in the course of a private civil claim in the national legal system (see **7.3**).

7.8.3 Example for particulars of claim

Facts

Two undertakings, All Ice plc and Barry Jones, enter a contract. All Ice agrees to supply Barry Jones with ice cream products. All Ice is a large-volume manufacturing company, specialising in ice creams but with interests in other frozen food products too. Barry Jones is a sole trader, operating newsagent/general stores in three villages. While the contract is still operating, Barry Jones is approached by a rival ice cream maker, Polar Glaces SA. Polar offers to supply its ice cream products to Barry Jones. Polar's range of products is similar to All Ice's but Polar is a foreign-based company, now seeking to establish itself in the UK. Polar currently has a low degree of brand recognition for its products in the UK and is willing to price its supplies to Barry Jones to reflect this. Barry Jones would like to take some of his requirement for ice cream from Polar but is unwilling to terminate his contract with All Ice as All Ice is the biggest supplier in the market, an established manufacturer who is well-known and has a wide range of the most popular brand names and products. Barry Jones' shop has space for only one ice cream freezer cabinet; currently that is supplied at a very low rental by All Ice, with a requirement that only All Ice products be stored there. Barry Jones has asked All Ice for permission to stock Polar's products and been turned down; in fact, All Ice threatened to take Barry Jones to court to enforce the exclusivity clause in the supply contract. Polar has encountered this situation in many locations across the UK and is having great difficulty in finding a viable number of retail outlets for its products.

Choices

Should Barry Jones sue All Ice, alleging that his contract with All Ice infringes Article 81(1) (ex 85(1))? Should Polar sue All Ice, alleging that the contract All Ice has with Barry Jones and/or many others infringes Article 81(1) (ex 85(1))? Would Polar be better advised to sue All Ice using Article 82 (ex 86), to allege that All Ice is abusing a dominant position (if All Ice in fact has a dominant position)? Should Barry Jones simply accept supplies from Polar and wait to see what action, if any, All Ice takes? These are all relevant questions but for our purposes we shall assume that Barry Jones has decided to sue All Ice, alleging an infringement of Article 81(1). We shall further assume that Barry Jones is quite happy to keep the All Ice contract going and keep the freezer, with its low rental cost — he just wants the freedom to store anyone's ice cream products in it.

IN THE HIGH COURT OF JUSTICE — Claim No: 2003 HC 1234

CHANCERY DIVISION

BETWEEN

BARRY JONES — Claimant

(a sole trader)

and

ALL ICE PLC — Defendant

PARTICULARS OF CLAIM

1. The Claimant owns 3 newsagent and general shops in and around Hadley, Hertfordshire, where he sells a variety of goods including ice creams. On the 4th March 2001, the Claimant entered into a written contract with the Defendants, whereby the Defendants would supply the Claimant with a range of their ice creams for sale in his shops. Such products would be for consumption either immediately ('impulse purchase') or away from the premises ('home consumption'). The Defendants are a public company engaged in the manufacture and distribution of various frozen food products, including industrially-produced ice cream products.
2. The following were material terms of the contract:
   (a) Clause 1.1 The Company [namely, the Defendants] will supply an extensive range of their ice cream products (hereafter 'products') to the Customer [namely, the Claimant]. Such supplies shall take place in quantities that the Company, in its experience, judges sufficient for the demand of the Customer.
   (b) Clause 1.2 The Company shall supply such of its range of ice cream products to the Customer as the Company considers appropriate. The Company retains complete discretion as to the brands and sizes of such products to be supplied.
   (c) Clause 2.3 The Customer shall observe all proper standards of hygiene and cleanliness in the storing and display of the products supplied to him by the Company, from time to time.
   (d) Clause 2.7 The Customer shall store and display the products in a freezer; such freezer to be of appropriate size and dimensions for the efficient resale of the products. The Company shall offer to supply to the Customer such a freezer, at a rental price of five pounds per month.
   (e) Clause 3.6 On agreeing to use a freezer supplied by the Company, the Customer will receive a 2.5% discount on every one hundred pounds of the Company's products that he buys.
   (f) Clause 3.7 When using a freezer supplied by the Company, the Customer agrees to keep only ice cream products therein; in particular, the Customer agrees to use the freezer exclusively for the purpose of storing and displaying the products of the Company.
3. The Claimant agreed to rent 3 freezers from the Defendants. Upon receipt of the freezers, the Claimant was obliged to re-order the shop fittings to accommodate the freezers. There is room for only one freezer and no other in each of the Claimant's shops.
4. On the 3rd February 2003, the Claimant approached the Defendants, seeking permission to store and display ice cream products manufactured in France by another company, Polar Glaces SA (hereafter 'Polar'). The Claimant had been offered supplies of ice creams by Polar in a range comparable to that of the Defendants but at prices which, on average, were 20% less than those charged to the Claimant for the Defendants' products. The Defendants refused permission and threatened to take legal action to enforce their exclusive access to the freezers.
5. The Claimant expected to sell Polar ice cream products in a ratio of 1:4 to those supplied by the Defendants.

6. The Claimant and the Defendants are and have been undertakings to which Article 81(1) of the European Community Treaty applies. The contract is an agreement between undertakings which has as its object or effect the restriction, distortion or prevention of trade between Member States of the European Community and which thereby infringes Article 81(1).

<u>Particulars of Infringement</u>

(1) *The market* The Defendants manufacture and sell ice cream products throughout the United Kingdom. Their share of industrial impulse and home consumption ice cream sales, of the type as are made through the Claimant's shops, was 35% in 2001.

(2) The contract entered into by the Claimant with the Defendants was in the standard form of contract used by the Defendants for the sale and supply of their ice cream products. The Defendants have placed their freezers in many shops and other retail outlets throughout the United Kingdom.

(3) *Restriction on trade* The operation of clauses 2.7 and 3.6 were such that the Claimant was induced to rent freezers from the Defendants. By virtue of his rental of freezers from the Defendants, together with the Defendants' insistence on applying clause 3.7, the Claimant is prevented from selling ice cream products from other manufacturers, in particular Polar. Further, such manufacturers and other suppliers are thereby denied access to the market, namely sales of industrial impulse and home consumption ice cream products to retail outlets.

(4) *Effect on trade between Member States* Polar is, and other manufacturers and suppliers may be, based in Member States of the Community other than the United Kingdom.

7. In the premises, clause 3.7 of the contract between the Claimant and the Defendant is prohibited and void, by the operation of Article 81(1) and 81(2) of the European Community Treaty.

8. The infringement of Article 81(1) has caused the Claimant loss and damage. The Claimant contends that he would have been able to obtain cheaper supplies of ice cream products from other sources, in the absence of the infringement, in particular from Polar.

<u>Particulars of Loss and Damage</u>

From 3rd February 2003 to date
30 weeks at an estimated loss of profits of £ *a* per week £ [30 x *a* = current total] and continuing.

[*We need to get a figure for £ a from Barry Jones to insert into the Particulars*]

9. Further the Claimant claims interest on the sums found due to him pursuant to section 35A of the Supreme Court Act 1981 at such rate and for such period as this Court shall think fit.

AND the Claimant claims:

(1) A declaration that clause 3.7 of the contract between the Claimant and the Defendants is prohibited and void as contrary to Article 81(1) of the European Community Treaty, and that the Claimant is no longer bound by it.

(2) Damages for the infringement of Article 81(1).

(3) Interest pursuant to section 35A of the Supreme Court Act 1981.

[Statement of truth]
The Claimant believes that the facts stated in these particulars of claim are true. I am duly authorised by the Claimant to sign this statement.

Denise Smith

Of Sime, Blake and Rose

D Smith [signed by counsel]

SERVED this 5th day of September 2003 by Sime, Blake & Rose of 600 Gray's Inn Road, London, Solicitors for the Claimant.

7.8.4 Example for an Opinion

7.8.4.1 Introduction

What follows (in **7.8.4.2**) is a set of instructions to Counsel, to advise a client and then draft a Defence and Counterclaim. Preliminary work on an Opinion is set out after the Particulars of Claim (in **7.8.4.3**); this Opinion is necessarily in draft form because one would never be able to give definite advice on many topics until after a full interview with, in this case, the Managing Director of the client company.

The set of instructions is of a simple nature, which could easily be given to someone new to practice on. If you are a newcomer to this area, you may want to use the instructions in this case to practice your analytical skills. If so, don't immediately read the draft Opinion that follows the Instructions to Counsel, try to jot down your own conclusions and questions. Think about how you might structure an Opinion for the client company. Try to spot and address all the issues raised by the Instructions, both explicit and implicit. Then read the draft Opinion in **7.8.4.3** and see how it compares with your work: it is not intended to be some sort of perfect model but rather a work in progress. Some paragraphs are not set out in any detail as a basic knowledge of opinion writing is assumed. The Instructions, and specifically the Particulars of Claim contained in them, have been used again as the basis for a 'first draft' Defence and Counterclaim; this is set out in **7.8.5**.

7.8.4.2 Instructions to Counsel

DEEPDIN UK LIMITED

AND

ARNOLD'S WORLD OF SOUND LIMITED

INSTRUCTIONS TO COUNSEL TO

With these Instructions, Counsel has:

(1) copy agreement

(2) statement of Terry Arnold

(3) copies of correspondence

(4) particulars of claim.

Instructing Solicitors represent Arnold's World of Sound Ltd ('AWS'). On the 2 January 2001, AWS entered an exclusive purchase agreement with Deepdin UK, manufacturer of the well-known Deepdin range of hi-fi equipment. Prior to the agreement, and for a time thereafter, the business of AWS was conducted exclusively within the United Kingdom. Until earlier this year, Instructing Solicitors are informed, the agreement operated to the apparent satisfaction of both parties. Over the last few months, however, there has been a breakdown in the relationship. This has arisen over the refusal of Deepdin to permit AWS to export its products outside the United Kingdom; the correspondence refers. To summarise, a company selling Deepdin products in France, HappiSound SA, wrote to AWS placing an order for the sale and delivery to them of 100 Deepdin CD Triple X hi-fi systems. Subsequently, on the 23 May 2003, AWS contacted Deepdin seeking permission to fulfil the order. Permission was denied by letter. Thereafter Mr Arnold rang Deepdin and told them he was determined to go ahead and fulfil the order from HappiSound.

The result is that Deepdin have started proceedings against AWS in the High Court. Counsel will find enclosed Particulars of Claim, seeking an injunction forcing AWS to comply with the terms of the agreement, in particular clause 2(11). We have been informed by Browning Lloyd, Deepdin's solicitors, that they will be applying for an interim injunction quite soon.

We have advised AWS that they may have a defence, and possibly a claim too, based on Article 81 of the EC Treaty. Counsel is asked to advise on the status of the export clause (2(11)). In fact, Mr Arnold is emphatic that he wants to end the entire agreement. He now feels that AWS would be more profitable if it was free to sell hi-fi equipment from several different manufacturers.

Instructing Solicitors have done some preliminary work, looking into the nature of the hi-fi market in the United Kingdom. Through perusing the trade journals, it appears that there are the following manufacturers:

Rebound	12%
Whatmore	25%
Goodsound	27%
Deepdin	8%
Other makes	28%

According to AWS the wholesale price of Deepdin hi-fi equipment is higher in other Member States of the European Union than in the United Kingdom. This explains the purchase order from HappiSound in France.

Counsel is requested to draft a Defence and Counterclaim in this matter. Counsel is further requested to advise:

— generally
— in particular, whether or not a complaint should be made to the European Commission
— on the steps to be taken in relation to (i) a complaint, if so advised, and (ii) the High Court proceedings.

[Copy agreement]

This PURCHASE AGREEMENT dated 2 January 2001 between DEEPDIN UK LIMITED Deepdin House Swaledale Estate Barnsley Yorkshire and ARNOLD'S WORLD OF SOUND LIMITED Tottenham Court Road London WC2

WHEREBY: DEEPDIN UK LIMITED ('the Company') and ARNOLD'S WORLD OF SOUND LIMITED ('the Exclusive Purchaser') have agreed that the Company will supply Deepdin hi-fi equipment to the Exclusive Purchaser upon the terms and conditions set out herein

INTRODUCTION

(a) The Company produces high quality and technically complex consumer hi-fi products. They are subject to continuous technological development.

(b) Consumers of the Company's products require informed and expert advice prior to making their purchase decision. They also require installation services and a full after sales service, including warranty service.

(c) The Company has established a network of exclusive purchasers for Deepdin products in order to provide all the services required by consumers.

AGREED TERMS:

1. The Company undertakes and agrees with the Exclusive Purchaser that the Company will

(i) supply the Exclusive Purchaser with all hi-fi products for sale in the exclusive Purchaser's business

(ii) not sell Deepdin products by way of retail to the Exclusive Purchaser's customers, except with the prior consent of the Exclusive Purchaser

(iii) use all reasonable endeavours to ensure that other exclusive purchasers do not sell Deepdin products by way of retail to the Exclusive Purchaser's customers.

2. In consideration of the above undertakings and obligations on the part of the Company, the Exclusive Purchaser hereby undertakes and agrees with the Company:

(1) For a period of five years from the date hereof to purchase from the Company all hi-fi products to be sold in its business;

(2) To pay the Company for all Deepdin products purchased by the exclusive Purchaser from the Company not later than the Saturday of the week following delivery thereof to the Exclusive Purchaser;

(3) To use its best endeavours to increase the sale of Deepdin products in its business;

(4) To give the Company at least one month's written notice of the exclusive Purchaser's wish to dispose of all or any part of the goodwill of its business or any interest therein;

(5) Upon any sale by the Exclusive Purchaser of the whole or a substantial part of its business to apply the proceeds of such sale in the discharge of any sums due to the Company from the Exclusive Purchaser;

(6) Not to manufacture or distribute hi-fi products which compete with Deepdin products;

(7) To purchase hi-fi products from across the Company's complete range;

(8) To purchase from the Company Deepdin products to the value of at least £100,000 within the period of five years;

(9) Not to tamper with or obliterate the trademark 'Deepdin';

(10) To provide installation services and a full after sales service including a warranty service to the Exclusive Purchaser's customers;

(11) Not to export any Deepdin products outside the territory of the United Kingdom without the prior written consent of the Company. Any enquiries for orders from outside the United Kingdom should be forwarded to the Company at its registered address.

3. The Company will provide training, information, guidance and promotional material relating to the sale and servicing of Deepdin products.

4. Either party may terminate this agreement forthwith if the other party commits an irremediable breach of any of its provisions.

5. Upon termination the Exclusive Purchaser will return or dispose of, in accordance with the Company's instructions, all promotional materials, specifications, and other documents and offer for sale back to the Company all Deepdin products belonging to the Exclusive Purchaser at a price equal to that which the Exclusive Purchaser paid for them.

THIS AGREEMENT constitutes the entire contract between the parties and may not be varied except by written agreement between them.

Deepdin products are the consumer electronic products sold under the Deepdin Trademark or Deepdin brand name which include Colour Televisions, Video Cassette Recorders, Camcorders, Hi-Fi Systems.

In witness whereof

STATEMENT OF TERRY ARNOLD

I am the Managing Director of Arnold's World of Sound. Two years ago we agreed with Deepdin UK that we would buy all our hi-fi requirements from them. They make hi-fi equipment at the quality end of the market, with basic equipment starting at about £1,000 wholesale. For their very top range, prices can be about ten times that. How much we paid for orders from Deepdin was dependent on the particular range we ordered from. As examples, a complete Deepdin Mashup sound system has a current cost price to us of £800 per unit, a Deepdin CD Triple X system costs £850 and the Deepdin Quality Airtime costs £2,385 each. To start with, the arrangement with Deepdin worked well. In the first trading year we bought in excess of £350,000 worth of Deepdin product.

At the start of this year, I attended the Paris Audio Vision Fair. This attracts manufacturers and dealers from all over Europe, as well as other major brand names. Whilst there, I learnt from other Deepdin dealers that the cost of Deepdin products varied considerably. Generally, they were higher than I was paying in the UK — for example, in France wholesale prices were on average 6–8% higher and in Germany they could be higher still. I spoke informally with several foreign Deepdin dealers in Paris and then in April this year I received a letter from M. Happi of HappiSound SA. He wanted to place an order with AWS for Deepdin products, to be supplied to him in July this year. Given the price differentials, it seemed to make sense for both of us, so I wrote to Deepdin asking for permission to supply the equipment. Deepdin turned me down pretty abruptly. I didn't like their response so I rang their MD, Oliver Din, and told him I was going to fulfil the order regardless. I could not see how he could stop HappiSound getting their stock. A week or so later I got their Particulars of Claim in the post.

I don't want to carry on with this agreement now, it seems too restrictive. AWS would be better off financially if we could sell hi-fi equipment across several brands and manufacturers. If needed, I can confirm that from some research we've done. I have written to M. Happi asking him to supply details of sales of Deepdin in France.

HappiSound SA

Avenue Coeur de Lion
Paris
France

30 April 2003

Arnold's World of Sound Ltd
1193 Tottenham Court Road
London
WC2

Dear Mr Arnold

We would be grateful if you would supply to us at HappiSound in July 2003, 100 CD Deepdin Triple X stereo sound systems at your quoted price of £1,100 per unit.

Yours sincerely,

Maurice Happi

Arnold's World of Sound Limited

Tottenham Court Road
London
WC2

23 May 2003

Mr O. Din
Deepdin UK Limited
Deepdin House
Swaledale Estate
Barnsley
Yorkshire

Dear Oliver,

Please find enclosed a request which we have received from HappiSound SA, a French dealer. We would be grateful to have your permission to fulfil this order.

Best wishes,

Terry Arnold

Deepdin UK Limited

Deepdin House
Swaledale Estate
Barnsley
Yorkshire

28 May 2003

Mr Terry Arnold
Arnold's World of Sound Ltd
1193 Tottenham Court Road
London
WC2

Dear Sir

Thank you for your letter of 23 May. In the circumstances, I am afraid that we cannot agree to your company fulfilling this order. We shall be instructing our French distributor to enquire of HappiSound SA whether they wish to purchase from our French agents.

Yours faithfully

Oliver Din

IN THE HIGH COURT OF JUSTICE — Claim No: 2003 HC 3217

QUEEN'S BENCH DIVISION

BETWEEN

DEEPDIN UK LIMITED — Claimant

and

ARNOLD'S WORLD OF SOUND LIMITED — Defendant

PARTICULARS OF CLAIM

1. At all material times the Claimants have carried on business as suppliers of hi-fi equipment. The Defendants have carried on a hi-fi distribution business.
2. By an agreement in writing dated 2nd January 2001 made between the Claimants and the Defendants, it was agreed that the Defendants would purchase for a period of five years Deepdin hi-fi products only from the Claimants.
3. It was an express term of the agreement that the Defendants would not sell Deepdin hi-fi equipment outside the United Kingdom without the prior written consent of the Claimants.
4. Notwithstanding that written term, the Defendants have threatened to act in breach of contract by selling a quantity of Deepdin hi-fi equipment to a French company, HappiSound SA.

PARTICULARS OF BREACH OF CONTRACT

(a) On 30th April 2003 a French company HappiSound SA requested the Defendants to provide it with 100 CD Deepdin Triple X sound systems.

(b) By letter dated 23rd May 2003, the Defendants requested permission from the Claimants to fulfil the order. By letter dated 28th May 2003, permission was refused.

(c) By telephone conversation Mr Arnold, the Managing Director of the Defendants, informed Mr Oliver Din of the Claimants that he would nevertheless satisfy the order from HappiSound.

5. In the premises, the Defendants threaten and intend unless restrained by injunction to sell Deepdin hi-fi equipment to HappiSound SA in breach of contract.
6. In the alternative, the Claimants will suffer loss and damage.

PARTICULARS

Full particulars will be provided in due course.

7. Further the Claimants claim interest on the amount found due to them pursuant to section 35A of the Supreme Court Act 1981 and/or the inherent jurisdiction of the Court.

AND the Claimants claim:

(1) An Order that the Defendants be restrained from exporting Deepdin hi-fi products.

(2) Alternatively, damages.

(3) Interest.

LOUDON PROWD

[statement of truth omitted]

SERVED this 5th day of June 2003 by BROWNING LLOYD of Lincoln's Inn, Solicitors for the Claimants.

7.8.4.3 Suggested Opinion

This is a draft Opinion, very much in the style of a first draft. It is intended to start you thinking about the structure of such an Opinion (not very different from those on many other, more familiar, areas of law). Also, it should show some of the issues that a client will need advice on, together with the identification of some gaps or ambiguities that will need to be resolved through a conference with the client.

DEEPDIN UK LIMITED v ARNOLD'S WORLD OF SOUND LIMITED

DRAFT OPINION

1. [Introductory paragraph, setting out who is represented, the contract and the basic allegations made by Deepdin in its S/C.]

2. [Again, probably just setting out the issues on which advice is being sought/given]
   - generally
   - whether a complaint should be made to the EC Commission
   - steps to take re (i) any complaint and (ii) the H/C proceedings.

3. [Perhaps a summary of the advice and/or steps to be taken]
   - Deepdin should get NO injunction and NO damages because there has been no breach of a contract term. Cl. 2(11) is void as an export ban, prohibited by Article 81(1).
   - Counterclaim for a declaration that the contract is void, by virtue of Article 81(1) and (2). Severance of the offending clause is not being sought [although query whether it might be so sought by Deepdin in any Reply]. Damages might be counterclaimed for the lost deal with HappiSound SA but we would need to check if the deal had actually fallen through. There is also a possible problem about *ex turpi causa* re the damages — if we are a willing party to a prohibited contract.
   - A complaint to the EC Commission is unnecessary. The High Court has the power to declare Article 81(1) applicable and thus a contract clause void. In cases of doubt, reference should be made to the Notice on Cooperation between national courts and the Commission. The High Court proceedings may be stayed while advice is sought from the Commission.

- The block exemption 2790/99 on vertical agreements is inapplicable. Reason — [state very briefly, cross-refer to paragraph 5 for full detail].
- *De minimis* is not a problem [again, state why briefly, cross-refer to paragraph 8].
- The action brought by Deepdin may also be an abuse of a dominant position because we suggest the relevant product market is top-range, premium hi-fi equipment and they are one of the two biggest players in that market in the UK. However, much more information is needed on market structure (including the geographical market) before anything definite can be decided on Article 82.
- Steps to be taken are — [concise list, drawn from the body of the Opinion].

4. Article 81 [Good idea to use headings — helps to focus reader's attention; provides easy access later.] [Tick off the elements and evidence for an Article 81(1) allegation]

- Agreement between undertakings — as stated in the Particulars of Claim.
- Effect on trade between Member States — the deal between AWS and HappiSound SA in particular, and other price differentials disclosed by Terry Arnold's statement; this raises issues about intra-brand competition being stifled. We might also want to advance an argument over the foreclosure of AWS as a distributor of hi-fi equipment from other manufacturers and suppliers to make a point about inter-brand competition (taking our cue from the *Delimitis v Henninger Braü* case).
- Object or effect — export ban in Cl. 2(11) probably qualifies under both now. Would have been *object* initially but now, in light of the refusal by Deepdin to allow AWS to export, it is also *effect*.
- Restriction, etc of competition — maintaining price differentials between Member States, thwarting creation of single market, reference to French distributor in Deepdin's letter is a naked attempt to maintain a price structure for resales and prevent parallel imports.

  Price differentials between Member States *might* be explicable as the result of different national tastes or just higher transport costs to distant markets but the way Cl. 2(11) is set up (coupled with the reaction of Deepdin to such a request) shows that price-fixing and market protection is the objective.

  Cl. 2(11) operates in a similar fashion to so-called 'English' clauses, whereby a company (under the guise of offering a better deal to its customers) optimises its information about demand and is able to stifle intra-brand competition.

  Note that Cl. 1(iii) seeks to limit competition between the exclusive purchase network at the retail level but is silent on intra-network competition at the distribution/wholesale level.
- Some analysis of the rest of the contract might be expected. This is not necessary for the purpose of defending the action but may be very relevant if we try to persuade a judge at trial that the entire contract is void (because AWS want to get out of it). For example:
- Cl. 2(1) — the *term* of the agreement is 5 years (probably OK) and sets up the exclusive purchase which is *prima facie* anti-competitive, hence the need for a Block Exemption
- Cl. 2(6) — a non-competition clause. AWS may be unlikely to go into manufacturing but distribution is obviously its business. Likely to be OK as to do

otherwise would defeat the purpose of the contract; likewise, Cl. 2(3) re use of *best endeavours*. Both seem limited to the life of the contract.

- Cl. 2(7) — full-range forcing. May be seen as restrictive of competition but obviously serves the needs of the consumer. Condemnation depends on whether the rule of reason applies at the stage of Article 81(1) or only comes in at Article 81(3).
- Cl. 2(8) is a minimum quantity requirement. Allows Deepdin to predict future demands with greater certainty and make more efficient use of resources (thus keeping prices lower).
- Cl. 2(8) — displaying supplier's trademark is probably not anti-competitive. Query silence of the clause regarding identification of AWS on the products. Cf. the Block Exemption on technology transfer (240/96).
- Cl. 2(10) — probably not anti-competitive. Smacks of selective distribution but no problem regarding 'tying' as customers are not obligated to enter a service/installation agreement or necessarily make use of such services from AWS after purchase.

5. The Block Exemption on Vertical Agreements — Regulation 2790/99

[In dealing with the application of the relevant block exemption in your Opinion, you should show a thorough knowledge of the regulation and how to use it. Reference has already been made above and will not be repeated here. You may want to show a similar structure. It is important to remember, though, that you cannot base an argument for infringement solely on the ground that an agreement does not come within the protection of a block exemption. No agreement was ever prohibited by Article 81(1) just because it was outside a block exemption; the argument for infringement has still to be made out.]

6. Individual exemption

[You should consider whether Deepdin has an individual exemption already; or would get one if it applied now. Both seem unlikely but it might be wise to ask AWS what they know of this; also, perhaps, approach the Commission. Deepdin may have gone through a notification before AWS entered this contract (which appears to be a standard form agreement).]

7. Article 82

[You may want to say something about abusive behaviour in this Opinion. I don't think it would be prudent to just skip over it and say nothing, based on what you currently know. It may be one of the implicit points that the instructions raise, so make a note to ask questions (in interview or in writing) in terms of seeking any further information which may be relevant. Initially, you would want to determine whether you could run an argument that Deepdin holds a dominant position. So the information you seek might include definition of the relevant product market, the structure of the market (eg does Deepdin's 8% of the whole UK hi-fi market translate into something more like a dominating market share if we use a more refined definition?).]

8. Remedies

[You should deal with the application of Article 81(1); also the fact that application of Article 81(3) to this contract is unlikely. It is void, subject to any severance. Severance should be dealt with because Deepdin are almost certainly going to raise it in any Reply and Defence to Counterclaim. I think severance is a possibility here. It might be worth pointing out to AWS that, if everything goes according to plan and Deepdin's attempt to compartmentalise the market and discriminate on prices is prohibited, the export market may lose the value that it currently has for AWS because the price differentials may fall or even disappear.]

The fact that the contract is void constitutes a defence to the action. A declaration to this effect in a counterclaim would allow AWS to walk away from it, as they wish, subject to severance. In any event, the fact that Cl. 2(11) is void also provides a good defence to the action.

Damages may be sought, if any have been sustained, probably via the lost HappiSound SA deal, but AWS should be asked for details of other export deals that have not been taken. Also, any projections or estimates about future earnings from developing an export market. A note of caution should be sounded on the likelihood of actually getting an award of damages.

9. *De minimis*

[You should consider this but I don't think there is a definite answer available on the information you have. Market share looks to be above the threshold in the Notice on Agreements of Minor Importance. If the market is defined as expensive, top-quality hi-fis, then market share is probably in excess of 10% anyway. There is a lack of information on turnover — this gap needs to be filled. You can show a practical approach in your Opinion through suggestions as to how this information may be acquired.]

Tentatively, if market definition goes the way we want, then Deepdin's market share will prevent this agreement falling through the net. Figures for Deepdin's turnover should be sought — through company reports, surveys by merchant banks, MMC reports on the industry, etc We also want to know the turnover figures for AWS: ask Mr Arnold.

10. Complaint to the Commission

[You should decide whether this offers any benefits to AWS. One benefit might be the investigative powers of the Commission and its expertise. Also, the low cost to AWS of making a complaint. However, the information which the Commission gets will not be available to the parties in *Deepdin v AWS* (see case-law of the ECJ), any fine will not go to AWS and no damages will be awarded by the Commission. In any event, the High Court claim needs to be defended. I can't see any great benefit to be got from complaining but it wouldn't hurt AWS. It may be that any findings of fact which the Commission made against Deepdin would be treated as conclusive evidence in the High Court proceedings but that would be a long time coming (see *Iberian UK v BPB Industries*). A complaint (or the threat thereof) may be a bargaining chip to use in the High Court action, against Deepdin.]

11. Steps to be taken regarding the High Court action

[Serve the enclosed Defence and Counterclaim. Seek information re lost deals from AWS. Seek information re market share of Deepdin from AWS and other sources. Advise AWS of the need to commission a report from an expert on the relevant market, unless one exists already that you can use. Any other questions that you want answers to? If so, specify what they are and, if you can, who to ask.]

Signed by counsel

7.8.5 Example for a defence and counterclaim

What follows is a first draft for this pleading, based purely on the information supplied in the instructions to counsel in **7.8.4.2**. It simply shows one way in which the material averments might be set out. It is quite acceptable (although not used here) for sub-headings to be used, within the heading of 'Particulars of infringement', to divide up the allegations into the following categories:

- restrictive clauses in the exclusive purchase agreement;
- restriction of competition within the common market;
- effect on trade between Member States.

Comments have been added in square brackets to explain why certain things have been said or appear where they do. Obviously, these would not appear on the real thing.

IN THE HIGH COURT OF JUSTICE — Claim No: 2003 HC 3217

QUEEN'S BENCH DIVISION

BETWEEN

DEEPDIN UK LIMITED — Claimant/Part 20 Defendants

and

ARNOLD'S WORLD OF SOUND LIMITED — Defendants/Part 20 Claimants

DEFENCE AND COUNTERCLAIM

DEFENCE

1. Paragraphs 1 and 2 of the Particulars of Claim are admitted. In particular, the Claimants have carried on business as manufacturers and suppliers of high quality hi-fi equipment which retails in the premium price ranges. At all material times, the Claimants maintained a network of such exclusive purchasers in the Member States of the European Union, in particular in France. The agreement was in the standard form used by the Claimants in all such agreements for the exclusive purchase of their products.

[*This is important to put in as we need to persuade the judge of a 'network effect' regarding any restriction on competition. It cannot be just Deepdin and AWS as this will be economically insignificant. Cf. the Delimitis case. We will need to try and check that this is a standard form contract. We also need to make a start on defining the relevant market with more precision.*]

2. Paragraph 3 of the Particulars of Claim is admitted, except that the term, namely Clause 2(11), is prohibited and void by virtue of Article 81(1) and (2) of the Treaty of Rome.

PARTICULARS OF BREACH OF ARTICLE 81, EC TREATY

(a) the contract between the Claimants and the Defendants is an agreement between undertakings;

(b) clause 2(11) has as its object the restriction, prevention or distortion of competition within the common market in that its aim is to prevent the Defendants from fulfilling orders placed by customers in other Member States, at prices lower than those offered by the Claimants to such customers;

(c) clause 2(11) has the effect of preventing, restricting or distorting competition within the common market since the Claimants have relied on this clause to stop the Defendants from fulfilling an order from an undertaking situated in another Member State, without good reason;

(d) in the absence of clause 2(11), the Defendants would seek to export the goods which are the subject-matter of the contract to customers situated in other Member States.

[*I think it is important to set out the particulars which rebut the cause of action here, in the Defence; however, some people would simply cross-refer to the salient paragraph in the Counterclaim.*]

3. Clause 2(11) of the contract restricts competition in a manner which is not exempted by the Block Exemption for vertical agreements, Regulation 2790/99 of the European Commission. In consequence thereof, the contract does not benefit from the Block Exemption at all.

[*Strictly speaking, we don't need to mention the Block Exemption in the Defence, we could wait and see if the Claimant tries to rely on it in any Reply. But I think it may help to make the defence seem stronger, at least in the mind of the Claimant.*]

4. Paragraphs 4 and 5 of the Particulars of Claim are admitted, except that it is denied that the actions of the Defendants were, are or will be in breach of the contract for the reasons set out above.

[*Basically, we agree that the Particulars of Claim accurately represent what we want(ed) to do but it is not a breach of contract to do so.*]

5. Paragraph 6 of the Particulars of Claim is not admitted.

[*What else can be said here? We have no details of the alleged loss. In any event, what loss could Deepdin suffer? Either it sells 100 units of the Triple X system to HappiSound SA through its French distributor or through AWS.*]

6. [*Plead counterclaim as a set-off. Standard form paragraph.*]

COUNTERCLAIM

7. The Defendants repeat paragraphs 1–5 of the Defence to this action.

[*These paragraphs are equally relevant to the claim we want to make for AWS against Deepdin.*]

8. Further or in the alternative, the following clauses of the contract are prohibited and void, by virtue of the operation of Article 81(1) and (2).

PARTICULARS OF BREACH OF ARTICLE 81, EC TREATY

(a) clause 2(1) obliges the Defendants for the duration of the contract, namely five years, to purchase all hi-fi products to be sold in their business from the Claimants;

(b) clause 2(6) obliges the Defendants not to compete with the Claimants through the manufacture or distribution of hi-fi products;

(c) clause 2(7) obliges the Defendants to purchase hi-fi products from across the Claimants' complete range;

(d) clause 2(8) obliges the Defendants to purchase a minimum quantity of the Claimants' products, namely to the value £100,000, within the term of the contract;

(e) the specified clauses had as their object, the prevention, restriction or distortion of competition within the common market;

(f) in all the circumstances, other manufacturers and distributors of branded, high quality hi-fi equipment were prevented from selling their products to the Defendants and to all such dealers within the Claimants' network. Such manufacturers and distributors are based both in the United Kingdom and elsewhere within the common market.

[*Here, we are specifying the other anti-competitive clauses, in the hope that the number of them will help us to make out the argument that the whole contract is void and severance is impractical. The consequences of such clauses, which are largely concerned with denying access to the market to Deepdin's competitors, are also alluded to, as is the possible effect on inter-State trade.*]

9. In the premises, the contract between the Claimants and the Defendants is prohibited and void in its entirety.

10. By reason of the unlawful actions of the Claimants, namely the insertion of clause 2(11) into the contract and the subsequent refusal of the Claimants to consent to the sale by the Defendants of hi-fi products to a French company, HappiSound SA, the Defendants have suffered loss and damage.

PARTICULARS OF LOSS AND DAMAGE

(a) sale of 100 units of the CD Deepdin Triple X system to HappiSound SA

Cost per unit to the Defendants	£850
Sale price per unit	£1,100
Total Profit	£15,000

(b) [maybe details of any other potential sales lost in consequence of C's attitude?]

[*Particulars need to be given of any loss for which we seek damages. We could get away with 'Full particulars will be supplied in due course' but as we have some specific information now, we may as well provide it.*]

11. Further the Defendants claim interest on the amounts found due to them pursuant to section 35A of the Supreme Court Act 1981 and/or the inherent jurisdiction of the Court.

AND the Defendants counterclaim:

(1) A Declaration that the contract between the Defendants and the Claimants is prohibited and void, and that the Defendants are no longer bound by it.

(2) Damages.

(3) Interest.

WATSON EARDRUM

[statement of truth omitted]

DATED etc

7.9 Remedies

7.9.1 Damages

Damages are often a remedy desired by clients. That they should be available to compensate those harmed by an infringement of the EC competition rules seems almost beyond doubt. Regarding English courts, you can rely on the speech of Lord Diplock in *Garden Cottage Foods*; this dealt explicitly with the notion that damages were a remedy available for the 'victim' of an abuse of a dominant position, pursuant to Article 82 (ex 86). As for the European Court, cases such as *Brasserie du Pêcheur v Germany* (C-46/93) [1996] ECR I-1029 can clearly be read as recognising the right of individuals to recover damages against other individuals (and not just Member States) for breaches of Community law. The view of the Commission is set out in the Notice it issued in 1993 on cooperation between itself and the national courts:

> [I]t is the right of parties subject to Community law that national courts should take provisional measures, that an effective end should be brought, by injunction, to the infringement of Community competition rules of which they are victims, and that *compensation should be awarded for the damage suffered as a result of infringements, where such remedies are available in proceedings relating to similar national law.*

(Paragraph 11 of the Notice, OJ 1993 C38/6)

One further possible obstacle to an award of damages arises in Article 81 (ex 85) cases: namely, where both claimant and defendant are parties to the agreement which, it is alleged, infringes Article 81(1) (ex 85(1)). When one party alleges that the contract is prohibited and void, it can be a little difficult to see why one party to a void contract should have to compensate the other and, indeed, why one of them should be seen as the victim of the other's infringement; after all, Article 81 (ex 85) hits at collusive anti-competitive behaviour. This 'obstacle' was considered by the Court of Appeal in *Gibbs Mew v Gemmell* [1999] 1 EG 117.

Gibbs Mew was a case about a pub. The brewer sued for possession and damages when the tenant fell into arrears with his rent. The tenant defended the claim and counterclaimed with allegations that the beer tie in the lease offended against Article 81(1) (ex 85(1)). The tenant argued that he was entitled to claim damages and set them off against the unpaid rent. The Court of Appeal found against the tenant — the claimant brewing company had such a small market share as to exclude the agreement from the operation of Article 81(1) (ex 85(1)) on the ground of *de minimis*. That much was uncontentious. Three further points were contained in the Court's judgment, though.

First, the Court of Appeal held that the block exemption regulation on beer ties, Regulation 1984/83, should be interpreted in a manner contrary to that set out by the Commission in its guidance on the regulation, issued in 1984. The Court of Appeal justified this on the (correct) basis that the notice was only persuasive and not binding upon national courts. In law, this analysis cannot be argued with, but it does fly in the face of the purposive interpretation of EC law which has long been the hallmark of the European Court. The relevant issue in the case is relatively insignificant (whether specifying tied beers by type rather than by brand or denomination prevented application of the block exemption) but this seemed to be an uncontentious issue, accepted by those who had to work with the block exemption, and the decision of this Court of Appeal is perhaps unlikely to accord with decisions of other national courts on the point. The Court refused leave to appeal to the House of Lords and also refused to make a preliminary reference to the European Court. Leave to appeal was subsequently also refused by the House of Lords.

Secondly, the Court of Appeal determined the 'obstacle' point raised above, namely, whether a party to a contract can argue successfully that the contract (or clause within it) is prohibited and void and yet claim damages upon it. The Court of Appeal decided that breach of statutory duty did not apply on the facts; the tenant was simply claiming for damages or restitution, arising from an illegal agreement to which he was a party. English law did not permit damages to be recovered in such circumstances. Like the first point mentioned above, this decision could have been foreseen. It is important to note that the case did not turn upon Article 82 (ex 86), which does not necessarily rely upon collusive behaviour. One might object that the decision does not reflect the spirit behind Article 81(1) (ex 85(1)) and does little to encourage enforcement of the Article at a national level. However, most noteworthy is the final decision of the Court of Appeal in the case.

Thirdly, the Court held that it was inappropriate for the tenant to rely upon Article 81 (ex 85) to claim any remedy from the courts. The Article was intended to protect one's competitors, either actual or potential. All the parties to a prohibited agreement were 'the cause not the victims' of the anti-competitive behaviour and its consequences. This decision has huge significance for the ability of English courts to enforce the EC competition rules. Certainly, it seems to have put a stop to undertakings using Article 81 (ex 85) as the basis of a claim against their contract partners. Arguably, it still allows defensive use of Article 81 (ex 85), if one simply denies liability by relying on the unenforceability of the contract and does not seek any remedy as such. Most intriguingly, the judgment could be interpreted as an encouragement to competing undertakings to sue their fellows, alleging that an arrangement that the defendant company has with another, or others, is prohibited by Article 81(1) (ex 85(1)). This suggests a whole new cause of action, different from statutory duty, but it also raises some familiar obstacles to a successful claim. For example, opening the floodgates — how many of your competitors could sue your company? Also, how would the court quantify the losses? Would there be problems over issues such as remoteness and causation? It would be optimistic to think that the Court of Appeal was encouraging a new area of enforcement to open up, but it seems more likely that the effect of this judgment will be to diminish the chances of effective enforcement of Article 81 (ex 85) (at least) in England for some time to come.

One possible way around this problem had already been closed off — namely, that the three decisions taken in Gibbs Mew might come to be regarded as *obiter dicta*. That hope was dashed by a subsequent decision of the Court, in *Trent Taverns Ltd v Sykes* The Times, 5 March 1999. This case was decided on 22 January 1999, with similar facts to the *Gibbs Mew* case. A differently constituted Court held that the observations in *Gibbs Mew* were not *obiter*. The Court in *Trent Taverns* did consider that a preliminary reference might be helpful but declined to order one as the *Gibbs Mew* case was still pending before the House of Lords who might order a reference. In fact, as noted above, the House of Lords did not order a preliminary reference when they rejected an application for leave to appeal.

Finally, a preliminary reference was made in another 'pub' case, *Courage Ltd v Crehan* [2001] All ER (EC) 886. The Court of Justice decided that (para 26–36):

> The full effectiveness of Article 85 of the Treaty and, in particular, the practical effect of the prohibition laid down in Article 85(1) would be put at risk if it were not open to any individual to claim damages for loss caused to him by a contract or by conduct liable to restrict or distort competition.
>
> ... actions for damages before the national courts can make a significant contribution to the maintenance of effective competition in the Community.
>
> There should not therefore be any absolute bar to such an action being brought by a party to a contract which would be held to violate the competition rules.

However, in the absence of Community rules governing the matter, it is for the domestic legal system of each Member State to designate the courts and tribunals having jurisdiction and to lay down the detailed procedural rules governing actions for safeguarding rights which individuals derive directly from Community law, provided that such rules are not less favourable than those governing similar domestic actions (principle of equivalence) and that they do not render practically impossible or excessively difficult the exercise of rights conferred by Community law (principle of effectiveness) (see *Palmisani* (C-261/95) [1997] ECR I-4025, para 27).

In that regard, the Court has held that Community law does not prevent national courts from taking steps to ensure that the protection of the rights guaranteed by Community law does not entail the unjust enrichment of those who enjoy them (see, in particular *Ireks-Arkady v Council and Commission* (238/78) [1979] ECR 2955, para 14, *Just* (68/79) [1980] ECR 501, para 26, and *Michaïlidis* (Joined Cases C-441/98 and C-442/98) [2000] ECR I-7145, para 31).

Similarly, provided that the principles of equivalence and effectiveness are respected (see *Palmisani*, cited above, para 27), Community law does not preclude national law from denying a party who is found to bear significant responsibility for the distortion of competition the right to obtain damages from the other contracting party. Under a principle which is recognised in most of the legal systems of the Member States and which the Court has applied in the past (see *Commission v Italy* (39/72) [1973] ECR 101, para 10), a litigant should not profit from his own unlawful conduct, where this is proven.

In that regard, the matters to be taken into account by the competent national court include the economic and legal context in which the parties find themselves and, as the United Kingdom Government rightly points out, the respective bargaining power and conduct of the two parties to the contract. In particular, it is for the national court to ascertain whether the party who claims to have suffered loss through concluding a contract that is liable to restrict or distort competition found himself in a markedly weaker position than the other party, such as seriously to compromise or even eliminate his freedom to negotiate the terms of the contract and his capacity to avoid the loss or reduce its extent, in particular by availing himself in good time of all the legal remedies available to him.

Referring to the judgments in *Brasserie de Haecht* (23/67) [1967] ECR 127 and *Delimitis* (C-234/89) [1991] ECR I-935, para 14 to 26, the Commission and the United Kingdom Government also rightly point out that a contract might prove to be contrary to Article 85(1) of the Treaty for the sole reason that it is part of a network of similar contracts which have a cumulative effect on competition. In such a case, the party contracting with the person controlling the network cannot bear significant responsibility for the breach of Article 85, particularly where in practice the terms of the contract were imposed on him by the party controlling the network.

Contrary to the submission of Courage, making a distinction as to the extent of the parties' liability does not conflict with the case-law of the Court to the effect that it does not matter, for the purposes of the application of Article 85 of the Treaty, whether the parties to an agreement are on an equal footing as regards their economic position and function (see *inter alia Consten and Grundig v Commission* (Joined Cases 56/64 and 58/64) [1966] ECR 382). That case-law concerns the conditions for application of Article 85 of the Treaty while the questions put before the Court in the present case concern certain consequences in civil law of a breach of that provision.

Having regard to all the foregoing considerations, the questions referred are to be answered as follows:

- a party to a contract liable to restrict or distort competition within the meaning of Article 85 of the Treaty can rely on the breach of that Article to obtain relief from the other contracting party;
- Article 85 of the Treaty precludes a rule of national law under which a party to a contract liable to restrict or distort competition within the meaning of that provision is barred from claiming damages for loss caused by performance of that contract on the sole ground that the claimant is a party to that contract;
- Community law does not preclude a rule of national law barring a party to a contract liable to restrict or distort competition from relying on his own unlawful actions to obtain damages where it is established that that party bears significant responsibility for the distortion of competition.

That would appear to sound the death knell for the *Gibbs Mew* judgment.

7.9.2 Injunctions

English courts can grant injunctions, both interim and final, in cases concerning breaches of EC law. In *Garden Cottage Foods v Milk Marketing Board* [1984] AC 130, the House of Lords refused to grant an interlocutory injunction to the plaintiff (now 'claimant'), who alleged a breach of Article 86 (now 82) by the defendant. The reason for the refusal was not that there was no jurisdiction to grant the order but that damages were available as a remedy for the plaintiff at trial and would be an adequate remedy for the plaintiff. Therefore, on straightforward principles (see *American Cyanamid Co v Ethicon Ltd* [1975] AC 396), the application was rejected. Conversely, in *Cutsforth v Mansfield Inns Ltd* [1986] 1 WLR 558, an interlocutory injunction was sought by a firm which supplied fruit machines to several pubs, ultimately owned by the defendant brewery. The brewery, on recently taking over the pubs, had told its tenants that they must take fruit machines only from a list of specified suppliers, which did not include the plaintiffs. The judge was explicit in stating that the question of whether to grant the application had to be considered in the light of the principles laid down in *American Cyanamid*. Recognising that damages were available as a remedy, and that the defendant brewery could afford to pay them, the judge nevertheless found that 'damages would not be an adequate remedy for the plaintiffs because the denial of interim relief would virtually put an end to [their] business' and granted the application.

It must be remembered that if the applicant fails to demonstrate a 'serious question to be tried' (namely, some sort of prima facie case that the respondent has infringed the EC competition rules), no interim injunction will be granted. Thus, the plaintiffs failed in *Cutsforth* under Article 86 (now 82) when the judge held that the area of the North of England covered by the defendant's pubs was not a 'substantial part of the common market'; fortunately for the plaintiffs, the judge was persuaded that there was a serious question to be tried under Article 85 (now 81).

Lastly, on the subject, we should note the ground-breaking impact of the *Factortame* litigation. In particular, the ruling of the Court of Justice that the enforcement of a British Act of Parliament could be suspended by means of an interim injunction notwithstanding the long-settled British rule which prohibited such relief. See *R v Secretary of State for Transport, ex p Factortame* (C-213/89) [1990] ECR I-2433.

7.9.3 Declarations

7.9.3.1 The agreement is valid

A declaration is perhaps of most use where the party relying upon EC competition law is a party to a contract, and wishes that contract to continue, notwithstanding that one or more clauses in the contract are void for infringement of Article 81(1) (ex 85(1)) or 82 (ex 86). An application for severance will normally accompany a declaration in such circumstances. If the claimant and defendant are in a customer-supplier relationship, it may be that the claimant/customer does not want a complete termination of dealings. An award of damages might antagonise the defendant/supplier, who may have considerably more bargaining power than the claimant; whereas a simple declaration is merely 'an authoritative statement of the relevant legal position on which the parties can base their future actions' (D. Harris, *Remedies in Contract and Tort*, Weidenfeld & Nicolson, 1988).

7.9.3.2 The agreement is void

In *Passmore v Morland plc* [1998] 4 All ER 468, Laddie J held that an agreement could move into and out of nullity, as it fell within Article 81(1) (ex 85(1)) and then without it. He based this decision on the need to undertake an economic assessment of the circumstances prior to deciding whether the agreement was anti-competitive or not. If the circumstances changed, then so might the enforceability of the agreement.

On the facts of *Passmore*, the original lessor of the pub was Inntrepreneur Beer Supply Ltd. Its share of the UK retail beer market was such in 1991 that the exclusive beer purchase obligation in the lease might have contributed to a foreclosure of the market, ie, be anti-competitive. This point was conceded by the defence, for the purposes only of the hearing. However, in 1992 Inntrepreneur assigned its interests in the lease to Morland plc. Morland is a small company and again it was conceded, for the purpose of the hearing, that an agreement between the tenant and Morland would not infringe Article 81(1) (ex 85(1)) because the size of Morland's tied estate is such that it does not contribute significantly to foreclosure of the market. The pub tenant argued that, if the lease was prohibited by Article 81 (ex 85) in the hands of Inntrepreneur, it was void *ab initio* and could not be assigned to anyone. In 1998, the tenant sued Morland and Inntrepreneur, seeking damages, restitution and a declaration that the beer tie was ineffective.

It should be noted that this was not an agreement whose 'object' was anti-competitive. It was alleged only that it had anti-competitive effects. The main argument for the tenant was that once an agreement fell foul of Article 81 (ex 85), it could have no further 'life' and would be void, unenforceable. For an agreement with an anti-competitive 'object', it would be null from its inception but other agreements would become void only once their 'effects' became anti-competitive (which would be a question of fact in each case). The tenant argued that once an agreement has anti-competitive effects, it becomes void 'as if a guillotine comes down and it does not revive subsequently'.

Counsel for the tenant relied upon a quote from the European Court of Justice (in *Société de Vente de Ciments et Bétons de l'Est SA v Kerpen & Kerpen GmbH & Co KG* (319/82) [1983] ECR 4173), where the Court said that an agreement which is prohibited under Article 81(1) (ex 85(1)) is void and 'the nullity is absolute'. On the other hand, Morland plc argued that 'the statutory prohibition in Article [81] operates periodically, ie, it can be turned on and off depending on the surrounding facts'. This argument was the one favoured by Laddie J. The agreement may have been void in the hands of Inntrepreneur but that ceased to be so once Inntrepreneur assigned the lease to Morland plc; thus, the beer tie was not currently unenforceable. The tenant's claim against Morland was struck out. *Passmore* was applied subsequently, in another pub case heard in the Chancery Division, in *Inntrepreneur Pub Co (CPC) Ltd v Price* The Times, 4 December 1998.

This issue clearly calls for an interpretation of Article 81(2) (ex 85(2)), but no preliminary reference was made in either *Passmore* or *Price*; nor was any advice sought from the Commission under the 1993 cooperation guidelines. In passing, one might note the view of the Commission on the matter, expressed most recently in its White Paper on Modernisation, published in April 1999. When introducing the notion of 'restrictive practices', the Commission ventured that 'such practices are void *ab initio*', that is, from the start. In the same White Paper, the Commission is concerned about what might happen to consistency of interpretation, if and when the application of Articles 81 (ex 85) and 82 (ex 86) is 'decentralised' (ie, the burden of enforcement is transferred to the national bodies from the Commission). It notes that to achieve consistency and to lend support, mechanisms would need to be set up for cooperation between the courts and the Commission. For example, national courts could be obliged to inform the Commission of any cases involving Articles 81 (ex 85) and 82 (ex 86):

> so that it is made aware of any problems of textual interpretation or lacunae in the legislative framework ... The Commission should also be allowed, subject to the leave of the court, to intervene in judicial proceedings that come to its attention as a result ... Allowing it intervene as *amicus curiae* would be an effective way of helping to maintain consistency in the application of the law.

At the time of writing, there still has not been a preliminary reference specifically on the point of nullity. However, in *Courage Ltd v Crehan* (C-453/99) [2001] All ER (EC) 886, the Court of Justice stated that:

> Since the nullity referred to in Article 85(2) is absolute, an agreement which is null and void by virtue of this provision has no effect as between the contracting parties and cannot be set up against third parties (see the judgment in *Béguelin v SAGL Import Export* (22/71) [1971] ECR 949, para 29). Moreover, it is capable of having a bearing on all the effects, either past or future, of the agreement or decision concerned (see the judgment in *Brasserie de Haecht v Wilkin II* (48/72) [1973] ECR 77, para 26).

Unfortunately, this is still rather ambiguous and further clarification is awaited.

7.10 Cooperation between national courts and the Commission

Some English courts have taken to the notion of cooperation with some enthusiasm. It has been held, albeit at first instance in the Chancery Division, that where the Commission has made findings of fact in a procedure in which the claimant and defendant participated, then those findings are conclusive evidence (and not merely admissible) in subsequent proceedings before the English court. See Laddie J in *Iberian UK Ltd v BPB Industries plc* [1996] 2 CMLR 601. The reason for this is given as the need for legal certainty and the desire to avoid reaching decisions which conflict; the same principle applied to findings by the Court of First Instance and the Court of Justice in competition proceedings. Certainly, one can see the sense in this, as both parties will have had a right to be heard during the Commission procedure under Regulation 1 and, if dissatisfied with the outcome, could (and perhaps did) appeal to the European Court. As Laddie J said:

> [I]t would be contrary to public policy to allow persons who have been involved in competition proceedings in Europe to deny here the correctness of the conclusions reached there.

This was only a decision at first instance, though, and one should be a little cautious before relying too heavily on it. It does seem safe to regard the Commission's findings of fact as *admissible* evidence but beyond that, one must bear in mind other, earlier, first instance decisions which appear to contradict Laddie J. One example is *Merson v Rover Group*, 22 May 1992, unreported (distinguished by Laddie J), where the judge held he was not bound by findings of fact from the European Court of Justice that the defendant company had infringed Article 86 (now 82). The defendant denied there had been an Article 86 (now 82) abuse and the judge refused an application for summary judgment, finding the defendant's present position did not constitute an abuse of the process of the court. One could assume that this judge would have been equally dismissive of any decision from the Commission.

The Commission takes a rather humble position on the subject. It issued a Notice on Cooperation in 1993 (OJ 1993 C39/6) in which it declared that, before a national court decides the question of whether there is an infringement of Article 81(1) (ex 85(1)) or 82 (ex 86), it should first find out if the alleged infringement has been considered already by the Commission. It may be that the Commission has already issued:

> a decision, opinion or other official statement ... Such statements provide national courts with significant information for reaching a judgment, even if they are not formally bound by them (paragraph 20).

It is worth noting that the Notice goes on to distinguish cases which have been closed with a formal decision and those where a comfort letter is used. Recognising that such letters do not bind national courts, the Commission continued:

> the Court of Justice has ... stated that the opinion expressed by the Commission constitutes a factor which the national courts may take into account in examining whether the agreements or conduct in question are in accordance with the provisions of Article 85 [now 81].

There seems no reason why this should not apply also to comfort letters dealing with Article 82 (ex 86).

More generally, the Notice observes that, while the power to grant an exemption under Article 81(3) (ex 85(3)) is exclusively within the competence of the Commission, with that exception the Commission and national courts have concurrent powers to apply Article 81(1) (ex 85(1)) and Article 82 (ex 86). The Commission is keen to encourage national courts to deal with such matters themselves, invoking the notion of subsidiarity and encouraging would-be complainants to turn instead to the appropriate national court:

> The Commission intends ... to concentrate on notifications, complaints and own-initiative proceedings [which have] particular political, economic or legal significance for the Community. Where these features are absent in a particular case, notifications will normally be dealt with by means of a comfort letter and complaints should, as a rule, be handled by national courts or authorities.
>
> The Commission considers that there is not normally a sufficient Community interest in examining a case when the [complainant] is able to secure adequate protection of his rights before the national courts. In these circumstances the complaint will normally be filed (paragraphs 14, 15 of the Notice).

It is important to avoid the possibility of conflicting decisions being reached by the national court and the Commission on the same facts. One way to this has been mentioned already — checking whether the Commission has already reached a decision (formal or informal) on the subject-matter (paragraph 20 of the Notice). If no such decision has been reached but the Commission has started a procedure under Regulation 1/2003, the court can choose to go ahead and rule on the existence of an infringement itself or stay the proceedings to await the decision of the Commission. Where a case is stayed for this reason, the Commission will try to 'fast-track' it (see Commission Notice, paragraph 37).

An example of a situation where a court might decide to stay proceedings is where:

- it felt that Article 81(1) (ex 85(1)) was infringed; but that
- an exemption was probably merited under Article 81(3) (ex 85(3)); and
- the agreement has been properly notified to the Commission.

In the absence of proper notification to the Commission, no exemption would be possible in this example and the national court should simply rule the agreement void, pursuant to Article 81(2) (ex 85(2)). Similarly, if the court felt that the agreement could not be granted an exemption, a stay would be unnecessary.

If the agreement was one which fell within the scope of a block exemption, then that could be applied by the national court (regardless of any notification) and a stay would be unnecessary. In cases of complexity, where the application of Article 81(1) (ex 85(1)) or Article 82 (ex 86) 'gives rise to legal or economic difficulties', a court can make a preliminary reference to the Court of Justice, seeking its opinion, or seek assistance from the Commission. The latter possibility represents a novel opportunity for English courts (which has been taken on at least one occasion already; see the Commission's XXIVth Report on Competition Policy 1994). Assistance is offered, initially, through the block exemptions and notices issued by the Commission; also, a court could refer to previous published decisions of the Commission and its annual reports on competition policy. If these are inadequate then a court can, 'within the limits of [its] national procedural law', seek information from the Commission. Three types of information are offered:

- Procedural information about the case, eg has there been a notification? Has the Commission sent a comfort letter? How long will it take the Commission to decide on an exemption?
- Legal advice, eg what are the criteria for determining whether a restriction on competition is appreciable or not? In such cases, the Commission is not concerned with the facts, or merits, of the particular case but the court may also ask for an interim opinion on whether an agreement is likely to get exemption under Article 81(3) (ex 85(3)). In that situation, the Commission will look at the circumstances of the case in question. The national court retains the right to seek a preliminary ruling from the European Court under Article 234 (ex 177), EC Treaty.
- Factual information, specifically 'statistics, market studies and economic analyses'. This is subject to the Commission actually having the information in its possession and compliance with the rules on confidentiality (see Article 287 (ex 214), EC Treaty; Article 28, Regulation 1/2003).

7.11 Actions against a Member State

Private litigants have brought actions against Member States on several occasions. Sometimes the individual is a national of that State (eg *Francovich and others v Italian Republic* (C-6/90 and 9/90) [1991] ECR I-5357), on other occasions the claimant is a foreign national (eg the *Factortame* cases in the UK, eg *R v Secretary of State for Transport, ex p Factortame Ltd (No 4)* [1986] 2 WLR 506). All Member States of the European Union are under an enforceable obligation to abide by the EC Treaty and implement such measures, as they are required to, as part of their national laws (cf Article 226 (ex 169) (and see further **8.6**), EC Treaty which empowers the Commission to take enforcement action in the European Court). Failure to act on the part of the Member State may result in liability; similarly, acting in contradiction of EC law may result in liability. In addition to the remedies of a declaration of the correct legal position, or the implementation of amending legislation, the successful private claimant may also claim damages from the Member State to compensate for losses suffered.

8

Cases involving the competition rules in the European Court

8.1 Introduction

There are several different procedures which can be used in order to seek some form of redress from the European Court. Some are 'direct' actions, others are 'indirect'. Usually, the initial venue for EC-level litigation will be the Court of First Instance (which has been in existence only since 1989). From there, appeal lies to the European Court of Justice but only on matters of law and only insofar as the Court of First Instance has erred; the Court of Justice is not concerned with examining factual arguments which have already had two airings, once before the Commission and again in the Court of First Instance. A private litigant (a natural or legal person) will by-pass the Court of First Instance and go straight to the Court of Justice in only one situation — on a preliminary reference under Article 234 (ex 177), EC Treaty. This might make it seem that the Article 234 (ex 177) reference is the 'direct' action referred to earlier but this is not correct. The Article 234 (ex 177) reference is an interlocutory step in other litigation; that litigation is a proceeding in a court or tribunal of a Member State and will continue after the preliminary ruling of the Court of Justice. So, it is the preliminary reference under Article 234 (ex 177) by a national court or tribunal which is the 'indirect' action; the other forms of procedure dealt with in this chapter are 'direct' actions, so-called because they start and end in the European Court.

Chapter 7 looked at the ways in which private litigants might use the EC competition rules in the courts of the Member States. Such litigation may be brought against a fellow private individual or against a Member State. No doubt, there have been many cases where a dissatisfied litigant has left the court, feeling that the judge did not understand the law as it applied to their case. If their lawyer could have persuaded the judge that he or she did not understand the EC law point argued in the case, then the court might have made a preliminary reference so that the Court of Justice could give its ruling on the interpretation of the Treaty or the validity or interpretation of the acts of the EC institutions. Such a ruling might have helped to resolve the national litigation with a different outcome; on the other hand, it may not have changed the result even if it changed the way the result was arrived at. What the Court of Justice does on a preliminary ruling does not dispose of the issues in the domestic action, it merely clarifies them; the Court of Justice is not functioning as an appeal court in Article 234 (ex 177) proceedings.

What happens if an undertaking feels aggrieved at something which the Commission has done, or not done, in connection with these same rules? In other words, the target of the displeasure is not a fellow private individual, nor a Member State but is the European Commission. The European Court is given a supervisory role by Article 220 (ex 164), EC Treaty:

The Court of Justice shall ensure that in the interpretation and application of this Treaty the law is observed.

The two main procedures which are created by the Treaty to enable this supervisory role to be fulfilled are the action to annul (under Article 230 (ex 173), EC Treaty; **8.2**) and the action for a failure to act (under Article 232 (ex 175), EC Treaty; **8.3**).

All of these procedures will be examined briefly in the following sections of this chapter. Further detail should be sought in works such as Schermers and Waelbroeck, *Judicial Protection in the European Communities*, Kluwer, 1991; there are also many useful insights to be found in *Procedure and Enforcement in EC and US Competition Law*, edited by Slot and McDonnell, Sweet & Maxwell, 1993.

Note that there might be costs implications for a party using these procedures. As well as bearing one's own costs, an unsuccessful party may end up being ordered to pay the (successful) Commission's costs. See, for example, *International Express Carriers Conference v Commission* (C-449/98 P) [2001] ECR I-3875, an appeal from Court of First Instance to European Court of Justice; and *Roberts v Commission* (T-25/99) [2001] ECR II-1881, a case under Article 230.

8.2 Action to annul: Article 230

There are two basic hurdles which must be cleared by an applicant if the action to annul is to succeed. First, is the act or measure which the applicant seeks to have annulled one which is susceptible to annulment? Fortunately in competition matters, measures which directly affect individuals or undertakings usually emanate from the Commission (see eg Regulation 1/2003, Article 7, **Appendix 1**); acts of the Commission are reviewable. Further, does the act have any legal effect? If it is merely a preliminary or administrative measure which is simply advisory (like a report of the Hearing Officer) then it cannot be annulled.

The second hurdle is to establish a sufficient interest in the applicant to mount a challenge to the measure. Privileged parties (the Council, Commission and Member States) are assumed to have sufficient interest. Private applicants (natural or legal persons) must demonstrate an interest in the measure. In competition cases, they can usually do so as being the addressee of the measure (a decision finding an infringement of Article 81(1) (ex 85(1)), say, and imposing a fine) or as the complainant. Complainants have an almost automatic sufficient interest in the case generated by their complaint and should have no trouble showing that a decision (perhaps to close the Commission's file in a case) is of 'direct and individual concern' to them (cf *Metro SB-Grossmarkte v Commission* (26/76) [1977] ECR 1875).

There is a limitation period of two months, which usually runs from the date of publication of the measure. The safest course is to start proceedings as soon as the adverse decision is discovered by the applicant. The four grounds on which the act may be annulled are:

(a) Lack of competence (similar to *ultra vires* in English administrative law).

(b) Infringement of an essential procedural requirement (whether any particular procedural requirement will be seen as 'essential' is determined on a case-by-case approach; case-law precedent is a good guide but one example would be the suspect undertaking's right to be heard in a competition investigation).

(c) Infringement of the EC Treaty itself or a rule of law relating to its application (this might include a challenge to a Commission decision finding an infringement of Article 81(1) (ex 85(1)) on its merits, for example; or a general principle of law may be used, such as *proportionality*, to attack the amount of a fine in a competition case).

(d) Misuse of power (the motives of the institution or official responsible for the measure will be examined).

As the comments perhaps indicate, grounds (b) and (c) are those most often used by aggrieved parties in competition cases. In the event of success, the measure is annulled. That does not prevent the institution from having another go. So if an 'improved' repetition of the relevant procedure can cure the previous infringement of an essential procedural requirement, the same measure may be promulgated for a second time and the applicant has won the battle but still lost the war (cf the *Polypropylene Cartel* cases where decisions involving millions of ECU were annulled but then re-appeared with the complaint cured and the fines still as high as they had been in the first decision; see *Commission v BASF AG* (C-137/92P) [1994] ECR I-2555).

8.3 Failure to act: Article 232

This procedure is used to try to compel an EC institution (in competition cases, usually the Commission) to act. The applicant must therefore show the absence of an act, that the institution was under a duty to act and that this duty was to address an act to the applicant. The duty may be imposed on the institution either by the Treaty or under secondary legislation. Natural or legal persons may use Article 232 (ex 175). The applicant should write to the institution, requiring it to 'define its position' and giving it two months to do so. The court procedure under Article 232 (ex 175) can be launched in the absence of satisfactory action by the end of that two-month period. It should be noted that, in competition cases, a complainant cannot oblige the Commission to launch an investigation into their complaint. See *Automec srl v Commission* (T-24/90) [1992] ECR II-2223:

> Where a complaint has been submitted to the Commission under Article 3 of Regulation No 17, it is not bound either to give a decision on the existence of the alleged infringement unless the subject-matter of the complaint falls within its exclusive purview, as in the case of the withdrawal of an exemption granted under Article 85(3) [now 81(3)] of the Treaty, or to conduct an investigation.

8.4 Action for damages: Article 288(2)

This procedure can be found in Article 288(2) (ex 215(2)), EC Treaty and is used to determine the non-contractual liability of the EC. The EC is required to 'make good any damage caused by its institutions or by its servants in the performance of their duties'. To succeed in a claim, an applicant must satisfy four criteria.

(a) damage must have been suffered, usually by the applicant;

(b) a Community institution or its servants must have acted, or omitted to act, in the performance of its duties;

(c) there must be a causal connection between the act (or omission) and the damage;

(d) the act or omission must be 'wrongful', ie there must be an element of 'fault' involved.

See eg, *Campagnia Italiana Alcool SAS Di Mario Mariano & Co v Commission* (C-358/90) [1992] 2 CMLR 876. To date, this action has not been of particular use in connection with acts or omissions of the Commission in its application of the competition rules; it is rarely used and even more rarely successful.

8.5 Appeals from the Court of First Instance to the Court of Justice

As mentioned earlier, private litigants who use Articles 230 (ex 173) or 232 (ex 175) in competition cases will begin their claims in the Court of First Instance (CFI). An unsuccessful litigant may appeal to the Court of Justice. Such appeal is to be made within two months of the appellant being notified of the final decision of the CFI. One may also appeal against a decision of the CFI on preliminary issues, such as lack of competence or inadmissibility (see Article 49, Protocol on the Statute of the Court of Justice of the EEC). It must be noted that appeals to the Court of Justice are limited to points of law only. The Court of Justice is vigilant to dismiss appeals on the ground that they ask the Court to re-try issues of fact.

8.6 Compelling Member States to act

Member States are often under an obligation to act, pursuant to the EC Treaty. This may be in the context of implementing directives into national law, for example. An action may be brought against a Member State for its failure to act as required. The action is brought either by the Commission (under Article 226 (ex 169), EC Treaty) or another Member State (under Article 227 (ex 170), EC Treaty). Due to political sensitivities, the Commission invokes proceedings under Article 226 rarely and, perhaps to avoid casting the first stone, Article 227 is hardly ever used by Member States. These procedures are not open to natural or legal persons. However, such individuals may still obtain redress for damage suffered as the result of a Member State's failure to act. This has been established clearly by the preliminary rulings of the Court of Justice in *Francovich v Italy* and *Brasserie du Pêcheur*. If a Member State is under a duty to implement an EC measure into its national legal system and fails to do so by the appointed date, then anyone who suffers damage as the result of such non-implementation may bring an action against the State and the State will effectively be estopped from denying liability. This type of direct redress may prove to be more efficacious than the procedures provided in the Treaty for ensuring that the Member States fulfil their obligations.

8.7 Preliminary references: Article 234

A preliminary reference is sought at the instigation of a court or tribunal of a Member State in the course of domestic litigation. The reference may be sought by one or both parties to the litigation, or on the national court's own initiative, but only a judicial body can make the reference. The reference may be made prior to trial of a domestic claim, or afterwards as part of an appeal within the national legal system. An English lawyer will find rules governing preliminary references in RSC Ord 114 (which can still be found, in Sch 1 of the Civil Procedure Rules) and in the Criminal Appeal (References to the European Court) Rules 1972. The procedure has three stages:

(a) the national court makes the reference;

(b) the national proceedings are 'stayed', or suspended, until such time as the preliminary ruling is received from the Court of Justice;

(c) the national court applies EC law, as interpreted by the preliminary ruling, to the facts in the case and continues to judgment.

Important issues when considering asking a court to make a preliminary reference are:

- Is the national forum a court or tribunal of a Member State? This has been interpreted quite broadly so there should not usually be a problem.
- Does the national court have a discretion to refer or can it be compelled to do so? Only courts against whose decisions there is no judicial remedy must make a reference, all others have a discretion.
- Is a preliminary ruling on the EC point necessary to enable the national court to give a judgment in the case? If not, then no reference should be made. This issue is one that tends to deter first instance courts from making references, as they will not usually have found the material facts in the case by the time they must decide if the EC point is 'necessary' or not.

When a preliminary ruling is received by a national court, it is binding in those proceedings. It is not binding in other litigation but the judgment of the Court of Justice in the case will usually have several points of general application. Private individuals and Member States are usually well-advised to heed such rulings even though they were not parties to the original action.

See also **Chapter 33** of the ***Advocacy Manual***; **Chapter 18** of the ***Remedies Manual***.

9

The relationship between the competition rules, rules on free movement of goods and intellectual property rights

9.1 The rules on free movement

The Treaty rules on the free movement of goods are often understood to be those contained in Articles 28–31 (ex 30–37) of the Treaty. However, these Articles are simply 'Chapter 2' of a larger body of Articles which begins with Article 23 (ex 9). Article 23 appears under the heading 'Title I Free Movement of Goods'; the Articles with which we are concerned appear under the rather daunting heading of 'Prohibition of Quantitative Restrictions between Member States'.

The basic principle relates to the concept of a 'common market', and in Article 3(a) of the Treaty, the Community is set the task of ensuring the elimination (as between Member States) of quantitative restrictions on the import and export of goods, and of all other measures having equivalent effect (see **1.2.2** above). In essence, this elimination is carried into effect by Article 28 (ex 30) of the Treaty. Although some of the terminology may seem prolix, we are really concerned with one of the two main ways in which countries seek to protect their domestic economy. One way is to impose tariffs on imports from other countries: the removal of such tariffs (or customs duties) is the aim of Articles 23–25 (ex 9–17) of the Treaty. Articles 28–31 (ex 30–37) deal with the other basic way to stop imports: the use of quotas.

9.2 Article 28: no quantitative restrictions

It seems that Article 28 (ex 30) has been used by litigants in national courts with much greater frequency than the EC competition rules. Partly this is no doubt due to expediency: there is no enforcement mechanism equivalent to Regulation 1/2003 in this field; so if firms want to have the benefit of the principle of free movement, they must invoke it for themselves in the courts of the Member States. This is possible since, from the end of the transitional period (1 January 1962), Article 28 (ex 30) has been directly effective in the national legal systems of the Member States.

Use of Article 28 (ex 30) by individuals in national courts tends to be defensive: often the owner of, say, a patent will start an action alleging infringement of the patent by a rival who is importing the offending product into the country from another Member

State. The defendant may rely on Article 28 to try and overcome the (national) right to exclusivity held by the patentee. See, for example, *Allen & Hanburys Ltd v Generics (UK) Ltd* [1989] 1 WLR 414. In such a situation, the litigation is a purely private matter (albeit that the challenge to the exercise of the patent right involves a challenge to the State through its law on patents). An alternative, still using Article 30 defensively, is where an individual or firm faces prosecution by either central or local government for commission of a regulatory offence.

Examples of such use occurring in the United Kingdom include *R v Henn and Darby* (34/79) [1979] ECR 3795. This case turned on the conflict between the basic EC freedom to import into a Member State goods which have been legally put onto the market in another Member State and the UK rules on the importation of obscene material. A highly-publicised use of Article 28 (ex 30) came in the spate of prosecutions of shops for trading on Sundays, in contravention of the Shops Act 1950. The basic defence in most of these cases was Article 30 (now 28): the suggestion being that the inability to trade on Sundays meant fewer sales and therefore fewer imports (ie an indirect quota). See *Torfaen Borough Council v B & Q plc* (145/88) [1990] 2 QB 19; *WH Smith Do-It-All Ltd v Peterborough City Council* [1990] 3 WLR 1131; *Stoke-on-Trent City Council v B & Q plc* [1991] 2 WLR 42.

As may be seen above, the use of Article 28 (ex 30) has grown over the years, and sometimes in rather unexpected ways. This has been the result of imaginative use of a typically broad interpretation of Article 30 (now 28) by the ECJ several years ago in *Cassis de Dijon (Rewe-Zentral AG v Bundesmonopolverwaltung für Branntwein* (120/78) [1979] ECR 649). A later judgment of the ECJ seemed to mark a watering-down of the impact of Article 28 (ex 30) on the circulation of goods around the Community: see *Keck and Mithouard* (C-267 and 268/91) [1993] ECR I-6097. This case, which turned on French legislation prohibiting the use of 'loss leaders' in retailing, found the ECJ in retreat from *Cassis*. In *Keck*, the ECJ held that rules governing selling arrangements and which applied to all traders alike in the territory were not caught by Article 30 (now 28).

A more recent preliminary ruling by the Court of Justice perhaps shows that Article 28 (ex 30) still has quite a broad application. A French law allowed for the denomination *montagne* to be applied to food products. This was intended to denote that the product in question originated in a mountain region, thus making it perhaps more attractive to a consumer. The French law went on to restrict the use of this denomination to products made in France from domestic raw materials. Imported products could not benefit from this denomination and so:

> the measure in question facilitates the marketing of goods of domestic [ie French] origin to the detriment of imported goods. In such circumstances, the application of the measure, even if restricted to domestic producers, in itself creates and maintains a difference of treatment between those two categories of goods, hindering, at least potentially, intra-Community trade.

The Article was held to preclude the application of the French law, even though the defendants in the proceedings in question were French nationals being prosecuted in France for misapplication of the denomination, a breach of French law. Interestingly, the Advocate General (Francis Jacobs) had previously proposed in his Opinion that Article 30 (now 28) 'has no application to a national law in so far as that law applies to national products'. See *Criminal proceedings v Jacques Pistre and others* (C-321 to 324/94), [1997] ECR I-2343.

Useful article: Anthony Arnull, 'What shall we do on Sunday?', (1991) ELR 112.

9.3 Free movement and intellectual property rights

As stated above, Article 28 (ex 30) aims to stop quotas: that is, the ability of a Member State to limit the volume of imports into the country. The same effect as a quota can be achieved in a much more absolute fashion by reliance on intellectual property rights. These are held (usually) in the hands of natural or legal persons rather than the State, and are much more specific than State-imposed quotas. For example, AB plc may hold a UK patent for a baby buggy. They can then stop imports into the UK of buggies which infringe their patent, but not of other buggies. The State may (in theory) impose a quota limit on imports of *all* baby buggies if it chooses; or, to alter the illustration, the State may impose a blanket ban on the import of French baby buggies only: no individual intellectual property right holder could (or would) do this.

The main difference which usually exists between State action and that taken by individuals using intellectual property rights, is that the State will impose a quota (eg no more than 100,000 Korean-built cars will be imported into the UK in 2004), whereas the holder of an intellectual property right wants an absolute ban on all infringing goods. This total prohibition can in principle be attained, because intellectual property rights commonly give their owner a monopoly over the item protected by the right.

9.4 Intellectual property rights

When referring above to intellectual property rights, a universal approach was intended, covering all such rights. It is useful to explain, very briefly, what was meant by such an all-embracing term.

9.4.1 Patents

The relevant statute is the Patents Act 1977. A patent is the grant of a monopoly right to (usually) the inventor of a product or process for a definite length of time. The invention must be clearly defined in the application for a patent and, to quote from WR Cornish (in *Patents, Copyright, Trademarks and Allied Rights*, Sweet & Maxwell), the invention must be 'patentable, ie (i) it must be novel, (ii) it must involve an inventive step, (iii) it must be capable of industrial application, and (iv) it must not belong to one of the categories of excluded subject-matter' (see Patents Act 1977, s 1(1)).

Perhaps the most important consideration for us is the protection given by a patent to its owner. According to s 60 of the Patents Act 1977, the patent in a product is infringed if (without the patentee's consent) someone 'makes it; disposes of it; offers to dispose of it; uses it; imports it; or keeps it whether for disposal or otherwise'.

The duration of a United Kingdom patent is from the date of publication of its grant (in the Patent Comptroller's journal) until 20 years after the patent was applied for (s 25).

9.4.2 Copyright

The relevant statute is the Copyright, Designs and Patents Act 1988. Basically, copyright is an exclusive right to do certain specific acts in relation to specified types of work. For example, one may have the copyright in 'original literary, dramatic, musical or artistic works' (Copyright, Designs and Patents Act 1988, s 1(1)(a)). The copyright owner then has the exclusive right to do the following acts in the United Kingdom:

(a) to copy the work;

(b) to issue copies of the work to the public;

(c) to perform, show or play the work in public;

(d) to broadcast the work or include it in a cable programme service;

(e) to make an adaptation of the work or do any of the above in relation to an adaptation (s 16(1)).

For anyone else to do these acts without the licence of the copyright owner is an infringement of copyright, which may give rise to a claim for damages, an injunction and an account (see s 16(2) and s 96).

Copyright in a literary, dramatic, musical or artistic work expires at the end of 70 years after the death of the author (s 12, as amended pursuant to EC Council Directive 93/98).

9.4.3 Trademark

'Trademark' has a statutory definition in the Trademarks Act 1994. This can be summarised as:

> a mark ... used ... in relation to goods for the purpose of indicating a connection in the course of trade between the goods and some person having the right either as proprietor or as registered user to use the mark, whether with or without any identification of the identity of that person.

A mark includes 'a device, brand, heading, label, ticket, name, signature, word, letter, numeral, or any combination thereof'.

Marks applied to services are also protected. Trade marks are of unlimited duration.

9.4.4 Registered designs

The relevant statutes are the Registered Designs Act 1949 and the Copyright, Designs and Patents Act 1988. Often used to protect engineering drawings and the plans used when making a product (eg the 'blueprint' for an exhaust pipe on a particular model of car). A 'design right' (the 1988 Act, s 213) lasts for a maximum of 15 years from the first recording of the design or its first use, whichever was earlier (s 216). A 'registered design' lasts for five years from the date of registration (1949 Act, s 8). The problem with both types of design is that they may be used to make the product without permission. An alternative problem is 'reverse engineering': a 'pirate' manufacturer obtains the product, determines its precise dimensions and composition, etc and then makes it. The design owner could argue that this infringes the right in the design: see, for example, *British Leyland Motor Corp v Armstrong Patents Co Ltd* [1986] AC 577.

9.4.5 Foreign intellectual property law

Lastly, it should be noted that the above explanation is concerned with the position in English law. Definitions and the extent of protection given may vary from one country to another. It may be necessary in an individual case to have a knowledge of the particular intellectual property law of the country most closely connected with the proceedings (usually the country which granted the right under consideration). See, for example, the judgment of the ECJ in *Keurkoop v Nancy Kean Gifts* (144/81) [1982] ECR 2853 on the protection of designs and models in the Member States:

> in the present state of Community law and in the absence of Community standardization or harmonization of laws the determination of the conditions and procedures under which such

protection is granted is a matter for national rules. It is for the national legislature to determine which products qualify for protection, even if they form part of a unit already protected as such.

That was the position in 1982. There have been developments since then in terms of Community rights in intellectual property, in particular regarding harmonization of national rights. On 1 April 1996, the Office for Harmonization in the Internal Market ('OHIM') was opened in Alicante, Spain. This office deals with trademarks and is not part of the administrative structure based in Brussels. It aims to become self-financing through charging fees to register trade marks. The Community trademark was established in 1994 (see Regulation 40/94) and this is seen as most important in supporting the single internal market as it offers a single trademark for an EU market of 350 million consumers. The Community trademark gives its holder 'a uniform right applicable in all EU Member States on the strength of a single procedure which simplifies trademark policies at national level'. Noting that there are already more than three million trademarks in existence through the EU Member States, the OHIM is to take care that applications to register a sign do not duplicate signs already taken by prior rights. The OHIM also sees a role for itself in sharing 'with the courts in Member States the task of deciding on requests for invalidation of registered titles'. This carries echoes of the Notice issued by the Commission in 1993, on cooperation with national courts in enforcement of the competition rules. The OHIM's introductory document states that its activities are subject to Community law and the European Court is responsible for supervising the legality of OHIM decisions. The OHIM expects to apply existing Community jurisprudence in its decisions, including that on the exhaustion of rights. This can be seen in the OHIM declaration that:

> Where the proprietor of the trademark has proceeded or agreed to market goods under this trademark in a Member State of the European Union, he cannot prohibit their free movement in the European Union. This limitation on the rights conferred by the Community trademark is derived from the rule of exhaustion of those rights within the Community ... Parallel imports of products covered by the Community trademark from countries which are not members of the European Union are not subject to this rule and to this limitation ...

The OHIM may be accessed through the europa site on the Internet at http://europa.eu.int/agencies/ohim/english. This is an informative and helpful location for those interested in trademarks.

By comparison with the progress made on the Community trademark, the Community patent has stalled. There was a Convention on the Community Patent in 1975 and an Agreement relating to Community patents in 1989: neither was fully ratified. A Green Paper was published in 1997, by DGXV which is responsible for the single market, asking whether the Community Patent Convention of 1975 should be replaced by legislation which would allow innovators to obtain patent protection throughout the common market via a single application for a patent. As the (then) Commissioner for the single market has observed:

> The present system of patents in the Union is complex and expensive, and does not provide a unitary patent for all the member States. (Mario Monti.)

There is already a European patent, which is granted by the European Patent Office in Munich. In practice, this operates rather like a national patent. It does not give jurisdiction to the European Court to adjudicate on patent disputes; these continue to be justiciable in the national courts with all of the consequent problems of different procedures, limitation periods, etc The single EU patent, suggested in the 1997 Green Paper, would sweep away such difficulties but it still does not exist. In February 1999, DGXV recorded that the need for a unitary patent, covering the entire territory of the EU, was expressed clearly during consultations on the Green Paper. A proposal to establish such a patent was published in February 1999. Then-Commissioner for the Single Market, Mario Monti, stated that 'We have made the introduction of a unitary patent valid throughout the Single Market a political priority'. Thereafter, a deadline was set of the end of 2001 for the establishment of the Community patent. According to Commissioner Frits Bolkestein, Commissioner for the Internal Market, the Community Patent was identified as a key element in ensuring that the EU might become the most competitive and dynamic knowledge-based economy in the world within ten years. Heads of State and Government had underlined that Community-wide patent protection should be as simple and inexpensive to obtain and as comprehensive in its scope as the protection granted to key competitors in the UK and Japan. On 26 November 2001, the Internal Market Council of Ministers failed to reach agreement on the creation of a Community patent. Until such time as the proposal becomes law, the observation of the European Court in *Nancy Kean Gifts* remains pertinent.

9.5 Infringement of intellectual property rights

It is important to note that, in order to make their grant effective, intellectual property rights give their holder the ability to stop others from abusing the monopoly. This abuse could occur in a variety of ways: making a patented product or using a patented process, presenting someone else's copyright work as your own, placing someone else's trademark on your goods, or using another's registered design to make a product. All of these acts can occur without infringing an intellectual property right if the holder of the right has given permission for the act, usually on payment of a royalty. Problems occur when such acts take place without proper permission. The nature of intellectual property law is that the right holder can stop any infringing activity — eg, making, distributing or selling the offending articles — usually by getting a court injunction. This will forbid repetition, order the destruction of any remaining articles and require the infringer to account to the intellectual property right holder for the profits of the infringement.

9.6 Territorial scope of intellectual property rights

These rights are granted by the State and are usually good for the whole territory of that country. This results in the possibility that different firms or individuals will hold the same or very similar rights in different countries. There is also the possibility that, in a particular country, no one owns the intellectual property rights, or that no such right can be granted under the law of that country. Two examples may clarify the point:

(a) In the early years of the EC, Italy did not grant patent protection to pharmaceutical products. So, anyone could make a drug in Italy and sell it there without breaking Italian patent law. If company A imported the pharmaceutical product from Italy into the United Kingdom, where it was protected by a patent granted to company B, could B use its patent to stop the import?

(b) In Spain, it was not possible to obtain a patent for a new process, as distinct from a new product. If a Spanish firm used such a process to make product x, could the UK holder of a patent covering that process stop imports into the UK of the product from Spain?

The theory of a common market is that once goods are put into circulation legitimately in one Member State, they should be allowed to circulate through all other Member States. But to do so in these two examples would deprive the intellectual property right holder of the legitimate profits of his right. See, for example, the observation of the ECJ in the Italian Renault case (*Consorzio Italiano della Componentistica di Ricambio per Autoveicoli and SpA Maxicar v Regie Nationale des usines Renault* (53/87) [1988] ECR 6039):

> It should be noted ... that the authority of a proprietor of a protective right in respect of [a design] to oppose the manufacture by third parties, for the purposes of sale on the internal market or export, of products incorporating the design or to prevent the import of such products manufactured without its consent in other Member States constitutes the substance of his exclusive right. To prevent the application of the national legislation in such circumstances would therefore be tantamount to challenging the very existence of that right.

The history of Article 28 (ex 30) and its interpretation by the ECJ has largely revolved around the attempt to resolve the conflict between 'national' intellectual property rights and the 'supranational' Article 28 (ex 30). Those involved with intellectual property rights have tried to solve the problem by creating new intellectual property rights which have a Community-wide scope: eg, the single Community patent and the Community trademark which would apply across national boundaries. These steps should achieve greater harmonization in the protection of intellectual property rights.

9.7 Abuse of an intellectual property right

As well as 'gaps' in the protection of intellectual property, as indicated in **9.6**, there is also the possibility of intellectual property right holders abusing the protection the law gives them. Abuse is used subjectively here, to cover what might be seen as unjustifiable extensions of the exclusivity given by an intellectual property right. Examples of such behaviour can include the refusal without good reason to supply spare parts (where the design of the part is protected by an intellectual property right); charging an unfairly high price; or the deliberate splitting up of intellectual property rights held by the same firm in different countries in order to prevent parallel imports. A typical example of such market partitioning involved the German firm, Grundig.

Grundig had registered the trademark 'Gint' in several countries, including France. When it appointed an exclusive distributor of its products in France — Consten — it assigned its French trademark 'Gint' to Consten. In theory, this enabled Consten to stop any 'Gint'-marked goods being imported into France without its permission. If 'Gint' products were cheaper in Germany than in France, say, it might be profitable for someone outside the Grundig-Consten system to bulk buy the goods in Germany, then transport them into France and resell them there. This might result in Consten's prices being undercut but if Consten could bring a trademark infringement action to stop the unauthorised (parallel) imports, all would be well again for Consten. This was precisely what Consten attempted to do, with the result that the European Commission investigated and found that the two firms, Consten and Grundig, had infringed Article 85 (now 81) by having an agreement to stop parallel imports.

The ECJ has drawn a firm line between what it calls the existence and the exhaustion of intellectual property rights. Essentially, once a product has been put on the market in a Member State with the consent of (or by) the intellectual property right owner, the right is exhausted. That item is now in free circulation throughout the common market. The intellectual property right owner cannot use nationally-defined monopolies to stop parallel imports of the item. *But* whenever the product is marketed *without* the intellectual property owner's consent (eg pirate copies), the right has not been exhausted: any infringement may be stopped, using the appropriate national laws and remedies. As well as the *Consten and Grundig v Commission* (56 & 58/64) [1966] ECR 299 mentioned above, see also the *'Cassis de Dijon'* case: *Rewe-Zentral AG v Bundesmonopolverwaltung für Branntwein* (120/78) [1979] ECR 649.

The strict application of the doctrine of exhaustion of rights can be seen in the preliminary ruling of the Court of Justice in *Merck & Co Inc and others v Primecrown and others; Beecham Group plc v Europharm of Worthing Ltd* (C-267/95 and 268/95), 5 December 1996, unreported. The plaintiffs in the English proceedings, Merck and Beecham, had marketed their pharmaceutical products in Spain and Portugal at a time when drugs could not be patented in those countries (no longer the position). The defendants had bought up quantities of the drugs in Spain and Portugal, at prices lower than those charged in the UK. The defendants then sought to import them into the UK and the plaintiffs brought proceedings for patent infringement. The Court of Justice ruled that, by putting their products on the market in Spain and Portugal, the plaintiffs had exhausted their rights in those goods. The drugs could circulate freely within the single market. If they had been under a *legal* obligation to market the products in Spain and Portugal, the position would be different:

> he cannot be deemed to have given his consent to the marketing of the products concerned and he is therefore entitled to oppose importation and marketing of those products in the State where they are protected.

But it has to be a *legal* obligation. The drugs involved in the cases were for the treatment of:

- hypertension;
- prostate problems;
- glaucoma;

and an antibiotic.

The Court of Justice ruled that:

> *ethical* obligations to provide supplies of drugs in Member States where they are needed, even though they are not patentable there, cannot provide a basis for derogating from the rule on free movement of goods.

Appendices

The EC legislation contained in Appendices 3 and 4 appears in its original form (as intended by the Treaty of Amsterdam, Article 12(3)). When reading those Appendices you should note that, for example, references to Articles 85, 86 and 87 of the EC Treaty should be understood as references to Articles 81, 82 and 83 respectively, as renumbered by the Treaty of Amsterdam. References to other Articles, Titles and Sections of the EC Treaty have similarly been left unamended in these Appendices.

APPENDIX 1
REGULATION 1/2003

COUNCIL REGULATION (EC) No 1/2003
of 16 December 2002
on the implementation of the rules on competition laid down in Articles 81 and 82 of the Treaty
(Text with EEA relevance)

THE COUNCIL OF THE EUROPEAN UNION,

Having regard to the Treaty establishing the European Community, and in particular Article 83 thereof,

Having regard to the proposal from the Commission,

Having regard to the opinion of the European Parliament,

Having regard to the opinion of the European Economic and Social Committee,

Whereas:

(1) In order to establish a system which ensures that competition in the common market is not distorted, Articles 81 and 82 of the Treaty must be applied effectively and uniformly in the Community No 17 of 6 February 1962, First Regulation implementing Articles 81 and 82 of the Treaty, has allowed a Community competition policy to develop that has helped to disseminate a competition culture within the Community. In the light of experience, however, that Regulation should now be replaced by legislation designed to meet the challenges of an integrated market and a future enlargement of the Community.

(2) In particular, there is a need to rethink the arrangements for applying the exception from the prohibition on agreements, which restrict competition, laid down in Article 81(3) of the Treaty. Under Article 83(2)(b) of the Treaty, account must be taken in this regard of the need to ensure effective supervision, on the one hand, and to simplify administration to the greatest possible extent, on the other.

(3) The centralised scheme set up by Regulation No 17 no longer secures a balance between those two objectives. It hampers application of the Community competition rules by the courts and competition authorities of the Member States, and the system of notification it involves prevents the Commission from concentrating its resources on curbing the most serious infringements. It also imposes considerable costs on undertakings.

(4) The present system should therefore be replaced by a directly applicable exception system in which the competition authorities and courts of the Member States have the power to apply not only Article 81(1) and Article 82 of the Treaty, which have direct applicability by virtue of the case-law of the Court of justice of the European Communities, but also Article 81(3) of the Treaty.

(5) In order to ensure an effective enforcement of the Community competition rules and at the same time the respect of fundamental rights of defence, this Regulation should regulate the burden of proof under Articles 81 and 82 of the Treaty. It should be for the party or the authority alleging an infringement of Article 81(1) and Article 82 of the Treaty to prove the existence thereof to the required legal standard. It should be for the undertaking or association of undertakings invoking the benefit of a defence against a finding of an infringement to demonstrate to the required legal standard that the conditions for applying such defence are satisfied. This Regulation affects neither national rules on the standard of proof nor obligations of competition authorities and courts of the Member States to ascertain the relevant facts of a case, provided that such rules and obligations are compatible with general principles of Community law.

(6) In order to ensure that the Community competition rules are applied effectively, the competition authorities of the Member States should be associated more closely with their application. To this end, they should be empowered to apply Community law.

(7) National courts have an essential part to play in applying the Community competition rules. When deciding disputes between private individuals, they protect the subjective rights under Community law, for example by awarding damages to the victims of infringements. The role of the national courts here complements that of the competition authorities of the Member States. They should therefore be allowed to apply Articles 81 and 82 of the Treaty in full.

(8) In order to ensure the effective enforcement of the Community competition rules and the proper functioning of the cooperation mechanisms contained in this Regulation, it is necessary to oblige the competition authorities and courts of the Member States to also apply Articles 81 and 82 of the Treaty where they apply national competition law to agreements and practices which may affect trade between Member States. In order to create a level playing field for agreements, decisions by associations of undertakings and concerted practices within the internal market, it is also necessary to determine pursuant to Article 83(2)(e) of the Treaty the relationship between national laws and Community competition law. To that effect it is necessary to provide that the application of national competition laws to agreements, decisions or concerted practices within the meaning of Article 81(1) of the Treaty may not lead to the prohibition of such agreements, decisions and concerted practices if they are not also prohibited under Community competition law. The notions of agreements, decisions and concerted practices are autonomous concepts of Community competition law covering the coordination of behaviour of undertakings on the market as interpreted by the Community Courts. Member States should not under this Regulation be precluded from adopting and applying on their territory stricter national competition laws which prohibit or impose sanctions on unilateral conduct engaged in by undertakings. These stricter national laws may include provisions which prohibit or impose sanctions on abusive behaviour toward economically dependent undertakings. Furthermore, this Regulation does not apply to national laws which impose criminal sanctions on natural persons except to the extent that such sanctions are the means whereby competition rules applying to undertakings are enforced.

(9) Articles 81 and 82 of the Treaty have as their objective the protection of competition on the market. This Regulation, which is adopted for the implementation of these Treaty provisions, does not preclude Member States from implementing on their territory national legislation, which protects other legitimate interests provided that such legislation is compatible with general principles and other provisions of Community law. In so far as such national legislation pursues predominantly an objec-

tive different from that of protecting competition on the market, the competition authorities and courts of the Member States may apply such legislation on their territory. Accordingly, Member States may under this Regulation implement on their territory national legislation that prohibits or imposes sanctions on acts of unfair trading practice, be they unilateral or contractual. Such legislation pursues a specific objective, irrespective of the actual or presumed effects of such acts on competition on the market. This is particularly the case of legislation which prohibits undertakings from imposing on their trading partners, obtaining or attempting to obtain from them terms and conditions that are unjustified, disproportionate or without consideration.

(10) Regulations such as 19/65/EEC, (EEC) No 2821/71, (EEC) No 3976/87, (EEC) No 1534/91, or (EEC) No 479/92 empower the Commission to apply Article 81(3) of the Treaty by Regulation to certain categories of agreements, decisions by associations of undertakings and concerted practices. In the areas defined by such Regulations, the Commission has adopted and may continue to adopt so called 'block' exemption Regulations by which it declares Article 81(1) of the Treaty inapplicable to categories of agreements, decisions and concerted practices. Where agreements, decisions and concerted practices to which such Regulations apply nonetheless have effects that are incompatible with Article 81(3) of the Treaty, the Commission and the competition authorities of the Member States should have the power to withdraw in a particular case the benefit of the block exemption Regulation.

(11) For it to ensure that the provisions of the Treaty are applied, the Commission should be able to address decisions to undertakings or associations of undertakings for the purpose of bringing to an end infringements of Articles 81 and 82 of the Treaty. Provided there is a legitimate interest in doing so, the Commission should also be able to adopt decisions which find that an infringement has been committed in the past even if it does not impose a fine. This Regulation should also make explicit provision for the Commission's power to adopt decisions ordering interim measures, which has been acknowledged by the Court of Justice.

(12) This Regulation should make explicit provision for the Commission's power to impose any remedy, whether behavioural or structural, which is necessary to bring the infringement effectively to an end, having regard to the principle of proportionality. Structural remedies should only be imposed either where there is no equally effective behavioural remedy or where any equally effective behavioural remedy would be more burdensome for the undertaking concerned than the structural remedy. Changes to the structure of an undertaking as it existed before the infringement was committed would only be proportionate where there is a substantial risk of a lasting or repeated infringement that derives from the very structure of the undertaking.

(13) Where, in the course of proceedings which might lead to an agreement or practice being prohibited, undertakings offer the Commission commitments such as to meet its concerns, the Commission should be able to adopt decisions which make those commitments binding on the undertakings concerned. Commitment decisions should find that there are no longer grounds for action by the Commission without concluding whether or not there has been or still is an infringement. Commitment decisions are without prejudice to the powers of competition authorities and courts of the Member States to make such a finding and decide upon the case. Commitment decisions are not appropriate in cases where the Commission intends to impose a fine.

(14) In exceptional cases where the public interest of the Community so requires, it may also be expedient for the Commission to adopt a decision of a declaratory nature finding that the prohibition in Article 81 or Article 82 of the Treaty does not apply, with a view to clarifying the law and ensuring its consistent application throughout the

Community, in particular with regard to new types of agreements or practices that have not been settled in the existing case-law and administrative practice.

(15) The Commission and the competition authorities of the Member States should form together a network of public authorities applying the Community competition rules in close cooperation. For that purpose it is necessary to set up arrangements for information and consultation. Further modalities for the cooperation within the network will be laid down and revised by the Commission, in close cooperation with the Member States.

(16) Notwithstanding any national provision to the contrary, the exchange of information and the use of such information in evidence should be allowed between the members of the network even where the information is confidential. This information may be used for the application of Articles 81 and 82 of the Treaty as well as for the parallel application of national competition law, provided that the latter application relates to the same case and does not lead to a different outcome. When the information exchanged is used by the receiving authority to impose sanctions on undertakings, there should be no other limit to the use of the information than the obligation to use it for the purpose for which it was collected given the fact that the sanctions imposed on undertakings are of the same type in all systems. The rights of defence enjoyed by undertakings in the various systems can be considered as sufficiently equivalent. However, as regards natural persons, they may be subject to substantially different types of sanctions across the various systems. Where that is the case, it is necessary to ensure that information can only be used if it has been collected in a way which respects the same level of protection of the rights of defence of natural persons as provided for under the national rules of the receiving authority.

(17) If the competition rules are to be applied consistently and, at the same time, the network is to be managed in the best possible way, it is essential to retain the rule that the competition authorities of the Member States are automatically relieved of their competence if the Commission initiates its own proceedings. Where a competition authority of a Member State is already acting on a case and the Commission intends to initiate proceedings, it should endeavour to do so as soon as possible. Before initiating proceedings, the Commission should consult the national authority concerned.

(18) To ensure that cases are dealt with by the most appropriate authorities within the network, a general provision should be laid down allowing a competition authority to suspend or close a case on the ground that another authority is dealing with it or has already dealt with it, the objective being that each case should be handled by a single authority. This provision should not prevent the Commission from rejecting a complaint for lack of Community interest, as the case-law of the Court of justice has acknowledged it may do, even if no other competition authority has indicated its intention of dealing with the case.

(19) The Advisory Committee on Restrictive Practices and Dominant Positions set up by Regulation No 17 has functioned in a very satisfactory manner. It will fit well into the new system of decentralised application. It is necessary, therefore, to build upon the rules laid down by Regulation No 17, while improving the effectiveness of the organisational arrangements. To this end, it would be expedient to allow opinions to be delivered by written procedure. The Advisory Committee should also be able to act as a forum for discussing cases that are being handled by the competition authorities of the Member States, so as to help safeguard the consistent application of the Community competition rules.

(20) The Advisory Committee should be composed of representatives of the competition authorities of the Member States. For meetings in which general issues are being

discussed, Member States should be able to appoint an additional representative. This is without prejudice to members of the Committee being assisted by other experts from the Member States.

(21) Consistency in the application of the competition rules also requires that arrangements be established for cooperation between the courts of the Member States and the Commission. This is relevant for all courts of the Member States that apply Articles 81 and 82 of the Treaty, whether applying these rules in lawsuits between private parties, acting as public enforcers or as review courts. In particular, national courts should be able to ask the Commission for information or for its opinion on points concerning the application of Community competition law. The Commission and the competition authorities of the Member States should also be able to submit written or oral observations to courts called upon to apply Article 81 or Article 82 of the Treaty. These observations should be submitted within the framework of national procedural rules and practices including those safeguarding the rights of the parties. Steps should therefore be taken to ensure that the Commission and the competition authorities of the Member States are kept sufficiently well informed of proceedings before national courts.

(22) In order to ensure compliance with the principles of legal certainty and the uniform application of the Community competition rules in a system of parallel powers, conflicting decisions must be avoided. It is therefore necessary to clarify, in accordance with the case-law of the Court of Justice, the effects of Commission decisions and proceedings on courts and competition authorities of the Member States. Commitment decisions adopted by the Commission do not affect the power of the courts and the competition authorities of the Member States to apply Articles 81 and 82 of the Treaty.

(23) The Commission should be empowered throughout the Community to require such information to be supplied as is necessary to detect any agreement, decision or concerted practice prohibited by Article 81 of the Treaty or any abuse of a dominant position prohibited by Article 82 of the Treaty. When complying with a decision of the Commission, undertakings cannot be forced to admit that they have committed an infringement, but they are in any event obliged to answer factual questions and to provide documents, even if this information may be used to establish against them or against another undertaking the existence of an infringement.

(24) The Commission should also be empowered to undertake such inspections as are necessary to detect any agreement, decision or concerted practice prohibited by Article 81 of the Treaty or any abuse of a dominant position prohibited by Article 82 of the Treaty. The competition authorities of the Member States should cooperate actively in the exercise of these powers.

(25) The detection of infringements of the competition rules is growing ever more difficult, and, in order to protect competition effectively, the Commission's powers of investigation need to be supplemented. The Commission should in particular be empowered to interview any persons who may be in possession of useful information and to record the statements made. In the course of an inspection, offidals authorised by the Commission should be empowered to affix seals for the period of time necessary for the inspection. Seals should normally not be affixed for more than 72 hours. Officials authorised by the Commission should also be empowered to ask for any information relevant to the subject matter and purpose of the inspection.

(26) Experience has shown that there are cases where business records are kept in the homes of directors or other people working for an undertaking. In order to safeguard the effectiveness of inspections, therefore, officials and other persons authorised by the Commission should be empowered to enter any premises where business records may be

kept, including private homes. However, the exercise of this latter power should be subject to the authorisation of the judicial authority.

(27) Without prejudice to the case-law of the Court of Justice, it is useful to set out the scope of the control that the national judicial authority may carry out when it authorises, as foreseen by national law including as a precautionary measure, assistance from law enforcement authorities in order to overcome possible opposition on the part of the undertaking or the execution of the decision to carry out inspections in non-business premises. It results from the case-law that the national judicial authority may in particular ask the Commission for further information which it needs to carry out its control and in the absence of which it could refuse the authorisation. The case-law also confirms the competence of the national courts to control the application of national rules governing the implementation of coercive measures.

(28) In order to help the competition authorities of the Member States to apply Articles 81 and 82 of the Treaty effectively, it is expedient to enable them to assist one another by carrying out inspections and other fact-finding measures.

(29) Compliance with Articles 81 and 82 of the Treaty and the fulfilment of the obligations imposed on undertakings and associations of undertakings under this Regulation should be enforceable by means of fines and periodic penalty payments. To that end, appropriate levels of fine should also be laid down for infringements of the procedural rules.

(30) In order to ensure effective recovery of fines imposed on associations of undertakings for infringements that they have committed, it is necessary to lay down the conditions on which the Commission may require payment of the fine from the members of the association where the association is not solvent. In doing so, the Commission should have regard to the relative size of the undertakings belonging to the association and in particular to the situation of small and medium-sized enterprises. Payment of the fine by one or several members of an association is without prejudice to rules of national law that provide for recovery of the amount paid from other members of the association.

(31) The rules on periods of limitation for the imposition of fines and periodic penalty payments were laid down in Council Regulation (EEC) No 2988/74 which also concerns penalties in the field of transport. In a system of parallel powers, the acts, which may interrupt a limitation period, should include procedural steps taken independently by the competition authority of a Member State. To clarify the legal framework, Regulation (EEC) No 2988/74 should therefore be amended to prevent it applying to matters covered by this Regulation, and this Regulation should include provisions on periods of limitation.

(32) The undertakings concerned should be accorded the right to be heard by the Commission, third parties whose interests may be affected by a decision should be given the opportunity of submitting their observations beforehand, and the decisions taken should be widely publicised. While ensuring the rights of defence of the undertakings concerned, in particular, the right of access to the file, it is essential that business secrets be protected. The confidentiality of information exchanged in the network should likewise be safeguarded.

(33) Since all decisions taken by the Commission under this Regulation are subject to review by the Court of justice in accordance with the Treaty, the Court of Justice should, in accordance vvith Article 229 thereof be given unlimited jurisdiction in respect of decisions by which the Commission imposes fines or periodic penalty payments.

(34) The principles laid down in Articles 81 and 82 of the Treaty, as they have been applied by Regulation No 17, have given a central role to the Community bodies. This

central role should be retained, whilst associating the Member States more closely with the application of the Community competition rules. In accordance with the principles of subsidiarity and proportionality as set out in Article 5 of the Treaty, this Regulation does not go beyond what is necessary in order to achieve its objective, which is to allow the Community competition rules to be applied effectively.

(35) In order to attain a proper enforcement of Community competition law, Member States should designate and empower authorities to apply Articles 81 and 82 of the Treaty as public enforcers. They should be able to designate administrative as well as judicial authorities to carry out the various functions conferred upon competition authorities in this Regulation. This Regulation recognises the wide variation which exists in the public enforcement systems of Member States. The effects of Article 11(6) of this Regulation should apply to all competition authorities. As an exception to this general rule, where a prosecuting authority brings a case before a separate judicial authority, Article 11(6) should apply to the prosecuting authority subject to the conditions in Article 35(4) of this Regulation. Where these conditions are not fulfilled, the general rule should apply. In any case, Article 11(6) should not apply to courts insofar as they are acting as review courts.

(36) As the case-law has made it clear that the competition rules apply to transport, that sector should be made subject to the procedural provisions of this Regulation. Council Regulation No 141 of 26 November 1962 exempting transport from the application of Regulation No 17 should therefore be repealed and Regulations (EEC) No 1017/68, (EEC) No 4056/86 and (EEC) No 3975/87 should be amended in order to delete the specific procedural provisions they contain.

(37) This Regulation respects the fundamental rights and observes the principles recognised in particular by the Charter of Fundamental Rights of the European Union. Accordingly, this Regulation should be interpreted and applied with respect to those rights and principles.

(38) Legal certainty for undertakings operating under the Community competition rules contributes to the promotion of innovation and investment. Where cases give rise to genuine uncertainty because they present novel or unresolved questions for the application of these rules, individual undertakings may wish to seek informal guidance from the Commission. This Regulation is without prejudice to the ability of the Commission to issue such informal guidance,

HAS ADOPTED THIS REGULATION:

CHAPTER I
PRINCIPLES

Article 1 Application of Articles 81 and 82 of the Treaty

1. Agreements, decisions and concerted practices caught by Article 81(1) of the Treaty which do not satisfy the conditions of Article 81(3) of the Treaty shall be prohibited, no prior decision to that effect being required.

2. Agreements, decisions and concerted practices caught by Article 81(1) of the Treaty which satisfy the conditions of Article 81(3) of the Treaty shall not be prohibited, no prior decision to that effect being required.

3. The abuse of a dominant position referred to in Article 82 of the Treaty shall be prohibited, no prior decision to that effect being required.

Article 2 Burden of proof

In any national or Community proceedings for the application of Articles 81 and 82 of the Treaty, the burden of proving an infringement of Article 81(1) or of Article 82 of the

Treaty shall rest on the party or the authority alleging the infringement. The undertaking or association of undertakings claiming the benefit of Article 81(3) of the Treaty shall bear the burden of proving that the conditions of that paragraph are fulfilled.

Article 3 Relationship between Articles 81 and 82 of the Treaty and national competition laws

1. Where the competition authorities of the Member States or national courts apply national competition law to agreements, decisions by associations of undertakings or concerted practices within the meaning of Article 81(1) of the Treaty which may affect trade between Member States within the meaning of that provision, they shall also apply Article 81 of the Treaty to such agreements, decisions or concerted practices. Where the competition authorities of the Member States or national courts apply national competition law to any abuse prohibited by Article 82 of the Treaty, they shall also apply Article 82 of the Treaty.

2. The application of national competition law may not lead to the prohibition of agreements, decisions by associations of undertakings or concerted practices which may affect trade between Member States but which do not restrict competition within the meaning of Article 81(1) of the Treaty, or which fulfil the conditions of Article 81(3) of the Treaty or which are covered by a Regulation for the application of Article 81(3) of the Treaty. Member States shall not under this Regulation be precluded from adopting and applying on their territory stricter national laws which prohibit or sanction unilateral conduct engaged in by undertakings.

3. Without prejudice to general principles and other provisions of Community law, paragraphs 1 and 2 do not apply when the competition authorities and the courts of the Member States apply national merger control laws nor do they preclude the application of provisions of national law that predominantly pursue an objective different from that pursued by Articles 81 and 82 of the Treaty.

CHAPTER II
POWERS

Article 4 Powers of the Commission

For the purpose of applying Articles 81 and 82 of the Treaty, the Commission shall have the powers provided for by this Regulation.

Article 5 Powers of the competition authorities of the Member States

The competition authorities of the Member States shall have the power to apply Articles 81 and 82 of the Treaty in individual cases. For this purpose, acting on their own initiative or on a complaint, they may take the following decisions:

- requiring that an infringement be brought to an end,
- ordering interim measures,
- accepting commitments,
- imposing fines, periodic penalty payments or any other penalty provided for in their national law.

Where on the basis of the information in their possession the conditions for prohibition are not met they may likewise decide that there are no grounds for action on their part.

Article 6 Powers of the national courts

National courts shall have the power to apply Articles 81 and 82 of the Treaty.

CHAPTER III
COMMISSION DECISIONS

Article 7 Finding and termination of infringement

1. Where the Commission, acting on a complaint or on its own initiative, finds that there is an infringement of Article 81 or of Article 82 of the Treaty, it may by decision require the undertakings and associations of undertakings concerned to bring such infringement to an end. For this purpose, it may impose on them any behavioural or structural remedies which are proportionate to the infringement committed and necessary to bring the infringement effectively to an end. Structural remedies can only be imposed either where there is no equally effective behavioural remedy or where any equally effective behavioural remedy would be more burdensome for the undertaking concerned than the structural remedy. If the Commission has a legitimate interest in doing so, it may also find that an infringement has been committed in the past.

2. Those entitled to lodge a complaint for the purposes of paragraph 1 are natural or legal persons who can show a legitimate interest and Member States.

Article 8 Interim measures

1. In cases of urgency due to the risk of serious and irreparable damage to competition, the Commission, acting on its own initiative may by decision, on the basis of a prima facie finding of infringement, order interim measures.

2. A decision under paragraph 1 shall apply for a specified period of time and may be renewed in so far this is necessary and appropriate.

Article 9 Commitments

1. Where the Commission intends to adopt a decision requiring that an infringement be brought to an end and the undertakings concerned offer commitments to meet the concerns expressed to them by the Commission in its preliminary assessment, the Commission may by decision make those commitments binding on the undertakings. Such a decision may be adopted for a specified period and shall conclude that there are no longer grounds for action by the Commission.

2. The Commission may, upon request or on its own initiative, reopen the proceedings:

(a) where there has been a material change in any of the facts on which the decision was based;

(b) where the undertakings concerned act contrary to their commitments: or

(c) where the decision was based on incomplete, incorrect or misleading information provided by the parties.

Article 10 Finding of inapplicability

Where the Community public interest relating to the application of Articles 81 and 82 of the Treaty so requires, the Commission, acting on its own initiative, may by decision find that Article 81 of the Treaty is not applicable to an agreement, a decision by an association of undertakings or a concerted practice, either because the conditions of Article 81(1) of the Treaty are not fulfilled, or because the conditions of Article 81(3) of the Treaty are satisfied.

The Commission may likewise make such a finding with reference to Article 82 of the Treaty.

CHAPTER IV
COOPERATION

Article 11 Cooperation between the Commission and the competition authorities of the Member States

1. The Commission and the competition authorities of the Member States shall apply the Community competition rules in close cooperation.

2. The Commission shall transmit to the competition authorities of the Member States copies of the most important documents it has collected with a view to applying Articles 7, 8, 9, 10 and Article 29(1). At the request of the competition authority of a Member State, the Commission shall provide it with a copy of other existing documents necessary for the assessment of the case.

3. The competition authorities of the Member States shall, when acting under Article 81 or Article 82 of the Treaty, inform the Commission in writing before or without delay after commencing the first formal investigative measure. This information may also be made available to the competition authorities of the other Member States.

4. No later than 30 days before the adoption of a decision requiring that an infringement be brought to an end, accepting commitments or withdrawing the benefit of a block exemption Regulation, the competition authorities of the Member States shall inform the Commission. To that effect, they shall provide the Commission with a summary of the case, the envisaged decision or, in the absence thereof, any other document indicating the proposed course of action. This information may also be made available to the competition authorities of the other Member States. At the request of the Commission, the acting competition authority shall make available to the Commission other documents it holds which are necessary for the assessment of the case. The information supplied to the Commission may be made available to the competition authorities of the other Member States. National competition authorities may also exchange between themselves information necessary for the assessment of a case that they are dealing with under Article 81 or Article 82 of the Treaty.

5. The competition authorities of the Member States may consult the Commission on any case involving the application of Community law.

6. The initiation by the Commission of proceedings for the adoption of a decision under Chapter III shall relieve the competition authorities of the Member States of their competence to apply Articles 81 and 82 of the Treaty. If a competition authority of a Member State is already acting on a case, the Commission shall only initiate proceedings after consulting with that national competition authority.

Article 12 Exchange of information

1. For the purpose of applying Articles 81 and 82 of the Treaty the Commission and the competition authorities of the Member States shall have the power to provide one another with and use in evidence any matter of fact or of law, including confidential information.

2. Information exchanged shall only be used in evidence for the purpose of applying Article 81 or Article 82 of the Treaty and in respect of the subject-matter for which it was collected by the transmitting authority. However, where national competition law is applied in the same case and in parallel to Community competition law and does not lead to a different outcome, information exchanged under this Article may also be used for the application of national competition law.

3. Information exchanged pursuant to paragraph 1 can only be used in evidence to impose sanctions on natural persons where:

— the law of the transmitting authority foresees sanctions of a similar kind in relation to an infringement of Article 81 or Article 82 of the Treaty or, in the absence thereof,
— the information has been collected in a way which respects the same level of protection of the rights of defence of natural persons as provided for under the national rules of the receiving authority. However, in this case, the information exchanged cannot be used by the receiving authority to impose custodial sanctions.

Article 13 Suspension or termination of proceedings

1. Where competition authorities of two or more Member States have received a complaint or are acting on their own initiative under Article 81 or Article 82 of the Treaty against the same agreement, decision of an association or practice, the fact that one authority is dealing with the case shall be sufficient grounds for the others to suspend the proceedings before them or to reject the complaint. The Commission may likewise reject a complaint on the ground that a competition authority of a Member State is dealing with the case.

2. Where a competition authority of a Member State or the Commission has received a complaint against an agreement, decision of an association or practice which has already been dealt with by another competition authority, it may reject it.

Article 14 Advisory Committee

1. The Commission shall consult an Advisory Committee on Restrictive Practices and Dominant Positions prior to the taking of any decision under Articles 7, 8, 9, 10, 23, Article 24(2) and Article 29(1).

2. For the discussion of individual cases, the Advisory Committee shall be composed of representatives of the competition authorities of the Member States. For meetings in which issues other than individual cases are being discussed, an additional Member State representative competent in competition matters may be appointed. Representatives may, if unable to attend, be replaced by other representatives.

3. The consultation may take place at a meeting convened and chaired by the Commission, held not earlier than 14 days after dispatch of the notice convening it, together with a summary of the case, an indication of the most important documents and a preliminary draft decision. In respect of decisions pursuant to Article 8, the meeting may be held seven days after the dispatch of the operative part of a draft decision. Where the Commission dispatches a notice convening the meeting which gives a shorter period of notice than those specified above, the meeting may take place on the proposed date in the absence of an objection by any Member State. The Advisory Committee shall deliver a written opinion on the Commission's preliminary draft decision. It may deliver an opinion even if some members are absent and are not represented. At the request of one or several members, the positions stated in the opinion shall be reasoned.

4. Consultation may also take place by written procedure. However, if any Member State so requests, the Commission shall convene a meeting. In case of written procedure, the Commission shall determine a time-limit of not less than 14 days within which the Member States are to put forward their observations for circulation to all other Member States. In case of decisions to be taken pursuant to Article 8, the time-limit of 14 days is replaced by seven days. Where the Commission determines a time-limit for the written procedure which is shorter than those specified above, the proposed time-limit shall be applicable in the absence of an objection by any Member State.

5. The Commission shall take the utmost account of the opinion delivered by the Advisory Committee. It shall inform the Committee of the manner in which its opinion has been taken into account.

6. Where the Advisory Committee delivers a written opinion, this opinion shall be appended to the draft decision. If the Advisory Committee recommends publication of the opinion, the Commission shall carry out such publication taking into account the legitimate interest of undertakings in the protection of their business secrets.

7. At the request of a competition authority of a Member State, the Commission shall include on the agenda of the Advisory Committee cases that are being dealt with by a competition authority of a Member State under Article 81 or Article 82 of the Treaty. The Commission may also do so on its own initiative. In either case, the Commission shall inform the competition authority concerned.

A request may in particular be made by a competition authority of a Member State in respect of a case where the Commission intends to initiate proceedings with the effect of Article 11(6).

The Advisory Committee shall not issue opinions on cases dealt with by competition authorities of the Member States. The Advisory Committee may also discuss general issues of Community competition law.

Article 15 Cooperation with national courts

1. In proceedings for the application of Article 81 or Article 82 of the Treaty, courts of the Member States may ask the Commission to transmit to them information in its possession or its opinion on questions concerning the application of the Community competition rules.

2. Member States shall forward to the Commission a copy of any written judgment of national courts deciding on the application of Article 81 or Article 82 of the Treaty. Such copy shall be forwarded without delay after the full written judgment is notified to the parties.

3. Competition authorities of the Member States, acting on their own initiative, may submit written observations to the national courts of their Member State on issues relating to the application of Article 81 or Article 82 of the Treaty. With the permission of the court in question, they may also submit oral observations to the national courts of their Member State. Where the coherent application of Article 81 or Article 82 of the Treaty so requires, the Commission, acting on its own initiative, may submit written observations to courts of the Member States. With the permission of the court in question, it may also make oral observations.

For the purpose of the preparation of their observations only, the competition authorities of the Member States and the Commission may request the relevant court of the Member State to transmit or ensure the transmission to them of any documents necessary for the assessment of the case.

4. This Article is without prejudice to wider powers to make observations before courts conferred on competition authorities of the Member States under the law of their Member State.

Article 16 Uniform application of Community competition law

1. When national courts rule on agreements, decisions or practices under Article 81 or Article 82 of the Treaty which are already the subject of a Commission decision, they cannot take decisions running counter to the decision adopted by the Commission. They must also avoid giving decisions which would conflict with a decision contemplated by the Commission in proceedings it has initiated. To that effect, the national

court may assess whether it is necessary to stay its proceedings. This obligation is without prejudice to the rights and obligations under Article 234 of the Treaty.

2. When competition authorities of the Member States rule on agreements, decisions or practices under Article 81 or Article 82 of the Treaty which are already the subject of a Commission decision, they cannot take decisions which would run counter to the decision adopted by the Commission.

CHAPTER V
POWERS OF INVESTIGATION

Article 17 Investigations into sectors of the economy and into types of agreements

1. Where the trend of trade between Member States, the rigidity of prices or other circumstances suggest that competition may be restricted or distorted within the common market, the Commission may conduct its inquiry into a particular sector of the economy or into a particular type of agreements across various sectors. In the course of that inquiry, the Commission may request the undertakings or associations of undertakings concerned to supply the information necessary for giving effect to Articles 81 and 82 of the Treaty and may carry out any inspections necessary for that purpose.

The Commission may in particular request the undertakings or associations of undertakings concerned to communicate to it all agreements, decisions and concerted practices.

The Commission may publish a report on the results of its inquiry into particular sectors of the economy or particular types of agreements across various sectors and invite comments from interested parties.

2. Articles 14, 18, 19, 20, 22, 23 and 24 shall apply *mutatis mutandis*.

Article 18 Requests for information

1. In order to carry out the duties assigned to it by this Regulation, the Commission may, by simple request or by decision, require undertakings and associations of undertakings to provide all necessary information.

2. When sending a simple request for information to an undertaking or association of undertakings, the Commission shall state the legal basis and the purpose of the request, specify what information is required and fix the time-limit within which the information is to be provided, and the penalties provided for in Article 23 for supplying incorrect or misleading information.

3. Where the Commission requires undertakings and associations of undertakings to supply information by decision, it shall state the legal basis and the purpose of the request, specify what information is required and fix the time-limit within which it is to be provided. it shall also indicate the penalties provided for in Article 23 and indicate or impose the penalties provided for in Article 24. It shall further indicate the right to have the decision reviewed by the Court of Justice.

4. The owners of the undertakings or their representatives and, in the case of legal persons, companies or firms, or associations having no legal personality, the persons authorised to represent them by law or by their constitution shall supply the information requested on behalf of the undertaking or the association of undertakings concerned. Lawyers duly authorised to act may supply the information on behalf of their clients. The latter shall remain fully responsible if the information supplied is incomplete, incorrect or misleading.

5. The Commission shall without delay forward a copy of the simple request or of the decision to the competition authority of the Member State in whose territory the

seat of the undertaking or association of undertakings is situated and the competition authority of the Member State whose territory is affected.

6. At the request of the Commission the governments and competition authorities of the Member States shall provide the Commission with all necessary information to carry out the duties assigned to it by this Regulation.

Article 19 Power to take statements

1. In order to carry out the duties assigned to it by this Regulation, the Commission may interview any natural or legal person who consents to be interviewed for the purpose of collecting information relating to the subject-matter of an investigation.

2. Where an interview pursuant to paragraph 1 is conducted in the premises of an undertaking, the Commission shall inform the competition authority of the Member State in whose territory the interview takes place. If so requested by the competition authority of that Member State, its offidals may assist the offidals and other accompanying persons authorised by the Commission to conduct the interview.

Article 20 The Commission's powers of inspection

1. In order to carry out the duties assigned to it by this Regulation, the Commission may conduct all necessary inspections of undertakings and associations of undertakings.

2. The officials and other accompanying persons authorised by the Commission to conduct an inspection are empowered:

(a) to enter any premises, land and means of transport of undertakings and associations of undertakings;

(b) to examine the books and other records related to the business, irrespective of the medium on which they are stored;

(c) to take or obtain in any form copies of or extracts from such books or records;

(d) to seal any business premises and books or records for the period and to the extent necessary for the inspection;

(e) to ask any representative or member of staff of the undertaking or association of undertakings for explanations on facts or documents relating to the subject-matter and purpose of the inspection and to record the answers.

3. The officials and other accompanying persons authorised by the Commission to conduct an inspection shall exercise their powers upon production of a written authorisation specifying the subject matter and purpose of the inspection and the penalties provided for in Article 23 in case the production of the required books or other records related to the business is incomplete or where the answers to questions asked under paragraph 2 of the present Article are incorrect or misleading. In good time before the inspection, the Commission shall give notice of the inspection to the competition authority of the Member State in whose territory it is to be conducted.

4. Undertakings and associations of undertakings are required to submit to inspections ordered by decision of the Commission. The decision shall specify the subject matter and purpose of the inspection, appoint the date on which it is to begin and indicate the penalties provided for in Articles 23 and 24 and the light to have the decision reviewed by the Court of Justice. The Commission shall take such decisions after consulting the competition authority of the Member State in whose territory the inspection is to be conducted.

5. Officials of as well as those authorised or appointed by the competition authority of the Member State in whose territory the inspection is to be conducted shall, at the

request of that authority or of the Commission, actively assist the officials and other accompanying persons authorised by the Commission. To this end, they shall enjoy the powers specified in paragraph 2.

6. Where the officials and other accompanying persons authorised by the Commission find that an undertaking opposes an inspection ordered pursuant to this Article, the Member State concerned shall afford them the necessary assistance, requesting where appropriate the assistance of the police or of an equivalent enforcement authority, so as to enable them to conduct their inspection.

7. If the assistance provided for in paragraph 6 requires authorisation from a judicial authority according to national rules, such authorisation shall be applied for. Such authorisation may also be applied for as a precautionary measure.

8. Where authorisation as referred to in paragraph 7 is applied for, the national judicial authority shall control that the Commission decision is authentic and that the coercive measures envisaged are neither arbitrary nor excessive having regard to the subject matter of the inspection. In its control of the proportionality of the coercive measures, the national judicial authority may ask the Commission, directly or through the Member State competition authority, for detailed explanations in particular on the grounds the Commission has for suspecting infringement of Articles 81 and 82 of the Treaty, as well as on the seriousness of the suspected infringement and on the nature of the involvement of the undertaking concerned. However, the national judicial authority may not call into question the necessity for the inspection nor demand that it be provided with the information in the Commission's file. The lawfulness of the Commission decision shall be subject to review only by the Court of Justice.

Article 21 Inspection of other premises

1. If a reasonable suspicion exists that books or other records related to the business and to the subject-matter of the inspection, which may be relevant to prove a serious violation of Article 81 or Article 82 of the Treaty, are being kept in any other premises, land and means of transport, including the homes of directors, managers and other members of staff of the undertakings and associations of undertakings concerned, the Commission can by decision order an inspection to be conducted in such other premises, land and means of transport.

2. The decision shall specify the subject matter and purpose of the inspection, appoint the date on which it is to begin and indicate the right to have the decision reviewed by the Court of Justice. It shall in particular state the reasons that have led the Commission to conclude that a suspicion in the sense of paragraph 1 exists. The Commission shall take such decisions after consulting the competition authority of the Member State in whose territory the inspection is to be conducted.

3. A decision adopted pursuant to paragraph 1 cannot be executed without prior authorisation from the national judicial authority of the Member State concerned. The national judicial authority shall control that the Commission decision is authentic and that the coercive measures envisaged are neither arbitrary nor excessive having regard in particular to the seriousness of the suspected infringement, to the importance of the evidence sought, to the involvement of the undertaking concerned and to the reasonable likelihood that business books and records relating to the subject matter of the inspection are kept in the premises for which the authorisation is requested. The national judicial authority may ask the Commission, directly or through the Member State competition authority, for detailed explanations on those elements which are necessary to allow its control of the proportionality of the coercive measures envisaged.

However, the national judicial authority may not call into question the necessity for the inspection nor demand that it be provided with information in the Commission's file. The lawfulness of the Commission decision shall be subject to review only by the Court of Justice.

4. The officials and other accompanying persons authorised by the Commission to conduct an inspection ordered in accordance with paragraph 1 of this Article shall have the powers set out in Article 20(2)(a), (b) and (c). Article 20(5) and (6) shall apply *mutatis mutandis*.

Article 22 Investigations by competition authorities of Member States

1. The competition authority of a Member State may in its own territory carry out any inspection or other fact-finding measure under its national law on behalf and for the account of the competition authority of another Member State in order to establish whether there has been an infringement of Article 81 or Article 82 of the Treaty. Any exchange and use of the information collected shall be carried out in accordance with Article 12.

2. At the request of the Commission, the competition authorities of the Member States shall undertake the inspections which the Commission considers to be necessary under Article 20(1) or which it has ordered by decision pursuant to Article 20(4). The officials of the competition authorities of the Member States who are responsible for conducting these inspections as well as those authorised or appointed by them shall exercise their powers in accordance with their national law.

If so requested by the Commission or by the competition authority of the Member State in whose territory the inspection is to be conducted, officials and other accompanying persons authorised by the Commission may assist the officials of the authority concerned.

CHAPTER VI
PENALTIES

Article 23 Fines

1. The Commission may by decision impose on undertakings and associations of undertakings fines not exceeding 1% of the total turnover in the preceding business year where, intentionally or negligently.

(a) they supply incorrect or misleading information in response to a request made pursuant to Article 17 or Article 18(2);

(b) in response to a request made by decision adopted pursuant to Article 17 or Article 18(3), they supply incorrect, incomplete or misleading information or do not supply information within the required time-limit;

(c) they produce the required books or other records related to the business in incomplete form during inspections under Article 20 or refuse to submit to inspections ordered by a decision adopted pursuant to Article 20(4);

(d) in response to a question asked in accordance with Article 20(2)(e),
- they give an incorrect or misleading answer,
- they fail to rectify within a time-limit set by the Commission an incorrect, incomplete or misleading answer given by a member of staff, or
- they fail or refuse to provide a complete answer on facts relating to the subject-matter and purpose of an inspection ordered by a decision adopted pursuant to Article 20(4);

(e) seals affixed in accordance with Article 20(2)(d) by officials or other accompanying persons authorised by the Commission have been broken.

2. The Commission may by decision impose fines on undertakings and associations of undertakings where, either intentionally or negligently:

(a) they infringe Article 81 or Article 82 of the Treaty; or

(b) they contravene a decision ordering interim measures under Article 8; or

(c) they fail to comply with a commitment made binding by a decision pursuant to Article 9.

For each undertaking and association of undertakings participating in the infringement, the fine shall not exceed 10% of its total turnover in the preceding business year.

Where the infringement of an association relates to the activities of its members, the fine shall not exceed 10% of the sum of the total turnover of each member active on the market affected by the infringement of the association.

3. In fixing the amount of the fine, regard shall be had both to the gravity and to the duration of the infringement.

4. When a fine is imposed on an association of undertakings taking account of the turnover of its members and the association is not solvent, the association is obliged to call for contributions from its members to cover the amount of the fine.

Where such contributions have not been made to the association within a time-limit fixed by the Commission, the Commission may require payment of the fine directly by any of the undertakings whose representatives were members of the decision-making bodies concerned of the association.

After the Commission has required payment under the second subparagraph, where necessary to ensure full payment of the fine, the Commission may require payment of the balance by any of the members of the association which were active on the market on which the infringement occurred.

However, the Commission shall not require payment under the second or the third subparagraph from undertakings which show that they have not implemented the infringing decision of the association and either were not aware of its existence or have actively distanced themselves from it before the Commission started investigating the case.

The financial liability of each undertaking in respect of the payment of the fine shall not exceed 10% of its total turnover in the preceding business year.

5. Decisions taken pursuant to paragraphs 1 and 2 shall not be of a criminal law nature.

Article 24 Periodic penalty payments

1. The Commission may, by decision, impose on undertakings or associations of undertakings periodic penalty payments not exceeding 5% of the average daily turnover in the preceding business year per day and calculated from the date appointed by the decision, in order to compel them:

(a) to put an end to an infringement of Article 81 or Article 82 of the Treaty, in accordance with a decision taken pursuant to Article 7;

(b) to comply with a decision ordering interim measures taken pursuant to Article 8;

(c) to comply with a commitment made binding by a decision pursuant to Article 9;

(d) to supply complete and correct information which it has requested by decision taken pursuant to Article 17 or Article 18(3);

(e) to submit to an inspection which it has ordered by decision taken pursuant to Article 20(4).

2. Where the undertakings or associations of undertakings have satisfied the obligation which the periodic penalty payment was intended to enforce, the Commission may fix the definitive amount of the periodic penalty payment at a figure lower than that which would arise under the original decision. Article 23(4) shall apply correspondingly.

CHAPTER VII
LIMITATION PERIODS

Article 25 Limitation periods for the imposition of penalties

1. The powers conferred on the Commission by Articles 23 and 24 shall be subject to the following limitation periods:

(a) three years in the case of infringements of provisions concerning requests for information or the conduct of inspections;

(b) five years in the case of all other infringements.

2. Time shall begin to run on the day on which the infringement is committed. However, in the case of continuing or repeated infringements, time shall begin to run on the day on which the infringement ceases.

3. Any action taken by the Commission or by the competition authority of a Member State for the purpose of the investigation or proceedings in respect of an infringement shall interrupt the limitation period for the imposition of fines or periodic penalty payments. The limitation period shall be interrupted with effect from the date on which the action is notified to at least one undertaking or association of undertakings which has participated in the infringement. Actions which interrupt the running of the period shall include in particular the following:

(a) written requests for information by the Commission or by the competition authority of a Member State;

(b) written authorisations to conduct inspections issued to its officials by the Commission or by the competition authority of a Member State;

(c) the initiation of proceedings by the Commission or by the competition authority of a Member State;

(d) notification of the statement of objections of the Commission or of the competition authority of a Member State.

4. The interruption of the limitation period shall apply for all the undertakings or associations of undertakings which have participated in the infringement.

5. Each interruption shall start time running afresh. However, the limitation period shall expire at the latest on the day on which a period equal to twice the limitation period has elapsed without the Commission having imposed a fine or a periodic penalty payment. That period shall be extended by the time during which limitation is suspended pursuant to paragraph 6.

6. The limitation period for the imposition of fines or periodic penalty payments shall be suspended for as long as the decision of the Commission is the subject of proceedings pending before the Court of Justice.

Article 26 Limitation period for the enforcement of penalties

1. The power of the Commission to enforce decisions taken pursuant to Articles 23 and 24 shall be subject to a limitation period of five years.

2. Time shall begin to run on the day on which the decision becomes final.

3. The limitation period for the enforcement of penalties shall be interrupted:

(a) by notification of a decision varying the original amount of the fine or periodic penalty payment or refusing an application for variation;

(b) by any action of the Commission or of a Member State, acting at the request of the Commission, designed to enforce payment of the fine or periodic penalty payment.

4. Each interruption shall start time running afresh.

5. The limitation period for the enforcement of penalties shall be suspended for so long as:

(a) time to pay is allowed;

(b) enforcement of payment is suspended pursuant to a decision of the Court of Justice.

CHAPTER VIII
HEARINGS AND PROFESSIONAL SECRECY

Article 27 Hearing of the parties, complainants and others

1. Before taking decisions as provided for in Articles 7, 8, 23 and Article 24(2), the Commission shall give the undertakings or associations of undertakings which are the subject of the proceedings conducted by the Commission the opportunity of being heard on the matters to which the Commission has taken objection. The Commission shall base its decisions only on objections on which the parties concerned have been able to comment. Complainants shall be associated closely with the proceedings.

2. The rights of defence of the parties concerned shall be fully respected in the proceedings. They shall be entitled to have access to the Commission's file, subject to the legitimate interest of undertakings in the protection of their business secrets. The right of access to the file shall not extend to confidential information and internal documents of the Commission or the competition authorities of the Member States. In particular, the right of access shall not extend to correspondence between the Commission and the competition authorities of the Member States, or between the latter, including documents drawn up pursuant to Articles 11 and 14. Nothing in this paragraph shall prevent the Commission from disclosing and using information necessary to prove an infringement.

3. If the Commission considers it necessary, it may also hear other natural or legal persons. Applications to be heard on the part of such persons shall, where they show a sufficient interest, be granted. The competition authorities of the Member States may also ask the Commission to hear other natural or legal persons.

4. Where the Commission intends to adopt a decision pursuant to Article 9 or Article 10, it shall publish a concise summary of the case and the main content of the commitments or of the proposed course of action. Interested third parties may submit their observations within a time limit which is fixed by the Commission in its publication and which may not be less than one month. Publication shall have regard to the legitimate interest of undertakings in the protection of their business secrets.

Article 28 Professional secrecy

1. Without prejudice to Articles 12 and 15, information collected pursuant to Articles 17 to 22 shall be used only for the purpose for which it was acquired.

2. Without prejudice to the exchange and to the use of information foreseen in Articles 11, 12, 14, 15 and 27, the Commission and the competition authorities of the Member States, their officials, servants and other persons working under the supervision of these authorities as well as officials and civil servants of other authorities of the Member States shall not disclose information acquired or exchanged by them pursuant to this Regulation and of the kind covered by the obligation of professional secrecy. This obligation also applies to all representatives and experts of Member States attending meetings of the Advisory Committee pursuant to Article 14.

CHAPTER IX
EXEMPTION REGULATIONS

Article 29 Withdrawal in individual cases

1. Where the Commission, empowered by a Council Regulation, such as Regulations 19/65/EEC, (EEC) No 2821/71, (EEC) No 3976/87, (EEC) No 1534/91 or

(EEC) No 479/92, to apply Article 81(3) of the Treaty by regulation, has declared Article 81(1) of the Treaty inapplicable to certain categories of agreements, decisions by associations of undertakings or concerted practices, it may, acting on its own initiative or on a complaint, withdraw the benefit of such an exemption Regulation when it finds that in any particular case an agreement, decision or concerted practice to which the exemption Regulation applies has certain effects which are incompatible with Article 81(3) of the Treaty.

2. Where, in any particular case, agreements, decisions by associations of undertakings or concerted practices to which a Commission Regulation referred to in paragraph 1 applies have effects which are incompatible with Article 81(3) of the Treaty in the territory of a Member State, or in a part thereof, which has all the characteristics of a distinct geographic market, the competition authority of that Member State may withdraw the benefit of the Regulation in question in respect of that territory.

CHAPTER X
GENERAL PROVISIONS

Article 30 Publication of decisions

1. The Commission shall publish the decisions, which it takes pursuant to Articles 7 to 10, 23 and 24.

2. The publication shall state the names of the parties and the main content of the decision, including any penalties imposed. it shall have regard to the legitimate interest of undertakings in the protection of their business secrets.

Article 31 Review by the Court of Justice

The Court of Justice shall have unlimited jurisdiction to review decisions whereby the Commission has fixed a fine or periodic penalty payment. It may cancel, reduce or increase the fine or periodic penalty payment imposed.

Article 32 Exclusions

This Regulation shall not apply to:

(a) international tramp vessel services as defined in Article 1(3)(a) of Regulation (EEC) No 4056/86;

(b) a maritime transport service that takes place exclusively between ports in one and the same Member State as foreseen in Article 1(2) of Regulation (EEC) No 4056/86;

(c) air transport between Community airports and third countries.

Article 33 Implementing provisions

1. The Commission shall be authorised to take such measures as may be appropriate in order to apply this Regulation. The measures may concern, *inter alia*:

(a) the form, content and other details of complaints lodged pursuant to Article 7 and the procedure for rejecting complaints.,

(b) the practical arrangements for the exchange of information and consultations provided for in Article 11;

(c) the practical arrangements for the hearings provided for in Article 27.

2. Before the adoption of any measures pursuant to paragraph 1, the Commission shall publish a draft thereof and invite all interested parties to submit their comments within the time-limit it lays down, which may not be less than one month. Before publishing a draft measure and before adopting it, the Commission shall consult the Advisory Committee on Restrictive Practices and Dominant Positions.

CHAPTER XI
TRANSITIONAL, AMENDING AND FINAL PROVISIONS

Article 34 Transitional provisions

1. Applications made to the Commission under Article 2 of Regulation No 17, notifications made under Articles 4 and 5 of that Regulation and the corresponding applications and notifications made under Regulations (EEC) No 1017/68, (EEC) No 4056/86 and (EEC) No 3975/87 shall lapse as from the date of application of this Regulation.

2. Procedural steps taken under Regulation No 17 and Regulations (EEC) No 1017/68, (EEC) No 4056/86 and (EEC) No 3975/87 shall continue to have effect for the purposes of applying this Regulation.

Article 35 Designation of competition authorities of Member States

1. The Member States shall designate the competition authority or authorities responsible for the application of Articles 81 and 82 of the Treaty in such a way that the provisions of this regulation are effectively complied with. The measures necessary to empower those authorities to apply those Articles shall be taken before 1 May 2004. The authorities designated may include courts.

2. When enforcement of Community competition law is entrusted to national administrative and judicial authorities, the Member States may allocate different powers and functions to those different national authorities, whether administrative or judicial.

3. The effects of Article 11(6) apply to the authorities designated by the Member States including courts that exercise functions regarding the preparation and the adoption of the types of decisions foreseen in Article 5. The effects of Article 11(6) do not extend to courts insofar as they act as review courts in respect of the types of decisions foreseen in Article 5.

4. Notwithstanding paragraph 3, in the Member States where, for the adoption of certain types of decisions foreseen in Article 5, an authority brings an action before a judicial authority that is separate and different from the prosecuting authority and provided that the terms of this paragraph are complied with, the effects of Article 11(6) shall be limited to the authority prosecuting the case which shall withdraw its claim before the judicial authority when the Commission opens proceedings and this withdrawal shall bring the national proceedings effectively to an end.

Article 36 Amendment of Regulation (EEC) No 1017/68

Regulation (EEC) No 1017/68 is amended as follows:

1. Article 2 is repealed;

2. in Article 3(1), the words 'The prohibition laid down in Article 2' are replaced by the words 'The prohibition in Article 81(1) of the Treaty;

3. Article 4 is amended as follows:

(a) In paragraph 1, the words 'The agreements, decisions and concerted practices referred to in Article 2' are replaced by the words 'Agreements, decisions and concerted practices pursuant to Article 81(1) of the Treaty';

(b) Paragraph 2 is replaced by the following:

'2. if the implementation of any agreement, decision or concerted practice covered by paragraph 1 has, in a given case, effects which are incompatible with the requirements of Article 81(3) of the Treaty, undertakings or associations of undertakings may be required to make such effects cease.'

4. Articles 5 to 29 are repealed with the exception of Article 13(3) which continues to apply to decisions adopted pursuant to Article 5 of Regulation (EEC) No 1017/68

prior to the date of application of this Regulation until the date of expiration of those decisions;

5. in Article 30, paragraphs 2, 3 and 4 are deleted.

Article 37 Amendment of Regulation (EEC) No 2988/74

In Regulation (EEC) No 2988/74, the following Article is inserted:

> **'Article 7a Exclusion**
>
> This Regulation shall not apply to measures taken under Council Regulation (EC) No 1/2003 of 16 December 2002 on the implementation of the rules on competition laid down in Articles 81 and 82 of the Treaty.

Article 38 Amendment of Regulation (EEC) No 4056/86

Regulation (EEC) No 4056/86 is amended as follows:

1. Article 7 is amended as follows:

(a) Paragraph 1 is replaced by the following:

'1. *Breach of an obligation*

Where the persons concerned are in breach of an obligation which, pursuant to Article 5, attaches to the exemption provided for in Article 3, the Commission may, in order to put an end to such breach and under the conditions laid down in Council Regulation (EC) No 1/2003 of 16 December 2002 on the implementation of the rules on competition laid down in Articles 81 and 82 of the Treaty adopt a decision that either prohibits them from carrying out or requires them to perform certain specific acts, or withdraws the benefit of the block exemption which they enjoyed.

(b) Paragraph 2 is amended as follows:

(i) In point (a), the words 'under the conditions laid down in Section II' are replaced by the words 'under the conditions laid down in Regulation (EC) No 1/2003';

(ii) The second sentence of the second subparagraph of point (c)(i) is replaced by the following:

'At the same time it shall decide, in accordance with Article 9 of Regulation (EC) No 1/2003, whether to accept commitments offered by the undertakings concerned with a view, *inter alia*, to obtaining access to the market for non-conference lines.'

2. Article 8 is amended as follows:

(a) Paragraph 1 is deleted.

(b) In paragraph 2 the words 'pursuant to Article 10' are replaced by the words 'pursuant to Regulation (EC) No 1/2003'.

(c) Paragraph 3 is deleted;

3. Article 9 is amended as follows:

(a) In paragraph 1, the words 'Advisory Committee referred to in Article 15' are replaced by the words 'Advisory Committee referred to in Article 14 of Regulation (EC) No 1/2003';

(b) In paragraph 2, the words 'Advisory Committee as referred to in Article 15' are replaced by the words 'Advisory Committee referred to in Article 14 of Regulation (EC) No 1/2003';

4. Articles 10 to 25 are repealed with the exception of Article 13(3) which continues to apply to decisions adopted pursuant to Article 81(3) of the Treaty prior to the date of application of this Regulation until the date of expiration of those decisions;

5. in Article 26, the words 'the form, content and other details of complaints pursuant to Article 10, applications pursuant to Article 12 and the hearings provided for in Article 23(1) and (2)' are deleted.

Article 39 Amendment of Regulation (EEC) No 3975/87

Articles 3 to 19 of Regulation (EEC) No 3975/87 are repealed with the exception of Article 6(3) which continues to apply to decisions adopted pursuant to Article 81(3) of the Treaty prior to the date of application of this Regulation until the date of expiration of those decisions.

Article 40 Amendment of Regulations No 19/65/EEC, (EEC) No 2821/71 and (EEC) No 1534/91

Article 7 of Regulation No 19/65/EEC, Article 7 of Regulation (EEC) No 2821/71 and Article 7 of Regulation (EEC) No 1534/91 are repealed.

Article 41 Amendment of Regulation (EEC) No 3976/87

Regulation (EEC) No 3976/87 is amended as follows:

1. Article 6 is replaced by the following:

   'Article 6

   The Commission shall consult the Advisory Committee referred to in Article 14 of Council Regulation (EC) No 1/2003 of 16 December 2002 on the implementation of the rules on competition laid down in Articles 81 and 82 of the Treaty before publishing a draft Regulation and before adopting a Regulation.

2. Article 7 is repealed.

Article 42 Amendment of Regulation (EEC) No 479/92

Regulation (EEC) No 479/92 is amended as follows:

1. Article 5 is replaced by the following:

   'Article 5

   Before publishing the draft Regulation and before adopting the Regulation, the Commission shall consult the Advisory Committee referred to in Article 14 of Council Regulation (EC) No 1/2003 of 16 December 2002 on the implementation of the rules on competition laid down in Articles 81 and 82 of the Treaty

2. Article 6 is repealed.

Article 43 Repeal of Regulations No 17 and No 141

1. Regulation No 17 is repealed with the exception of Artide 8(3) which continues to apply to decisions adopted pursuant to Article 81(3) of the Treaty prior to the date of application of this Regulation until the date of expiration of those decisions.

2. Regulation No 141 is repealed.

3. References to the repealed Regulations shall be construed as references to this Regulation.

Article 44 Report on the application of the present Regulation

Five years from the date of application of this Regulation, the Commission shall report to the European Parliament and the Council on the functioning of this Regulation, in particular on the application of Article 11(6) and Article 17.

On the basis of this report, the Commission shall assess whether it is appropriate to propose to the Council a revision of this Regulation.

Article 45 Entry into force

This Regulation shall enter into force on the 20th day following that of its publication in the *Official Journal of the European Communities*.

It shall apply from 1 May 2004.

This Regulation shall be binding in its entirety and directly applicable in all Member States.

Done at Brussels, 16 December 2002.

For the Council
The President
M. FISCHER BOEL

APPENDIX 2
BLOCK EXEMPTION 2790/99

COMMISSION REGULATION (EC) No 2790/99 OF 22 DECEMBER 1999
on the application of Article 81(3) of the Treaty to categories of vertical agreements and concerted practices
(Text with EEA relevance)

THE COMMISSION OF THE EUROPEAN COMMUNITIES,

Having regard to the Treaty establishing the European Community,

Having regard to Council Regulation No 19/65/EEC of 2 March 1965 on the application of Article 85(3) of the Treaty to certain categories of agreements and concerted practices, as last amended by Regulation (EC) No 1215/1999, and in particular Article 1 thereof,

Having published a draft of this Regulation,

Having consulted the Advisory Committee on Restrictive Practices and Dominant Positions,

Whereas:

(1) Regulation No 19/65/EEC empowers the Commission to apply Article 81(3) of the Treaty (formerly Article 85(3)) by regulation to certain categories of vertical agreements and corresponding concerted practices falling within Article 81(1).

(2) Experience acquired to date makes it possible to define a category of vertical agreements which can be regarded as normally satisfying the conditions laid down in Article 81(3).

(3) This category includes vertical agreements for the purchase or sale of goods or services where these agreements are concluded between non-competing undertakings, between certain competitors or by certain associations of retailers of goods; it also includes vertical agreements containing ancillary provisions on the assignment or use of intellectual property rights; for the purposes of this Regulation, the term 'vertical agreements' includes the corresponding concerted practices.

(4) For the application of Article 81(3) by regulation, it is not necessary to define those vertical agreements which are capable of falling within Article 81(1); in the individual assessment of agreements under Article 81(1), account has to be taken of several factors, and in particular the market structure on the supply and purchase side.

(5) The benefit of the block exemption should be limited to vertical agreements for which it can be assumed with sufficient certainty that they satisfy the conditions of Article 81(3).

(6) Vertical agreements of the category defined in this Regulation can improve economic efficiency within a chain of production or distribution by facilitating better coordination between the participating undertakings; in particular, they can lead to a

reduction in the transaction and distribution costs of the parties and to an optimisation of their sales and investment levels.

(7) The likelihood that such efficiency-enhancing effects will outweigh any anti-competitive effects due to restrictions contained in vertical agreements depends on the degree of market power of the undertakings concerned and, therefore, on the extent to which those undertakings face competition from other suppliers of goods or services regarded by the buyer as interchangeable or substitutable for one another, by reason of the products' characteristics, their prices and their intended use.

(8) It can be presumed that, where the share of the relevant market accounted for by the supplier does not exceed 30%, vertical agreements which do not contain certain types of severely anti-competitive restraints generally lead to an improvement in production or distribution and allow consumers a fair share of the resulting benefits; in the case of vertical agreements containing exclusive supply obligations, it is the market share of the buyer which is relevant in determining the overall effects of such vertical agreements on the market.

(9) Above the market share threshold of 30%, there can be no presumption that vertical agreements falling within the scope of Article 81(1) will usually give rise to objective advantages of such a character and size as to compensate for the disadvantages which they create for competition.

(10) This Regulation should not exempt vertical agreements containing restrictions which are not indispensable to the attainment of the positive effects mentioned above; in particular, vertical agreements containing certain types of severely anti-competitive restraints such as minimum and fixed resale-prices, as well as certain types of territorial protection, should be excluded from the benefit of the block exemption established by this Regulation irrespective of the market share of the undertakings concerned.

(11) In order to ensure access to or to prevent collusion on the relevant market, certain conditions are to be attached to the block exemption; to this end, the exemption of non-compete obligations should be limited to obligations which do not exceed a definite duration; for the same reasons, any direct or indirect obligation causing the members of a selective distribution system not to sell the brands of particular competing suppliers should be excluded from the benefit of this Regulation.

(12) The market-share limitation, the non-exemption of certain vertical agreements and the conditions provided for in this Regulation normally ensure that the agreements to which the block exemption applies do not enable the participating undertakings to eliminate competition in respect of a substantial part of the products in question.

(13) In particular cases in which the agreements falling under this Regulation nevertheless have effects incompatible with Article 81(3), the Commission may withdraw the benefit of the block exemption; this may occur in particular where the buyer has significant market power in the relevant market in which it resells the goods or provides the services or where parallel networks of vertical agreements have similar effects which significantly restrict access to a relevant market or competition therein; such cumulative effects may for example arise in the case of selective distribution or non-compete obligations.

(14) Regulation No 19/65/EEC empowers the competent authorities of Member States to withdraw the benefit of the block exemption in respect of vertical agreements having effects incompatible with the conditions laid down in Article 81(3), where such effects are felt in their respective territory, or in a part thereof, and where such territory has the characteristics of a distinct geographic market; Member States should ensure that

the exercise of this power of withdrawal does not prejudice the uniform application throughout the common market of the Community competition rules or the full effect of the measures adopted in implementation of those rules.

(15) In order to strengthen supervision of parallel networks of vertical agreements which have similar restrictive effects and which cover more than 50% of a given market, the Commission may declare this Regulation inapplicable to vertical agreements containing specific restraints relating to the market concerned, thereby restoring the full application of Article 81 to such agreements.

(16) This Regulation is without prejudice to the application of Article 82.

(17) In accordance with the principle of the primacy of Community law, no measure taken pursuant to national laws on competition should prejudice the uniform application throughout the common market of the Community competition rules or the full effect of any measures adopted in implementation of those rules, including this Regulation,

HAS ADOPTED THIS REGULATION:

Article 1

For the purposes of this Regulation:

(a) 'competing undertakings' means actual or potential suppliers in the same product market; the product market includes goods or services which are regarded by the buyer as interchangeable with or substitutable for the contract goods or services, by reason of the products' characteristics, their prices and their intended use;

(b) 'non-compete obligation' means any direct or indirect obligation causing the buyer not to manufacture, purchase, sell or resell goods or services which compete with the contract goods or services, or any direct or indirect obligation on the buyer to purchase from the supplier or from another undertaking designated by the supplier more than 80% of the buyer's total purchases of the contract goods or services and their substitutes on the relevant market, calculated on the basis of the value of its purchases in the preceding calendar year,

(c) 'exclusive supply obligation' means any direct or indirect obligation causing the supplier to sell the goods or services specified in the agreement only to one buyer inside the Community for the purposes of a specific use or for resale;

(d) 'Selective distribution system' means a distribution system where the supplier undertakes to sell the contract goods or services, either directly or indirectly, only to distributors selected on the basis of specified criteria and where these distributors undertake not to sell such goods or services to unauthorised distributors;

(e) 'intellectual property rights' includes industrial property rights, copyright and neighbouring rights;

(f) 'know-how' means a package of non-patented practical information, resulting from experience and testing by the supplier, which is secret, substantial and identified: in this context, 'secret' means that the know-how, as a body or in the precise configuration and assembly of its components, is not generally known or easily accessible; 'substantial' means that the know-how includes information which is indispensable to the buyer for the use, sale or resale of the contract goods or services; 'identified' means that the know-how must be described in a sufficiently comprehensive manner so as to make it possible to verify that it fulfils the criteria of secrecy and substantiality;

(g) 'buyer' includes an undertaking which, under an agreement falling within Article 81(1) of the Treaty, sells goods or services on behalf of another undertaking.

Article 2

1. Pursuant to Article 81(3) of the Treaty and subject to the provisions of this Regulation, it is hereby declared that Article 81(1) shall not apply to agreements or concerted practices entered into between two or more undertakings each of which operates, for the purposes of the agreement, at a different level of the production or distribution chain, and relating to the conditions under which the parties may purchase, sell or resell certain goods or services ('vertical agreements').

This exemption shall apply to the extent that such agreements contain restrictions of competition falling within the scope of Article 81(1) ('vertical restraints').

2. The exemption provided for in paragraph 1 shall apply to vertical agreements entered into between an association of undertakings and its members, or between such an association and its suppliers, only if all its members are retailers of goods and if no individual member of the association, together with its connected undertakings, has a total annual turnover exceeding EUR 50 million; vertical agreements entered into by such associations shall be covered by this Regulation without prejudice to the application of Article 81 to horizontal agreements concluded between the members of the association or decisions adopted by the association.

3. The exemption provided for in paragraph 1 shall apply to vertical agreements containing provisions which relate to the assignment to the buyer or use by the buyer of intellectual property rights, provided that those provisions do not constitute the primary object of such agreements and are directly related to the use, sale or resale of goods or services by the buyer or its customers. The exemption applies on condition that, in relation to the contract goods or services, those provisions do not contain restrictions of competition having the same object or effect as vertical restraints which are not exempted under this Regulation.

4. The exemption provided for in paragraph 1 shall not apply to vertical agreements entered into between competing undertakings; however, it shall apply where competing undertakings enter into a non-reciprocal vertical agreement and:

(a) the buyer has a total annual turnover not exceeding EUR 100 million, or

(b) the supplier is a manufacturer and a distributor of goods, while the buyer is a distributor not manufacturing goods competing with the contract goods, or

(c) the supplier is a provider of services at several levels of trade, while the buyer does not provide competing services at the level of trade where it purchases the contract services.

5. This Regulation shall not apply to vertical agreements the subject matter of which falls within the scope of any other block exemption regulation.

Article 3

1. Subject to paragraph 2 of this Article, the exemption provided for in Article 2 shall apply on condition that the market share held by the supplier does not exceed 30% of the relevant market on which it sells the contract goods or services.

2. In the case of vertical agreements containing exclusive supply obligations, the exemption provided for in Article 2 shall apply on condition that the market share held by the buyer does not exceed 30% of the relevant market on which it purchases the contract goods or services.

Article 4

The exemption provided for in Article 2 shall not apply to vertical agreements which, directly or indirectly, in isolation or in combination with other factors under the control of the parties, have as their object:

(a) the restriction of the buyer's ability to determine its sale price, without prejudice to the possibility of the supplier's imposing a maximum sale price or recommending a sale price, provided that they do not amount to a fixed or minimum sale price as a result of pressure from, or incentives offered by, any of the parties;

(b) the restriction of the territory into which, or of the customers to whom, the buyer may sell the contract goods or services, except:

— the restriction of active sales into the exclusive territory or to an exclusive customer group reserved to the supplier or allocated by the supplier to another buyer, where such a restriction does not limit sales by the customers of the buyer,

— the restriction of sales to end users by a buyer operating at the wholesale level of trade,

— the restriction of sales to unauthorised distributors by the members of a selective distribution system, and

— the restriction of the buyer's ability to sell components, supplied for the purposes of incorporation, to customers who would use them to manufacture the same type of goods as those produced by the supplier;

(c) the restriction of active or passive sales to end users by members of a selective distribution system operating at the retail level of trade, without prejudice to the possibility of prohibiting a member of the system from operating out of an unauthorised place of establishment;

(d) the restriction of cross-supplies between distributors within a selective distribution system, including between distributors operating at different level of trade;

(e) the restriction agreed between a supplier of components and a buyer who incorporates those components, which limits the supplier to selling the components as spare parts to end-users or to repairers or other service providers not entrusted by the buyer with the repair or servicing of its goods.

Article 5

The exemption provided for in Article 2 shall not apply to any of the following obligations contained in vertical agreements:

(a) any direct or indirect non-compete obligation, the duration of which is indefinite or exceeds five years. A non-compete obligation which is tacitly renewable beyond a period of five years is to be deemed to have been concluded for an indefinite duration. However, the time limitation of five years shall not apply where the contract goods or services are sold by the buyer from premises and land owned by the supplier or leased by the supplier from third parties not connected with the buyer, provided that the duration of the non-compete obligation does not exceed the period of occupancy of the premises and land by the buyer;

(b) any direct or indirect obligation causing the buyer, after termination of the agreement, not to manufacture, purchase, sell or resell goods or services, unless such obligation:

— relates to goods or services which compete with the contract goods or services, and

— is limited to the premises and land from which the buyer has operated during the contract period, and

— is indispensable to protect know-how transferred by the supplier to the buyer,

and provided that the duration of such non-compete obligation is limited to a period of one year after termination of the agreement; this obligation is without prejudice to the possibility of imposing a restriction which is unlimited in time on the use and disclosure of know-how which has not entered the public domain;

(c) any direct or indirect obligation causing the members of a selective distribution system not to sell the brands of particular competing suppliers.

Article 6

The Commission may withdraw the benefit of this Regulation, pursuant to Article 7(1) of Regulation No 19/65/EEC, where it finds in any particular case that vertical agreements to which this Regulation applies nevertheless have effects which are incompatible with the conditions laid down in Article 81(3) of the Treaty, and in particular where access to the relevant market or competition therein is significantly restricted by the cumulative effect of parallel networks of similar vertical restraints implemented by competing suppliers or buyers.

Article 7

Where in any particular case vertical agreements to which the exemption provided for in Article 2 applies have effects incompatible with the conditions laid down in Article 81(3) of the Treaty in the territory of a Member State, or in a part thereof, which has all the characteristics of a distinct geographic market, the competent authority of that Member State may withdraw the benefit of application of this Regulation in respect of that territory, under the same conditions as provided in Article 6.

Article 8

1. Pursuant to Article 1a of Regulation No 19/65/EEC, the Commission may by regulation declare that, where parallel networks of similar vertical restraints cover more than 50% of a relevant market, this Regulation shall not apply to vertical agreements containing specific restraints relating to that market.

2. A regulation pursuant to paragraph 1 shall not become applicable earlier than six months following its adoption.

Article 9

1. The market share of 30% provided for in Article 3(1) shall be calculated on the basis of the market sales value of the contract goods or services and other goods or services sold by the supplier, which are regarded as interchangeable or substitutable by the buyer, by reason of the products' characteristics, their prices and their intended use; if market sales value data are not available, estimates based on other reliable market information, including market sales volumes, may be used to establish the market share of the undertaking concerned. For the purposes of Article 3(2), it is either the market purchase value or estimates thereof which shall be used to calculate the market share.

2. For the purposes of applying the market share threshold provided for in Article 3 the following rules shall apply:

(a) the market share shall be calculated on the basis of data relating to the preceding calendar year;

(b) the market share shall include any goods or services supplied to integrated distributors for the purposes of sale;

(c) if the market share is initially not more than 30% but subsequently rises above that level without exceeding 35%, the exemption provided for in Article 2 shall continue to apply for a period of two consecutive calendar years following the year in which the 30% market share threshold was first exceeded;

(d) if the market share is initially not more than 30% but subsequently rises above 35%, the exemption provided for in Article 2 shall continue to apply for one calendar year following the year in which the level of 35% was first exceeded.

(e) the benefit of points (c) and (d) may not be combined so as to exceed a period of two calendar years.

Article 10

1. For the purpose of calculating total annual turnover within the meaning of Article 2(2) and (4), the turnover achieved during the previous financial year by the relevant party to the vertical agreement and the turnover achieved by its connected undertakings in respect of all goods and services, excluding all taxes and other duties, shall be added together. For this purpose, no account shall be taken of dealings between the party to the vertical agreement and its connected undertakings or between its connected undertakings.

2. The exemption provided for in Article 2 shall remain applicable where, for any period of two consecutive financial years, the total annual turnover threshold is exceeded by no more than 10%.

Article 11

1. For the purposes of this Regulation, the terms 'undertaking', 'supplier' and 'buyer' shall include their respective connected undertakings.

2. 'Connected undertakings' are:

(a) undertakings in which a party to the agreement, directly or indirectly:
- has the power to exercise more than half the voting rights, or
- has the power to appoint more than half the members of the supervisory board, board of management or bodies legally representing the undertaking, or
- has the right to manage the undertaking's affairs;

(b) undertakings which directly or indirectly have, over a party to the agreement, the rights or powers listed in (a);

(c) undertakings in which an undertaking referred to in (b) has, directly or indirectly, the rights or powers listed in (a);

(d) undertakings in which a party to the agreement together with one or more of the undertakings referred to in (a), (b) or (c), or in which two or more of the latter undertakings, jointly have the rights or powers listed in (a);

(e) undertakings in which the rights or the powers listed in (a) are jointly held by:
- parties to the agreement or their respective connected undertakings referred to in (a) to (d), or
- one or more of the parties to the agreement or one or more of their connected undertakings referred to in (a) to (d) and one or more third parties.

3. For the purposes of Article 3, the market share held by the undertakings referred to in paragraph 2(e) of this Article shall be apportioned equally to each undertaking having the rights or the powers listed in paragraph 2(a).

Article 12

1. The exemptions provided for in Commission Regulations (EEC) No 1983/83, (EEC) No 1984/83 and (EEC) No 4087/88 shall continue to apply until 31 May 2000.

2. The prohibition laid down in Article 81(1) of the EC Treaty shall not apply during the period from 1 June 2000 to 31 December 2001 in respect of agreements already in force on 31 May 2000 which do not satisfy the conditions for exemption provided for in this Regulation but which satisfy the conditions for exemption provided for in Regulations (EEC) No 1983/83, (EEC) No 1984/83 or (EEC) No 4087/88.

Article 13

This Regulation shall enter into force on 1 January 2000.

It shall apply from 1 June 2000, except for Article 12(1) which shall apply from 1 January 2000.

This Regulation shall expire on 31 May 2010.

This Regulation shall be binding in its entirety and directly applicable in all Member States.

Done at Brussels, 22 December 1999.

For the Commission
Mario MONTI
Member of the Commission

APPENDIX 3
HEARING OFFICERS AND COMMISSION POLICY ON ACCESS TO THE FILE

A3.1 Extracts from Commission Decision 2001/462 on the terms of reference for hearing officers in certain competition proceedings

COMMISSION DECISION OF 23 MAY 2001
on the terms of reference of hearing officers in certain competition proceedings (notified under document number C(2001) 1461)
(Text with EEA relevance) (2001/462/EC, ECSC)

THE COMMISSION OF THE EUROPEAN COMMUNITIES,

Having regard to the Treaty establishing the European Community,

...

Whereas:

(1) The right of the parties concerned and of third parties to be heard before a final decision affecting their interests is taken is a fundamental principle of Community law... .

(2) The Commission must ensure that that right is guaranteed in its competition proceedings, having regard in particular to the Charter of Fundamental Rights of the European Union.

(3) The conduct of administrative proceedings should therefore be entrusted to an independent person experienced in competition matters who has the integrity necessary to contribute to the objectivity, transparency and efficiency of those proceedings.

(4) The Commission created the post of hearing officer for these purposes in 1982 and last laid down the terms of reference for that post in Commission Decision 94/810/ECSC, EC of 12 December 1994 on the terms of reference of hearing officers in competition procedures before the Commission.

(5) It is necessary to further strengthen the role of the hearing officer and to adapt and consolidate those terms of reference in the light of developments in competition law.

(6) In order to ensure the independence of the hearing officer, he should be attached, for administrative purposes, to the member of the Commission with special responsibility for competition. Transparency as regards the appointment, termination of appointment and transfer of hearing officers should be increased.

...

(8) The terms of reference of the hearing officer in competition proceedings should be framed in such a way as to safeguard the right to be heard throughout the whole procedure.

(9) When disclosing information on natural persons, particular attention should be paid to Regulation (EC) No 45/2001 of the European Parliament and of the Council of 18 December 2000 on the protection of individuals with regard to the processing of

personal data by the Community institutions and bodies and on the free movement of such data.

(10) This Decision should be without prejudice to the general rules granting or excluding access to Commission documents.

(11) Decision 94/810/ECSC, EC should be repealed,

HAS DECIDED AS FOLLOWS:

Article 1

The Commission shall appoint one or more hearing officers (hereinafter 'the hearing officer'), who shall ensure that the effective exercise of the right to be heard is respected in competition proceedings before the Commission under Articles 81 and 82 of the EC Treaty, Articles 65 and 66 of the ECSC Treaty, and Regulation (EEC) No 4064/89.

Article 2

1. The appointment of the hearing officer shall be published in the Official Journal of the European Communities. Any interruption, termination of appointment or transfer by whatever procedure, shall be the subject of a reasoned decision of the Commission. That decision shall be published in the Official Journal of the European Communities.

2. The hearing officer shall be attached, for administrative purposes, to the member of the Commission with special responsibility for competition (hereinafter 'the competent member of the Commission').

3. Where the hearing officer is unable to act, the competent member of the Commission, where appropriate after consultation of the hearing officer, shall designate another official, who is not involved in the case in question to carry out the hearing officer's duties.

Article 3

1. In performing his duties, the hearing officer shall take account of the need for effective application of the competition rules in accordance with the Community legislation in force and the principles laid down by the Court of Justice and the Court of First Instance of the European Communities.

2. The hearing officer shall be kept informed by the director responsible for investigating the case (hereinafter 'the director responsible') about the development of the procedure up to the stage of the draft decision to be submitted to the competent member of the Commission.

3. The hearing officer may present observations on any matter arising out of any Commission competition proceeding to the competent member of the Commission.

Article 4

1. The hearing officer shall organise and conduct the hearings provided for in the provisions implementing Articles 81 and 82 of the EC Treaty, Articles 65 and 66 of the ECSC Treaty and Regulation (EEC) No 4064/89, in accordance with Articles 5 to 13 of this Decision.

2. The provisions referred to in paragraph 1 are:

   (a) the first paragraph of Article 36 of the ECSC Treaty;
   (b) Regulation (EC) No 2842/98;
   (c) Regulation (EC) No 447/98.

Article 5

The hearing officer shall ensure that the hearing is properly conducted and contributes to the objectivity of the hearing itself and of any decision taken subsequently. The hearing officer shall seek to ensure in particular that, in the preparation of draft Commission decisions, due account is taken of all the relevant facts, whether favourable or unfavourable to the parties concerned, including the factual elements related to the gravity of any infringement.

Article 6

1. Applications to be heard from third parties, be they persons, undertakings or associations of persons or undertakings, shall be submitted in writing, together with a written statement explaining the applicant's interest in the outcome of the procedure.

2. Decisions as to whether third parties are to be heard shall be taken after consulting the director responsible.

3. Where it is found that an application has not shown a sufficient interest to be heard, he shall be informed in writing of the reasons for such finding. A time limit shall be fixed within which he may submit any further written comments.

Article 7

1. Applications to be heard orally shall be made in the applicant's written comments on letters which the Commission has addressed to him.

2. The letters referred to in paragraph 1 are those:

(a) communicating a statement of objections;

(b) inviting the written comments of a third party having shown sufficient interest to be heard;

(c) informing a complainant that in the Commission's view there are insufficient grounds for finding an infringement and inviting him to submit any further written comments.

3. Decisions as to whether applicants are to be heard orally shall be taken after consulting the director responsible.

Article 8

1. Where a person, an undertaking or an association of persons or undertakings has received one or more of the letters listed in Article 7(2) and has reason to believe that the Commission has in its possession documents which have not been disclosed to it and that those documents are necessary for the proper exercise of the right to be heard, access to those documents may be sought by means of a reasoned request.

2. The reasoned decision on any such request shall be communicated to the person, undertaking or association that made the request and to any other person, undertaking or association concerned by the procedure.

Article 9

Where it is intended to disclose information which may constitute a business secret of an undertaking, it shall be informed in writing of this intention and the reasons for it. A time limit shall be fixed within which the undertaking concerned may submit any written comments.

Where the undertaking concerned objects to the disclosure of the information but it is found that the information is not protected and may therefore be disclosed, that finding shall be stated in a reasoned decision which shall be notified to the undertaking concerned. The decision shall specify the date after which the information will be disclosed. This date shall not be less than one week from the date of notification.

The first and second paragraphs shall apply mutatis mutandis to the disclosure of information by publication in the Official Journal of the European Communities.

...

Article 11
Where appropriate, in view of the need to ensure that the hearing is properly prepared and particularly that questions of fact are clarified as far as possible, the hearing officer may, after consulting the director responsible, supply in advance to the parties invited to the hearing a list of the questions on which he wishes them to make known their views.
...

Article 12
1. After consulting the director responsible, the hearing officer shall determine the date, the duration and the place of the hearing. Where a postponement is requested, the hearing officer shall decide whether or not to allow it.
2. The hearing officer shall be fully responsible for the conduct of the hearing.
3. The hearing officer shall decide whether fresh documents should be admitted during the hearing, what persons should be heard on behalf of a party and whether the persons concerned should be heard separately or in the presence of other persons attending the hearing.
4. Where appropriate, in view of the need to ensure the right to be heard, the hearing officer may, after consulting the director responsible, afford persons, undertakings, and associations of persons or undertakings the opportunity of submitting further written comments after the oral hearing. The hearing officer shall fix a date by which such submissions may be made. The Commission shall not be obliged to take into account written comments received after that date.

Article 13
1. The hearing officer shall report to the competent member of the Commission on the hearing and the conclusions he draws from it, with regard to the respect of the right to be heard. The observations in this report shall concern procedural issues, including disclosure of documents and access to the file, time limits for replying to the statement of objections and the proper conduct of the oral hearing.
A copy of the report shall be given to the Director-General for Competition and to the director responsible.
2. In addition to the report referred to in paragraph 1, the hearing officer may make observations on the further progress of the proceedings. Such observations may relate among other things to the need for further information, the withdrawal of certain objections, or the formulation of further objections.
...

Article 15
The hearing officer shall, on the basis of the draft decision to be submitted to the Advisory Committee in the case in question, prepare a final report in writing on the respect of the right to be heard, as referred to in Article 13(1). This report will also consider whether the draft decision deals only with objections in respect of which the parties have been afforded the opportunity of making known their views, and, where appropriate, the objectivity of any enquiry within the meaning of Article 14.
The final report shall be submitted to the competent member of the Commission, the Director-General for Competition and the director responsible. It shall be communicated to the competent authorities of the Member States... .

Article 16
1. The hearing officer's final report shall be attached to the draft decision submitted to the Commission, in order to ensure that, when it reaches a decision on an individual case, the Commission is fully apprised of all relevant information as regards the course of the procedure and respect of the right to be heard.

2. The final report may be modified by the hearing officer in the light of any amendments to the draft decision up to the time the decision is adopted by the Commission.

3. The Commission shall communicate the hearing officer's final report, together with the decision, to the addressees of the decision. It shall publish the hearing officer's final report in the Official Journal of the European Communities, together with the decision, having regard to the legitimate interest of undertakings in the protection of their business secrets.

Article 17

Decision 94/810/ECSC, EC is repealed.

...

Done at Brussels, 23 May 2001.

For the Commission
Mario MONTI
Member of the Commission

A3.2 Commission Notice on the internal rules of procedure for processing requests for access to the file in cases pursuant to Articles 85 and 86 of the EC Treaty [1997] OJ C 25/3

INTRODUCTION

Access to the file is an important procedural stage in all contentious competition cases (prohibitions with or without a fine, prohibitions of mergers, rejection of complaints, etc). The Commission's task in this area is to reconcile two opposing obligations, namely that of safeguarding the rights of the defence and that of protecting confidential information concerning firms.

The purpose of this notice is to ensure compatibility between current administrative practice regarding access to the file and the case-law of the Court of Justice of the European Communities and the Court of First Instance, in particular the 'Soda-ash' cases. The line of conduct thus laid down concerns cases dealt with on the basis of the competition rules applicable to enterprises. Articles 85 and 86 of the EC Treaty, Regulation (EEC) No 4064/89 (hereinafter 'the Merger Regulation'), and Articles 65 and 66 of the ECSC Treaty.

Access to the file, which is one of the procedural safeguards designed to ensure effective exercise of the right to be heard provided for in Article 19(1) and (2) of Council Regulation No 17 and Article 2 of Commission Regulation No 99/63/EEC, as well as in the corresponding provisions of the Regulations governing the application of Articles 85 and 86 in the field of transport, must be arranged in all cases involving decisions on infringements, decisions rejecting complaints, decisions imposing interim measures and decisions adopted on the basis of Article 15(6) of Regulation No 17.

The guidelines set out below, however, essentially relate to the rights of the undertakings which are the subject of investigations into alleged infringements; they do not relate to the rights of third parties, and complainants in particular.

In merger cases, access to the file by parties directly concerned is expressly provided for in Article 18(3) of the Merger Regulation and in Article 13(3)(a) of Regulation (EC) No 3384/94 ('the Implementing Regulation').

I. SCOPE AND LIMITS OF ACCESS TO THE FILE

As the purpose of providing access to the file is to enable the addressees of a statement of objections to express their views on the conclusions reached by the Commission, the firms in question must have access to all the documents making up the 'file' of the Commission (DG IV), apart from the categories of documents identified in the *Hercules* judgment, namely the business secrets of other undertakings, internal Commission documents and other confidential information.

Thus not all the documents collected in the course of an investigation are communicable and a distinction must be made between non-communicable and communicable documents.

A. Non-communicable documents

1. Business secrets

Business secrets mean information (documents or parts of documents) for which an undertaking has claimed protection as 'business secrets', and which are recognised as such by the Commission.

The non-communicability of such information is intended to protect the legitimate interest of firms in preventing third parties from obtaining strategic information on their essential interests and on the operation or development of their business.

The criteria for determining what constitutes a business secret have not as yet been defined in full. Reference may be made, however, to the case-law, especially the Akzo and the BAT and Reynolds judgments, to the criteria used in anti-dumping procedures, and to decisions on the subject by the Hearing Officer. The term 'business secret' must be construed in its broader sense: according to Akzo, Regulation No 17 requires the Commission to have regard to the legitimate interest of firms in the protection of their business secrets.

Business secrets need no longer be protected when they are known outside the firm (or group or association of firms) to which they relate. Nor can facts remain business secrets if, owing to the passage of time or for any other reason, they are no longer commercially important.

Where business secrets provide evidence of an infringement or tend to exonerate a firm, the Commission must reconcile the interest in the protection of sensitive information, the public interest in having the infringement of the competition rules terminated, and the rights of the defence. This calls for an assessment of:

(i) the relevance of the information to determining whether or not an infringement has been committed;

(ii) its probative value;

(iii) whether it is indispensable;

(iv) the degree of sensitivity involved (to what extent would disclosure of the information harm the interests of the firm?);

(v) the seriousness of the infringement.

Each document must be assessed individually to determine whether the need to disclose it is greater than the harm which might result from disclosure.

2. Confidential documents

It is also necessary to protect information for which confidentiality has been requested.

This category includes information making it possible to identify the suppliers of the information who wish to remain anonymous to the other parties, and certain types of information communicated to the Commission on condition that confidentiality is observed, such as documents obtained during an investigation which form part of a firm's property and are the subject of a non-disclosure request (such as a market study commissioned by the firm and forming part of its property). As in the preceding case (business secrets), the Commission must reconcile the legitimate interest of the firm in protecting its assets, the public interest in having breaches of the competition rules terminated, and the rights of the defence. Military secrets also belong in the category of 'other confidential information'.

As a rule, the confidential nature of documents is not a bar to the disclosure if the information in question is necessary in order to prove an alleged infringement ('inculpatory documents') or if the papers invalidate or rebut the reasoning of the Commission set out in its statement of objections ('exculpatory documents').

3. Internal documents

Internal documents are, by their nature, not the sort of evidence on which the Commission can rely in its assessment of a case. For the most part they consist of drafts, opinions or memos from the departments concerned and relating to ongoing procedures.

The Commission departments must be able to express themselves freely within their institution concerning ongoing cases. The disclosure of such documents could also jeopardise the secrecy of the Commission's deliberations.

It should, moreover, be noted that the secrecy of proceedings is also protected by the code of conduct on public access to Commission and Council documents as set out in Commission Decision 94/90/ECSC, EC, Euratom, as amended by Decision 96/567/ECSC, EC, Euratom as are internal documents relating to inspections and investigations and those whose disclosure could jeopardise the protection of individual privacy, business and industrial secrets or the confidentiality requested by a legal or natural person.

These considerations justify the non-disclosure of this category of documents, which will, in future, be placed in the file of internal documents relating to cases under investigation, which is, as a matter of principle, inaccessible (see point II.A.2).

B. Communicable documents

All documents not regarded as 'non-communicable' under the abovementioned criteria are accessible to the parties concerned.

Thus, access to the file is not limited to documents which the Commission regards as 'relevant' to an undertaking's rights of defence.

The Commission does not select accessible documents in order to remove those which may be relevant to the defence of an undertaking. This concept, already outlined in the Court of First Instance judgments in Hercules and Cimenteries CBR, was confirmed and developed in the Soda-ash case, where the Court held that 'in the defended proceedings for which Regulation No 17 provides it cannot be for the Commission alone to decide which documents are of use for the defence .... The Commission must give the advisers of the undertaking concerned the opportunity to examine documents which may be relevant so that their probative value for the defence can be assessed' (Case T-30/91, paragraph 81).

Special note concerning studies:

It should be stressed that studies commissioned in connection with proceedings or for a specific file, whether used directly or indirectly in the proceedings, must be made accessible irrespective of their intrinsic value. Access must be given not only to the results of a study (reports, statistics, etc), but also to the Commission's correspondence with the contractor, the tender specifications and the methodology of the study.

However, correspondence relating to the financial aspects of a study and the references concerning the contractor remain confidential in the interests of the latter.

II. PROCEDURES FOR IMPLEMENTING ACCESS TO THE FILE

A. Preparatory procedure Cases investigated under Articles 85 and 86

1. Investigation file

1.1 Return of certain documents after inspection visits

In the course of its investigations under Article 14(2) and (3) of Regulation No 17, the Commission obtains a considerable number of documents, some of which may, following a detailed examination, prove to be irrelevant to the case in question. Such documents are normally returned to the firm as rapidly as possible.

1.2 Request for a nonconfidential version of a document

In order to facilitate access to the file at a later stage in proceedings, the undertakings concerned will systematically be asked to:

detail the information (documents or parts of documents) which they regard as business secrets and the confidential documents whose disclosure would injure them;
substantiate their claim for confidentiality in writing;
give the Commission a nonconfidential version of their confidential documents (where confidential passages are deleted).

As regards documents taken during an inspection (Article 14(2) and (3)), requests are made only after the inspectors have returned from their mission.

When an undertaking, in response to a request from the Commission, claims that the information supplied is confidential, the following procedure will be adopted:

(a) at that stage of the proceedings, claims of confidentiality which at first sight seem justified will be accepted provisionally. The Commission reserves the right, however, to reconsider the matter at a later stage of the proceedings;

(b) where it is apparent that the claim of confidentiality is clearly unjustified, for example where it relates to a document already published or distributed extensively, or is excessive where it covers all or virtually all the documents obtained or sent without any plausible justification, the firm concerned will be informed that the Commission does not agree with the scope of the confidentiality that is claimed. The matter will be dealt with when the final assessment is made of the accessibility of the documents (see below).

1.3 Final assessment of the accessibility of documents

It may prove necessary to grant other undertakings involved access to a document even where the undertaking that has issued it objects, if the document serves as a basis for the decision or is clearly an exculpatory document.

If an undertaking states that a document is confidential but does not submit a nonconfidential version, the following procedure applies:

the undertaking claiming confidentiality will be contacted again and asked for a reasonably coherent nonconfidential version of the document;

if the undertaking continues to object to the disclosure of the information, the competent department applies to the Hearing Officer, who will if necessary implement the procedure leading to a decision pursuant to Article 5(4) of Commission Decision 94/810/ECSC, EC of 12 December 1994 on the terms of reference of hearing officers in competition procedures before the Commission. The undertaking will be informed by letter that the Hearing Officer is examining the question.

1.4 Enumerative list of documents

An enumerative list of documents should be drawn up according to the following principles:

(a) the list should include uninterrupted numbering of all the pages in the investigation file and an indication (using a classification code) of the degree of accessibility of the document and the parties with authorised access;

(b) an access code is given to each document on the list:
— accessible document
— partially accessible document
— non-accessible document;

(c) the category of completely non-accessible documents essentially consists of documents containing 'business secrets' and other confidential documents. In view of the '*Soda-ash*' case-law, the list will include a summary enabling the content and subject of the documents to be identified, so that any firm having requested access to the file is able to determine in full knowledge of the facts whether the documents are likely to be relevant to its defence and to decide whether to request access despite that classification;

(d) accessible and partially accessible documents do not call for a description of their content in the list as they can be 'physically' consulted by all firms, either in their full version or in their non-confidential version. In the latter event, only the sensitive passages are deleted in such a way that the firm with access is able to determine the nature of the information deleted (eg turnover).

2. File of internal documents relating to ongoing cases

In order to simplify administration and increase efficiency, internal documents will, in future, be placed in the file of internal documents relating to cases under investigation (non-accessible) containing all internal documents in chronological order. Classification in this category is subject to the control of the Hearing Officer, who will if necessary certify that the papers contained therein are 'internal documents'.

The following, for example, will be deemed to be internal documents:

(a) requests for instructions made to, and instructions received from, hierarchical superiors on the treatment of cases;

(b) consultations with other Commission departments on a case;

(c) correspondence with other public authorities concerning a case;

(d) drafts and other working documents;

(e) individual technical assistance contracts (languages, computing, etc) relating to a specific aspect of a case.

B. Preparatory procedure — Cases examined within the meaning of the Merger Regulation

1. Measures common to the preparatory procedure in cases investigated pursuant to Articles 85 and 86

(a) Return of certain documents after an inspection

On-the-spot inspections are specifically provided for in Article 13 of the Merger Regulation: in such cases, the procedure provided for in point II.A.1.1 for cases examined on the basis of Articles 85 and 86 is applicable.

(b) Enumerative list of documents

The enumerative list of the documents in the Commission file with the access codes will be drawn up in accordance with the criteria set out in point II.A.1.4.

(c) Request for a non-confidential version of a document

In order to facilitate access to the file, firms being investigated will be asked to:

— detail the information (documents or parts of documents) they regard as business secrets and the confidential documents whose disclosure would injure them,

— substantiate their requests for confidentiality in writing,

— give the Commission a reasonably coherent non-confidential version of their confidential documents (where confidential passages are deleted).

This procedure will be followed in stage II cases (where the Commission initiates proceedings in respect of the notifying parties) and in stage I cases (giving rise to a Commission decision without initiation of proceedings).

2. Measures specific to preparatory procedures in merger cases

(a) Subsequent procedure in stage II cases

In stage II cases the subsequent procedure is as follows.

Where a firm states that all or part of the documents it has provided are business secrets, the following steps should be taken:

— if the claim appears to be justified, the documents or parts of documents concerned will be regarded as non-accessible to third parties,

— if the claim does not appear to be justified, the competent Commission department will ask the firm, in the course of the investigation and no later than the time at which the statement of objections is sent, to review its position. The firm must either state in writing which documents or parts of documents must be regarded as confidential, or send a non-confidential version of the documents.

If disagreement regarding the extent of the confidentiality persists, the competent department refers the matter to the Hearing Officer, who may if necessary take the decision provided for in Article 5(4) of Decision 94/810/ECSC, EC.

(b) Specific cases

Article 9(1) of the Merger Regulation provides that 'the Commission may, by means of a decision notified without delay to the undertakings concerned ... refer a notified concentration to the competent authorities of the Member State concerned'. In the context of access to the file, the parties concerned should, as a general rule be able to see the request for referral from a national authority, with the exception of any business secrets or other confidential information it may contain.

Article 22(3) of the Merger Regulation provides that 'If the Commission finds, at the request of a Member State, that a concentration (...) that has no Community dimension (...) creates or strengthens a dominant position (...) it may (...) adopt the decisions provided for in the second subparagraph of Article 8(2), (3) and (4)'. Such requests have the effect of empowering the Commission to deal with mergers which would normally fall outside its powers of review. Accordingly, the parties concerned should be granted right of access to the letter from the Member State requesting referral, after deletion of any business secrets or other confidential information.

C. Practical arrangements for access to the file

1. General rule: access by way of consultation on the Commission's premises

Firms are invited to examine the relevant files on the Commission's premises.

If the firm considers, on the basis of the list of documents it has received, that it requires certain non-accessible documents for its defence, it may make a reasoned request to that end to the Hearing Officer.

2. If the file is not too bulky, however, the firm has the choice of being sent all the accessible documents, apart from those already sent with the statement of objections or the letter rejecting the complaint, or of consulting the file on the Commission's premises.

As regards Articles 85 and 86 cases, contrary to a common previous practice, the statement of objections or letter of rejection will in future be accompanied only by the evidence adduced and documents cited on which the objections/rejection letter is based.

Any request for access made prior to submission of the statement of objections will in principle be inadmissible.

D. Particular questions which may arise in connection with complaints and procedures relating to abuse of a dominant position (Articles 85 and 86)

1. Complaints

While complainants may properly be involved in proceedings, they do not have the same rights and guarantees as the alleged infringers. A complainant's right to consult the files does not share the same basis as the rights of defence of the addressees of a statement of objections, and there are no grounds for treating the rights of the complainant as equivalent to those of the firms objected to.

Nevertheless, a complainant who has been informed of the intention to reject his complaint may request access to the documents on which the Commission based its position. Complainants may not, however, have access to any confidential information or other business secrets belonging to the firms complained of, or to third-party firms, which the Commission has obtained in the course of its investigations (Articles 11 and 14 of Regulation No 17).

Clearly, it is even more necessary here to respect the principle of confidentiality as there is no presumption of infringement. In accordance with the judgment in Fedetab, Article 19(2) of Regulation No 17 gives complainants a right to be heard and not a right to receive confidential information.

2. Procedures in cases of abuse of a dominant position

The question of procedures in cases of abuse of a dominant position was referred to by the Court of First Instance and the Court of Justice in the *BPB Industries and British Gypsum v Commission* case.

By definition, firms in a dominant position on a market are able to place very considerable economic or commercial pressure on their competitors or on their trading partners, customers or suppliers.

The Court of First Instance and the Court of Justice thus acknowledged the legitimacy of the reluctance displayed by the Commission in revealing certain letters received from customers of the firm being investigated.

Although it is of value to the Commission for giving a better understanding of the market concerned, the information does not in any way constitute inculpatory evidence, and its disclosure to the firm concerned might easily expose the authors to the risk of retaliatory measures.

APPENDIX 4
REGULATION 240/96: THE BLOCK EXEMPTION ON TECHNOLOGY TRANSFER

A4.1 Introduction

As we saw in **3.5.2**, block exemptions were introduced (through the medium of Commission regulations) in order to lighten the workload of the Commission. They have been adopted in several common types of business arrangement, most notably perhaps in the area of exclusive dealing. Here, after an initial single regulation covering exclusive dealing in its entirety (Regulation 67/67, which ran for 15 years), the Commission issued two further measures in 1983, one for exclusive distribution and a second for exclusive purchase (Regulations 1983/83 and 1984/83, respectively).

The Commission published a Notice to offer 'a certain amount of interpretative guidance' to the two 1983 block exemptions (OJ 1984 C101/2). This perhaps reflects a recognition that the format of the block exemptions did (and still does) not lend itself to immediate comprehension or practical application. As the Commission's Notice points out (at para 2):

> In determining how a given provision is to be applied, one must take into account, in addition to the ordinary meaning of the words used, the intention of the provision as this emerges from the preamble. For further guidance, reference should be made to the principles that have been evolved in the case law of the Court of Justice of the European Communities and in the Commission's decisions on individual cases.

One key piece of advice is offered in that passage. When trying to apply a block exemption, and divine its meaning, the reader should always try to cross-refer between the laws (the articles in a regulation) and the explanation of purpose (the preamble or recitals in a regulation). The latter often shed light on what a provision means or how it is intended to operate; often they make reference to a specific provision in an article. The other piece of advice that is on offer in this appendix is: try to understand how the conduct or contractual clause which a provision refers to will actually operate in practice. What sort of behaviour is being described in the article? Why is the Commission prepared to exempt it on an 'unseen' basis? The block exemptions can be extremely useful analytical tools if you are prepared to invest the time in understanding them and how to use them. As well as helping you to decide whether a particular clause, for example, is protected by a block exemption, your familiarity with the Commission's attitude to a method of doing business (eg distribution franchising will also help you when determining if a particular contract or conduct infringes Article 81(1) (ex 85(1)) or might qualify for individual exemption under Article 81(3) (ex 85(3)).

The rest of this appendix is intended to help you achieve greater familiarity with one of the block exemptions, namely Regulation 240/96 on technology transfer. In **A4.2**, you will find the text of the regulation, as issued by the Commission in 1996. Then in **A4.3** you will find a commentary on the regulation which, it is hoped, will help you to see one way of 'dissecting' the regulation and making it of practical application to you. It is hoped that, when reading the commentary, you will make copious cross-references to the text of the regulation itself.

A4.2 Regulation 240/96: the block exemption

COMMISSION REGULATION (EEC) NO 240/96 OF 31 JANUARY 1996
on the application of Article 85(3) of the Treaty to certain categories of technology transfer agreements
(Text with EEA relevance)
(OJ [1996] L 31/2)

THE COMMISSION OF THE EUROPEAN COMMUNITIES,

Having regard to the Treaty establishing the European Community,

Having regard to Council Regulation 19/65/EEC of 2 March 1965 on the application of Article 85(3) of the Treaty to certain categories of agreements and concerted practices, as last amended by the Act of Accession of Austria, Finland and Sweden, and in particular Article 1 thereof,

Having published a draft of this Regulation,

After consulting the Advisory Committee on Restrictive Practices and Dominant Positions,

Whereas:

(1) Regulation 19/65/EEC empowers the Commission to apply Article 85(3) of the Treaty by regulation to certain categories of agreements and concerted practices falling within the scope of Article 85(1) which include restrictions imposed in relation to the acquisition or use of industrial property rights — in particular of patents, utility models, designs or trademarks — or to the rights arising out of contracts for assignment of, or the right to use, a method of manufacture of knowledge relating to use or to the application of industrial processes.

(2) The Commission has made use of this power by adopting Regulation (EEC) 2349/84 of 23 July 1984 on the application of Article 85(3) of the Treaty to certain categories of patent licensing agreements, as last amended by Regulation (EC) 2131/95, and Regulation (EEC) 556/89 of 30 November 1988 on the application of Article 85(3) of the Treaty to certain categories of know-how licensing agreements, as last amended by the Act of Accession of Austria, Finland and Sweden.

(3) These two block exemptions ought to be combined into a single regulation covering technology transfer agreements, and the rules governing patent licensing agreements and agreements for the licensing of know-how ought to be harmonised and simplified as far as possible, in order to encourage the disseminaton of technical knowledge in the Community and to promote the manufacture of technically more sophisticated products. In those circumstances Regulation (EEC) 556/89 should be repealed.

(4) This Regulation should apply to the licensing of Member States' own patents, Community patents and European patents ('pure' patent licensing agreements). It should also apply to agreements for the licensing of non-patented technical information such as descriptions of manufacturing processes, recipes, formulae, designs or drawings, commonly termed 'know-how' ('pure' know-how licensing agreements), and to combined patent and know-how licensing agreements ('mixed' agreements), which are playing an increasingly important role in the transfer of technology. For the purposes of this Regulation, a number of terms are defined in Article 10.

(5) Patent or know-how licensing agreements are agreements whereby one undertaking which holds a patent or know-how ('the licensor') permits another undertaking ('the licensee') to exploit the patent thereby licensed, or communicates the know-how to it, in particular for purposes of manufacture, use or putting on the market. In the light of experience acquired so far, it is possible to define a category of licensing agreements covering all or part of the common market which are capable of falling within the scope of Article 85(1) but which can normally be regarded as satisfying the conditions laid down in Article 85(3), where patents are necessary for the achievement of the objects of the licensed technology by a mixed agreement or where know-how — whether it is ancillary to patents or independent of them — is secret, substantial and identified in any appropriate form. These criteria are intended only to ensure that the licensing of the know-how or the grant of the patent licence justifies a block exemption of obligations restricting competition. This is without prejudice to the right of the parties to include in the contract provisions regarding other obligations, such as the obligation to pay royalties, even if the block exemption no longer applies.

(6) It is appropriate to extend the scope of this Regulation to pure or mixed agreements containing the licensing of intellectual property rights other than patents (in particular, trademarks, design rights and copyrights, especially software protection), when such additional licensing contributes to the achievement of the objects of the licensed technology and contains only ancillary provisions.

(7) Where such pure or mixed licensing agreements contain not only obligations relating to territories within the common market but also obligations relating to non-member countries, the presence of the latter does not prevent this Regulation from applying to the obligations relating to territories within the common market. Where licensing agreements for non-member countries or for territories which extend beyond the frontiers of the Community have effects within the common market which may fall within the scope of Article 85(1), such agreements should be covered by this Regulation to the same extent as would agreements for territories within the common market.

(8) The objective being to facilitate the dissemination of technology and the improvement of manufacturing processes, this Regulation should apply only where the licensee himself manufactures the licensed products or has them manufactured for his account, or where the licensed product is a service, provides the service himself or has the service provided for his account, irrespective of whether or not the licensee is also entitled to use confidential information provided by the licensor for the promotion and sale of the licensed product. The scope of this Regulation should therefore exclude agreements solely for the purpose of sale. Also to be excluded from the scope of this Regulation are agreements relating to marketing know-how communicated in the context of franchising arrangements and certain licensing agreements entered into in connection with arrangements such as joint ventures or patent pools and other arrangements in which a licence is granted in exchange for other licences not related to improvements to or new applications of the licensed technology. Such agreements pose different problems which cannot at present be dealt with in a single regulation (Article 5).

(9) Given the similarity between sale and exclusive licensing, and the danger that the requirements of this Regulation might be evaded by presenting as assignments what are in fact exclusive licenses restrictive of competition, this regulation should apply to agreements concerning the assignment and acquisition of patents or know-how where the risk associated with exploitation remains with the assignor. It should also apply to licensing agreements in which the licensor is not the holder of the patent or know-how but is authorised by the holder to grant the licence (as in the case of sub-licences) and to

licensing agreements in which the parties' rights or obligations are assumed by connected undertakings (Article 6).

(10) Exclusive licensing agreements, ie, agreements in which the licensor undertakes not to exploit the licensed technology in the licensed territory himself or to grant further licences there, may not be in themselves incompatible with Article 85(1) where they are concerned with the introduction and protection of a new technology in the licensed territory, by reason of the scale of the research which has been undertaken, of the increase in the level of competition, in particular inter-brand competition, and of the competitiveness of the undertakings concerned resulting from the dissemination of innovation within the Community. In so far as agreements of this kind fall, in other circumstances, within the scope of Article 85(1), it is appropriate to include them in Article 1 in order that they may also benefit from the exemption.

(11) The exemption of export bans on the licensor and on the licensees does not prejudice any developments in the case law of the Court of Justice in relation to such agreements, notably with respect to Articles 30 to 36 and Article 85(1). This is also the case, in particular, regarding the prohibition on the licensee from selling the licensed product in territories granted to other licensees (passive competition).

(12) The obligations listed in Article 1 generally contribute to improving the production of goods and to promoting technical progress. They make the holders of patents or know-how more willing to grant licences and licensees more inclined to undertake the investment required to manufacture, use and put on the market a new product or to use a new process. Such obligations may be permitted under this Regulation in respect of territories where the licensed product is protected by patents as long as these remain in force.

(13) Since the point at which the know-how ceases to be secret can be difficult to determine, it is appropriate, in respect of territories where the licensed technology comprises know-how only, to limit such obligations to a fixed number of years. Moreover, in order to provide sufficient periods of protection, it is appropriate to take as the starting-point for such periods the date on which the product is first put on the market in the Community by a licensee.

(14) Exemption under Article 85(3) of longer periods of territorial protection for know-how agreements, in particular in order to protect expensive and risky investment or where the parties were not competitors at the date of the grant of the licence, can be granted only by individual decision. On the other hand, parties are free to extend the term of their agreements in order to exploit any subsequent improvement and to provide for the payment of additional royalties. However, in such cases, further periods of territorial protection may be allowed only starting from the date of licensing of the secret improvements in the Community, and by individual decision. Where the research for improvements results in innovations which are distinct from the licensed technology the parties may conclude a new agreement benefitting from an exemption under this Regulation.

(15) Provision should also be made for exemption of an obligation on the licensee not to put the product on the market in the territories of other licensees, the permitted period for such an obligation (this obligation would ban not just active competition but passive competition too) should, however, be limited to a few years from the date on which the licensed product is first put on the market in the Community by a licensee, irrespective of whether the licensed technology comprises know-how, patents or both in the territories concerned.

(16) The exemption of territorial protection should apply for the whole duration of the periods thus permitted, as long as the patents remain in force or the know-how

remains secret and substantial. The parties to a mixed patent and know-how licensing agreement must be able to take advantage in a particular territory of the period of protection conferred by a patent or by the know-how, whichever is the longer.

(17) The obligations listed in Article 1 also generally fulfil the other conditions for the application of Article 85(3). Consumers will, as a rule, be allowed a fair share of the benefit resulting from the improvement in the supply of goods on the market. To safeguard this effect, however, it is right to exclude from the application of Article 1 cases where the parties agree to refuse to meet demand from users or resellers within their respective territories who would resell for export, or to take other steps to impede parallel imports. The obligations referred to above thus only impose restrictions which are indispensable to the attainment of their objectives.

(18) It is desirable to list in this Regulation a number of obligations that are commonly found in licensing agreements but are normally not restrictive of competition, and to provide that in the event that because of the particular economic or legal circumstances they should fall within Article 85(1), they too will be covered by the exemption. This list, in Article 2, is not exhaustive.

(19) This Regulation must also specify what restrictions or provisions may not be included in licensing agreements if these are to benefit from the block exemption. The restrictions listed in Article 3 may fall under the prohibition of Article 85(1), but in their case there can be no general presumption that, although they relate to the transfer of technology, they will lead to the positive effects required by Article 85(3), as would be necessary for the granting of a block exemption. Such restrictions can be declared exempt only by an individual decision, taking account of the market position of the undertakings concerned and the degree of concentration on the relevant market.

(20) The obligations on the licensee to cease using the licensed technology after the termination of the agreement (Article 2(1)(3)) and to make improvements available to the licensor (Article 2(1)(4)) do not generally restrict competition. The post-term use ban may be regarded as a normal feature of licensing, as otherwise the licensor would be forced to transfer his know-how or patents in perpetuity. Undertakings by the licensee to grant back to the licensor a licence for improvements to the licensed know-how and/or patents are generally not restrictive of competition if the licensee is entitled by the contract to share in future experience and inventions made by the licensor. On the other hand, a restrictive effect on competition arises where the agreement obliges the licensee to assign to the licensor rights to improvements of the originally licensed technology that he himself has brought about (Article 3(6)).

(21) The list of clauses which do not prevent exemption also includes an obligation on the licensee to keep paying royalties until the end of the agreement independently of whether or not the licensed know-how has entered into the public domain through the action of third parties or of the licensee himself (Article 2(1)(7)). Moreover, the parties must be free, in order to facilitate payment, to spread the royalty payments for the use of the licensed technology over a period extending beyond the duration of the licensed patents, in particular by setting lower royalty rates. As a rule, parties do not need to be protected against the foreseeable financial consequences of an agreement freely entered into, and they should therefore be free to choose the appropriate means of financing the technology transfer and sharing between them the risks of such use. However, the setting of rates of royalty so as to achieve one of the restrictions listed in Article 3 renders the agreement ineligible for the block exemption.

(22) An obligation on the licensee to restrict his exploitation of the licensed technology to one or more technical fields of application ('fields of use') or to one or more

product markets is not caught by Article 85(1) either, since the licensor is entitled to transfer the technology only for a limited purpose (Article 2(1)(8)).

(23) Clauses whereby the parties allocate customers within the same technological field of use or the same product market, either by an actual prohibition on supplying certain classes of customer or through an obligation with an equivalent effect, would also render the agreement ineligible for the block exemption where the parties are competitors for the contract products (Article 3(4)). Such restrictions between undertakings which are not competitors remain subject to the opposition procedure. Article 3 does not apply to cases where the patent or know-how licence is granted in order to provide a single customer with a second source of supply. In such a case, a prohibition on the second licensee from supplying persons other than the customer concerned is an essential condition for the grant of a second licence, since the purpose of the transaction is not to create an independent supplier in the market. The same applies to limitations on the quantities the licensee may supply to the customer concerned (Article 2(1)(13)).

(24) Besides the clauses already mentioned, the list of restrictions which render the block exemption inapplicable also includes restrictions regarding the selling prices of the licensed product or the quantities to be manufactured or sold, since they seriously limit the extent to which the licensee can exploit the licensed technology and since quantity restrictions particularly may have the same effect as export bans (Article 3(1) and (5)). This does not apply where a licence is granted for use of the technology in specific production facilities and where both a specific technology is communicated for the setting-up, operation and maintenance of these facilities and the licensee is allowed to increase the capacity of the facilities or to set up further facilities for its own use on normal commercial terms. On the other hand, the licensee may lawfully be prevented from using the transferred technology to set up facilities for third parties, since the purpose of the agreement is not to permit the licensee to give other producers access to the licensor's technology while it remains secret or protected by patent (Article 2(1)(12)).

(25) Agreements which are not automatically covered by the exemption because they contain provisions that are not expressly exempted by this Regulation and not expressly excluded from exemption, including those listed in Article 4(2), may, in certain circumstances, nonetheless be presumed to be eligible for application of the block exemption. It will be possible for the Commission rapidly to establish whether this is the case on the basis of the information undertakings are obliged to provide under Commission Regulation (EC) 3385/94. The Commission may waive the requirement to supply specific information required in form A/B but which it does not deem necessary. The Commission will generally be content with communication of the text of the agreement and with an estimate, based on directly available data, of the market structure and of the licensee's market share. Such agreements should therefore be deemed to be covered by the exemption provided for in this Regulation where they are notified to the Commission and the Commission does not oppose the application of the exemption within a specified period of time.

(26) Where agreements exempted under this Regulation nevertheless have effects incompatible with Article 85(3), the Commission may withdraw the block exemption, in particular where the licensed products are not faced with real competition in the licensed territory (Article 7). This could also be the case where the licensee has a strong position on the market. In assessing the competition the Commission will pay special attention to cases where the licensee has more than 40% of the whole market for the licensed products and of all the products or services which customers consider interchangeable or substitutable on account of their characteristics, prices and intended use.

(27) Agreements which come within the terms of Articles 1 and 2 which have neither the object nor the effect of restricting competition in any other way need no longer be notified. Nevertheless, undertakings will still have the right to apply in individual cases for negative clearance or for exemption under Article 85(3) in accordance with Council Regulation No 17, as last amended by the Act of Accession of Austria, Finland and Sweden. They can in particular notify agreements obliging the licensor not to grant other licences in the territory, where the licensee's market share exceeds or is likely to exceed 40%.

HAS ADOPTED THIS REGULATION:

Article 1

1. Pursuant to Article 85(3) of the Treaty and subject to the conditions set out below, it is hereby declared that Article 85(1) of the Treaty shall not apply to pure patent licensing or know-how licensing agreements and to mixed patent and know-how licensing agreements, including those agreements containing ancillary provisions relating to intellectual property rights other than patents, to which only two undertakings are party and which include one or more of the following obligations:

(1) an obligation on the licensor not to license other undertakings to exploit the licensed technology in the licensed territory;

(2) an obligation on the licensor not to exploit the licensed technology in the licensed territory himself;

(3) an obligation on the licensee not to exploit the licensed technology in the territory of the licensor within the common market;

(4) an obligation on the licensee not to manufacture or use the licensed product, or use the licensed process, in territories within the common market which are licensed to other licensees;

(5) an obligation on the licensee not to pursue an active policy of putting the licensed product on the market in the territories within the common market which are licensed to other licensees, and in particular not to engage in advertising specifically aimed at those territories or to establish any branch or maintain an [sic] distribution depot there;

(6) an obligation on the licensee not to put the licensed product on the market in the territories licensed to other licensees within the common market in response to unsolicited orders;

(7) an obligation on the licensee to use only the licensor's trademark or get up to distinguish the licensed product during the term of the agreement, provided that the licensee is not presented from identifying himself as the manufacturer of the licensed products;

(8) an obligation on the licensee to limit his production of the licensed product to the quantities he requires in manufacturing his own product and to sell the licensed product only as an integral part of or a replacement part for his own products or otherwise in connection with the sale of his own products, provided that such quantities are freely determined by the licensee.

2. Where the agreement is a pure patent licensing agreement, the exemption of the obligations referred to in paragraph 1 is granted only to the extent that and for as long as the licensed product is protected by parallel patents, in the territories respectively of the licensee (points (1), (2), (7) and (8)), the licensor (point (3)) and other licensees (points (4) and (5)). The exemption of the obligation referred to in point (6) of paragraph 1 is granted for a period not exceeding five years from the date when the licensed product is first put on the market within the common market by one of the licensees, to the

extent that and for as long as, in these territories, this product is protected by parallel patents.

3. Where the agreement is a pure know-how licensing agreement, the period for which the exemption of the obligations referred to in points (1) to (5) of paragraph 1 is granted may not exceed ten years from the date when the licensed product is first put on the market within the common market by one of the licensees.

The exemption of the obligation referred to in point (6) of paragraph 1 is granted for a period not exceeding five years from the date when the licensed product is first put on the market within the common market by one of the licensees.

The obligations referred to in points (7) and (8) of paragraph 1 are exempted during the lifetime of the agreement for as long as the know-how remains secret and substantial.

However, the exemption in paragraph 1 shall apply only where the parties have identified in any appropriate form the initial know-how and any subsequent improvements to it which become available to one party and are communicated to the other party pursuant to the terms of the agreement and to the purpose thereof, and only for as long as the know-how remains secret and substantial.

4. Where the agreement is a mixed patent and know-how licensing agreement, the exemption of the obligations referred to in points (1) to (5) of paragraph 1 shall apply in Member States in which the licensed technology is protected by necessary patents for as long as the licensed product is protected in those Member States by such patents if the duration of such protection exceeds the periods specified in paragraph 3.

The duration of the exemption provided in point (6) of paragraph 1 may not exceed the five-year period provided for in paragraphs 2 and 3.

However, such agreements qualify for the exemption referred to in paragraph 1 only for as long as the patents remain in force or to the extent that the know-how is identified and for as long as it remains secret and substantial whichever period is the longer.

5. The exemption provided for in paragraph 1 shall also apply where in a particular agreement the parties undertake obligations of the types referred to in that paragraph but with a more limited scope than is permitted by that paragraph.

Article 2

1. Article 1 shall apply notwithstanding the presence in particular of any of the following clauses, which are generally not restrictive of competition:

(1) an obligation on the licensee not to divulge the know-how communicated by the licensor; the licensee may be held to this obligation after the agreement has expired;

(2) an obligation on the licensee not to grant sublicences or assign the licence;

(3) an obligation on the licensee not to exploit the licensed know-how or patents after termination of the agreement in so far and as long as the know-how is still secret or the patents are still in force;

(4) an obligation on the licensee to grant to the licensor a licence in respect of his own improvements to or his new applications of the licensed technology, provided:

— that, in the case of severable improvements, such a licence is not exclusive, so that the licensee is free to use his own improvements or to license them to third parties, in so far as that does not involve disclosure of the know-how communicated by the licensor that is still secret,

— and that the licensor undertakes to grant an exclusive or non-exclusive licence of his own improvements to the licensee;

(5) an obligation on the licensee to observe minimum quality specifications, including technical specifications, for the licensed product or to procure goods or services from the licensor or from an undertaking designated by the licensor, in so far as these quality specifications, products or services are necessary for:

(a) a technically proper exploitation of the licensed technology; or

(b) ensuring that the product of the licensee conforms to the minimum quality specifications that are applicable to the licensor and other licensees;

and to allow the licensor to carry out related checks;

(6) obligations:

(a) to inform the licensor of misappropriation of the know-how or of infringements of the licensed patents; or

(b) to take or to assist the licensor in taking legal action against such misappropriation or infringements;

(7) an obligation on the licensee to continue paying the royalties:

(a) until the end of the agreement in the amounts, for the periods and according to the methods freely determined by the parties, in the event of the know-how becoming publicly known other than by action of the licensor, without prejudice to the payment of any additional damages in the event of the know-how becoming publicly known by the action of the licensee in breach of the agreement;

(b) over a period going beyond the duration of the licensed patents, in order to facilitate payment;

(8) an obligation on the licensee to restrict his exploitation of the licensed technology to one or more technical fields of application covered by the licensed technology or to one or more product markets;

(9) an obligation on the licensee to pay a minimum royalty or to produce a minimum quantity of the licensed product or to carry out a minimum number of operations exploiting the licensed technology;

(10) an obligation on the licensor to grant the licensee any more favourable terms that the licensor may grant to another undertaking after the agreement is entered into;

(11) an obligation on the licensee to mark the licensed product with an indication of the licensor's name or of the licensed patent;

(12) an obligation on the licensee not to use the licensor's technology to construct facilities for third parties; this is without prejudice to the right of the licensee to increase the capacity of his facilities or to set up additional facilities for his own use on normal commercial terms, including the payment of additional royalties;

(13) an obligation on the licensee to supply only a limited quantity of the licensed product to a particular customer, where the licence was granted so that the customer might have a second source of supply inside the licensed territory; this provision shall also apply where the customer is the licensee, and the licence which was granted in order to provide a second source of supply provides that the customer is himself to manufacture the licensed products or to have them manufactured by a subcontractor;

(14) a reservation by the licensor of the right to exercise the rights conferred by a patent to oppose the exploitation of the technology by the licensee outside the licensed territory;

(15) a reservation by the licensor of the right to terminate the agreement if the licensee contests the secret or substantial nature of the licensed know-how or challenges the validity of licensed patents within the common market belonging to the licensor or undertakings connected with him;

(16) a reservation by the licensor of the right to terminate the licence agreement of a patent if the licensee raises the claim that such a patent is not necessary;

(17) an obligation on the licensee to use his best endeavours to manufacture and market the licensed product;

(18) a reservation by the licensor of the right to terminate the exclusivity granted to the licensee and to stop licensing improvements to him when the licensee enters into competition within the common market with the licensor, with undertakings connected with the licensor or with other undertakings inrespect of research and development, production, use or distribution of competing products, and to require the licensee to prove that the licensed know-how is not being used for the production of products and the provision of services other than those licensed.

2. In the event that, because of particular circumstances, the clauses referred to in paragraph 1 fall within the scope of Article 85(1), they shall also be exempted even if they are not accompanied by any of the obligations exempted by Article 1.

3. The exemption in paragraph 2 shall also apply where an agreement contains clauses of the types referred to in paragraph 1 but with a more limited scope than is permitted by that paragraph.

Article 3

Article 1 and Article 2(2) shall not apply where:

(1) one party is restricted in the determination of prices, components of prices or discounts for the licensed products;

(2) one party is restricted from competing within the common market with the other party, with undertakings connected with the other party or with other undertakings in respect of research and development, production, use or distribution of competing products without prejudice to the provisions of Article 2(1)(17) and (18);

(3) one or both of the parties are required without any objectively justified reason:

(a) to refuse to meet orders from users or resellers in their respective territories who would market products in other territories within the common market;

(b) to make it difficult for users or resellers to obtain the products from other resellers within the common market, and in particular to exercise intellectual property rights or take measures so as to prevent users or resellers from obtaining outside, or from putting on the market in the licensed territory products which have been lawfully put on the market within the common market by the licensor or with his consent;

or do so as a result of a concerted practice between them;

(4) the parties were already competing manufacturers before the grant of the licence and one of them is restricted, within the same technical field of use or within the same product market, as to the customers he may serve, in particular by being prohibited from supplying certain classes of user, employing certain forms of distribution or, with the aim of sharing customers, using certain types of packaging for the products, save as provided in Article 1(1)(7) and Article 2(1)(13);

(5) the quantity of the licensed products one party may manufacture or sell or the number of operations exploiting the licensed technology he may carry out are subject to limitations, save as provided in Article (1)(8) and Article 2(1)(13);

(6) the licensee is obliged to assign in whole or in part to the licensor rights to improvements to or new applications of the licensed technology;

(7) the licensor is required, albeit in separate agreements or through automatic prolongation of the initial duration of the agreement by the inclusion of any new improvements, for a period exceeding that referred to in Article 1(2) and (3) not to

license other undertakings to exploit the licensed technology in the licensed territory, or a party is required for a period exceeding that referred to in Article 1(2) and (3) or Article 1(4) not to exploit the licensed technology in the territory of the other party or of other licensees.

Article 4

1. The exemption provided for in Articles 1 and 2 shall also apply to agreements containing obligations restrictive of competition which are not covered by those Articles and do not fall within the scope of Article 3, on condition that the agreements in question are notified to the Commission in accordance with the provisions of Articles 1, 2 and 3 of Regulation (EC) 3385/94 and that the Commission does not oppose such exemption within a period of four months.

2. Paragraph 1 shall apply, in particular, where:

(a) the licensee is obliged at the time the agreement is entered into to accept quality specifications or further licences or to procure goods or services which are not necessary for a technically satisfactory exploitation of the licensed technology or for ensuring that the production of the licensee conforms to the quality standards that are respected by the licensor and other licensees;

(b) the licensee is prohibited from contesting the secrecy or the substantiality of the licensed know-how or from challenging the validity of patents licensed within the common market belonging to the licensor or undertakings connected with him.

3. The period of four months referred to in paragraph 1 shall run from the date on which the notification takes effect in accordance with Article 4 of Regulation (EC) 3385/94.

4. The benefit of paragraphs 1 and 2 may be claimed for agreements notified before the entry into force of this Regulation by submitting a communication to the Commission referring expressly to this Article and to the notification. Paragraph 3 shall apply *mutatis mutandis*.

5. The Commission may oppose the exemption within a period of four months. It shall oppose exemption if it receives a request to do so from a Member State within two months of the transmission to the Member State of the notification referred to in paragraph 1 or of the communication referred to in paragraph 4. This request must be justified on the basis of considerations relating to the competition rules of the Treaty.

6. The Commission may withdraw the opposition to the exemption at any time. However, where the opposition was raised at the request of a Member State and this request is maintained, it may be withdrawn only after consultation of the Advisory Committee on Restrictive Practices and Dominant Positions.

7. If the opposition is withdrawn because the undertakings concerned have shown that the conditions of Article 85(3) are satisfied, the exemption shall apply from the date of notification.

8. If the opposition is withdrawn because the undertakings concerned have amended the agreement so that the conditions of Article 85(3) are satisfied, the exemption shall apply from the date on which the amendments take effect.

9. If the Commission opposes exemption and the opposition is not withdrawn, the effects of the notification shall be governed by the provisions of Regulation No 17.

Article 5

1. This Regulation shall not apply to:

(1) agreements between members of a patent or know-how pool which relate to the pooled technologies;

(2) licensing agreements between competing undertakings which hold interests in a joint venture, or between one of them and the joint venture, if the licensing agreements relate to the activities of the joint venture;

(3) agreements under which one party grants the other a patent and/or know-how licence and in exchange the other party, albeit in separate agreements or through connected undertakings, grants the first party a patent, trademark or know-how licence or exclusive sales rights, where the parties are competitors in relation to the products covered by those agreements;

(4) licensing agreements containing provisions relating to intellectual property rights other than patents which are not ancillary;

(5) agreements entered into solely for the purpose of sale.

2. This Regulation shall nevertheless apply:

(1) to agreements to which paragraph 1(2) applies, under which a parent undertaking grants the joint venture a patent or know-how licence, provided that the licensed products and the other goods and services of the participating undertakings which are considered by users to be interchangeable or substitutable in view of their characteristics, price and intended use represent:

— in case of a licence limited to production, not more than 20%, and

— in case of a licence covering production and distribution, not more than 10%;

of the market for the licensed products and all interchangeable or substitutable goods and services;

(2) to agreements to which paragraph 1(1) applies and to reciprocal licences within the meaning of paragraph 1(3), provided the parties are not subject to any territorial restriction within the common market with regard to the manufacture, use or putting on the market of the licensed products or to the use of the licensed or pooled technologies.

3. This Regulation shall continue to apply where, for two consecutive financial years, the market shares in paragraph 2(1) are not exceeded by more than one-tenth; where that limit is exceeded, this Regulation shall continue to apply for a period of six months from the end of the year in which the limit was exceeded.

Article 6

This Regulation shall also apply to:

(1) agreements where the licensor is not the holder of the know-how or the patentee, but is authorised by the holder or the patentee to grant a licence;

(2) assignments of know-how, patents or both where the risk associated with exploitation remains with the assignor, in particular where the sum payable in consideration of the assignment is dependent on the turnover obtained by the assignee in respect of products made using the know-how or the patents, the quantity of such products manufactured or the number of operations carried out employing the know-how or the patents;

(3) licensing agreements in which the rights or obligations of the licensor or the licensee are assumed by undertakings connected with them.

Article 7

The Commission may withdraw the benefit of this Regulation, pursuant to Article 7 of Regulation 19/65/EEC, where it finds in a particular case that an agreement exempted by this Regulation nevertheless has certain effects which are incompatible with the conditions laid down in Article 85(3) of the Treaty, and in particular where:

(1) the effect of the agreement is to prevent the licensed products from being exposed to effective competition in the licensed territory from identical goods

or services or from goods or services considered by users as interchangeable or substitutable in view of their characteristics, price and intended use, which may in particular occur where the licensee's market share exceeds 40%;

(2) without prejudice to Article 1(1)(6), the licensee refuses, without any objectively justified reason, to meet unsolicited orders from users or resellers in the territory of other licensees;

(3) the parties;

(a) without any objectively justified reason, refuse to meet orders from users or resellers in their respective territories who would market the products in other territories within the common market; or

(b) make it difficult for users or resellers to obtain the products from other resellers within the common market, and in particular where they exercise intellectual property rights or take measures so as to prevent resellers or users from obtaining outside, or from putting on the market in the licensed territory products which have been lawfully put on the market within the common market by the licensor or with his consent;

(4) the parties were competing manufacturers at the date of the grant of the licence and obligations on the licensee to produce a minimum quantity or to use his best endeavours as referred to in Article 2(1), (9) and (17) respectively have the effect of preventing the licensee from using competing technologies.

Article 8

1. For purposes of this Regulation:

(a) patent applications;
(b) utility models;
(c) applications for registration of utility models;
(d) topographies of semiconductor products;
(e) certificats d'utilité and certificats d'addition under French law;
(f) applications for certificats d'utilité and certificats d'addition under French law;
(g) supplementary protection certificates for medicinal products or other products for which such supplementary protection certificates may be obtained;
(h) plant breeder's certificates,

shall be deemed to be patents.

2. This Regulation shall also apply to agreements relating to the exploitation of an invention if an application within the meaning of paragraph 1 is made in respect of the invention for a licensed territory after the date when the agreements were entered into but within the time-limits set by the national law or the international convention to be applied.

3. This Regulation shall furthermore apply to pure patent or know-how licensing agreements or to mixed agreements whose initial duration is automatically prolonged by the inclusion of any new improvements, whether patented or not, communicated by the licensor, provided that the licensee has the right to refuse such improvements or each party has the right to terminate the agreement at the expiry of the initial term of an agreement and at least every three years thereafter.

Article 9

1. Information acquired pursuant to Article 4 shall be used only for the purposes of this Regulation.

2. The Commission and the authorities of the Member States, their officials and other servants shall not disclose information acquired by them pursuant to this Regulation of the kind covered by the obligation of professional secrecy.

3. The provision of paragraphs 1 and 2 shall not prevent publication of general information or surveys which do not contain information relating to particular undertakings or associations of undertakings.

Article 10

For purposes of this Regulation:

(1) 'know-how' means a body of technical information that is secret, substantial and identified in any appropriate form;

(2) 'secret' means that the know-how package as a body or in the precise configuration and assembly of its components is not generally known or easily accessible, so that part of its value consists in the lead which the licensee gains when it is communicated to him; it is not limited to the narrow sense that each individual component of the know-how should be totally unknown or unobtainable outside the licensor's business;

(3) 'substantial' means that the know-how includes information which must be useful, ie, can reasonably be expected at the date of conclusion of the agreement to be capable of improving the competitive position of the licensee, for example by helping him to enter a new market or giving him an advantage in competition with other manufacturers or providers of services who do not have access to the licensed secret know-how or other comparable secret know-how;

(4) 'identified' means that the know-how is described or recorded in such a manner as to make it possible to verify that it satisfies the criteria of secrecy and substantiality and to ensure that the licensee is not unduly restricted in his exploitation of his own technology, to be identified the know-how can either be set out in the licence agreement or in a separate document or recorded in any other appropriate form at the latest when the know-how is transferred or shortly thereafter, provided that the separate documents or other record can be made available if the need arises;

(5) 'necessary patents' are patents where a licence under the patent is necessary for the putting into effect of the licensed technology in so far as, in the absence of such a licence, the realisation of the licensed technology would not be possible or would be possible only to a lesser extent or in more difficult or costly conditions. Such patents must therefore be of technical, legal or economic interest to the licensee;

(6) 'licensing agreement' means pure patent licensing agreements and pure know-how licensing agreements as well as mixed patent and know-how licensing agreements;

(7) 'licensed technology' means the initial manufacturing know-how or the necessary product and process patents, or both, existing at the time the first licensing agreement is concluded, and improvements subsequently made to the know-how or patents, irrespective of whether and to what extent they are exploited by the parties or by other licensees;

(8) 'the licensed products' are goods or services the production or provision of which requires the use of the licensed technology;

(9) 'the licensee's market share' means the proportion which the licensed products and other goods or services provided by the licensee, which are considered by users to be interchangeable or substitutable for the licensed products in view of their characteristics, price and intended use, represent the entire market for the licensed products and all other inter-changeable or substitutable goods and services in the common market or a substantial part of it;

(10) 'exploitation' refers to any use of the licensed technology in particular in the production, active or passive sales in a territory even if not coupled with manufacture in that territory, or leasing of the licensed products;

(11) 'the licensed territory' is the territory covering all or at least part of the common market where the licensee is entitled to exploit the licensed technology;

(12) 'territory of the licensor' means territories in which the licensor has not granted any licenses for patents and/or know-how covered by the licensing agreement;

(13) 'parallel patents' means patents which, in spite of the divergences which remain in the absence of any unification of national rules concerning industrial property, protect the same invention in various Member States;

(14) 'connected undertakings' means:

(a) undertakings in which a party to the agreement, directly or indirectly:

— owns more than half the capital or business assets, or

— has the power to exercise more than half the voting rights, or

— has the power to appoint more than half the members of the supervisory board, board of directors or bodies legally representing the undertaking, or

— has the right to manage the affairs of the undertaking;

(b) undertakings which, directly or indirectly, have in or over a party to the agreement the rights or powers listed in (a);

(c) undertakings in which an undertaking referred to in (b), directly or indirectly, has the rights or powers listed in (a);

(d) undertakings in which the parties to the agreement or undertakings connected with them jointly have the rights or powers listed in (a): such jointly controlled undertakings are considered to be connected with each of the parties to the agreement;

(15) 'ancillary provisions' are provisions relating to the exploitation of intellectual property rights other than patents, which contain no obligations restrictive of competition other than those also attached to the licensed know-how or patents and exempted under this Regulation;

(16) 'obligation' means both contractual obligation and a concerted practice;

(17) 'competing manufacturers' or manufacturers of 'competing products' means manufacturers who sell products which, in view of their characteristics, price and intended use, are considered by users to be interchangeable or substitutable for the licensed products.

Article 11

1. Regulation (EEC) 556/89 is hereby repealed with effect from 1 April 1996.
2. Regulation (EEC) 2349/84 shall continue to apply until 31 March 1996.
3. The prohibition in Article 85(1) of the Treaty shall not apply to agreements in force on 31 March 1996 which fulfil the exemption requirements laid down by Regulation (EEC) 2349/84 or (EEC) 556/89.

Article 12

1. The Commission shall undertake regular assessments of the application of this Regulation, and in particular of the opposition procedure provided for in Article 4.
2. The Commission shall draw up a report on the operation of this Regulation before the end of the fourth year following its entry into force and shall, on that basis, assess whether any adaptation of the Regulation is desirable.

Article 13

This Regulation shall enter into force on 1 April 1996.

It shall apply until 31 March 2006.

Article 11(2) of this Regulation shall, however, enter into force on 1 January 1996.

This Regulation shall be binding in its entirety and directly applicable in all Member States.

Done at Brussels, 31 January 1996.

A4.3 A commentary on the regulation

The subject of technology transfer is largely about licensing others to exploit your technological progress. This may occur by transferring 'know-how' to the licensee or permitting them to exploit a patent that you hold, or both. Originally, there was just a block exemption on patent licensing (Regulation 2349/84). That was due to expire at the end of 1994 but its 'life' was subsequently extended three times. The Commission subsequently issued a block exemption on 'know-how' transfer agreements (Regulation 556/89). That was not due to expire until 31 December 1999 but was relatively short-lived because on 31 January 1996, the Commission promulgated a new block exemption on technology transfer agreements (see OJ 1996 L31/2).

Regulation 240/96 came into effect on 1 April 1996, with a 10-year life. It replaced both the patent licensing block exemption and the know-how block exemption; as recital (3) to the Regulation states, the Commission felt that the two sets of rules ought to be harmonized and simplified as far as possible, in order to encourage the dissemination of technical knowledge in the Community and to promote the manufacture of technically more sophisticated products (see also recital 8). With those objectives in mind, agreements which are solely for the purpose of sale are excluded (recital (8)). The Commission endeavoured to show why an exemption was merited for this type of agreement; as with all of the block exemptions, the four criteria in Article 85(3) (now 81(3)) had to be satisfied. Taking them in turn, the Commission said that:

(i) the obligations ... in Article 1 generally contribute to improving the production of goods and to promoting technical progress. They make the holders of patents or know-how more willing to grant licences and licensees more inclined to undertake the investment required to manufacture, use and put on the market a new product or to use a new process;

(ii) consumers will, as a rule, be allowed a fair share of the benefit resulting from the improvement in the supply of goods on the market but to ensure they do ...

(iii) ... it is right to exclude from the application of Article 1 cases where the parties agree to refuse to meet demand from users or resellers within their respective territories who would sell for export, or to take other steps to impede parallel imports. The obligations referred to above [ie in Article 1] only impose restrictions which are indispensable to the attainment of their objectives.

(iv) in connection with the need to ensure that the agreement does not offer the opportunity to eradicate a significant portion of the 'competition', the Commission may withdraw the benefit of the block exemption. This may happen 'in particular where the licensed products are not faced with real competition in the licensed territory' and 'could also be the case where the licensee has a strong position on the market' (defined as a market share in excess of 40%).

See recitals 12, 17 and 26.

The new block exemption is not intended to be more restrictive than its predecessors: agreements which were in force on 31 March 1996 and fulfilled the requirements of either Regulation 2349/84 or 556/89 continue to be exempt (Article 11(3), Regulation 240/96). References to articles or recitals (in the preamble) in this chapter can be assumed to refer to Regulation 240/96 unless the contrary is stated.

A4.3.1 What agreements are coverd by the block exemption?

The block exemption applies to:

- pure patent licensing agreements;
- know-how licensing agreements; and
- mixed patent and know-how licensing agreements.

See Article 1(1) and the definition of licensing agreement in Article 10(6).

A4.3.2 What is a patent?

One might have thought this was quite straightforward but there is a rather broad list in Article 8 which includes 'topographies of semiconductor products' and 'plant breeder's certificates'. All of these items are described as 'industrial property rights' in recital 1. Curiously, recital 1 also includes trademarks although these really only appear as *ancillary* intellectual property rights in the rest of this block exemption. Recital 4 specifies that the exemption applies to patents granted by Member States, Community patents and European patents.

A4.3.3 What is know-how?

Know-how is defined in Article 10. One should note its component parts, it must be:

(a) Technical information.

(b) Secret, that is:

  (i) not generally known or easily accessible;

  (ii) its communication gives the licensee a 'lead' over others;

  (iii) it is not limited to situations where each element of know-how is totally unknown or unobtainable outside the licensor's business.

(c) Substantial: it must be useful, either regarding entry to new markets or gaining a competitive edge.

(d) Can be identified in any form:

  (i) which allows it to be verified as secret and substantial;

  (ii) to ensure the licensee is not unduly restricted in exploitation of his own technology (ie it is not a backwards step really);

  (iii) identification can be in the licence agreement or a separate document or recorded in any other appropriate form, which can be made available if the need arises.

Know-how may be found in 'descriptions of manufacturing processes, recipes, formulae, designs or drawings'; see recital (4).

A4.3.4 Basic overview of Regulation 240/96

Article 1 sets out the 'white list': clauses which automatically qualify for exemption.

Article 2 sets out the 'grey list': clauses which are not generally restrictive of competition but which are exempted in case circumstances arise which make them restrictive.

Article 3 sets out the 'black list': clauses, the presence of which, will take the agreement outside the block exemption.

Article 4 contains the opposition procedure. What if you have clauses which are restrictive of competition but which are not saved by Articles 1 or 2? So long as they do not fall within Article 3, you can notify the Commission, on Form A/B, and if the Commission raises no opposition within four months, you get the exemption.

Article 5 lists categories of agreement to which the block exemption does not apply (see also recital 8). Essentially, these are agreements for pooling patents or know-how. Such agreements are likely to frustrate technological progress by the partners and certainly act as a substantial barrier to anyone outside the pool. Also excluded are patent swaps; substantial licences of other intellectual property rights; and agreements purely for the purpose of sale. However, many of these apparently prohibited agreements can still be rescued in certain circumstances: see Article 5(2).

Article 6 lists further categories of agreement to which the block exemption applies. There are three:

(a) where the licensor is not the intellectual property holder;

(b) assignments where the risk stays with the assignor (typically his royalties depend on the degree of successful exploitation by the licensee);

(c) situations where the risks or obligations of either licensor or licensee are assumed by connected undertakings.

Article 7 provides for withdrawal of the exemption if the Commission finds a specific agreement should not qualify (ie it actually examines that agreement). See also recital 26.

Article 8, as mentioned already, allows a liberal application of the block exemption (and see recital 4). It provides a broad definition of 'patent'; covers agreements to exploit an invention where no patent exists but one is timeously applied for; and agreements for an indefinite term may be covered in certain circumstances.

Article 9 specifies the use that may be made of information that the Commission acquires through use of the opposition procedure.

Article 10 is a 'definitions' article.

Article 11 repeals the old block exemptions from 1 April 1996.

Article 12 provides for reviews by the Commission of how the block exemption is working.

A4.3.5 Key articles from the Regulation in more detail

A4.3.5.1 Article 1: the white list

There must be only two undertakings as parties to the agreement. There is nothing unusual in this; it is typical for block exemptions to contain this limitation. The article allows a degree of exclusivity (or market protection):

(a) **For the licensee:**

(i) The licensor is not to *license others for exploitation* within the licensed territory (Article 1, para 1(1)).

(ii) The licensor is not to *exploit* the technology himself in the licensed territory (Article 1, para 1(2)).

(b) **For the licensor:**

(i) The licensee is not to *exploit* the technology within the licensor's territory (Article 1, para 1(3)).

(c) **For other licensees:**

(i) The licensee is not to *manufacture or use* the licensed *product* or use the licensed *process* in other licensees' territories (Article 1, para 1(4)).

(ii) *An active sales ban,* ie the licensee must not actively *put the product on the market* in territories of other licensees and must not target such areas through advertising (Article 1, para 1(5)).

(iii) *A passive sales ban* (Article 1, para 1(6)). Where the agreement is a *pure patent licence,* this ban applies only to territories if they are covered by parallel patents and (in any event) expires five years after the licensed product was first put on the market by a licensee (see Article 1, para 2). If the agreement is a *pure know-how licence,* this ban expires five years after the licensed product was first put on the market by a licensee (see Article 1, para 3). Where the agreement is a mixed patent and know-how licence, this ban expires *at the latest* five years after the licensed product was first put on the market by a licensee (and earlier if the patent expires *and* the know-how becomes 'worthless'; see Article 1, para 4).

Article 1 also deals with **trade marks.** The licensee can be obliged to apply *only the licensor's trademark* or get-up, so long as the licensee can identify itself as the manufacturer (Article 1, para 1(7)). There is nothing new here. It respects the function of a trademark, while allowing a degree of protection for the licensee against suffering a terminal drop in market share once the agreement ends.

Article 1 also contains a (sort of) **field-of-use** provision (for true field-of-use restrictions, see Article 2, para 1(8)). The licensee may be restricted to selling the licensed product only as an integral part of (or replacement part for) his own products and not to produce any surplus (ie the licensor can prevent a separate market opening up). The licensee must remain free to determine the quantities he needs for this purpose. (See Article 1, para 1(8).)

Article 1 stipulates that there are time limits on the exemptions. If the agreement is a *pure patent licence* agreement, the restrictions in Article 1, para 1(1), (2), (3), (4), (5), (7) and (8) are permitted only for so long as there is a *parallel patent in force* in the protected territory (see Article 1, para 2). If the agreement is a *pure know-how licence* agreement, the restrictions in Article 1, para 1(1)–(5) are permitted for a *maximum of 10 years* from the date of first marketing by a licensee. The restrictions in para 1(7) and (8) can subsist for the *lifetime* of the agreement, *so long as* the know-how stays secret and substantial (see Article 1, para 3). If the agreement is a *mixed patent and know-how licence* agreement, then the restrictions in para 1(1)–(5) and (7)–(8) can last for the lifetime of the patent in territories where there is patent protection, or 10 years from the date of first marketing by a licensee, whichever is the longer. If the patent expires but the know-how is still secret and substantial, the protection continues; conversely, if the know-how becomes public but the patent remains, the protection continues. If the patent expires and the know-how becomes public, the protection stops forthwith. (See Article 1, para 4; recital 16.) It does not follow that longer periods of exclusivity are not allowed, but they can only be granted by *individual* exemption (see recital 14).

A4.3.5.2 Article 2: the grey list

This Article contains a long list of obligations which are not normally restrictive of competition. They are included in the regulation in order to clarify that, 'in the event that because of the particular economic or legal circumstances they should fall within Article 85(1) [now 81(1)], they too will be covered by the exemption' (recital 18). These obligations include:

(a) Protection of **confidentiality** in the form of:
- (i) non-disclosure (Article 2, para 1(1) — this can continue post-termination);
- (ii) non-exploitation; and
- (iii) enforcement. The licensee can be obliged to tell the licensor of any 'leak' of know-how or patent infringement; and participate in taking legal action against the offender. See Article 2, para 1(6).

There are several examples of non-exploitation given:
- (i) *Simple* non-exploitation. See Article 2, para 1(3); recital 20. This applies post-termination for the lifetime of the patent or as long as the know-how is still secret.
- (ii) Article 2, para 1(12): the licensee can be obliged not to use the licensed technology to build *facilities for third parties*. The licensee can, however, expand or build additional facilities *for himself*.
- (iii) The licensor can reserve the right to pursue a *patent infringement action against the licensee*, should the licensee seek to exploit the patent/technology *outside the licensed territory* (maybe by going somewhere without patent protection or short-life patents). See Article 2, para 1(14).
- (iv) The licensor can require the licensee to prove that the know-how is not being used in connection with non-licensed products where the licensee gets involved with *competing products*. See Article 2, para 1(18); also see 'non-competition' below.

(b) Power to control **who holds a licence** (see Article 2, para 1(2)).

(c) **Grant-back** licences regarding improvements or new applications discovered by the licensee. But these are approved only if the licensor agrees to grant a licence (exclusive or otherwise) to the licensee for his own improvements. Also, if the improvement is severable, the licence grant-back must not be exclusive; ie the licensee must remain free to use his own improvements or even licence them to third parties, if he can do so without disclosing still-secret know-how.

(d) Methods of ensuring **quality control** over the licensed product or technology. These can include observance of minimum quality specifications, technical specifications, or sourcing goods/services from nominated suppliers. See Article 2, para 1(5). Cf. *assignment* of improvements *forbidden* by Article 3(6).

(e) Issues over *royalty* payments:
- (i) **guaranteeing income** for the licensor in the form of a minimum royalty or an obligation to produce a minimum quantity of the licensed product or to use the licensed technology a minimum number of times (see Article 2, para 1(9));

(ii) **spreading royalties** over the duration of the agreement, even if the patents have expired (because to do so may 'facilitate' payment; see Article 2, para 1(7)(b)); and

(iii) requiring the licensee to pay royalties in accordance with the terms of the agreement throughout the life of the agreement, **even though** the **know-how** has become **public** (so long as publication has not been by action of the licensor). Clearly, if know-how has been published by action of the licensee, there may be a claim for additional damages by the licensor against the licensee. See Article 2, para 1(7)(a); recital 21.

(f) (True) **field-of-use** restrictions on licensee. See Article 2, para 1(8); recital 22.

(g) '**Most favoured partner**' status for the licensee. In other words, if some later licensee cuts a better deal, then the previous one(s) also get the benefit. This is useful because, as time goes by, circumstances may change; a licensee would not want to suffer by being the first in line. It is an added incentive to be first in line — it encourages and accelerates exploitation of the licensed product or technology. See Article 2, para 1(10).

(h) Obligation to **identify** the licensor and/or the patent by a mark. Not, presumably, the licensor's trademark since that was covered by Article 1, para 1(7). This must be a little broader. See Article 2, para 1(11).

(i) **Limits on quantity** to be supplied to a customer. This applies only to particularised customers and where the licence was only granted to provide for possible shortfalls in the quantity that might be supplied to that customer by another licensee in that territory (ie the limited licensee is created as a fall-back or second-source supplier). See Article 2, para 1(13); recital 23.

(j) **Non-challenge** clauses. This seems a very strange provision. If the licensee contests whether the know-how is secret or substantial, or challenges the validity of the patent, or claims the patent is unnecessary, the licensor may have reserved the right to terminate the agreement. One might have thought this was forbidden, since it is not in society's interests for people to pay money for unnecessary information or for monopoly profits to be earned from an unwarranted patent. The licensee is usually in the best position to raise such a claim. Is this simply a pragmatic recognition by the Commission that licensors will not licence without such 'protection'? See Article 2, para 1(15) and (16).

(k) Limited form of **non-competition** clauses. The licensee may be required to use *best endeavours* to make and market the licensed product. See Article 2, para 1(17). Further, the licensor may reserve the right to *terminate* the licensee's *exclusivity* and *stop licensing improvements* to him if the licensee starts to *compete* with the licensor within the common market. Such competition could be in research and development, or production, use or distribution of the product. In such circumstances, the licensor can put the licensee to proof that licensed know-how is not being misused. See Article 2, para 1(18). Cf. Article 3(2): the agreement cannot actually prohibit competition by the licensee.

A4.3.5.3 Article 3: the 'black list'

These are the 'no-no' clauses; if any of them are included in the agreement then the benefit of the block exemption is lost. As well as Article 3, see recital 19.

(a) **Price fixing** is the first entry and is still clearly forbidden. See Article 3(1); recital 24. By way of comparison, in its recent Green Paper on Vertical Restraints, the

Commission noted that when an agreement exceeds the *de minimis* rules Article 81(1) (ex 85(1)) will apply 'virtually automatically to certain vertical agreements which by their very nature can only distort competition, in particular ... agreements which limit the freedom of distributors to set their resale prices (Resale Price Maintenance)'.

(b) **Non-competition** is next. Any restriction on the ability of either party to compete is forbidden (whether it applies to research and development, production, use or distribution of competing products). Clearly, the behaviour permitted by Article 2, para 1(17) and (18) is not seen as restrictive. See Article 3(2).

(c) Hindering **parallel imports** must not occur. Where either party is required to (or does so as the result of a concerted practice)

  (i) refuse orders from customers who wish to market products in other territories in the common market (this covers simple re-selling of the product and using it as a component of some new product); or

  (ii) use intellectual property rights to prevent lawful marketing

  then, in the absence of 'any objectively justified reason', the agreement does not benefit from the block exemption. See Article 3(3).

(d) **Restrictions on customers**. Where the parties to the agreement were competing manufacturers before the licence, there shall be no restriction on (or sharing out of) customers, except as permitted by Article 2, para 1(13) and by Article 1, para 1(7) (dealing with trademarks and the get-up of the product). An example of what is forbidden is the reservation of different classes of customer to the licensor. See Article 3(4); recital 23.

(e) **Maximum quantities**. Other than limiting the licensee to only making as much as he needs (Article 1, para 1(8)) and limiting the amount that a secondary supplier can make for a particular customer (Article 2, para 1(13)), there can be no upper limit on the quantity of the licensed product made or the number of times that a licensed technology is used. See Article 3(5); recital 24.

(f) **Obligatory assignment** of improvements or new applications should not appear. See Article 3(6); recital 20.

(g) **Prolonging territorial protection**. If there is an attempt to prolong exclusivity, whether of the licensor or licensee, beyond the periods permitted for 'pure' agreements then the benefit of the block exemption is lost. Such an attempt might include prolonging exclusivity as the result of communicating improvements. See Article 3(7); recital 14.

The other major 'no-no' that one might have expected to find in the black list is absolute territorial protection. One sees in the Commission Green Paper on Vertical Restraints, para 21, that agreements which establish absolute territorial protection 'by their very nature can only distort competition'. However, although that point is 'central to Commission policy', it is mentioned only in the context of distribution. A different line has often been taken with technically innovative licences. An early example came with the judgment of the Court of Justice in *Nungesser and Eisele v Commission* (258/78) [1982] ECR 2015; this is echoed in recital (10) of Regulation 240/96:

> exclusive licensing agreements ... may not be in themselves incompatible with Article 85(1) [now 81(1)] [again, signs of a rule of reason approach] where they are concerned with the introduction and protection of a new technology in the licensed territory, by reason of the scale of the research which has been undertaken, of the increase in the level of competition, in particular

inter-brand competition, and of the competitiveness of the undertakings concerned resulting from the dissemination of innovation within the Community.

A4.3.5.4 Article 4: the opposition procedure

Parties to a licensing agreement are encouraged to use the opposition procedure in two specific instances:

(a) Where the licensee is obliged to accept licences, or procure goods or services, which are not necessary for a technically satisfactory exploitation of the licensed technology or for ensuring respect for quality standards. These are forms of **tie** which previously have been black-listed (cf. the patent licensing regulation 2349/84 at Article 3(4) and (9); the know-how regulation 556/89 at Article 3(3)). In the block exemptions for patent licensing and know-how, such obligations were prohibited unless they were necessary for a technically satisfactory exploitation of the licensed invention, or perhaps necessary to ensure respect for quality standards during production. See Article 4, para 2(a).

(b) Where the licensee is prohibited from contesting the licensed know-how or challenging the validity of the licensed patent. Again, this prohibition was black-listed in the patent and know-how block exemptions (see Article 3(1) and Article 3(4), respectively). In both cases, the licensor was allowed to retain a right to terminate the licence in the event of such a challenge. See Article 4, para 2(b); recital 25.

APPENDIX 5
GLOSSARY

Absolute territorial protection
A clause in a distribution agreement whereby a supplier agrees not to supply to others who will sell in the same territory as the first buyer. This is usually accompanied by another clause in the agreement, defining the territory within which the first buyer will operate. This type of protection may involve a ban on passive as well as active sales.

Chiselling
When an individual covertly undercuts the prices agreed by an unlawful cartel of producers/ sellers. It is sometimes suggested that the likelihood of chiselling is so great that cartels do not pose a long-term threat to competition. Since, the theory goes, the cartel members are necessarily prepared to act in an underhand fashion and rip off their customers (in the form of agreed higher prices), they will feel little hesitation in ripping off their fellow cartel members (eg, by offering secret discounts to customers) and thereby increasing their market share.

Competition
A perfectly competitive market is unattainable in practice. It is a situation towards which one can aim without ever getting there. In a competitive market, no single producer can influence the price of the product: there are enough competitors or competing products to ensure that the quantity sold by a producer does not affect the price. The lack of influence which an individual firm has in a competitive market is best illustrated by the demand curve for a firm in a competitive industry (see **Figure A** below). This shows that for this firm there is effectively a set price for the product. As long as it does not try to sell above this price, it can sell as much of the product as it can produce. Once it puts its price above the level indicated, it will sell nothing as there are plenty of available and acceptable substitutes around. Note that for a competitive *industry*, the demand curve will be like that in **Figure B** (see demand curve over). See also **Marginal costs and revenue, Figure C**.

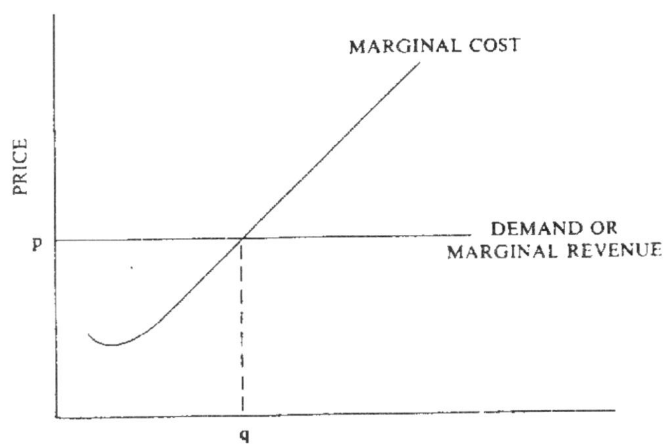

Figure A Output of a firm in a competitive industry

Demand curve

Economists are often concerned about the 'demand' for a product. When determining levels of demand, a demand curve is usually constructed. This is simply a graph illustrating the relationship between the number of items that a consumer will buy and the price charged for the item. The demand curve is usually on a negative slope (see **Figure B**) because the more you get, the less you want. For example, as the price of coats drops, so the number of coats sold increases, but if you bought, say, two coats at £100 each, you are unlikely to buy yourself another coat unless the price drops. Thus, in order to sell more coats, the seller has to reduce the price. If he charges £150, you'll buy one; if he drops the price to £100, you'll buy two; but you'll only buy three if he drops the price to £70.

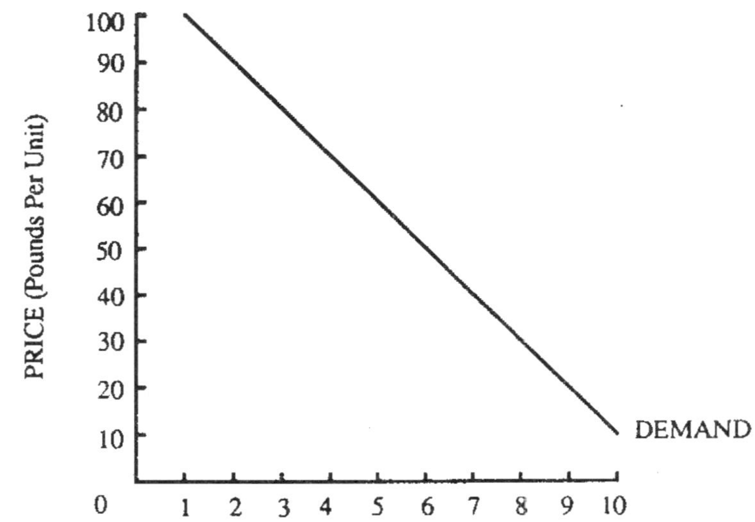

Figure B The demand curve

DG IV

The department of the Commission which deals with competition matters, especially investigations. In 1999, the long-term Commissioner in charge of competition matters, Karel Van Miert, of Belgium, was replaced by Mario Monti, of Italy, as part of large-scale changes to the membership of the Commission.

DG XV

The department of the Commission which deals with the single market. In particular, it is responsible for industrial and intellectual property rights, and issues concerning the free movement of goods. In 1999, its Commissioner, Mario Monti, switched to become the Commissioner for Competition.

Exclusionary rebates and discounts

Fidelity rebates (ie keep buying from me and you get a rebate); rebates based on improving your volume of purchases from a particular supplier above last year's levels. Basically, financial incentives to stay with a particular supplier and even buy more of his product. These tactics tie up distributors and make it difficult for other suppliers to find an outlet for their products.

Exclusive dealer/distributor

This is an independent distributor who agrees to stock the goods of a particular supplier in return for a promise that the supplier will not supply those goods to another distributor within a defined territory. The distributor is restricted to that territory for his sales. The distributor may also agree to stock the full range of the supplier's goods and not to stock any competing products. Such agreements are regarded by the European

Commission as having competitive advantages in certain circumstances: this led the Commission to issue block exemptions in this field, notably Regulation 1983/83 (now replaced by Regulation 2790/99).

Exclusive purchase

Originally exclusive distribution and exclusive purchasing were treated by the Commission as a single form of business conduct — exclusive dealing (see Regulation 67/67). From 1983 to 2000, two block exemptions existed in this field, with Regulation 1984/83 covering exclusive purchasing agreements. As the Commission observed,

> Regulations ... 1983/83 and ... 1984/83 are both concerned with exclusive agreements between two undertakings for the purpose of the resale of goods.

In an exclusive purchase agreement, the purchaser (or reseller) agrees to buy the relevant goods only from that supplier. Unlike exclusive distribution, the purchaser has no exclusive territory and this has two effects. First, the supplier can supply the same goods to others operating in the vicinity of the exclusive purchaser; secondly, the purchaser is not restricted to a particular area for his sales efforts.

Two particular types of exclusive purchase agreement which were especially dealt with in Regulation 1984/83 were those for the supply of beer in pubs etc and of petrol in service stations.

Export bans

A contract clause forbidding the purchaser from reselling outside his territory (which may be anything from a 100-metre radius around his shop to the territory of a member state). Such bans may be on active sales only or passive sales, or both. A ban on active sales outside one's territory would prevent the opening of additional shops, for example. A ban on passive sales would prevent one from selling to a customer who came in from outside the allotted territory.

Geographical market

Relevant to the issue of whether there is an effect on trade between Member States. See also **Market share analysis**.

Horizontal agreement

Simply an agreement between companies operating at the same level of the market, eg, manufacturers of a product (as in *ICI v Commission* (48/69) [1972] ECR 619). Compare **Vertical agreement**.

Marginal costs and revenue

These terms refer to the additional costs incurred or revenue raised by producing and selling each additional item. Profits are maximised if one sells the quantity at the price indicated by the place where marginal costs and revenue are equal. See **Figure C**.

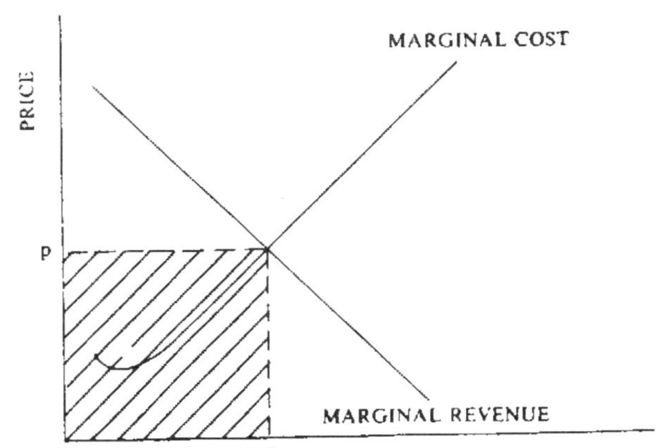

Figure C Profit maximisation by a firm

Market share analysis

When determining, for example, whether a company has a dominant position in a market (for use in proceedings under Article 82 (ex 86), EC Treaty), it is necessary to decide on the nature of both the product market and the geographical market. In *United Brands v Commission* (27/76) the relevant product was bananas, not all soft fruits and certainly not all fruits; in *Michelin v Commission* (322/81) [1983] ECR 3461 the relevant product was tyres for heavy trucks, not all truck tyres and not all motor vehicle tyres. The geographical market in *Michelin* was The Netherlands, rather than, say, the Benelux countries; in *United Brands* sales of bananas in France, the UK and Italy were excluded from consideration because of different trading conditions from the other six Member States.

Once the relevant product and geographical markets have been determined, one can gather evidence on the percentage share (either in terms of finance or volume) of that market held by the suspect firm. This is commonly used by the Commission as an indicator of the presence (or absence) of a dominant position. In *United Brands*, the company was found to possess a significant market share and hold a dominant position, even though for at least some of the time it had been incurring losses.

Monopoly

In very simple terms, a monopolist has freedom to charge a price he chooses for his product and (usually) sell less of it, regardless of his competitors' actions and the demands of consumers: he is independent of the other 'players' in that market. One evil of such domination, according to economic theory, is that resources will be misused: higher prices will be charged by the monopolist and some potential customers will either go unsatisfied or will buy inappropriate substitutes. Either way, there is an inefficient allocation of resources ('welfare loss'). Also, the lack of any competition means that the monopolist has less incentive to improve his product or be innovative: this is a disadvantage to consumers.

Some economists argue that monopolies are not necessarily all bad. For example, the greater profits generated may lead both directly and indirectly to more investment in research and development, either by the monopolist or by potential competitors who would like to enter the market and share the profits.

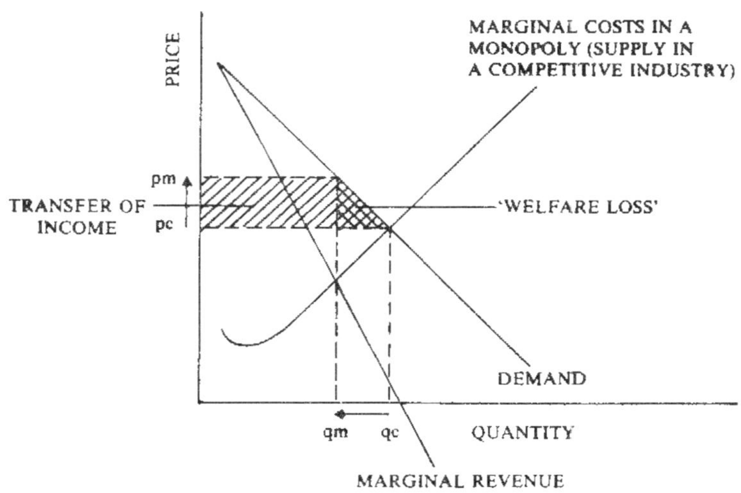

Figure D Comparing monopoly with a competitive industry

Figure D represents the situation in a perfect monopoly. Note that price and quantity are determined by the spot where marginal costs equal marginal revenue (because this is where profits are maximised). In a competitive industry, marginal revenue and the demand curve are the same so that demand is satisfied. In a monopoly the marginal revenue is always lower than the demand so that when the monopolist maximises profits there is an unsatisfied demand.

The EC prohibits abuse, but not the mere attainment, of a dominant position. Dominant position is not necessarily the same as a monopoly — if a company has a monopoly, then almost certainly it will have a dominant position; but there have been cases in the EC where a company does not seem to have a monopoly but has nevertheless been held to be dominant (see *United Brands*).

New agreement
One made since March 1962, when the competition rules took effect. Alternatively, one made after the date of accession of a Member State if one of the parties operates in the new Member State and the agreement took effect there. They were specifically dealt with in Article 4, Regulation 17/62, and should be compared with **'old' agreements**.

Non-challenge clause
Basically, this concerns the licensing of intellectual property rights (eg, patents). (See, eg, *Bayer AG v Sullhofer* (65/86) [1988] ECR 5249.) The licensor permits the licensee to have access to his patent and manufacture the patented goods, subject to the requirement not to challenge the grant of the patent to the licensor. A licensee might want to do this because, if he could show the patent was invalid, he could make the goods without having to pay a royalty to the licensor. This type of clause is often seen as anti-competitive, although it may not be where the patent licence was granted compulsorily rather than voluntarily.

Non-competition clause
A contract clause requiring one party not to compete with the other or sometimes with third parties. An example is a standard franchise agreement. It may last for the duration of the agreement or extend beyond the lifetime of the agreement. Essentially, the longer it lasts, the more it is likely to be regarded as anti-competitive. Such clauses were considered by the Court of Justice in *Kai Ottung v Klee & Weillback A/S and Thomas Schmidt A/S* (320/87) [1990] 4 CMLR 67 in the context of a licence for a patented invention. The Court observed that if the licensee was prohibited from manufacture and marketing after termination of the licence, he would be at a disadvantage because, once the patent had expired, others would be free to make and market the product. In such circumstances, the clause would be anti-competitive. It might be saved, though, if the clause were limited in time to the duration of the patent. See also Regulation 240/96, the block exemption on technology transfers.

Old agreement
One which was made between undertakings prior to March 1962 and therefore predated the operation of the EC competition rules. See Article 5 of Regulation 17/62 and **provisional validity**.

Predatory pricing
This is the name given to a theory that a company will reduce the price of its product to below its marginal costs (ie deliberately make a loss on each sale) in order to attract many customers to it. In order for its competitors to survive, they too will have to slash prices and face losses. Sooner or later, one of the companies will either go out of business or get out of that product. Either way, that leaves the market free of competition for the survivor who can then charge a monopoly price for the product. After a while, the survivor will recoup his losses and start to make monopoly profits.

This theory has been the subject of some debate. Some economists consider that the theory is unrealistic — once monopoly prices were charged, other companies would be attracted to enter the market. The consequence would then be a drop in price towards that originally charged and the survivor would be unable to recoup the losses in full or make monopoly profits. These views seem to be accepted in the USA (see e.g, *Matsushita Electrical Industries Co v Zenith Radio Corp* (1986) 106 S Ct 1348). In the European Community, predatory behaviour (including pricing policy) is acknowledged as a fact. See, eg, the investigation of AKZO Chemie by the European Commission (1986), and the 1989 report on predatory pricing by the OECD.

Price fixing
Price fixing has traditionally been condemned by both the Commission and the ECJ. They are often concerned with agreements between competitors (ie horizontal agreements or cartels) to sell their products at the same prices: this may occur with homogenous products (like chemical dyes) or similar products (like personal stereos). Such agreements usually cover the whole range of the parties' relevant products. The theory is that such agreements are anti-competitive because the consumer cannot benefit from competition on prices: he cannot purchase the goods cheaper in the store down the road. If the Commission finds competitors even exchanging information about their respective future prices, it may suspect (at the least) a concerted practice which infringes Article 81 (ex 85).

Such horizontal agreements may occur at the level of manufacturers (see, eg, *ICI v Commission* (48/69) [1972] ECR 619; *Ahlström Oy v Commission* (C-89, 104, 114, 116–7/85, C-125-129/85) [1993] 4 CMLR 407); or distributors; or retailers. The economic impact of a similar (but vertical) agreement between, say, a manufacturer and one of its distributors to fix the resale prices for the distributor is likely to be less than if all distributors of competing products agree on prices: that single distributor will face price competition from other distributors. One can distinguish vertical agreements from horizontal ones and argue that price fixing is less significant in vertical arrangements.

However, one manufacturer may fix the resale prices for all of its distributors: this entirely removes competition on prices for that product, although it may still face such competition from distributors of substitute products. This control over resale prices is still forbidden by the Commission and the ECJ, and they will be alert to find even indirect control being exercised over prices. See, for example, *Pronuptia de Paris* (161/84) [1986] ECR 353, where the ECJ stated that for a franchisor to *merely* recommend prices to its franchisee was acceptable; what would infringe Article 85 would be where a concerted practice existed between franchisor and franchisee (vertical) or between franchisees (horizontal) to apply the 'recommended' prices as actual prices. A concerted practice of this sort between franchisor and franchisee might be found to exist where the franchisor maintained control over the franchisee's publicity and promotional material (including statements about prices). See also **Chiselling**.

Product market
See Market share analysis.

Provisional validity
A term applied to 'old' agreements, referring to a form of prima facie legality which they have. See Regulation 17/62.

Royalties
Often used in patent licences. Considered by the Court of Justice in *Kai Ottung* where it was held that generally a royalty clause which required payments to continue after expiry of the patent would infringe Article 81(1) (ex 85(1)). However, if the licensee

could freely terminate the licence agreement on reasonable notice, an obligation to continue paying for the duration of the licence (ie for an indeterminate period) was not prohibited by Article 81(1) (ex 85(1)).

Selective distribution systems

As the name implies, what is involved in this type of business is the appointment of several distributors to a network, who are engaged in reselling a product. The distributor must meet certain criteria, imposed by the supplier, in order to qualify for appointment. These criteria might include fitting out a retail shop in a specific way (eg, *Yves Rocher* shops: see OJ 1987 L8/49), or giving specific training to sales staff, or providing an after-sales service to customers. Such networks may fall foul of Article 81(1) (ex 85(1)), in particular if the supplier requires distributors to satisfy quantitative criteria in order to be appointed, rather than qualitative criteria. See now Regulation 2790/99 on vertical agreements.

Ties

The notion that a seller with market power can force an unwilling buyer to buy more products than are actually wanted. So if seller S has a monopoly in, say, nail guns (maybe a patent for them) and requires every purchaser of nail guns to buy their supply of nails from him too, even though they could get the nails from another supplier, this represents a tie-in. This type of requirement is often seen as anti-competitive.

Vertical agreement

An agreement made between undertakings operating at different levels of the market, eg, a manufacturer makes an agreement with a distributor to distribute his products. See the block exemption for vertical agreements — Regulation 2790/99 — and the Commission Guidelines on Vertical Agreements, published in 2000.

APPENDIX 6
OVERVIEW OF EUROPEAN COMMUNITY LAW

The information which follows is designed only as an introduction to European Community law. It merely outlines the basic concepts, structure and operation of the Community legal order and gives extracts from some source material.

A6.1 The importance of European Community law to the UK practitioner

European Community law became enforceable law in the UK by virtue of the European Communities Act 1972 (ECA 1972). Every year, thousands of decisions based on the Community treaties are made by Community institutions which affect the Member States and the lives of their citizens. An individual citizen of a Member State is not only subject to national law but is also affected by European Community law. Practitioners should be well-informed about the Community legal order as well as the national law which affect their clients. For example, in a recent case involving the Tipp-Ex Company, the company was fined heavily for a breach of Community law notwithstanding its illegal action had been approved (wrongly) by their lawyer!

A barrister will be expected to advise on a point of European Community law when it arises in a case, to decide if the client or his opponent can rely on it in their claim or defence and perhaps to deal with the point in the national court or before the European Court.

A Community law point may arise in a variety of topics with which the ordinary legal practitioner has to deal and is not limited to the commercial sphere only. The practitioner is expected to recognise that a European Community matter has arisen, know where to go to obtain further information about it, how to handle it in person or when to seek specialist advice in relation to it.

A6.2 The Community is a supranational legal order

The Community is often described as a supranational legal order. This is because it is an association of states endowed with autonomous legal authority. Although it was created like a traditional international organisation by international treaties, it is more developed. The same founding documents which established the Community bestowed on it its own sovereign rights and competence. The Community legal system is independent of and superior to those of the Member States. In exchange for membership to the Community, Member States have relinquished some of their own legislative powers and transferred them to the Community institutions which are empowered to enact an autonomous body of Community law. Member States and their citizens are subject to

Community law in matters over which the Community has competence. The objectives of the Community are pursued by means of Community legislation and case law and enforced by both the ECJ, the Court of First Instance and the national courts (*Van Gend en Loos* (26/62) [1963] CMLR 105).

A6.3 Legislative powers of the Community institutions

The EC Treaty sets out the Community's aims. The Community institutions are left to fill in the details by enacting legislation. As the EC Treaty covers a wide variety of matters, an almost unlimited potential exists for Community legislation (subject to the requirement that the Community institutions may only act within the areas and power laid down by the EC Treaty).

Some Treaty provisions are precise enough not to need further implementation (eg, the competition rules, Articles 81 (ex 85) and 82 (ex 86)). Others specifically call for, or simply require, further measures to be passed. The Council, acting in conjunction with the Commission and the Parliament, has an implicit power to legislate if action by the Community should prove necessary to attain one of the objectives of the Community and the Treaty has not provided the necessary powers (Article 308 (ex 235), EC Treaty).

To facilitate the Community in carrying out its policies towards third countries, the EC Treaty bestows legal personality on the Community (Article 281 (ex 210)), enables the Commission to negotiate on its behalf and the Council, after consulting with the Parliament where so required by the Treaty, to conclude Treaties between the Community and third countries or international organisations (Article 300 (ex 228)).

By reason of the broad power of the Community institutions to legislate in many areas covered by the EC Treaty, the practitioner has to be constantly alert to keep up to date with the legislation being passed. The best way to do so is through the Official Journal (OJ), published by the Community. Ignorance of EC law is no defence — *Tipp-Ex* case (C-279/87) [1990] ECR I-261).

Member States must be vigilant that they are not breaking Community legislation so that an infringement action is not brought against them. The practitioner may need to advise on such a matter also.

A6.4 How is legislation made in the Community?

The legislative process in the Community is based on a division of power between the Commission and the Council. There are only a few cases in which the Commission alone may exercise legislative power. In most cases the Commission proposes and the Council disposes. Before the Council can take a final decision, depending on the subject-matter of the measure, it has to consult the Parliament and sometimes the Economic and Social Committee. The Treaty of European Union strengthened the legislative powers of the Parliament considerably. It acquired a power of 'co-decision' with the Council on areas such as health, culture and research. Under the 'cooperation procedure' the Parliament is able to amend draft legislation sent by the Council (the result is that unanimity is then required in the Council to pass the legislation, rather than a qualified majority). Under further changes, contained in the Amsterdam Treaty 1997, co-decision will become the norm in many areas. However, in the key fields of economic and monetary union, the cooperation procedure will continue to define the roles of the Parliament and Council.

Although the Council is in the strongest position in the decision-making process, the Commission has some tactical advantages. No decision can be taken by the Council without the Commission taking the initiative by proposing the draft Community measure in question. The Commission can amend its proposal up to the time the final decision is made; the Council can only do so by unanimous vote.

A6.5 Legislative measures that the Community institutions can make

The legislative measures or acts which the Community institutions have power to enact are regulations, directives, decisions, recommendations and opinions. Only the first three are legally binding. All five are described in Article 249 (ex 189), EC Treaty:

> *In order to carry out their task and in accordance with the provisions of the Treaty, the European Parliament acting jointly with the Council and the Commission shall make regulations and issue directives, take decisions, make recommendations or deliver opinions.*
>
> *A regulation shall have general application. It shall be binding in its entirety and directly applicable in all Member States.*
>
> *A directive shall be binding, as to the result to be achieved, upon each Member State to which it is addressed, but shall leave to the national authorities the choice of form and methods. A decision shall be binding in its entirety upon those to whom it is addressed.*
>
> *Recommendations and opinions shall have no binding force.*

A Regulation is best described as a normative measure, laying down general rules which apply to anyone who falls within their scope (like a public Act of Parliament in the UK). They do not need additional implementation to take effect.

A directive may be addressed to all Member States, or an individual Member State. It requires implementation by the Member State(s) before it has the force of law, unless it meets the criteria for direct effect. See **A6.9**. The method of implementation is left to the Member State but the result to be achieved is binding.

A decision is an individual act addressed to a specific person or to a Member State. It has the force of law without further enactment. Its nature is essentially administrative, usually affecting just the addressees. It can have judicial undertones, too: see Article 230 (ex 173).

The EC Treaty lays down safeguards in the adoption of these measures. The measures must state the reasons on which they are based and refer to any proposals or opinions which were required to be obtained by the Treaty (Article 253 (ex 190)). Any act which fails to follow this procedural requirement is at risk of annulment (see Article 230 (ex 173)). Another safeguard is publication: see Article 254 (ex 191) for details.

Despite Article 249 (ex 189), the ECJ has held that the true nature of an act is determined by its substance and object, and not its form and label (*Confédération Nationale des Producteurs de Fruits et Legumes v Council* (C-16 and 17/62) [1963] CMLR 160); *International Fruit Co NV v Commission (No 1)* (C-41-4/70) [1975] 2 CMLR 515). The ECJ will re-classify specific measures according to their nature, as distinct from the description applied by the Commission or Council. The ECJ has also developed a category of EC acts which are *sui generis* and not in Article 249 (ex 189) at all. (See *Commission of the European Communities v Council of the European Communities* (22/78) [1971] ECR 263, [1971] CMLR 335.)

A6.6 Sources of Community law

The sources of law, in the sense of the legal rules that form the Community legal order and bind the Community, its institutions, the Member States and (in some instances) individuals, are the following: the founding treaties; the legal acts of the Community; international agreements entered into by the Community institutions on behalf of the Community; the judgments of the ECJ (and the Court of First Instance) and general principles of law. Member States are obliged by Article 10 (ex 5) (see **1.2.3.1** above) to 'take all appropriate measures, whether general or particular, to ensure fulfilment' of the obligations which these sources of law impose.

A6.6.1 The founding treaties

The founding treaties are a primary source of Community law. They were created directly by the Member States themselves. They are the EC Treaty and Protocols as amended by subsequent Treaties: the Merger Treaty 1965; Acts of Accession 1972 (UK, Ireland, Denmark), 1979 (Greece), 1985 (Spain, Portugal), 1995 (Austria, Finland and Sweden); Budgetary Treaties 1970, 1975; Single European Act 1986; the Treaty on European Union 1992; and the Treaty of Amsterdam 1997. They form a constitutional skeleton for the Community by setting out the objectives of the Community, its mechanisms, the timetable within which the objectives are to be achieved, and setting up its institutions and conferring on them legislative and administrative powers.

A6.6.2 Secondary legislation of the Community

The acts of the Community institutions form an important source of Community law (see **A6.5**). Note that:

(a) Regulations are directly applicable in national legal systems and apply throughout the Community in all the Member States. Many have direct effect, conferring rights and duties on individuals who can rely on them in the same way as domestic law in their national courts. Unlike national law, however, they have not been passed by the national legislature.

(b) Directives are often used for coordinating the laws of Member States (Article 94 (ex 100), EC Treaty). Member States may be obliged to introduce new legislation or redraft or amend existing national legislation and administrative rules to conform to the objectives of a directive. They may have direct effect in certain circumstances.

(c) Decisions are administrative measures. Sometimes the Community institutions themselves are responsible for implementing the treaties or regulations. They can make decisions binding on individuals, firms or Member States. A directive usually requires the addressee to perform some action or refrain therefrom. It also may confer rights or impose obligations on those to whom it is addressed.

A6.6.3 International agreements between the EC and non-Member States

The international agreements that the Community enters into with non-Member States and other international organisations on behalf of the Community are a third source of Community law. Such agreements may be new, such as the Rome Convention 1979, or existing agreements for which the Community takes responsibility from Member States on their accession to the Community, such as the General Agreement on Tariffs and Trade (GATT). This agreement was established before the Community existed, but all the Member States were parties to it and it concerned matters over which the Community has competence. 'In so far as the Community has assumed the powers previously exercised by Member States in the area governed by the General Agreement, the provisions of that agreement have the effect of binding the Community' (*International Fruit Company v Produktschap voor Groenten en Fruit* (C-21-4/72) [1972] ECR 1439, para 18).

A6.6.4 International agreements between Member States

International agreements between Member States may be concluded on any topic, within or without the scope of Community law only if their subject-matter is within the jurisdiction of the Community, as defined by the Treaty of Rome and subsequent legislation.

Member States may be under an obligation to reach agreement on a topic as part of a programme determined by the Treaty of Rome. In certain cases these additional conventions are intended to supplement its provisions. For example, Article 293 (ex 220), EC Treaty enables the Member States to enter into treaties and conventions on specific matters listed in the Article. Two conventions have been concluded: one on the Mutual Recognition of Companies and Legal Persons and a second, on Jurisdiction and the Enforcement of Judgments in Civil and Commercial Matters (both 1968). These agreements are regarded as Community law.

Alternatively, the States may achieve a binding consensus on a topic entirely of their own choosing. If this has no connection with the work of the Community, then it should not be regarded as a source of Community law. As the Community institutions draw on the fundamental aims and objectives set out in the Treaty of Rome (eg in the Single European Act), the topics where Member States have a 'free hand' will be restricted.

In some areas, the Member States seem to have accepted the desirability of broadening the application of European Community law. For example, the Member States have set out to create new intellectual property rights, the Community patent and the Community trademark, which are closely connected to the concept of a single community.

The Treaty of Rome imposes no obligation on Member States to create these new property rights and it might be thought that they are, therefore, no part of Community law. However, the relationship with the Community is clear.

The geographical limit of these intellectual property rights is defined as that of the Community's Member States; the right is described in the agreement as a Community patent (for example). The countries which are involved are all of the existing Member States (and no one else); the European Commission was brought in to advise on the proposed agreement; the European Court of Justice is given jurisdiction over the agreement; and there is a clear connection between the aims of the Community on free movement of goods and services around the common market (and fair competition) and the establishment of a single Community-wide patent together with the single application needed to obtain it. This type of international agreement should clearly be seen as a source of Community law, although subordinate to the Treaty of Rome and its subsequent secondary legislation.

A6.7 Judicial legislation

The entire jurisprudence of the ECJ, including the general principles of law it has recognised and the doctrines it has developed, forms an important source of Community law. This has recently been enlarged by the developing case law of the Court of First Instance.

A6.7.1 General principles of law

The notion of general principles of law has been developed by the ECJ in its judgments; they are often regarded as a separate source of Community law and are based on concepts of law and justice found in most legal systems.

The EC Treaty makes indirect reference to general principles of law in several of its articles. For example:

(a) Article 220 (ex 164) states that the 'Court of Justice shall ensure that in the interpretation and application of this Treaty the law is observed'. 'Law' here suggests a law which transcends the text of the EC Treaty itself. The practical application of this abstract notion is shown in (b) and (c).

(b) Article 230 (ex 173) permits the Court of Justice to declare Community acts illegal if, eg, an act infringes a rule of law relating to the application of the Treaty. This has meant that private or legal persons (if they have locus standi) may challenge a Commission decision on the ground that it infringes a general principle of law, such as equality or legitimate expectations.

(c) Article 288(2) (ex 215(2)) provides that the non-contractual liability of the Community shall be based on 'the general principles common to the law of the Member States'. For example, the Community is only liable for unlawful acts of a legislative nature (ie regulations) if the Court of Justice decides that the act infringed a 'superior rule of law' which was intended to protect the individual, since this is a common basis for state liability for such acts in national courts of the Member States (*Aktien-Zuckerfabrik Schöppenstedt v Council* (5/71) [1971] ECR 975).

The particular principles are inspired by those common to the legal systems of Member States and are recognised or developed by the ECJ when required in cases before it. Although the categories of general principles which the ECJ will use are not closed, those which have been considered by the ECJ in its case law, and thus recognised as sources of Community law, have arisen in an *ad hoc* fashion.

(a) The restrictive nature of the Community's non-contractual liability for legislative acts of its institutions (see *Schöppenstedt*).

(b) Legality in administration (ie, the institutions comply with the set procedures and act reasonably).

(c) Proportionality: action must be proportionate to the end it seeks to achieve. See *Internationale Handelsgesellschaft* (11/70) [1970] ECR 1125 and *Bela-Muhle Josef Bergman v Grows-Farm* (114/76) [1977] ECR 1211.

(d) Legal certainty. See *Germany v Commission* (44/81) [1982] ECR 1855 and *Simmenthal* (92/78) [1979] ECR 811.

(e) Protection of legitimate expectations. See *Amylum v Council* (108/81) [1982] ECR 2107, para 4–17 and *CNTA v Commission* (74/74) [1975] ECR 533.

(f) Non-discrimination and equality of treatment. See *Sabbatini v European Parliament* (20/71) [1972] ECR 345, *Prais v Council* (130/75) [1976] ECR 1589 and *Bela-Muhle Josef Bergman v Grows-Farm* (114/76) [1977] ECR 1211.

(g) Entitlement to a hearing. See *Transocean Marine Paint v Commission* (17/74) [1974] ECR 1063.

(h) Professional legal privilege in anti-competition investigations by the Commission. See *AM & S* (155/79) [1982] ECR 1575.

(i) The right to be assisted by counsel. See *Demont* (15/80) [1981] ECR 3147.

(j) The fundamental human rights upon which the constitutional law of Member States is based. See *Stauder v City of Ulm* (29/69) [1969] ECR 419, *Internationale Handelsgesellschaft* (11/70) [1970] ECR 1125 and *Nold v Commission* (4/73) [1974] ECR 491.

It is not possible to explain all of these principles here. An explanation of two will illustrate their use.

A6.7.1.1 Equality

The principle of equality or non-discrimination means that the Community institutions must act without regard to sex or nationality.

Mrs Sabbatini challenged the Community staff regulation which provided that only 'a head of family' was entitled to an expatriation allowance. The regulation defined this phrase in such a way that only men could receive the allowance. Her claim, based on the general principle of equality, succeeded. Ms Prais challenged the Council's decision to hold a competitive examination on the date of a Jewish festival as religious discrimination. The ECJ held that religious freedom was a general principle of law but on the facts discrimination had not been made out in Ms Prais' case. In *Bela-Muhle Josef Bergman v Grows-Farm* (otherwise known as the *Skimmed Milk Powder* case) the Council passed a measure to force animal feed producers to use skimmed milk in their feed rather than soya. The result of this was to increase the price of animal feed thus harming livestock farmers. The only farmers who benefited from this were dairy farmers as their product was being used in the feedstuffs. The claim that the policy was discriminatory between the two categories of farmers succeeded.

Specific non-discrimination is mentioned in two important EC Treaty Articles. Article 12 (ex 7) prohibits discrimination on the ground of nationality in the application of the Treaty. (This has especially been relied on in relation to the free movement of workers (Article 39 (ex 48)) and services (Article 49 (ex 59)).) Article 141 (ex 119) provides for equal pay for men and women who do equal work. (Directives also specifically deal with equal treatment between men and women in social security matters, occupational pension schemes and in self-employment.)

A6.7.1.2 Human rights

There is no written list of fundamental rights and freedoms in Community law. Some basic rights however were mentioned in the original EC Treaty: freedom of movement of workers (Article 39 (ex 48)); the right of establishment (Article 43 (ex 52)); the freedom to provide services (Article 49 (ex 59)); the freedom of movement of goods (Article 23 (ex 9)); the right of association (Article 140 (ex 118(1)); the protection of business and professional secrets (Article 287 (ex 214)); and numerous prohibitions on discrimination (Articles 12, 13, 39, 43, 50, 81 and 141 (ex 7, 48, 52, 60, 85 and 119)).

However, the ECJ has developed the Community's unwritten fundamental rights in its case law.

Stauder was the first case in which it declared that a respect for human rights was a fundamental general principle of Community law that the ECJ would safeguard. In *Internationale Handelsgesellschaft* the ECJ made clear that Community measures would not be judged by the human rights concepts of the national constitutions of Member States, but would be judged by its own concept of human rights. However, Community concepts which the ECJ will protect are those which are common to the constitutions of Member States. These act as inspiration to the development of the Community's concepts (*Nold*). International conventions concerning the protection of human rights to which Member States are parties or have acceded also serve as guidelines for the

Community concepts (*Nold*). In *Rutili v Minister for the Interior* (36/75) [1975] ECR 1219 specific reference in this respect was made to the European Convention on Human Rights.

Examples of human rights concepts that the ECJ has recognised, in addition to the ones which overlap with some of the general principles already listed and discussed above, are the right of ownership, the general right of privacy, freedom to engage in business and to choose and practise a profession, freedom of association, privacy and correspondence.

The ECJ's process of evolving 'European fundamental rights' is a continuing and piecemeal process. The ECJ has been unable to develop rights for all areas in which this might be necessary or desirable because its judgments are confined to the particular cases which are brought before it. In this context, one should see now also Article 6 (ex F) of the Treaty on European Union (**1.2.1**). It should be noted that, in an Opinion delivered on 28 March 1996 (2/94), the ECJ responded to a request from the Council of Ministers, which sought advice on whether accession by the European Community to the European Convention on Human Rights would be compatible with the EC Treaty. The ECJ stated that, in the present state of Community law, the Community would have 'no competence' to accede to the ECHR. Subsequently, the EU has embraced both the concept of human rights and the ECHR itself, through changes wrought by the Treaty of Amsterdam. See Articles 6 (ex 3c) and 46 (ex 56), EC Treaty.

A6.8 Community law in our national legal system

A6.8.1 International law and the English legal system

Under English law, international laws (specifically treaties) may be binding on the State and subject to enforcement by legal process. An example is the European Convention on Human Rights and Fundamental Freedoms (ECHR). But international law is unlikely to create rights for individuals which can be enforced through our own courts or tribunals. Again, using the example of the ECHR, a complainant must use the procedures and institutions established by the ECHR in order to complain about a violation of the Convention.

An English court might take note of the principles of the ECHR, especially when interpreting an Act of Parliament as our Parliament is not to be understood as passing legislation which is contrary to the international obligations of the UK unless the Act expresses this intention. But if the victim of an act which was contrary to the ECHR seeks relief from the English courts, the cause of action must be one known to English law (eg, assault; false imprisonment; a claim for judicial review based on a denial of natural justice): a writ which simply alleges an infringement of the Convention will be struck out as disclosing no cause of action.

So, international laws generally have no effect on individuals in the UK: they give no rights, impose no obligations, which can be relied on in our courts. These laws bind only the State and are enforceable against the State through procedures totally distinct from our legal system. European Community law is different: it can give rights to individuals or impose obligations on individuals and the State which are enforceable through our courts. It does this by virtue of the European Communities Act 1972 (ECA). Since this was originally written, the UK Parliament has passed the Human Rights Act 1998. Some of the ECHR Articles are now part of the English legal system.

A6.8.2 The European Communities Act 1972

The laws of the European Community became a part of our domestic legal system as a result of the European Communities Act 1972. So, the articles of the EC Treaty and the secondary legislation of the Community institutions are as much a part of our legal system as is an Act of Parliament, an Order in Council or a decision of the House of Lords.

Under s 2(1) of the ECA 1972:

> *all such rights, powers, obligations and restrictions from time to time created or arising* [from the EC Treaty, amongst others], *and all … remedies and procedures* [provided for by the Treaty] *as in accordance with [the Treaty] are without further enactment to be given legal effect or used in the United Kingdom shall be recognised and available in law, and be enforced … and followed accordingly …*

The important element here is that some Community laws may give rights and obligations without further enactment, that is they become a part of our laws without any statute or Order in Council to implement them.

By s 2(2) of the ECA 1972, the Government is empowered to pass secondary legislation, when appropriate, to implement any Community obligation of the UK. By s 2(4) any such legislation (and Acts of Parliament) passed or to be passed 'shall be construed and have effect subject to the foregoing provisions of this section'. This subsection is often relied on as implicitly establishing the supremacy of Community law over English law by 'entrenching' its position.

A6.8.3 The European Communities Act and English courts

Whenever a question arises in legal proceedings as to the interpretation or effect of the EC Treaty (or as to the validity, effect or interpretation of EC secondary legislation), this shall be treated as a question of law, not of fact. The question should either be referred to the European Court of Justice (ECJ) for its opinion or determined by the English judge 'in accordance with the principles laid down by and any relevant decision of the European Court' (s 3(1) of the ECA 1972). This seems to establish the primacy of the ECJ and its case law in relation to our own courts.

In a similar vein, s 3(2) requires an English judge to take judicial notice of (ie be bound by):

(a) the Community Treaties;

(b) the Official Journal of the Communities; and

(c) 'any decision of, or expression of opinion by, the European Court' on the questions of law referred to in s 3(1).

The two most important 'decisions' by the ECJ, which English judges are bound by are: (a) that Community law takes precedence over national law where the two are in conflict; and (b) that some Community laws give rights or obligations to individuals which can be enforced in our courts without the need for implementing legislation. These two decisions are examined below.

A6.9 The direct effect of Community law

Under Article 249 (ex 189) of the EC Treaty, regulations are directly applicable in the Member States. No other type of Community law is thus described. But the ECJ has evolved a concept of 'direct effect': by this it means that Community laws which meet certain criteria may be used by individuals in national courts. Sometimes such laws may only be used against the State (ie they impose no obligation on individuals) — perhaps to claim damages or certiorari; other laws proscribe certain conduct — they may be used by one individual to sue another or as a defence to litigation. Some examples may help.

A6.9.1 Some examples

Example 1

A UK Government minister bans imports of French turkeys. His action is designed to support UK turkey breeders at the expense of French producers. Article 28 (ex 30) of the EC Treaty establishes the principle of free circulation of goods between the Member States of the Community. The ECJ has held this article to be directly effective. The French turkey producers sue the minister in the English High Court for damages, relying on his alleged infringement of Article 30 (now 28). They establish the right to a declaration that the ban is illegal but the remedy of damages is denied by the court. The case is subsequently settled out of court.

See *Bourgoin v Ministry of Agriculture, Fisheries and Food* [1986] QB 716.

Example 2

A woman works for a local health authority. When she reaches the age of 62, she is dismissed from her job. There is no reason for this, other than her age. The policy of the health authority is to dismiss female staff when they reach 60, male staff at age 65. She makes a claim in the Employment Tribunal, alleging that her dismissal contravenes a Community Directive, No 76/207. This provides that male and female employees shall receive equal treatment in their conditions of work, including dismissal. The question of whether the directive is directly effective is referred to the ECJ. The ECJ decides that it is enforceable against the state (in this case represented by the health authority). The Employment Tribunal then upholds her claim and awards her several thousand pounds compensation.

See *Marshall v Southampton and SW Hants AHA* [1986] QB 401.

Example 3

A French national gets a place at an English university to read for a degree in electrical engineering. His application to the relevant UK Government department for payment of his tuition fees and maintenance grant is refused because he does not meet the requirements for foreign students' grants. He sues the responsible Government minister, claiming that the requirements discriminate against him on the ground of his nationality, contrary to Articles 12 (ex 6) and 39 (ex 48) of the EC Treaty. Both Articles are directly effective, according to the case law of the ECJ. During the proceedings, the Government changes the rules regarding payment of tuition fees for EC nationals; a reference to the ECJ establishes the right of EC workers to move to another Member State and get a maintenance grant from their 'host' country.

See *Brown v Secretary of State for Scotland* [1988] ECR 3237.

Example 4

An English company makes dairy products, using milk supplied by the Milk Marketing Board (MMB). The MMB announces it will no longer sell directly to the company; the company must now buy from a middle man with higher prices. The company sues the MMB in the High Court for damages, alleging breach of Article 82 (ex 86) of the Treaty (anti-competitive conduct). The ECJ has held previously that Article 82 is directly effective. The English courts hold that a breach of Article 82 is actionable (as a breach of statutory duty) and can be used to claim damages.

See *Garden Cottage Foods v Milk Marketing Board* [1984] AC 130.

Example 5

An English company owns the patent in a pharmaceutical substance 'S'. Another company applies for a licence to import 'S' into the UK from another Member State (Italy). Before the licence is granted (or refused), the applicant starts importing 'S'. The patentee sues in the High Court, alleging infringement of its patent. It claims an injunction to stop the imports. The importer's defence states that its imports have been bought quite lawfully in Italy, although 'S' is not patented there, and it relies on Article 28 (ex 30) of the Treaty (free circulation of goods). A reference to the ECJ makes it clear that the injunction would contradict Article 28 so the English court refuses to grant the injunction.

See *Allen & Hanburys Ltd v Generics (UK) Ltd* [1989] 1 WLR 414.

Example 6

Two men are prosecuted for breaking the laws on importation of obscene material. They have imported pornographic literature from another Member State where it is lawfully on sale. Their defence is that they bought the literature legitimately and, under Article 28 (ex 30) of the Treaty, are allowed to export it to any other Member State. This would have succeeded, as Article 28 is directly effective, save that there is an exception to the basic right of free circulation, contained in Article 30 (ex 36). This allows States to derogate from the right on the ground of public morality.

See *R v Henn and Darby* [1981] AC 850.

A6.9.2 Which Community laws are directly effective?

A list of all the Treaty Articles and secondary legislation that have been held to be directly effective would be too long for insertion here. The ECJ has held that several articles of the Treaty are directly effective; also certain regulations, directives and decisions. However, each article, regulation, etc will be examined individually by the ECJ to see whether it meets the criteria for direct effect. Thus, the contents of a list of directly effective laws is governed by which measures have been referred by national courts to the ECJ for its opinion on the matter. The criteria are examined in **A6.9.3** onwards.

A6.9.3 Directly effective Articles of the Treaty

The following Articles have been held to be of direct effect:

(a) Article 12 (ex 6) (non-discrimination between EC nationals on grounds of nationality); *Gravier v City of Liege* [1985] ECR 593.

(b) Article 25 (ex 12) (ban on introduction of new customs duties on imports from one Member State to another); *Van Gend en Loos* [1963] ECR 1.

(c) Article 28 (ex 30) (elimination of quantitative restrictions on the free movement of goods between Member States); *Ianelli & Volpi Spa v Ditta Paola Meroni* [1977] ECR 557.

(d) Article 39 (ex 48) (freedom of workers who are EC nationals to move to another Member State to work there); *Van Duyn v Home Office* [1974] ECR 1337.

(e) Article 43 (ex 52) (freedom of EC nationals who are self-employed or members of a profession, or EC companies, to set themselves up in another Member State); *Reyners v Belgian State* [1974] ECR 631.

(f) Article 49 (ex 59) (freedom of EC nationals to move temporarily to another Member State in order to provide (or receive) a service there); *Van Binsbergen* [1974] ECR 1299.

(g) Articles 81 (ex 85) and 82 (ex 86) (prohibition on conduct which restricts or distorts competition in the common market); *BRT v SABAM* [1974] ECR 51.

(h) Article 141 (ex 119) (equal pay for male and female staff who do equal work); *Defrenne v Sabena* [1976] ECR 455.

The criteria for Articles to be directly effective were first established by the ECJ in the *Van Gend en Loos* case (26/62) and have since been modified. The wording of the Article must be:

(a) clear and unambiguous;

(b) unconditional (on the exercise of a power or discretion by, for example, a Member State or the European Commission);

(c) not dependent on further action.

Clarity and lack of ambiguity are not features of Community law that the man in the street might subscribe to. These features can by supplied by the ECJ, though, often when an EC measure is referred to it for interpretation under Article 234 (ex 177) of the Treaty. The ECJ has also occasionally interpreted an Article in such a way that it has direct effect in certain circumstances but not others. A typical example of this is the litigation between Ms Defrenne and the Belgian national airline, *Sabena* (43/75). The ECJ was concerned to interpret Article 141 (ex 119) regarding the principle of equal pay for equal work. The ECJ held that it was directly effective so far as 'direct' discrimination was concerned but not for 'indirect' discrimination. The distinction was based on the premise that in some situations discrimination could be determined simply on a legal analysis (direct discrimination) while in others a more complex determination would be required which a court might be ill-equipped to perform (indirect discrimination). So, if Miss A works alongside Mr B doing the same job, they should both receive the same wage, subject to proper reasons for distinction like seniority. On the other hand, if Miss A is a canteen assistant in a shipyard, while Mr B is a welder there, a job evaluation scheme is required to see if their jobs are of equal value; or Miss A may do a job which only women have done for that employer but seeks to argue that, if a man had the job, he would be paid more. Both of the latter examples are indirect discrimination according to the ECJ and Article 141 (ex 119) will not help.

If an Article requires further action, for example by a Member State, then usually it has no direct effect. However, in this situation the Member State would not be allowed to reap the benefit of its own inaction. If a time limit was expressed in the Article (or could be implied) for the further action to be taken but none was, the ECJ is likely to hold that (subject to the first two criteria being satisfied) the Article is now directly effective insofar as it may be enforced against the defaulting Member State. In such circumstances, the Member State might be liable to compensate individuals for any losses caused by its default: see *Brasserie du Pêcheur SA v Germany* (C-46/93) [1996] 2 WLR 506.

A6.9.4 Directly effective regulations

Similar provisions have been held by the ECJ to exist for regulations as have been considered in **A6.9.3** for Articles of the Treaty. The regulation must be clear and unambiguous, it must be unconditional and not require further action to be taken.

A6.9.5 Directly effective directives and decisions

The ECJ has held that directives can have direct effect, a good example being the *Marshall* case, referred to above. Unlike regulations, which are not meant to require any action on the part of Member States to implement them into national law, directives usually specify an aim or general principles and leave choices to the Member States. A good example is the Commission's Directive on Product Liability which allowed

Member States to take several different options as to liability. The UK enacted the Consumer Protection Act 1987 to implement it.

This might be thought to indicate that a directive should not have direct effect but the ECJ has said that to deprive directives of direct effect would lead to their avoidance by Member States, again through inactivity. This has led the ECJ to declare that once the time limit for implementation of a directive has passed without any (or any proper) implementation, an individual may rely on the directive against the Member State, providing it is clear and precise. The idea is that the Member State cannot rely on its own failure to deprive the individual of a right or remedy. However, the same policy argument cannot be used against another individual; it is not Mr Brown's fault if the UK Parliament has not enacted Directive 90/123, for example. This has led the ECJ to declare that directives have vertical direct effect (ie, impose obligations on the State, give rights to individuals) but not horizontal direct effect (ie, do not impose obligations on individuals). This view was recently reaffirmed by the ECJ in *Paola Faccini Dori v Recreb Srl* [1995] All ER (EC) 1. The obligation imposed on the Member State may include a liability to pay damages to individuals: see *Francovich v Italy* (C-6/90) [1991] ECR I-5357.

One result has been several cases in the UK where individual litigants have tried to rely on EC directives against a defendant arguing that the defendant is an 'emanation of the State' and thus subject to vertical direct effect. Two notable cases involved a (then) nationalised corporation, British Gas, and a company wholly-owned by the British Government, Rolls-Royce. They were sued by their employees, who relied on EC directives about equal pay or treatment. Both employees lost since the courts decided that neither organisation represented the State (unlike the area health authority in the *Marshall* case).

Lastly, decisions may have direct effect. The criteria are the same as for directives. See, for example, the case of *Grad v Finanzamt Traunstein* (9/70) [1971] CMLR 1.

For further reading, see Josephine Steiner, 'Coming to Terms with EEC Directives' (1990) 106 LQR 144.

A6.10 Supremacy of Community law

There are two points of view to be considered here. First, that of the European Community, second, that of the Member State. The European Community has always taken the view that its law takes precedence over any conflicting national law (see, eg, the second Simmenthal case (*Amministrazione delle Finanze dello Stato v Simmenthal SpA* (106/77) [1978] ECR 629)), whether the national law is precedent in time or not. The ECJ is firmly of the opinion that national courts should not apply national law on an issue where a Community measure could be applied.

The doctrine developed by the ECJ is that Community law has primacy over national law. The doctrine of Community primacy was first clarified by the ECJ in a preliminary ruling on a reference from a Milan Justice of the Peace in *Costa v ENEL* (6/64) [1964] ECR 585.

When Italy nationalised the production and supply of electricity and transferred the management of it to ENEL, Mr Costa, a shareholder in the Edison Volta company felt that his interests had been adversely affected. He refused to pay his electricity bill which was only a few hundred lire. His defence before the Milan justice was, inter alia, that the nationalisation of the electricity industry infringed several articles of the EC Treaty. When asked to interpret these Articles in a preliminary reference by the justice, the ECJ used the opportunity to stress that:

> The integration into the Laws of each Member State of provisions which derive from the Community, and more generally the terms and spirit of the Treaty, make it impossible for the States, as a corollary, to accord precedence to a unilateral and subsequent measure over a legal system accepted by them on a basis of reciprocity. The executive force of Community law cannot vary from one State to another in deference to subsequent domestic laws, without jeopardising the attainment of the objectives of the Treaty set out in Article 5(2) [now 10(2)] and giving rise to discrimination prohibited by Article 7 [now 12].

Another important ECJ case on this concept is *Internationale Handelsgesellschaft* (11/70) [1970] ECR 1125.

The doctrine of supremacy of EC law has found expression in the Member States in different ways according to their different constitutions (Trevor Hartley's book, *Foundations of European Community Law* has a good chapter reviewing the Member States' constitutions). In the UK s 2(4) of the ECA 1972 seems to establish the supremacy of Community law. Sometimes this concept has been accepted with apparent enthusiasm by English courts (see, eg, *Pickstone v Freemans plc* [1988] 3 WLR 265), but on other occasions a rather narrower view has prevailed (eg, *Duke v GEC Reliance Systems Ltd* [1988] 2 WLR 359). One way to encourage acceptance is through preliminary references by national courts to the ECJ under Article 234 (ex 177) of the EC Treaty. A problem exists with this, though. Such references are usually made at the discretion of the court then dealing with the case; they cannot be insisted upon by the parties to litigation. The more xenophobic a State's judges are, the less likely is any reference to the ECJ where a ruling on supremacy (or at least on an interpretation inconsistent with national law) might emerge. In the long term, the European community can really only rely on the States and all their institutions (including the courts) being '*communautaire*' and embracing the philosophy of the supranational single common market, with all the consequent loss of national sovereignty which that implies.

APPENDIX 7
THE COURT OF JUSTICE OF THE EUROPEAN COMMUNITIES

The Treaties, the Statutes of the Court annexed as Protocols to the Treaties, and the Rules of Procedure of the Court provide the framework in which the European Court operates. Originally, the EC Treaty created the European Court of Justice (ECJ). More recently, an inferior court has also been created: the Court of First Instance (CFI). The June 1996 issue of *European Law Review* (Vol 21 No 3) contains several articles with radical proposals for the future of the European Court.

A7.1 The jurisdiction of the European Court

The supranational aspect of the Community constitution is safeguarded by the ECJ. For the purposes of this appendix, the two courts of the Community — the Court of Justice and the Court of First Instance — have not usually been differentiated. The ECJ ensures that Community law is interpreted and applied uniformly throughout the Member States of the Community. It has sole jurisdiction to decide on the validity of Community legislation. It acts as referee in disputes between the institutions *inter se*, between the Community and Member States, and protects the rights of the individual against the Community bureaucracies, an important role as the democratic element is still quite weak within the Community.

The EC Treaty gives the ECJ a general duty to ensure that, in the interpretation and application of the EC Treaty, Community law is observed (Article 220 (ex 164)). This does not mean that the ECJ has a general power to determine any case submitted to it. It has jurisdiction only in the specific topics and procedures which the Treaty has indicated. The kinds of proceedings that may be dealt with by the ECJ are:

(a) Infringement actions brought against Member States for failing to fulfil their obligations under the EC Treaty or the law derived therefrom (Articles 226_227 (ex 169-170)).

(b) Annulment actions (Article 230 (ex 173)). The ECJ can review the legality of the acts of the institutions on the grounds mentioned in Article 230 (ex 173). If the act is found to be illegal, the European Court can declare it void (Article 231 (ex 174)). The institution concerned is required to take the necessary measures to comply with the Court's judgment (Article 233 (ex 176)).

(c) An action for failure of an institution to act (Articles 232 (ex 175) and 233 (ex 176)).

(d) An action for damages for the non-contractual liability of the Community (Articles 235 (ex 178) and 288(2) (ex 215(2))).

(e) A reference by a national court or tribunal for a preliminary ruling on the interpretation and validity of Community provisions (Article 234 (ex 177)).

(f) The adjustment of penalties provided for in Council regulations. For example, Regulation 1/2003 (on competition), allows the European Court to adjust fines or periodic penalties imposed by the Commission for infringements of the competition rules.

(g) Staff cases. The European Court has jurisdiction to resolve disputes between the Community institutions and its servants (Article 236 (ex 179)).

(h) Contractual liability of the Community (Articles 238 (ex 181) and 288 (ex 215)). A contract concluded by the Community may give the ECJ jurisdiction to hear disputes arising in relation to the contract.

(i) Opinions pursuant to Article 300(1) (ex 228(1)) (eg, the ECJ may give an opinion as to whether a proposed agreement to be concluded by the Community with a third country or international organisation is compatible with EC law).

The SEA 1986 provided for a Court of First Instance to determine certain classes of action or proceedings brought by national or legal persons. The Court first sat in September 1989. The actions it hears are staff cases, competition and coal and steel cases brought by individuals under Article 230 (ex 173) or 232 (ex 175). Actions started by Member States or the Community institutions and preliminary rulings are expressly excluded from the jurisdiction of the Court of First Instance.

The Court of First Instance looks at the facts in each case in greater detail than formerly happened in the ECJ. An illustration can be found in the *BASF AG v Commission* case (T-79/89 etc) where the annulment of a Commission decision was sought before the Court. The application was dismissed as inadmissible because the decision was so flawed in content and creation as to be legally non-existent thus rendering any annulment unnecessary. The case went on appeal to the ECJ. The ECJ disagreed with the CFI and quashed the Commission's decision on the ground of infringement of an essential procedural requirement (see (137/92) [1994] ECR I-2555).

The Court of First Instance is perhaps intended to be less 'judicially creative' than the ECJ, although the Decision of the Council which established the Court recited that:

> in respect of actions requiring close examination of complex facts, the establishment of a second court [Court of First Instance] will improve the judicial protection of individual interests.

A7.2 The composition and organisation of the European Court

The ECJ has 15 judges and nine Advocates-General. The qualifications for appointment are similar for both. They must be:

> *persons whose independence is beyond doubt and who possess the qualifications required for appointment to the highest judicial offices in their respective countries or who are jurisconsults of recognised competence.* (Article 223 (ex 167).)

Jurisconsults can include academic lawyers. Appointment is 'by common accord of the Governments of the Member States' for a period of six years and is renewable. In practice one Judge is appointed from each Member State; traditionally there is an additional post which is rotated between the different Member States. Every three years there is a partial replacement of six or seven judges and three Advocates-General. A President of the Court is elected by the judges themselves.

An Advocate-General is not a judge but he has equal status. After parties' written and oral submissions have been given in a case and before the judges deliberate, the Advocates-General appointed to the case gives an Opinion in open court. His Opinion on the case is fully reasoned, impartial and independent and recommends to the judges the decision to take. It need not be followed by the judges but it often is. It is published together with the judgment in the law reports and may be cited by counsel and Advocates-General in future cases.

A Judge Rapporteur is chosen by the President of the Court for each case. The Judge Rapporteur has the responsibility of seeing the case through the various stages of the proceedings and preparing reports on the case at different stages. After the Advocate-General's Opinion, the Judge Rapporteur drafts a judgment on which the other judges deliberate before a final, collective, judgment is reached by them.

The Registrar of the ECJ is responsible for the administration of the court and the reception, transmission and custody of documents relating to the cases.

Cases are decided either in plenary session (ie a quorum of nine judges) or in Chambers of three or five judges.

The Court of First Instance consists of 15 members, but has no permanent Advocates-General. Instead, any member of the Court may be called upon to perform the task of an Advocate-General in each case (he may not then participate in judging that case). The Court sits in chambers of three or five judges and their decisions may be the subject of an appeal to the ECJ. The Fifth and Sixth Chambers consist of seven judges each (of whom, five will sit in a given case), while the First, Second, Third and Fourth Chambers sit with three judges each. The first UK appointment to the Court of First Instance was David Edward QC, a Scots advocate. Following the appointment of Sir Gordon Slynn as a Law Lord, David Edward was appointed as a judge of the ECJ and Christopher Bellamy QC replaced him in the Court of First Instance.

A7.3 The practice and procedure of the European Court

The rules of procedure of the ECJ in relation to its jurisdiction under the EC Treaty can be found in the Protocol on the Statute of the Court of Justice, which is annexed to the EC Treaty, and in the Rules of Procedure of the Court.

The ECJ has jurisdiction over two types of action: direct and indirect. Direct actions commence and end in the ECJ, subject to the work of the Court of First Instance. References for preliminary rulings are indirect actions, which begin and end in the national court. The preliminary ruling of the ECJ is only a step in the proceedings before the national court.

In both types of action greater emphasis is placed on written procedure than oral hearings and the approach at the relatively short oral stage is inquisitorial, not adversarial.

An extremely informative article on the working of the Court of Justice has been written by David Edward and can be found in (1995) *European Law Review* 539.

A7.3.1 Direct actions

A7.3.1.1 Written procedure

Direct actions are initiated by a written application addressed to the President and Members of the ECJ, which is sent to the Registrar of the ECJ. The content of the application is governed by Article 38 of the Rules. Its main function is to define the issues between the parties, set out the grounds on which the application is based, the form of order sought and the nature of evidence relied upon. The Registrar effects service of the documents. The defendant must lodge a defence within a month of the application being served. A default judgment can be obtained. The defendant can contest the admissibility of an action as a preliminary objection by making a separate application to the ECJ. Further optional pleadings can be made, eg, a reply by the applicant and a rejoinder by the defendant.

A7.3.1.2 Fact finding

The ECJ may decide that a preparatory inquiry is necessary to clarify issues of fact. Article 45 of the Rules provides for various 'measures of inquiry', in practice the most usual being written questions devised by the Court and sent to the parties concerned. The parties reply in writing.

A7.3.1.3 The oral hearing

A public hearing is held at which oral submissions are made by representatives of the parties. These are relatively short as the Court has already studied the more lengthy written submissions. Members of the Bench sometimes interrupt counsel's speeches to ask questions. Usually their questions are put after all the submissions have been made.

A7.3.1.4 The opinion of the Advocate-General

The Advocate-General then delivers his Opinion which can be either *ex tempore* or delivered in open court at a later date.

A7.3.1.5 Deliberation and judgment

The Court deliberates in secrecy. Its decision may be taken by majority vote although it is always presented as a collective judgment with all the judges signing it. No individual judgments, eg, dissenting judgments, are given. As compromises have to be made this may explain why a judgment (or parts of it) sometimes lacks clarity and cohesion.

A judgment usually has three parts: the first contains a statement of the facts and a summary of the arguments of the parties; the second contains the reasons for the judgment in numbered paragraphs; and the third is the actual decision. The form of the judgment is terse, formal and abstract like a French court judgment. The short operative third part of the judgment is delivered in open court.

A7.3.1.6 Interim relief

The ECJ can provide interim relief (Articles 242 (ex 185) and 243 (ex 186)). In practice it is sought most often when a company challenges a Commission decision that the company has infringed the Community rules on competition (*United Brands v Commission* (27/76) [1978] ECR 207). The rules governing interim measures are found in the Rules of Court (especially Articles 83 and 85) and in ECJ case law (eg, *Camera Care v Commission* (792/79R) [1980] ECR 119, *Ford of Europe Inc and Forde Werke AG v Commission* (228/82) [1982] ECR 3091, *Finsider SPA v Commission* (392/85) [1986] 2 CMLR 290, *Brass Band Instruments Ltd v Boosey and Hawkes Plc* [1988] 4 CMLR 67).

A7.3.1.7 Intervention

Member States and institutions of the Community have a right to intervene in proceedings between other parties. Private parties may intervene in an action brought by another private party for annulment, failure to act or for damages, if the private intervener has an interest in the outcome of the case itself (Article 37 of the Statute).

A7.3.2 References for preliminary rulings

Article 20 of the Statute and Article 103 of the Rules govern the procedure before the ECJ.

A7.3.2.1 Making the reference

The parties to the national proceedings cannot initiate proceedings for preliminary rulings. The national court can alone make an order for reference. It will ask questions on the interpretation or validity of Community law. In the English High Court, see RSC Ord 114, CPR Sch 1.

A7.3.2.2 Written procedure

There are no formal pleadings as the proceedings are not contentious. The ECJ is not asked to decide the merits of the dispute between the parties. Its function is simply to assist the national court on the questions asked. It makes no inquiry as to the facts. A statement of agreed or decided facts should be found in the reference for the order or the national court's file on the case.

The Registrar will transmit copies of the preliminary reference to the parties in the national proceedings, to the Member State, the Commission (and to the Council, if the reference concerns an act of the Council). Those notified may submit written observations to the ECJ but there is no obligation on them to do so.

A7.3.2.3 Oral procedure

Those notified may also attend the oral hearing and make submissions. The procedure is similar to that for direct actions. After the Advocate-General's Opinion the oral proceedings are closed.

A7.3.2.4 Deliberations and judgment

The procedure is the same as for direct actions.

When the preliminary ruling is sent back to the national court, the case before the national court is resumed (proceedings having usually been suspended, pending the outcome of the preliminary reference).

A7.3.3 The language of the case

The language of the case (ie that in which the proceedings should be drafted) may be any one of the eleven official Community languages and Irish. In a direct action the applicant can choose the language of the case. However, where the action is brought against a Member State, it is the official language of that State. In references for preliminary rulings the language of the case is the language of the referring court (Rules, Article 29).

The working language of the ECJ is French, although the Advocates-General draft and deliver their Opinions in their own languages. The judgments are drafted and deliberated in French but the authentic version of the judgment will be in the language of the case. If that is not French, it will be a translation into that language from French.

A7.3.4 Representation before the European Court

Member States and Community institutions are represented by an agent who is often assisted by an advisor or lawyer entitled to practise before a Court in a Member State (eg, an agent from the Treasury Solicitor's Department, assisted by a barrister). Other parties in direct actions are represented by a lawyer entitled to practise in the courts of a Member State (Article 17 of the Statute). In preliminary rulings the ECJ is to take account of the rules of procedure of the national court making the reference (Rules, Article 194(2)).

A7.3.5 Costs

In direct actions the unsuccessful party shall be ordered to pay costs, if these have been asked for in the pleadings. A successful party may however be ordered to pay costs which the ECJ considers to have been unreasonably or vexatiously caused to the opponent (Rules, Article 69).

In references for preliminary rulings the question of costs is to be determined by the national court or tribunal in question (Rules, Article 104(3)). However, costs incurred by Community institutions or Member States which intervene in such proceedings are not recoverable, ie they must be borne by the intervener.

A7.3.6 Legal aid

In direct actions the ECJ may grant legal aid to a party 'who is wholly or in part unable to meet the cost of the proceedings' (Rules, Article 76).

In references for a preliminary ruling, parties to the national proceedings may be eligible under national law for public funding in respect of proceedings before the ECJ. For example, in *R v Marlborough Street Stipendiary Magistrates, ex p Bouchereau* [1977] ECR 1999 an existing legal aid certificate for the case before the national court was held to cover proceedings for a preliminary reference. In exceptional cases the ECJ may also grant legal aid.

A7.4 Interpretation of the Treaties and Community legislation by the European Court

The ECJ in some ways takes the same approach as an English court: it looks at the words used. It also considers their meaning in the context of the instrument as a whole (contextual interpretation). However, where the contextual interpretation is not helpful it uses the teleological method of interpretation. This means that the ECJ interprets the provision so that it fits into the general aims of the Community legal order, what the Court thinks the Community should be trying to achieve and the needs of the Community. The ECJ differs from the English courts in the extent to which it readily departs from the literal meaning and resorts to the teleological approach and the use of policy in arriving at its decisions.

A7.5 Policy and decision-making in the European Court

One of the distinguishing features of the ECJ is the extent to which the ECJ relies on policy considerations in its decisions. Its policy is the promotion of European integration by:

(a) strengthening the Community and its supranational elements;

(b) developing the scope and effectiveness of Community law;

(c) increasing the powers of the Community institutions.

For example, in *Parti Ecologiste 'Les Verts' v European Parliament* (294/83) [1987] 2 CMLR 343, the ECJ extended its power of judicial review to cover the legality of acts of the European Parliament as well as those of the Commission and the Council, the only institutions actually mentioned in Article 230 (ex 173), EC Treaty. It did this because it thought that such acts ought to be reviewable.

The principle of effectiveness (ie a provision is to be interpreted in the way that enables it to achieve its objective as effectively as possible), has been used by the ECJ to develop the doctrine of direct effect for directives.

Sometimes the Advocates-General make a comparative study of national provisions in order to find a solution which best fits the purposes of Community law (eg, *AM & S Europe Ltd v Commission* (155/79) [1982] ECR 1575).

The ECJ introduces new doctrines gradually, initially as a general principle subject to qualifications. In later cases it re-affirms the principle and slowly decreases the qualifications. This was its approach to the treaty-making power of the Community and the doctrine of direct effect (eg, *Defrenne v Sabena* (43/75) [1976] ECR 455).

The original EC Treaty had little to say on the subject of human rights. The subject had been covered already, in the European Convention on Human Rights and Fundamental Freedoms of 1950, and the EC Treaty was more concerned with economic matters. Following amendments to the EC Treaty by the Treaty of Amsterdam (effective from 1 May 1999), the European Court is now required to respect fundamental rights, as guaranteed by the European Convention on Human Rights. This enshrines in the Treaty what had been developed gradually in the case-law of the European Court over many years. In fact, other amendments of the EC Treaty expand upon this formalisation of the role of human rights within the European Union. Article 12 (ex 6) EC states clearly that the EU is based upon principles of liberty, democracy, respect for human rights and fundamental freedoms, and the rule of law. Article 46 (ex 56) EC places responsibility on the European Court to ensure that the acts of the Community institutions show respect for fundamental rights.

A7.6 The doctrine of precedent in the European Court

There is no formal doctrine of *stare decisis* but the ECJ tends to follow its previous decisions in most cases. Its case law is instrumental in developing Community law. Only rarely does it refer to previous cases in its judgment, although sometimes it may repeat parts of a previous judgment without quotation marks or without mentioning the name of the case. On rare occasions it may not follow precedent, eg, where the circumstances have changed or the views of the judges have altered. In such situations the ECJ does not overrule or distinguish the previous case. It merely ignores it. The Opinions of Advocates-General are often cited by lawyers appearing before the ECJ.

APPENDIX 8
FLOWCHARTS

The following flowcharts are provided as a quick and simple aid to analysis, when using the competition rules. You may find it useful to see if you can improve them or devise new ones.

A8.1 Is the behaviour prohibited by Article 81(1)?

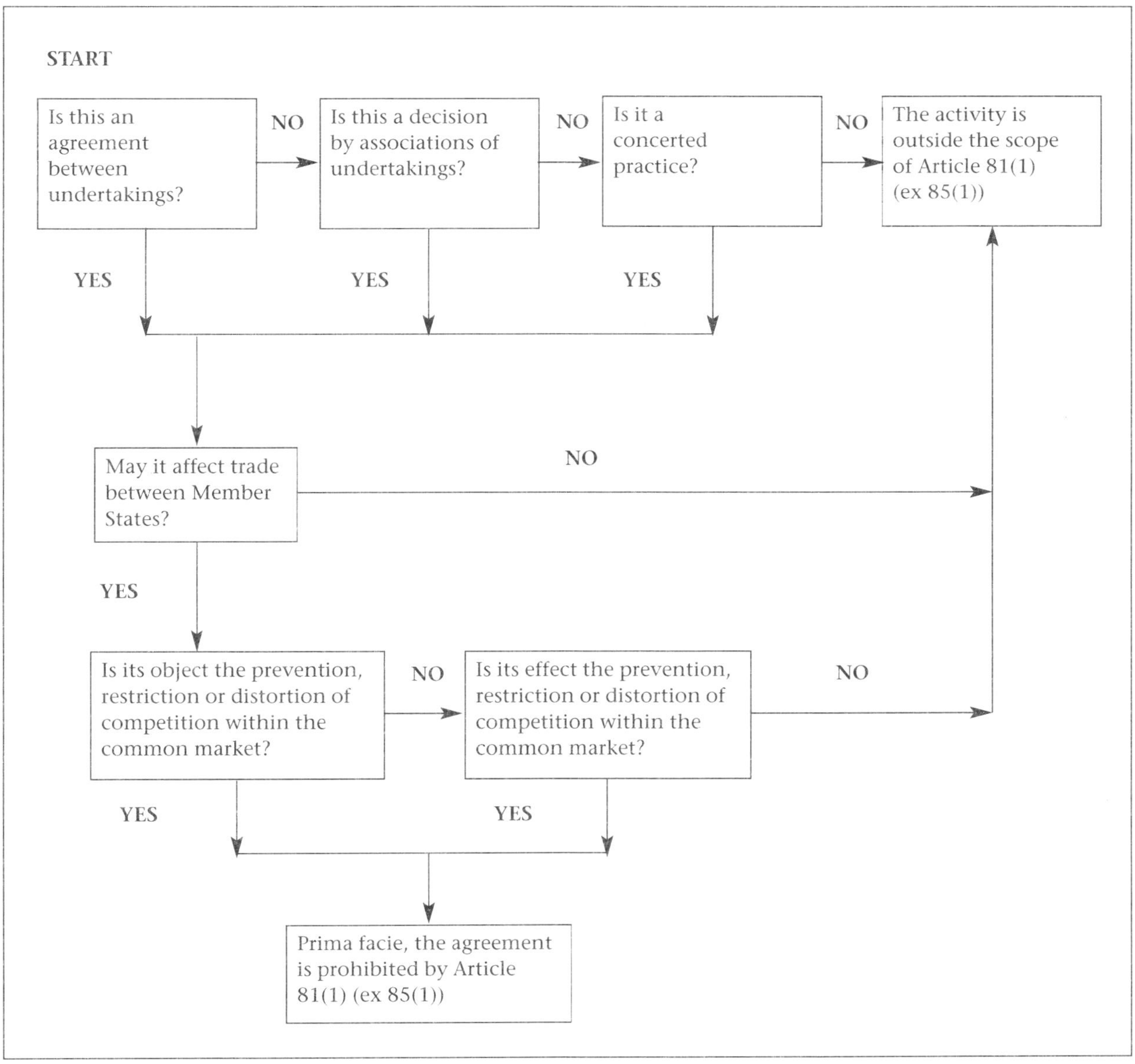

A8.2 Is the behaviour rendered void by Article 81(2)?

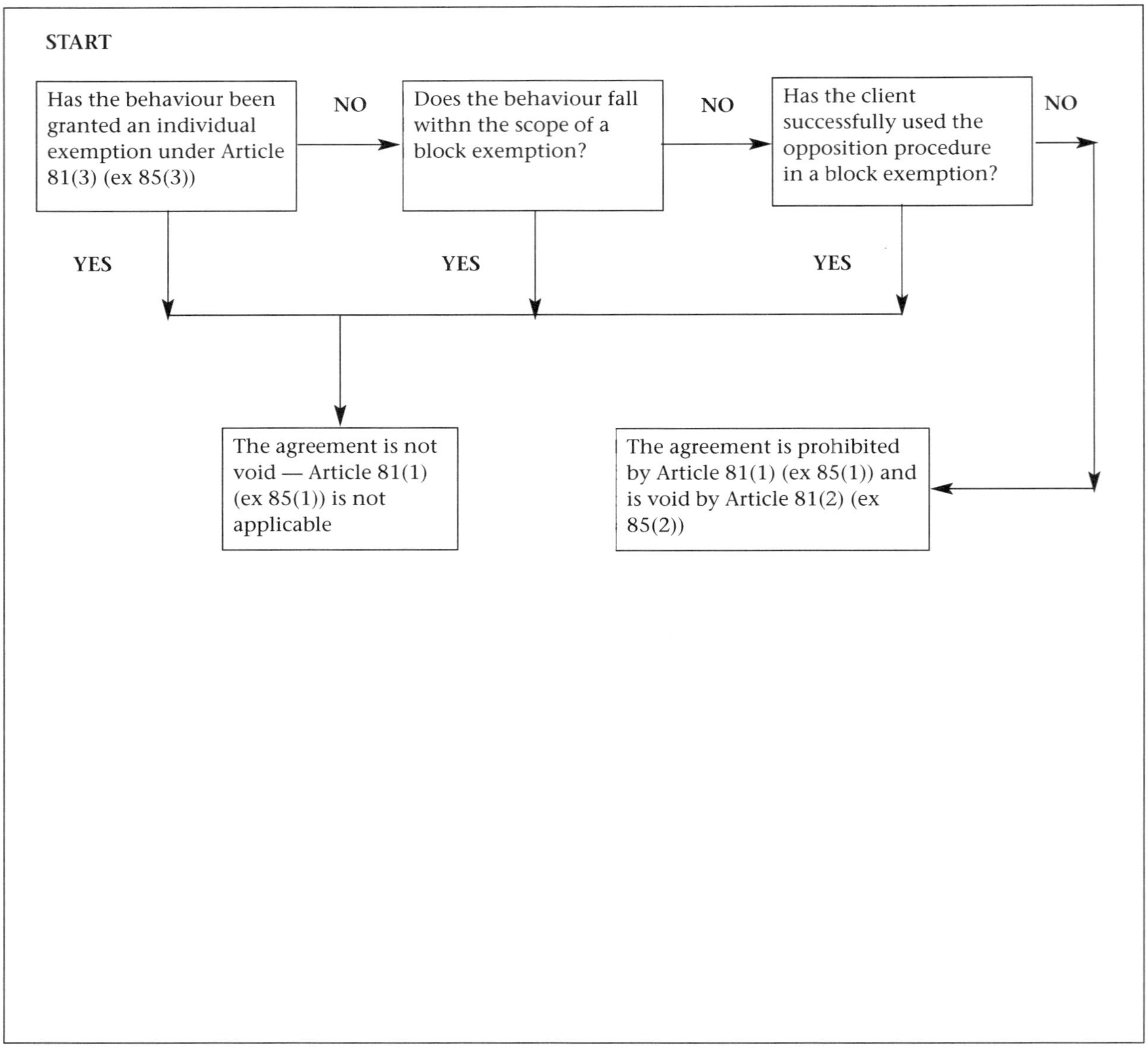

A8.3 Individual exemption: Article 81(3)

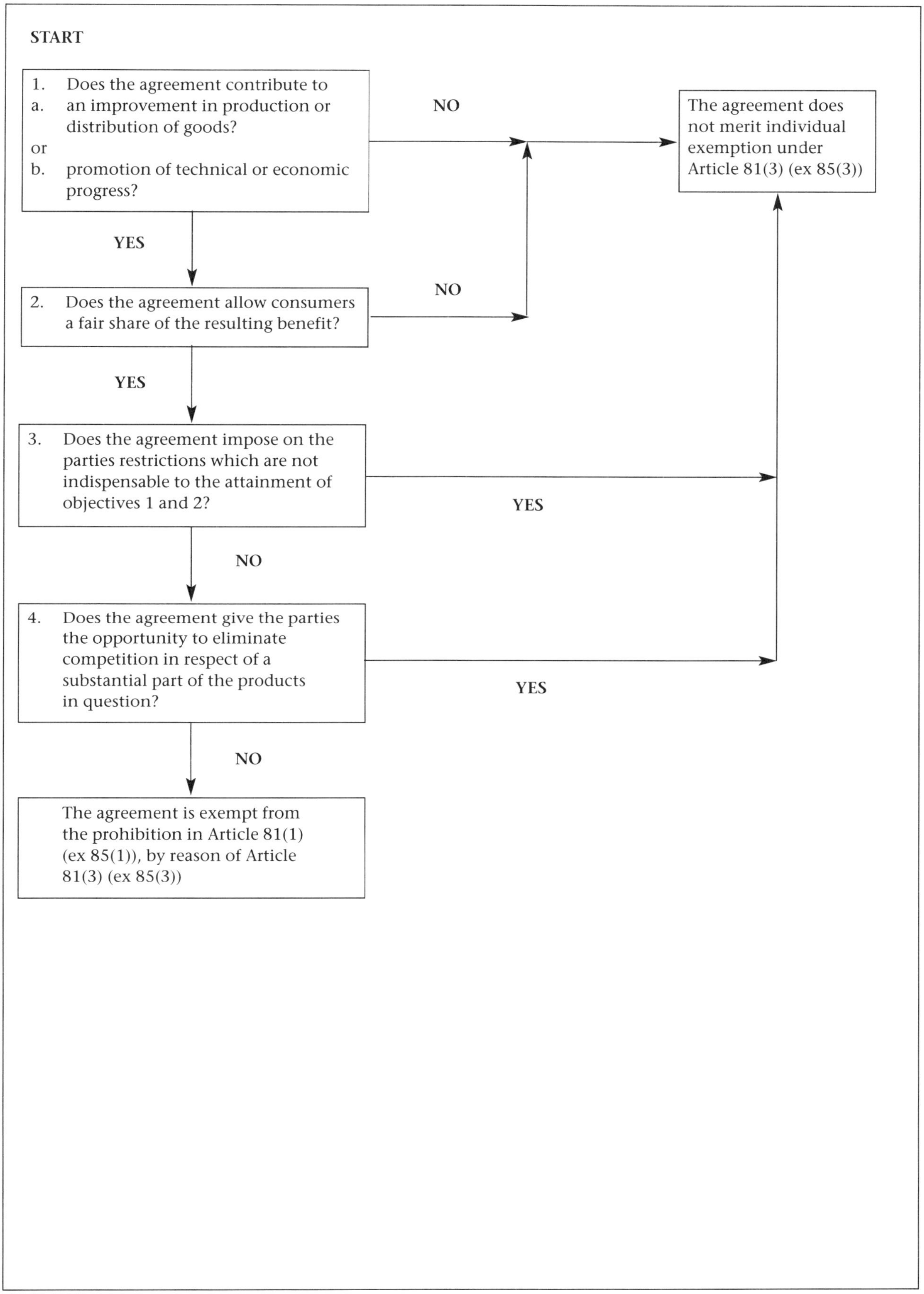

APPENDIX 9
BIBLIOGRAPHY

A9.1 Treaties, statutes, protocols, rules

Treaties establishing the European Communities: eg The European Economic Community Treaty 1957.

The Single European Act 1986.

Protocol of the Statute of the Court of Justice of the European Economic Community.

Rules of Procedure of the Court.

The European Communities Act 1972.

Rules of Civil Procedure, Sch 1, ord. 114.

Treaty on European Union, Maastricht 1992.

Treaty of Amsterdam 1997.

A9.2 Books on competition law

There are both specialist and general books which deal with EC competition law. In the following selection, (G) indicates a book containing a section on competition law, (S) indicates a book devoted to competition law.

Bellamy and Child, *Common Market Law of Competition* 5th edn, 2001, Sweet & Maxwell. (S)

Brown and Jacobs, *The Court of Justice of the European Communities*, 5th edn, 2001, Sweet & Maxwell. (G)

Craig and De Burca, *EU Law: Text, Cases and Materials*, 3rd edn, 2002, Oxford University Press. (G)

Goyder, J., *EEC Competition Law*, 1988, Clarendon Press. (S)

Green, N., *Commercial Agreements and Competition Law*, 1986, Graham & Trotman. (S)

Hawk, B., *United States, Common Market and International Antitrust — a Comparative Guide* (especially vol. II), Law & Business Inc./Harcourt Brace Jovanovich. (S)

Kapteyn and Verloren van Themaat, *Introduction to the Law of the European Communities: after the coming into force of the Single European Act*, 1989, Kluwer Publishers. (G)

Korah, V., *An Introductory Guide to EC Competition Law and Practice*, 7th edn, 2000, Hart Publishing. (S)

Ritter, Braun and Rawlinson, *European Competition Law: A Practitioner's Guide*, 2nd edn, 2000, Kluwer Law International (S).

Slot, P.-J., and McDonnell, A. (eds), *Procedure and Enforcement in EC and US Competition Law*, 1993, Sweet & Maxwell. (S)

Steiner, J., Woods, L. and Twigg-Flesner, C., *Textbook on EC Law*, 8th edn, 2003, Oxford University Press. (G)

Van Bael, I. and Bellis, J.-F., *Competition Law of the EEC*, 1995, CCH Illinois. (S)

Vaughan, D. (edn), *Law of the European Communities*, 2 vols, 1997, Butterworths. (G)

Weatherill, S. and Beaumont, P., *EC Law*, 2nd edn, 1998, Penguin. (G)

Wesseling, *The Modernisation of EC Antitrust Law*, 2000, Hart Publishing (S).

Whish, R., *Competition Law*, 5th edn, 2003, Butterworths. (S)

Wyatt and Dashwood, *European Union Law* 4th edn, 2001, Sweet & Maxwell. (G)

A9.3 Practitioners' works

Anderson, *References to the European Court*, 1995, Sweet & Maxwell.

Halsbury's Laws, Vols 51 and 52.

Vaughan, *The Law of the European Communities* (1986) 2 vol. (reprint of the relevant volumes of Halsbury's Laws), Butterworths.

Lasok, *The European Court of Justice: Practice and Procedure*, 2nd edn, 1994, Butterworths.

Usher, *European Court Practice*, 1983, Sweet & Maxwell.

Kapteyn and Verloran Van Themaat, *Introduction to the law of the European Communities*, 2nd edn, Kluwer.

D'Sa, *European Community Law and Civil Remedies in England and Wales*, 1994, Sweet & Maxwell.

Brealey & Hoskins, *Remedies in EC Law: Law and Practice in the English and EC Courts*, 1994, FT Law & Tax.

A9.4 Periodical reports and journals (English language)

Common Market Law Reports (much more up-to-date than the paper European Court Reports), published by European Law Centre Ltd monthly. Has a special series devoted to competition matters. Reports cases in the Court of Justice and cases in national courts which have a EC significance.

Common Market Law Review, covers the whole spectrum of Community affairs; often very good articles on competition matters.

European Competition Law Review, good articles on competition and free movement of goods; good case digests.

European Court Reports (official law reports of the Court of Justice), English-language version is always about two years behind; off-prints of individual cases are usually available from the Court (usually in French) after date of judgment until publication in the ECR.

European Intellectual Property Review, a specialist journal which deals with Community competition matters via case summaries, reports of Community press releases, articles. Also deals with issues concerning free movement of goods.

Official Journal (often abbreviated to OJ, or JO in French texts), this is the organ through which official announcements are made. These may be formal notices in a competition investigation, a declaration of a decision to exempt a company from Article 85(1), or other, legislative, matters. Series L covers the legislation of the Community, divided into those measures which must be published and those which need not be but are published; Series C covers everything else.

A9.5 Journal articles on competition law

Easterbrook, Frank H., On identifying exclusionary conduct, [1986] Notre Dame LR 972: an article by a judge on the 7th Circuit Court of Appeals; a radical look at the abuse of a dominant position in US terms.

Farr, Sebastian, Abuse of a Dominant Position — the *Hilti* case [1992] 4 ECLR 174.

Fox, Eleanor M., Monopolization and dominance in the United States and the European Community: efficiency, opportunity and fairness, [1986] Notre Dame 981: a good comparative study, of use when looking at Article 86, EC Treaty.

Furse, Mark, Fines and the Commission's discretion [1995] ECLR 1A9.

Green, Nicholas, Article 85 in perspective: stretching jurisdiction, narrowing the concept of a restriction and plugging a few gaps, [1988] ECLR 190: looks at actual and potential developments in the application of Article 85.

Hawk, Barry, The American (anti-trust) revolution: lessons for the EEC? [1988] ECLR 53: deals with the changes in competition law enforcement in the USA caused by new economic ideas, and their potential impact for the European Community.

Maitland-Walker, Julian, A Step Closer to a Definitive Ruling on a Right in Damages for Breach of the EC Competition Rules [1992] 1 ECLR 3.

Oliver, Peter, Enforcing Community rights in the English Courts, (1987) 50 MLR 881: looks at some aspects of the use of EC rights in English courts. One case dealt with in some detail is *Bourgoin v MAFF* [1986] QB 716.

Robertson, Aiden and Williams, Mark, An Ice-Cream War: The Law and Economics of Freezer Exclusivity [1995] 1 ECLR 7.

Smith, Helen, The *Francovich* Case: State Liability and the Individual's Right to Damages [1992] 3 ECLR 129.

Steiner, Josephine, How to make the action suit the case — domestic remedies for breach of EEC Law, (1987) 12 *European Law Review* 102: examination of the remedies available in English courts when an alleged breach of EC law is used as a cause of action.

Van Bael, Ivo, Fining à la carte: the lottery of EU competition law [1995] 4 ECLR 237.

Whish, Richard, The enforcement of EC competition law in the domestic courts of Member States [1994] 2 ECLR 60.

N.B. Other articles are referred to in relevant chapters.

A9.6 Other sources on competition law

Areeda & Turner, *Antitrust Law: an analysis of antitrust principles and their application*: regarded as an authority on the economic thinking behind the laws on competition; an American work.

Bork, R., *The Antitrust Paradox*: further reading on American challenges to traditional economic thinking; a representative of the 'Chicago' school of economic theory.

Celex: a computer database, see europa.eu.int/celex/htm/celex–en.htm.

europa.eu.int/eur-lex/en: the 'Portal to European Union Law'.

European Communities Legislation Current Status, Butterworths, updated work.

Foster, Nigel, *Blackstone's EC Legislation*, 14th edn, 2003, Blackstone Press: an abundance of primary and secondary legislation in the main 'European' areas, including competition and industrial/intellectual property.

Gellhorn, Ernest, *Antitrust Law and Economics* (in the US 'Nutshell' series): concentrates on competition law and economic theory in the USA but with good, concise sections on basic economic concepts. Available in London through Hammicks

curia.eu.int: material on the Court of Justice including the recent case-law.

Internet sites:

- europa — this takes you into an enormous range of sites and information about everything connected with the EU — http://europa.eu.int.
- particular sites of interest to competition lawyers are the DG IV site (for competition matters) — http://europa.eu.int/comm/competition/index–en.htm and DG XV site (free movement of goods and intellectual property rights) — http://europa.eu.int/comm/dg15/en.
- for national competition matters, refer to the UK Office of Fair Trading — http://www.open.gov.uk/oft/oft home.htm.

Rudden & Wyatt, *EU Treaties and Legislation*, 8th edn, 2003, Oxford University Press: a materials book containing significant secondary legislation.

A9.7 Student textbooks

Hartley, *The Foundation of European Community Law*, 5th edn, 2003, Oxford University Press.

Steiner, Woods and Twigg-Flesner, *Textbook on EC Law*, 8th edn, 2003, Oxford University Press.

Weatherill and Beaumont, *EC Law*, 2nd edn, 1996, Penguin.

Wyatt and Dashwood, *European Union Law*, 4th edn, 2001, Sweet & Maxwell.

INDEX

D